THE CAMPUS COLOR LINE

The Campus Color Line

COLLEGE PRESIDENTS AND
THE STRUGGLE FOR BLACK FREEDOM

EDDIE R. COLE

PRINCETON UNIVERSITY PRESS
PRINCETON & OXFORD

Requests for permission to reproduce material from this work
should be sent to permissions@press.princeton.edu

Published by Princeton University Press
41 William Street, Princeton, New Jersey 08540
6 Oxford Street, Woodstock, Oxfordshire OX20 1TR

press.princeton.edu

ISBN 9780691206745
ISBN (e-book) 9780691206752

British Library Cataloging-in-Publication Data is available

Editorial: Peter Dougherty, Alena Chekanov
Production Editorial: Terri O'Prey
Jacket/Cover Design: Chris Ferrante
Production: Erin Suydam
Publicity: Alyssa Sanford, Amy Stewart
Copyeditor: Molan Goldstein

Jacket image: From *Sit-Ins: The Student Report*, published by the Congress of
Racial Equality, May 1960. Courtesy of the State Archives of Florida

This book has been composed in Arno

Printed on acid-free paper. ∞

Printed in the United States of America

10 9 8 7 6 5 4 3 2 1

CONTENTS

THE IDEA for this book is a natural extension of my own Black educational genealogy. I grew up in Boligee, Alabama. It is a small town located in the Alabama Black Belt. There, my parents were school teachers. Each worked more than thirty years across the Greene and Sumter county school systems. Before them, my father's parents were also rural west Alabama teachers, starting their careers in one- and two-room schoolhouses. They were also graduates of Black colleges and members of the state's Black teacher association. Combined, their careers made clear the role of education in the Black freedom struggle, and their lives molded me.

By the time I started formal education, the de jure school segregation that my parents and grandparents experienced in the Jim Crow South had long been exchanged for de facto practices. For instance, the all-Black public high school that I attended in nearby Eutaw, Alabama, was located around the corner from a smaller, yet defiant, majority-white private academy. The short, slender Woodfield Avenue was our *color line*. That was an accepted norm in the Alabama Black Belt; however, it sparked my intellectual curiosity about the decisions made by past educational leaders, and how those choices shaped the present. This book takes up those same questions within the context of higher education.

Today, the debate continues over who should or should not be admitted to certain colleges and universities. The relationship between expanding urban campuses and bordering neighborhoods remains contentious. There is still uncertainty over where hate speech begins and free speech ends. Black students are demanding an end to racism on majority-white campuses. Questions over the legality of affirmative action are entering yet another decade. And campus relationships with law enforcement are under renewed scrutiny. All the while, elected officials regularly resuscitate old questions about Historically Black Colleges and Universities (HBCUs) and the vitality, funding, and governance of those institutions. These are serious issues. But these contemporary issues have long histories.

Several college presidents are just now, in the twenty-first century, acknowledging how their institutions benefited from slavery and, at last, beginning to make symbolic and practical reparations. This reconciliation has been 175 years in the making; however, one does not have to go back that far to see how academic leaders have impacted the struggle for Black freedom, past or present. Therefore, if we are just beginning to unspool and make right the injustices from the mid-1800s, what does that mean for reconciling more recent college presidents' decisions?

Perhaps now, more than ever, we need to understand how college presidents have influenced racial policies and practices. This book is being released amid a global health and racial pandemic that will likely permanently change education, and the accompanying economic uncertainty resulting from this crisis has, once again, turned our attention to university leaders. The decisions made by college presidents today will have long-term racial implications, but we can better examine those decisions when we frame them within the history of their predecessors' actions for or against racial equity.

In closing this preface, I am reminded of what Frederick Douglass argued in 1881: "slavery, ignorance, stupidity, servility, poverty, dependence, are undesirable conditions. When these shall cease to be coupled with color, there will be no color line drawn." But when shall the twenty-first-century renditions of those conditions cease? I wrote this book as a challenge to the global citizenry to critically self-reflect on the ongoing struggle for Black freedom and how academic leaders have held, or are holding, the *campus color line*—a division that has shaped generations.

ACKNOWLEDGMENTS

THIS BOOK would not be before you if not for support from countless family members, friends, mentors, former professors, colleagues, conference discussants, and archivists.

My parents—Eddie (formally, I am Eddie II) and Nancy Cole—are the best. Mom has always been careful and attentive to details, while dad has always offered big-picture perspectives on Black life in the United States. What a much younger me once considered to be insignificant parental character traits, I have drawn on them to complete this book. Furthermore, my *big* sisters—Latryce and Charlene—set a high bar that I am still trying to reach. Thank you!

My formal introduction to the study of higher education started at Indiana University (IU). Since then, several IU alumni and past and present faculty continue to cheer on my career. This includes Shaun R. Harper, Thomas F. Nelson Laird, Robin Hughes, Megan Palmer, Donald Hossler, Danielle DeSawal, Andrea Walton, Nancy Chism, and Vasti Torres. Beyond the IU School of Education, I had insightful, supportive conversations about my study of college presidents and the Black Freedom Movement with Valerie Grim, James Wimbush, Khalil Muhammad, Marvin Sterling, and John Lucaites. These individuals may not realize the impression they left on me, but I have always valued their most casual conversations that pushed my thinking. Of course, there is no IU faculty member who has been more impactful on my life than Dionne Danns. In more ways than I can articulate, this book is a testament to her friendship, advice, sharpness, and ongoing support—thank you.

Additionally, I owe a great amount of debt to the people I met as an IU graduate student. Although I had no initial desire to live in Bloomington, it turned out to be one of the best decisions of my life. I continue to admire and appreciate Adrian D. Land, Nadrea R. Njoku, Carl Suddler, Cameron J. Harris, Mahauganee D. Shaw Bonds, and Rubin Pusha III. As my time at IU progressed, I found unwavering support in Jessica C. Harris, Katherine I. E. Wheatle, Francisco Ramos, and Brian L. McGowan. I am grateful for each of you.

I also offer my sincerest thanks to the staff of the Spencer Foundation and members of the National Academy of Education (NAEd). In 2015, my NAEd/Spencer Postdoctoral Fellowship supported the early development of this book, which required a substantial amount of travel across the United States. In total, I visited twenty-seven colleges and universities, as well as state archives and local historical societies, as part of my national archival exploration. I am equally grateful to the staff of the Woodrow Wilson National Fellowship Foundation. In 2017, I was named a Mellon Emerging Faculty Leader (formerly the Nancy Weiss Malkiel Award), which offered invaluable support for follow-up archival visits and manuscript revision. The University of Chicago's Robert L. Platzman fellowship, Princeton University Library grant, and the University of Wisconsin-Madison Library grant were also instrumental.

Those fellowships also presented opportunities to meet and be mentored by many accomplished scholars whose research has inspired me. By way of the NAEd, Gloria Ladson-Billings, James D. Anderson, Patricia Albjerg Graham, William J. Reese, James A. Banks, Shirley Brice Heath, and Carol Lee have unknowingly poured so much into me and my work. It was a career-changing opportunity and I am forever grateful for the incomparable James Earl Davis (also a former NAEd/Spencer postdoctoral fellow) for first encouraging me to apply for that fellowship. Also, through the Woodrow Wilson Foundation, Nancy Weiss Malkiel and Michael R. Winston offered their careful eyes and attentive ears to help make this manuscript stronger. I am grateful for these distinguished scholars. Truly, I found myself in an intellectual playground working on this project. There are also a number of other researchers whose scholarship and general kindness have motivated me. I remain appreciative of the History of Education Society. There are too many historians to name, but Joy Williamson-Lott, Vanessa Siddle Walker, Linda Eisenmann, Derrick P. Alridge, Christopher Span, Julie A. Reuben, Stefan M. Bradley, Jon Hale, and Ibram X. Kendi have all, even if only briefly, made time to converse about my work. Any good that comes of this book is because of these scholars' generosity.

The same can be said for many of my professional colleagues turned friends, and friends turned professional colleagues. Jamel K. Donnor, Robert Trent Vinson, William A. Smith, James P. Barber, Jeremy Stoddard, Jason Chen, and Brian A. Burt have each provided feedback on various aspects of this book, whether fellowship proposals or casual conversations. Ideas, as Jamel always says, are priceless. Jessica C. Harris also offered an unmatched, much-needed critical perspective. Chad Roberts, too, has rallied behind this project since its beginning. I offer my gratitude and a toast for their insights and friendship.

Of course, the research conducted for this book would not be possible without dedicated archivists. Those archivists welcomed me into campus special collections at opening and bid me farewell at closing. Truly, no token of appreciation can capture what these thoughtful staff members have done to aid my research. This includes the following staffs: Beulah Davis Research Room, Morgan State University; Special Collections Research Center, University of Chicago Library; UCLA Library Special Collections, Charles E. Young Research Library; University of Mississippi, J. D. Williams Library Archives and Special Collections; University of Alabama, W. S. Hoole Special Collections Library; Princeton University Department of Rare Books and Special Collections, Seeley G. Mudd Manuscript Library; University of Wisconsin-Madison Archives, Steenbock Library; and the Wisconsin Historical Society. As mentioned earlier, I visited more campuses, historical societies, and state archives than only these collections, but the bulk of the sources used in the book came from the aforementioned locations.

I must also thank the wonderful editorial insights offered by the phenomenally talented team at Princeton University Press. I will always remember November 9, 2016—the day after the 2016 presidential election—when editor Jessica Yao first contacted me. With the election of Donald J. Trump as a backdrop, our ensuing conversation was a turning point for this book. She was intrigued by my initial vision for this book, but later encouraged me to "be even more ambitious" because "this may properly be a somewhat bigger book with a broader scope." Since then, I have not been disappointed by any aspect of working with this publisher. My editor, Peter Dougherty, is sharp, precise, and offers a keen big-picture view of this book. Indeed, this is a "big history," and he is one of the best in publishing. I am also grateful for the chance to work with Terri O'Prey, the managing editor who shepherded this manuscript with care and flexibility all the way to print; Chris Ferrante, who designed a cover that captured a student scene that college presidents across the nation feared; and many others at Princeton University Press.

Finally, and most importantly, I thank my wife, Melanie, and our son, Beau. They are the stars of a story I will always tell, and the happiest of everyone that this book is *finally* done. This book required time and their selflessness never went unnoticed. I love them.

THE CAMPUS COLOR LINE

Introduction

"YOU PEOPLE SEEM to have been born into a time of crisis," Edwin D. Harrison told the students gathered inside the old gymnasium at the Georgia Institute of Technology the morning of January 17, 1961. Wearing a dark suit and tie squarely positioned over a white shirt, the forty-five-year-old college president stood behind a skinny lectern, flanked by a microphone to his right. Students squeezed into the crowded bleachers. Others sat on tables, leaving their legs swinging beneath, while the rest sat on the gym floor. The students leaned forward with uneasy frowns or held their heads with worried, aimless gazes.

Harrison hosted an informal meeting every quarter to provide an opportunity for students to chat with him about any topic. But this assembly was different. Roughly two thousand students attended, a record number for an open forum. Therefore, when Harrison stepped before the crowd of somber young white faces, he took the first steps to address what would become "Georgia Tech's toughest test"—desegregation.[1]

The uneasiness that hovered over the gymnasium came with the swirling suspicion that Georgia Tech, a state-supported university, would succumb to the same racial violence that had occurred a week earlier only seventy miles east of its Atlanta campus. In Athens, a white mob overran the University of Georgia after a federal court order allowed two Black students, Charlayne Hunter and Hamilton Holmes, to enroll. Several white students and Ku Klux Klan members rioted in tandem. They set fire to Hunter's residence hall, launched makeshift missiles, and tossed bricks and rocks at local police officers

---

1. This January 1961 quarterly meeting is notable for both the record attendance and the decision to record the transcript of President Edwin D. Harrison's conversation with the students, which was later printed with photographs in the Georgia Tech alumni magazine. For more, see "Approach to a Crisis," *Alumni Magazine*, March/May 1961, Location UA003, 6:4; 33:1, 3, Georgia Institute of Technology Archives & Records Management (location hereafter cited as GT).

and journalists. Afterward, allegations spread that Georgia's segregationist governor, Ernest Vandiver, intentionally delayed dispatching state law enforcement to help control the mob violence.[2]

The events in Athens prompted Georgia Tech students to rattle off a barrage of inquiries as soon as Harrison opened the floor for questions. One student asked, "How has the racial crisis affected Tech's ability to attract and retain a competent faculty?" Another asked, "What can we do to show our displeasure at being forced into an integrated situation?" And another question: "In some northern universities, some of the student organizations have been forced to integrate or get off campus. Do you think that is apt to happen here?"[3]

Then more questions came in rapid fire: What would happen to students who protested the enrollment of Black students? What was the university's policy to stop outsiders like Klansmen from causing trouble on campus? What challenges did Harrison anticipate Black students would bring to Georgia Tech besides potential violence? Since the press had worsened the Athens situation, according to one student's assessment, could journalists be banned from Georgia Tech? One after another, student questions revolved around desegregation: how, if, and when. But Harrison's answers demonstrated that desegregation was a far more complex issue for college presidents than the students could imagine.[4]

With each response, Harrison introduced a new issue he was dealing with regarding civil rights. He explained that Georgia Tech was the only technological institute in the South with a respected national academic reputation. In fact, non-Georgians widely believed it was a private university because of the stigma carried by state-supported southern white colleges of being social clubs rather than intellectual hubs. The exceptional academic performance of Georgia Tech students also led nonsouthern companies to hire its graduates. Yet, he said, mob violence would certainly damage this reputation.[5]

In answering another student question, Harrison pondered local residents' varying opinions on desegregation and whether the rapport between campus and the community would worsen depending on how the university managed desegregation. Additionally, when considering the consequences of violence,

---

2. For an account of the University of Georgia riot, see Daniels, *Horace T. Ward*, pp. 154–155. The violence at the University of Georgia often takes a backseat to other violent moments in higher education's racial history, such as the sit-ins in 1960, the Freedom Rides of 1961, or the University of Mississippi's desegregation in 1962. Regarding the national significance of the Georgia riot, see Pratt, *We Shall Not Be Moved*, pp. 103–106.

3. "Approach to a Crisis," *Alumni Magazine*.

4. Ibid.

5. Ibid.

Harrison explained how outside journalists—those in New York, Philadelphia, Boston, and Chicago—regularly critiqued white southerners' resistance to desegregation. He then gingerly weighed the idea of banning journalists from campus alongside concerns about freedom of the press. This answer dovetailed with his bolder threat to expel any student demonstrators.[6]

Those issues aside, another student question prompted Harrison to note the Ford Foundation's recent $690,000 grant to Georgia Tech to support doctoral programs; however, those funds could be jeopardized if the institution mishandled desegregation. Media influence, community relations, freedom of expression, academic freedom, and private donors were just some of the sources of pressure that emerged alongside concerns about student resistance. "Any actions and activities which you could undertake if and when a crisis should arise on our campus," Harrison advised students, "will affect greatly the future of the institution."[7]

As news of Harrison's remarks to Georgia Tech students spread throughout the region, James E. Walter, president of Piedmont College, a segregated white college in Demorest, Georgia, immediately wrote Harrison. "Power to you as you carry the ball for many of us," Walter remarked. A similar message came from Florida, where Franklyn A. Johnson, president of the segregated Jacksonville University, concluded, "I have no doubt that we here will grapple with this sort of a situation sooner or later."[8]

From the largest to the smallest institutions, private or state-supported, the academic leaders of segregated white campuses knew the first presidents tasked with addressing desegregation were simply that: the first. They were attentive to the long-anticipated race question at white institutions, but no amount of anticipation would prepare them for the actual pressures of the day. Thus, as Joe W. Guthridge, Harrison's assistant and Georgia Tech's director of development, warned Harrison the day following the quarterly student meeting, "we should not be led into a sense of false security based on the positive reaction we received."[9]

6. Ibid.

7. Ibid. For specific information about Georgia Tech's academic reputation, see O'Mara, *Cities of Knowledge*, pp. 182–185. Georgia Tech was also considered unique among southern universities because it enrolled a significantly high number of out-of-state students. For more, see Daniels, *Horace T. Ward*, p. 155.

8. James E. Walter to Edwin D. Harrison, January 18, 1961, E. D. Harrison Collection, Desegregation File, GT (collection hereafter cited as Harrison Collection); Franklyn A. Johnson to Edwin D. Harrison, January 18, 1961, Harrison Collection, GT.

9. Joe W. Guthridge to Edwin D. Harrison, January 18, 1961, Harrison Collection, GT.

The Campus Color Line is a history of the Black Freedom Movement as seen through the actions of college presidents. The most pressing civil rights issues—desegregation, equal educational and employment opportunity, fair housing, free speech, economic disparities—were intertwined with higher education. Therefore, the college presidency is a prism through which to disclose how colleges and universities have challenged or preserved the many enduring forms of anti-Black racism in the United States. Through this book, the historic role of college presidents is recovered and reconstructed. It expands understanding regarding college presidents and racial struggles, and it breaks down our regional conceptions while broadening our perspective on how these academic leaders navigated competing demands.[10]

Historical accounts of the Black Freedom Movement have suggested that the nation's college presidents—as a national collective—were neither protagonists nor antagonists in the debate over racial equality. Institutional histories and individual presidents' biographies demonstrate that there are some exceptions, but overall, college presidents as a group are not portrayed as directly responsible for racial segregation, nor were they expected to lead the challenge against segregation. In essence, college presidents walked a fine line between constituents on opposite sides to protect themselves and their institutions from reprisal. This captivating narrative demonstrates the precarious position of these academic leaders; however, it is incomplete. There is more to learn about the broader struggle for Black freedom through college presidents.[11]

The Black Freedom Movement presented numerous new challenges for college presidents. Student and faculty demonstrations were perhaps the most visible, but they were not the only cause for concern. How a college president managed racial tensions also affected the recruitment and retention of faculty. The support of local entities—businesses, churches, and civic organizations—also hinged on where academic leaders stood on racial advancement. Journalists from local and national media outlets frequented campuses to assess how college presidents were handling racial crises; in turn, college presidents became increasingly focused on maintaining good publicity.

10. On the term "anti-Black racism" and its use as a theoretical framework, see Benjamin, "The Black/Jamaican Criminal," particularly pp. 60–89.

11. My use of "college presidents," as well as "academic leaders," refers to chief administrative officers (i.e., president, chancellor) as a group. When referring to a specific campus, I use the local term associated with that chief officer, which may be president or chancellor, because the individuals featured in this book led institutions of varying histories, sizes, and governance structures. Therefore, terminology varied by institution, and I incorporate the terms of the specific institutions being discussed.

Trustees and alumni donors stirred new questions about higher education governance, and college presidents were forced to mold new university practices around free speech and academic freedom. College presidents also exchanged pleasantries with the executives at private foundations to stay on the good side of philanthropists. Meanwhile, those same philanthropists' dollars helped fund the physical growth of universities and, subsequently, strained relationships between academic leaders and local residents.

These issues and others demonstrate why President Harrison's open forum with Georgia Tech students is significant. It was a rare moment when a college president publicly discussed the breadth of challenges associated with desegregation and broader civil rights struggles. College presidents usually held such conversations behind closed doors, through private correspondence, or within mediums limited to academic circles. But Harrison stood before the Georgia Tech student body and candidly laid bare some of the issues college presidents quietly managed. During struggles for racial equality, college presidents played varied roles, from mitigating free speech concerns to soliciting private foundations to fund racial initiatives, occasionally reaching beyond their campuses to shape urban renewal programs.[12]

University leaders continue to play these roles today, as racism, racial tensions, and racial violence resonate loudly on college campuses once more. Education researchers have found that current college presidents sometimes alienate members of their campus communities when they respond to racial unrest—suggesting that campus officials do not always understand or utilize history well. Legal scholars have assessed that college presidents' mishandling of contemporary racial unrest have resulted in "millions of tuition dollars lost,

---

12. Black college presidents frequently used the *Journal of Negro Education*, founded in 1932, as an outlet to discuss desegregation. Many of them published scholarly studies and commentaries that assessed or offered opinions regarding the future of Black colleges in a desegregated America. It is also notable that administrators at southern white institutions anticipated Black students in an effort to refine their strategies to stay segregated. I offer two examples, one during Reconstruction and the other following World War II, both key periods in Black citizens' fight for equality. In September 1870, University of Mississippi chancellor John N. Waddel said his university "never, for a moment, conceived it possible or proper that a Negro should be admitted to its classes, graduated with its honors, or presented with its diplomas." John N. Waddel to R. S. Hudson, September 28, 1870, J. D. Williams Collection, Box 6, Folder 4, University of Mississippi, Archives and Special Collections. In November 1949, University of Alabama dean A. B. Moore anticipated that some people would "expect Negroes to be admitted to state universities, as has been done in three states." A. B. Moore to John R. McLure, November 17, 1949, Frank A. Rose Papers, Box 6, Location 084–079, Folder: Integration Plans, University of Alabama, W. S. Hoole Special Collections Library.

statewide and national reputation[s] harmed, [and] relations with [legislatures] damaged." Journalists have also deemed recent campus unrest "a second civil rights movement" and "a rebirth of the civil rights movement." But these contemporary assessments are shaped by a long history of racism, and college presidents' responses to it, on college campuses.[13]

———

The Campus Color Line builds upon and intervenes in existing literature, ideas, and arguments about the Black Freedom Movement. Many scholars have rightfully centered Black colleges when interrogating mid-twentieth-century racial struggles. This has been critical for understanding the power and agency of Black college students, not just formal civil rights leaders. In centering Black colleges, scholars have also challenged the broad summations of Black college presidents during the movement. For instance, in 1964, former Spelman College professor Howard Zinn stated, "Presidents of state-supported Negro colleges, with an eye on trustees, regents, and state legislatures, lashed out at their student rebels." This was a common sweeping appraisal—one that drew a distinctive line between private and state-supported Black colleges; however, scholars have offered more nuanced accounts about these presidents over the years.[14]

For example, historian Jelani M. Favors has argued that Black colleges were "the most important space for sheltering budding activists, inculcating a second curriculum of racial consciousness, and providing the communitas necessary to generate the sense of solidarity and connections sufficient to launch a full frontal assault on white supremacy." That study focuses on activism and further solidified Black college students' legacy as leaders; however, in explaining how Black colleges cultivated activists, Favors also offered insight into Black college presidents' support of students. In a history of the movement in Greensboro, William H. Chafe illustrated not only how President Willa B. Player at Bennett College, a private Black college, was a pivotal figure but also

13. Douglas, Lane-Bonds, and Freeman, "There Is No Manual"; Cole and Harper, "Race and Rhetoric"; Trachtenberg, "The 2015 University of Missouri Protests." For descriptions of recent racial unrest as the second civil rights movement, see both Chuck Hobbs, "Missouri Football and the Second Civil Rights Movement," *The Hill*, November 10, 2015, http://thehill.com/blogs/pundits-blog/civil-rights/259670-missouri-football-and-the-second-civil-rights-movement (accessed February 17, 2017); and Joseph P. Williams, "Welcome to Missouri, and Civil Rights 2.0," *US News & World Report*, January 5, 2016, http://www.usnews.com/news/the-report/articles/2016/01/05/welcome-to-missouri-and-civil-rights-20 (accessed February 17, 2017).

14. Zinn, *SNCC*, p. 30.

how the president of the state-supported North Carolina A&T surprised local whites when he refused to reprimand Black students for the lunch counter sit-ins.[15]

Joy Ann Williamson-Lott further demonstrated the complexity of the Black college presidency in a study of Mississippi. There, to prevent the president of a state-supported Black college from even thinking of empowering student activists, white leaders vetted potential candidates to ensure that the most accommodating Black leaders were hired. As a result, white supremacists positioned themselves to encourage those state-supported Black college presidents to reprimand student and faculty activists through firings, suspensions, or expulsions—more akin to Zinn's assessment. Yet, although some presidents of private Black colleges utilized their more independent governance structures to support civil rights efforts, Williamson-Lott explained that even the presidents of private Black colleges were not immune from being fired for aiding the movement. What remains widely unexplored within institutional and state-level histories, or individual biographies are the collective strategies and intraregional networks that southern Black college presidents used to navigate the constraints of white supremacy.[16]

Beyond Black colleges, scholars acknowledge white college presidents when discussing the tensions between federal and state officials over the desegregation of white state-supported institutions in the South. Supreme Court rulings in the 1930s through the 1950s gradually opened graduate and professional programs to Black students at some southern white universities, but the scholarship on the desegregation of these universities is typically about specific institutions in the Deep South. Thus, the bulk of scholarly attention to white southern presidents is concentrated where white resistance was most pronounced. In Alabama, Mississippi, and Georgia, for instance, the presidents of the leading white state-supported universities are often noted as having failed to halt the white mobs who violently resisted desegregation, or as being removed from any substantial decision-making as segregationist governors sparred with federal officials. Yet, deeper insight into the Black Freedom Movement is gained by interrogating these institutions before and after desegregation.[17]

15. Favors, *Shelter in a Time of Storm*, p. 11; Chafe, *Civilities and Civil Rights*, pp. 95–97.

16. Williamson, *Radicalizing the Ebony Tower*, pp. 97–105, 114–119; Williamson-Lott, *Jim Crow Campus*, pp. 51–57, 64–71; Williamson, "'This Has Been Quite a Year.'"

17. See chapters 4 and 5 of this book for an examination of college presidents during the pre- and post-desegregation of state-supported white universities. There are also a number of institutional histories that briefly discuss desegregation, and references to college presidents are just as brief. For example, University of South Carolina president Thomas F. Jones consulted

For example, David G. Sansing's comprehensive history of Mississippi higher education is a deeply valuable and serious investigation of a complex state. Yet, there is an intriguing leap in his book, *Making Haste Slowly*, from James Meredith enrolling as the first Black student in September 1962 directly to Meredith studying for his final exams before his August 1963 graduation. For Sansing and many others, there is only brief reference to the difficulties University of Mississippi academic leaders faced after the campus riot during the 1962–63 academic year; however, *The Campus Color Line* provides an account of southern higher education from the perspective of the white presidents who failed to halt racial violence and those who successfully prevented it.[18]

As we consider how college presidents are positioned within the prevailing historical narrative, we might surmise that this is why the general populace is more familiar with the tactics of segregationist governors or prominent student activists like Diane Nash, John Lewis, Patricia and Priscilla Stephens, or Stokely Carmichael. But college presidents during the mid-twentieth-century fight for racial equality remain virtually nameless when we remember higher education's role in civil rights struggles. For instance, the Greensboro lunch counter sit-ins and the four freshmen at North Carolina A&T are commemorated every February. Yet, who was the president of that state-supported Black college that did not reprimand the students? The violent desegregation of the University of Mississippi conjures memories of Governor Ross Barnett, US president John F. Kennedy, and James Meredith, the Black admitted student, but the chancellor's name does not immediately roll off the casual reader's tongue. The same is evident at the University of Alabama, where Governor George C. Wallace's "stand in the schoolhouse door" is remembered more than the university president's months of planning for peaceful desegregation.

There have been numerous books and scholarly articles written about these watershed moments in US history, but college presidents as a group have not emerged as a focal point. Therefore, it is unsurprising that Edwin D. Harrison is largely unknown despite leading Georgia Tech to become the first Deep

---

Georgia Tech president Edwin D. Harrison, who "managed desegregation at that school quietly and without incident," but Henry H. Lesesne's history of the university does not interrogate the details of the strategizing between the two presidents. For more, see Lesesne, *History of the University of South Carolina*, p. 141.

18. Sansing, *Making Haste Slowly*. For the specifics of discussing Meredith's enrollment and graduation, see ibid., chaps. 11 and 12. The presidents of white segregated private colleges faced similar pressures as their colleagues at state-supported white institutions. For more, see Kean, *Desegregating Private Higher Education*.

South university to desegregate without violence or a court order. He was regularly sought out among southerners for his counsel on how to admit Black students peacefully, but our collective memories have not done the likes of Harrison and other college presidents justice for their roles in shaping how the nation engaged the race question.[19]

That said, the most glaring historiographical lapse regarding the college presidency and race might be that what we *do* know is almost exclusively southern. This is important, considering the significance of the fight for racial equality in other regions. Thomas J. Sugrue, a historian of race and public policy, argued that studying civil rights beyond the South "opens up new ways of exploring the most important, and still unfinished, history of race, rights, and politics in modern America." There is significant room for further understanding of social movements and racial initiatives on nonsouthern campuses before the "Black Revolution on Campus," as described in historian Martha Biondi's book about the Black student activism of the late 1960s and early 1970s.[20]

More recently, Stefan M. Bradley has documented Black student resistance at Ivy League institutions from the 1940s to the 1970s. Therefore, just as scholars have wisely framed the southern movement as the culmination of decades of Black resistance, the post-1965 racial unrest in the Northeast, Midwest, and West was also an extension of years of racial frustration in those regions. It is important to study the Black Freedom Movement nationally to challenge assumptions around racial policies and practices based on geography, space, place, and time. Historian Matthew D. Lassiter argued that "[r]acial inequality is a constant theme in American history, but the manifestations of racism are evolving and multifaceted, refracted through frameworks such as economics

19. "In 1961, Georgia Tech became the first university in the Deep South to open its doors to African American students without a court order." For more, see Georgia Tech Division of Student Life, "History and Traditions," http://studentlife.gatech.edu/content/history-and -traditions (accessed March 12, 2019); Ibram X. Kendi also noted that Georgia Tech first "peacefully" opened its doors to Black students in the Deep South when violence and other forms of white resistance were common at other southern institutions. For more, see Kendi, *The Black Campus Movement*, pp. 26–27.

20. On the importance of studying racial struggles outside of the South, see Sugrue, *Sweet Land of Liberty*, p. xxviii. An additional scholarly argument is the need to expand the narrow conception of region. See Nickerson and Dochuk, *Sunbelt Rising*, specifically pp. 13–15, for the benefits of doing away with the strict "regional concept" in exchange for the "conceptional region." This is important because of the connectedness of college presidents across the nation from an ideological standpoint more than a geographic one. For a national survey of the Black student unrest in the late 1960s and early 1970s, see Kendi, *The Black Campus Movement*, and Biondi, *The Black Revolution on Campus*.

and geography." Therefore, college presidents outside of the South were engaged in different types of racial struggle but were influential nonetheless.[21]

For example, nonsouthern academic institutions have been described as being focused on technological and scientific advances during the Cold War. Those universities, often considered as more advanced than their southern counterparts, secured the bulk of government defense contracts, and their college presidents were touted as the leaders of intellectual engines. The critical question that remains unknown, however, is how did those college presidents engage the white powerbrokers who wanted to ensure that civil rights pressures in the Northeast, Midwest, and West did not negatively impact federal grants, private foundation funds, wealthy alumni donors, and urban renewal projects tied to university campuses.[22]

The Campus Color Line examines a national cohort of college presidents' strategies amid unrest over desegregation. It explores how that unrest impacted their relationships with local community leaders, trustees, faculty members, business leaders, alumni, journalists, state and federal officials, and students alongside concerns about governance, public relations, free speech, academic freedom, and fundraising. This account of academic leaders offers a panoramic view of American higher education from the 1940s through the 1960s and transcends regional boundaries to demonstrate how college presidents handled intensified questions about race and racism. This book turns attention toward college presidents' offices, where numerous racial practices were conceived and facilitated. In doing so, it argues college presidents were a driving force behind many of the social changes, initiatives, and struggles that emerged during this era as they actively, though often quietly, shaped racial policy both inside and outside of the educational sphere.

———

In investigating the actions of college presidents, the following chapters examine the philosophical, social, economic, and political elements that shaped the American higher education system during the mid-twentieth century. There was greater public interest in higher education as student enrollments increased, and dramatic societal shifts beyond the college campus resulted in more cross-sector communication. Academic, corporate, state, and federal leaders worked together to protect the nation's interests because the global

21. Bradley, *Upending the Ivory Tower*; Lassiter, *The Silent Majority*, p. 4.

22. O'Mara, *Cities of Knowledge*; Levin, *Cold War University*; Winling, *Building the Ivory Tower*.

perception of US race relations belied the nation's espoused commitment to democracy and undermined its standing around the world. The international pressure that accompanied World War II and the Cold War resulted in a remarkable amount of power and influence bestowed upon college presidents. As a result, many presidents utilized their new realm of influence to mold institutional, state, and national racial policies and practices.

This book begins in the 1940s and progresses into the 1960s. Black presidents used silent networks to shape policy in segregated states while strategically not appearing too radical. These strategies were essential mechanisms that presidents of state-supported Black colleges used to mold racial practices. Networking was also present among their southern white counterparts. Although much less covert, the presidents of segregated white universities, particularly state-supported campuses, were not the hands-off actors typically depicted in history.

Beyond the South, the urban renewal program's displacement of Black communities is well documented, but it was elite private university presidents who coordinated federal, state, and local funding to redevelop urban centers at the expense of Black and underserved citizens. At nonsouthern state-supported universities, presidents developed university systems and launched campus initiatives touted as more racially inclusive than those of segregated white universities; however, those same academic leaders contradicted themselves when demands for Black liberation emerged on campuses in the Midwest, Northeast, and West. Each chapter follows college presidents' actions as a lens to examine a larger theme about racism and higher education and demonstrates the varied roles academic leaders accepted in shaping racial policy.

The first chapter explores how Black college presidents negotiated several pressures in order to help maintain control of their institutions, secure money from white legislators, fight back against racists, and balance student demands with other demands—and they relied on silent networks to accomplish these tasks. Focused on Martin D. Jenkins, president of Morgan State College in Baltimore, the chapter challenges the perception of Black college presidents, especially those at state-supported institutions, as being publicly deferential to white officials. By contrast, Jenkins was a prolific scholar who advised white state and federal officials on racial inequalities. His survey research on Black youth also helped him build relationships with Black teacher associations and civic groups. Combined, his professional and personal networks made him a sought-after speaker from Maryland in ways unimaginable to the presidents of state-supported Black campuses in the Deep South. Thus, the chapter allows us to see that Black college presidents' most defiant intellectual and political efforts to support the Black freedom struggle often occurred offstage.

Chapter 2 examines chancellors Lawrence Kimpton and George Beadle at the University of Chicago and how urban university presidents shaped unfair housing policies in the United States. Following the New Deal in the 1930s, whites took advantage of new federal home loan policies and developed local housing practices that systematically discriminated against Black residents. Restrictive covenants were paired with redlining to segregate neighborhoods by race. By the 1950s, however, the postwar migration of Black southerners increased Chicago's population without increasing the number of neighborhoods willing to welcome Black residents. In response, academic leaders sought to protect the university from the encroaching Black "slums" and coordinated a nationwide effort among other urban university presidents to acquire slum properties. Universities across the nation followed Chicago's lead and displaced thousands of Black residents in the name of urban renewal. The peak of this effort, called "Negro removal" by its opponents, was a result of Chicago chancellors' large-scale, public relations–friendly commitment to racial equality to downplay concerns about gentrifying Black communities—a method that would be duplicated across the nation.

In chapter 3, the university president/campus chancellor governance structure is evaluated for its strategic use to stifle Black liberation and maintain white supremacy. In the 1950s, state officials crafted the California Master Plan for Higher Education, touted as the nation's premier higher education system. This created widespread conflict, as the plan outlined three college systems for the state—one for two-year colleges, another for state colleges, and a third for the University of California campuses. New racial concerns emerged: Was this tiering higher education? Would fewer Black and low-income students be admitted to UC campuses? As state officials and residents critiqued the plan, Franklin D. Murphy, the new chancellor of the University of California, Los Angeles, sought complete autonomy—starting with ending racial discrimination on campus and supporting students' civil rights activities. Yet, conservative California leaders and the UC president Clark Kerr did not agree with Murphy's support of UCLA students' demands for racial equality. The university system's structure added new layers of organizational complexity regarding how, or even if, the chief academic leader of an individual campus could support students' grassroots efforts to address racism.

Chapter 4 analyzes the continued fight for the autonomy to lead a state-supported institution through the chancellorship of John Davis Williams at the University of Mississippi. In 1962, Governor Ross Barnett stripped Williams of any authority to decide if James Meredith, a Black applicant, could enroll. By the time Barnett reinstated the chancellor's authority, it was too late to prevent violence as a white mob battled federal troops dispatched to the campus by US president John F. Kennedy. In the process, the regional accrediting agency threatened to remove the university's accreditation if it did not maintain an environment conducive to learning: free of violence, without state officials' interference, and protective of academic freedom. Afterward, Williams immediately started a statewide campaign that gained a regional and then national reach to reframe the "Mississippi story." His efforts were significant to how university leaders could recover from campus racism and violence and restore its public image, but only when concerns of academic freedom and race are addressed.

Chapter 5 dissects how, shortly after the violence in Mississippi, the academic leaders of other segregated white universities began implementing preventative measures on their campuses. This proactivity of college presidents is important as seen through University of Alabama president Frank A. Rose's strategic efforts to ensure that his campus remained peaceful during desegregation. He coordinated a statewide call for "law and order" and worked with the state's most influential business leaders to establish a shared understanding that racial violence was bad for the state's economy. Rose then convinced the national alumni association to have each local alumni chapter condemn any violent resistance to desegregation, and similar messages were shared among faculty, students, and local residents. But the 1963 inauguration of segregationist governor George C. Wallace made maintaining peace more complex. Wallace vowed to keep Alabama segregated, and Rose was left to play the middleman between the governor and federal officials. In the end, Alabama became the site of Wallace's dramatic-but-nonviolent "Stand in the Schoolhouse Door," but it was Rose's relationships with the private sector and public officials—including those in the White House—that established the college president as the key facilitator in preventing racial violence.

The next chapter analyzes the tension between free speech protections and racial and intellectual diversity in higher education as white supremacists were invited to speak on campuses where academic leaders were also recruiting more Black students. At Princeton University, President Robert F. Goheen managed this free speech crisis years before the Free Speech Movement at the University of California, Berkeley. He advocated for racial equality, but the student debate society's invitation to Mississippi governor Ross Barnett to speak at Princeton created a dilemma. After his failed but defiant effort to keep Mississippi colleges segregated, Barnett was invited to speak across the nation, and Goheen was conflicted about whether to allow the governor to speak at Princeton or condemn his appearance as counter to the university's efforts to diversify the student body. Goheen chose both. He angered Princeton's influential southern alumni base when he denounced Barnett's racist ideas but appeased them by allowing him to address the campus. With racial tensions at their peak, Goheen's hands-on coordination resulted in a peaceful Barnett public address before a standing-room-only audience, but his greatest coup was using the controversial speaker as the impetus for racial advances in campus admissions and Princeton borough's business, housing, and employment practices.

Bringing the book full circle, chapter 7 evaluates the nation's first higher education affirmative action programs—mostly geared toward strengthening Black colleges and universities. Yet, white college presidents quickly dismantled the initial system-wide affirmative action goals and made those programs solely focused on objectives applicable to their individual campuses. For instance, University of Wisconsin president Fred Harvey Harrington aimed to position his university as the nation's leading institution in addressing the racial challenges Black citizens faced. He used the national interest in affirmative action to solicit private foundations—Ford, Carnegie, Rockefeller, and others—to fund Wisconsin's racial initiatives. Harrington also coordinated similar efforts among other midwestern universities to follow Wisconsin's lead, but with millions of dollars available, white college presidents soon competed among one another. The self-serving motives of those academic leaders derailed the broader affirmative action goals that included the nation's Black colleges. This decision set the stage for the Black campus movement of the late 1960s, and race-based admissions practices became the surviving original program—making affirmative action solely about a select few white colleges and universities.

———

Due to the national scope of this book, I use "civil rights" in the broadest sense. In the South, it meant challenging legalized racial discrimination. In nonsouthern states, people joined the civil rights efforts intent on racial equality despite there being no formal laws that mandated the segregation that existed. Therefore, civil rights may convey a nuanced meaning throughout the book based on the particular issue and locale being discussed.

Additionally, a number of historians and other commentators on the Black Freedom Movement describe the United States with binary terms: "North" and "South." What is not the South is simply referred to as "the North"—a mythical region that spans from Maine to California; however, with the exception of direct quotes, I use the terms Northeast, Midwest, and West to more accurately locate accounts of college presidents and racial unrest.

It is also important to note that only the first of the seven chapters focuses solely on Black colleges, despite this book being about the Black Freedom Movement—a social movement intertwined with Black institutions. Beginning with a Black president centers Black colleges in the movement, and Martin D. Jenkins's frequent travel and speaking engagements made him an intellectual leader and an activist—descriptors not commonly assigned to Black presidents during this era or today. Therefore, he is a unique figure as the leader of a state-supported Black college, and he sets the foundation for understanding the multifaceted roles of college presidents. From there, the remaining chapters exhibit how white academic leaders determined how the rest of American higher education responded to and engaged the movement.

A final point of interest is the variety of colleges and universities examined in this book. This approach offers a robust opportunity to learn more about higher education and racism by looking across the spectrum of institutional types and regional differences. These presidents led prestigious private or state-supported institutions as well as regional colleges, commuter campuses, and aspiring research universities. There are numerous institutional histories but nothing so broad as this book in demonstrating the shared role of the collective American higher education system during the Black Freedom Movement.

———

In the mid-twentieth century, higher education inherited a broader meaning as a cultural structure and distinctive aspect of a democratic society, and each chapter conveys a multifaceted tale of the college presidency and its new and competing pressures. *The Campus Color Line* illustrates the variety of challenges academic leaders confronted and the range of strategies they employed as they ushered the full range of institutions into new social and political significance and influenced how municipal, state, and federal officials engaged racial policy and practices. There are lessons to be learned from how these individuals negotiated organizational needs and pressures that conflicted with academic missions and espoused institutional values. This national study of the college presidency—from smaller colleges to elite universities—conveys historical accounts that must be reckoned with if we are to ever envision college presidents better equipped to effectively address racism, racial tensions, and racial violence in US higher education.

1

"This Is a Good Movement"

BLACK PRESIDENTS AND THE DISMANTLING OF SEGREGATION

"IT IS MORE desirable at this time to advance the interests of the institution now committed to our care than to engage in controversy," Morris A. Soper advised Martin D. Jenkins. This caution came on April 29, 1948, two days after Jenkins accepted the presidency of Morgan State College in Baltimore, where Soper, a white man, was chair of the Black college's board of trustees. Black college presidents like Jenkins were critical actors in the shaping of racial policy and practices across the South and within the federal government. These academic leaders regularly advised white elected officials on issues pertaining to segregated white colleges and universities. They helped formulate the parameters of out-of-state scholarship programs that supported southern Black students' enrollment at desegregated institutions. Black presidents also molded public discourse around the governance of Black colleges. And notably, they often championed the direct action campaigns and student demonstrations that challenged segregation; however, much of this work was done with extreme caution and out of plain sight.[1]

This was necessary because Black presidents were also the most scrutinized subset of academic leaders. When southern higher education was faced with the question of desegregation, white leaders were suspicious of Black leaders'

The Martin D. Jenkins collection was being reprocessed by Morgan State archivist Ida Jones in 2018. Therefore, the archival collection locations (e.g., box, folder) used in the notes may have changed.

1. Morris A. Soper to Martin D. Jenkins, April 29, 1948, Morris A. Soper, Morgan Christian Center, and Morgan Board of Trustees Collection, Box 2–5, Folder: 7, Beulah Davis Research Room, Morgan State University (archival collection and location hereafter cited as Soper Collection and MSU).

ideas, arguments, and perceived radical acts. Therefore, Black presidents regularly relied on hidden networks to negotiate several pressures in order to help maintain control of their institutions, secure money from white legislators, and fight back against racists. They utilized personal and professional relationships to communicate among themselves and convey messages to white powerbrokers as needed. Black presidents' efforts to challenge white supremacy was dangerous work and required meticulous attention to details and well-calculated strategies, whether leading a state-supported or private Black campus.

These were the harrowing realities of segregation, particularly in the Deep South, but a broader perspective on Black presidents is gained from Maryland—the last state to provide its Black residents with access to state-supported higher education. Morgan State was initially a private college but was later purchased by the State of Maryland and converted into a state-supported institution. This created unique tensions between white officials and the college's Black leaders who were accustomed to independence and unwilling to concede their self-governed organizational structure to state control. With Maryland offering unimaginable concessions, Jenkins emerged as an intellectual leader and activist, and he used a silent network to influence policies and practices that advanced racial equality in Maryland and elsewhere throughout the South—demonstrating how Black college presidents supported Black liberation.

The Making of a Scholar

Martin David Jenkins was born September 11, 1904, in Terre Haute, Indiana, a small town tightly nestled along the Wabash River near the Illinois state line. There, his father David Jenkins started a business as a contractor working with the State Highway Commission of Indiana and the State of Illinois. The company specialized in roads, bridges, and general construction, and by age fourteen, Martin spent his summers on Indiana and Illinois highways working with his father. Just as childhood moved quickly into summers working, life also did not slow down for the younger Jenkins during the academic year. He was a sprinter and served as captain of Wiley High School's mostly white track team and led it to win the city track championship in 1921. An apprentice and foreman during the summer and a sprinter during the school year, Jenkins had a clear path to follow in his father's footsteps.[2]

---

2. For biographical information, see Jenkins, Martin David (biographical clipping), n.d., Martin D. Jenkins Collection, Box: Personal Papers, Folder: Biographical, Newspaper, and

After high school, he attended Howard University in Washington, DC, and majored in mathematics with a minor in industrial arts/commerce amid plans to return home to work with his father's highway and bridge construction company. In fact, Jenkins returned from Washington, DC, to Terre Haute every summer to work the family business until he graduated from Howard in 1925, and by 1927, then well acquainted with the family business, the firm was renamed—David Jenkins and Son. The two were officially co-partners.[3]

Traveling along those highways, however, in and around the rolling hills of southern Indiana and elsewhere in the region, was no easy feat for Black people. At Howard, a hub of Black intelligentsia, Jenkins had spent his college years within the confines of the private, federally subsided university, where several students—particularly Black women students—were redefining what it meant to be full citizens in America, but when he returned home, Indiana was leading the post-Reconstruction resurgence of the Ku Klux Klan. There were roughly 194,000 registered Klan members living in Indiana. In Terre Haute, there were two chapters—one with a membership of 7,250 whites and another with 990 whites on its roster—with the majority of candidates for public office in town as members. This is the social environment that hovered over Jenkins as he settled into his role alongside his father, and after two years, he stopped working as a co-partner. Education had taken the younger Jenkins's heart as he enrolled at Indiana State Teachers College in Terre Haute and earned a second bachelor's degree in 1930.[4]

Equipped with two bachelor's degrees, Jenkins moved to Petersburg, Virginia, where, from 1930 to 1932, he was an instructor at Virginia State College for Negroes. But not satisfied with merely being an instructor, Jenkins returned to the Midwest during the Great Depression. There, he pursued graduate studies in education at Northwestern University in Evanston, Illinois, during the economic downturn and earned a master's degree in 1933 and a

---

Picture Clippings, MSU (collection hereafter cited as Jenkins Collection); "Wiley High, City Champions, Finish Second to Garfield in District Track and Field Meet," *Terre Haute Tribune,* May 15, 1921.

3. For employment history, see Notarized Statement, December 21, 1939, Jenkins Collection, Box 14–14a–15, Folder 187, MSU. For academic credentials, see Martin D. Jenkins Dissertation Announcement and Transcript, 1935, Jenkins Collection, Box 14–14a–15, Folder 187, MSU.

4. Jeffrey C. Stewart wrote, "As the only bona fide Black university in America, Howard possessed a respected medical school, a well-regarded law school, and a federal subsidy that made it one of the most secure academic institutions in Black higher education." For more, see Stewart, *The New Negro,* p. 236. On Black women's activities at Howard during Jenkins's undergraduate studies, see Lindsey, *Colored No More,* especially pp. 25–39; Roznowski, *An American Hometown,* pp. 22–23.

doctor of philosophy degree in education in 1935. He was a straight-A student while studying under Professor Paul A. Witty, his Northwestern advisor and dissertation committee chair.[5]

Witty was also born in Terre Haute and graduated from Indiana State, and the two cultivated a relationship around their commonalities and shared interests. Witty was a renowned scholar who challenged popular beliefs about giftedness in children, and like his advisor, Jenkins also studied gifted education with a focus on Black youth. Jenkins launched a prolific scholarly career following the successful defense of his dissertation, "A Socio-Psychological Study of Negro Children of Superior Intelligence," on May 24, 1935.[6]

After Northwestern, Jenkins followed a common path for Black academics who earned doctorates at research universities in the Midwest and Northeast during this era. Regardless of how Black students excelled as doctoral students, those institutions were liberal only in enrolling them, not in employing or supporting Black graduates. For instance, between 1930 and 1943, 317 Black scholars earned PhDs. The University of Chicago, Columbia University, and the University of Pennsylvania awarded the most earned doctorates to Black scholars during that period. But the white scholars at these institutions had a long history, even prior to Jenkins's era, of shunning Black intellectuals or stealing their intellectual contributions and leaving them uncredited. In the early 1900s, W. E. B. Du Bois, who earned his doctorate at Harvard University, was not credited for his ideas that became key to the emerging field of sociology. Likewise, Georgiana Rose Simpson earned her doctorate in German at Chicago, but she was forced to live off campus and her career was largely ignored by the university. As a result, these scholars often found their professional homes at Black colleges.[7]

Jenkins's first job post-Northwestern was at the Negro Agricultural and Technical College of North Carolina in Greensboro, where he was the registrar and an education professor. There, he honed his administrative prowess as registrar, but he also maintained an unusually close scholarly relationship with his former Northwestern advisor. Generational contemporaries, with Witty only six years older, they co-authored a study published in the *Journal of*

5. Jenkins (biographical clipping); Jenkins Dissertation Announcement; Press Release, June 12, 1978, Jenkins Collection, Box: Personal Papers, Folder: In Memoriam, MSU.

6. Ibid. Regarding Paul A. Witty's background, see Jolly and Bruno, "Paul A. Witty," p. 14.

7. For more about mid-twentieth-century Black scholars, see Winston, "Through the Back Door," particularly p. 693 on number of degrees conferred. Regarding W. E. B. Du Bois and sociology, see Morris, *The Scholar Denied*, and Du Bois, "A Negro Student at Harvard." Only recently has the University of Chicago recognized Georgiana Rose Simpson. For more, see Lolly Bowean, "U. of C. Statue Gives Black Scholar Her Place in History," *Chicago Tribune*, November 27, 2017.

Psychology in 1936. Their study challenged the prominent argument that Black people were intellectually inferior to whites. Witty and Jenkins found that intelligence was attributable to a child's environment more than race, thus the amount of white ancestry that a Black child possessed had no impact. Their study had national implications for the use of intelligence testing in schools and earned widespread media coverage, especially among the Black press.[8]

A few months later, in October 1936, Jenkins published in the *Journal of Negro Education* his first in a series of annual assessments of current trends and events in Black higher education. This initial evaluation focused on the scholarly activities among the "few Negro colleges making provision for the publication of faculty research." His review of research activities highlighted research projects and recent publications by Howard and West Virginia State professors and discussed potential for research partnerships and grants for Black colleges. His commitment to scholarship and Black colleges' intellectual contributions spoke to the longstanding ideological debate over the purpose of Black higher education.[9]

At the turn of the century, Booker T. Washington had risen to national prominence among white philanthropists and government officials. Born into slavery, he pursued his education at Hampton Institute and later founded Tuskegee Institute. From there, he promoted a program of industrial education for Black students, and whites backed his call for Black people to build their own independence to support themselves through industrial vocations. This appealed to southern and northern whites as philanthropists supported Washington and this educational plan.[10]

Du Bois led a contingent against Washington's ideals. He argued that Washington's own institution could not exist without the full-fledged colleges—those that offered more than vocational studies—that trained the faculty who taught at Tuskegee. He also cited whites' efforts to politically disenfranchise

8. Jenkins (biographical clipping); Jolly and Bruno, "Paul A. Witty"; Witty and Jenkins, "Intra-race Testing and Negro Intelligence"; "Colored People with Most White Blood Not Smartest," *Baltimore Afro-American*, April 4, 1936 (newspaper hereafter cited as *Afro*).

9. Jenkins published annually about Black colleges in the *Journal of Negro Education* from 1936 until the *Brown v. Board of Education* decision in 1954. See his first article on the topic: Jenkins, "Negro Higher Education."

10. Washington, *Up from Slavery*. Regarding Washington's effectiveness at fundraising, Michael Bieze wrote, "As America's first black media celebrity, Washington was a master of appealing to white northerners by sending paradoxical messages." For more, see Bieze, "Booker T. Washington," p. 42; As an extension of Washington's success, in the early 1900s, the General Education Board surpassed churches as the largest funder of Black education. For more, see Rooks, *White Money/Black Power*, p. 104.

Black people, the treatment of Black people as second-class citizens, and the withdrawal of aid from Black colleges as evidence that Washington's views stifled Black liberation. "These movements are not, to be sure, direct results of Mr. Washington's teachings," Du Bois argued in 1903, "but his propaganda has, without a shadow of doubt, helped their speedier accomplishment."[11]

This debate over the future of Black higher education framed the careers of the next generation of Black college educators like Jenkins, whose early career trajectory aligned more with Du Bois. Jenkins was interested in publishing his research and promoting more scholarly output at Black colleges. In 1937, he left North Carolina A&T to become the dean of instruction at Cheyney Training School for Teachers, a Black college in Pennsylvania. But Cheyney, like North Carolina A&T, did not offer the opportunity to connect his emerging scholarly profile with a well-established university. In 1938, however, he secured a faculty job at Howard—one of the few Black institutions offering graduate-level curricula. In fact, in 1926, when Mordecai W. Johnson became president, Howard received $218,000 in federal appropriations, and that amount only increased during his presidency. Jenkins's skills and Howard's infrastructure were an excellent match, and when he accepted the job, Johnson told him, "I rejoice. Your coming to us will be warmly welcomed by students, faculties, and trustees."[12]

11. Du Bois, *The Souls of Black Folk*, pp. 43–61. The book was originally published in 1903. Also refer to Du Bois, "The Talented Tenth." Over the past century, numerous scholarly discussions have added more nuance to the characterizations of Du Bois and Washington. For instance, historian Robert J. Norrell noted that the two men were friendly before a series of events led to the perception of betrayal. There was an attempted "truce," but it failed. "The estrangement between the two was personal before it became ideological." For more, see Norrell, *Up from History*, pp. 224–228, 268. Conversely, Ibram X. Kendi has argued that the debate between Du Bois and Washington has been "overplayed." Instead, the issue with Black education was "the pervasive sway of white capitalists and paternalists." For more, see Kendi, *The Black Campus Movement*, p. 17.

12. Jenkins (biographical clipping); James D. Anderson's seminal history of Black education in the South details the struggles of Black schools and how few Black colleges offered an actual collegiate-level curriculum well into the twentieth century. For more, see Anderson, *Education of Blacks in the South*, p. 238. Several scholars have noted that due to limited educational opportunities during slavery, the first schools established for Blacks focused on primary and secondary education. Specific to Black education in Maryland, which is the focus of this chapter, see Wheatle, "'Ward of the State,'" p. 128–129. On accepting the Howard job, see Mordecai W. Johnson to Martin D. Jenkins, May 10, 1938, Jenkins Collection, Box: Correspondence Ha–Pu, Folder: Johnson, Mordecai W., MSU (correspondence boxes hereafter cited by alphabetical label, and folder hereafter cited as Johnson).

Once he arrived in Washington, DC, Jenkins's impact as a scholar was felt at Howard and beyond. He conducted a national study on gifted Black youth, utilizing connections at larger white universities established with his advisor Paul A. Witty. By 1942, Jenkins had published twenty-six articles that spanned both white and Black academic circles. His scholarly arguments appeared in white-run journals, such as *School and Society* and the *Journal of Higher Education*, the latter housed at Ohio State University, and in Black-run outlets like the *Journal of Negro Education* and the *Crisis*, the official magazine of the National Association for the Advancement of Colored People. Jenkins moved in two worlds. Yet, he never sacrificed the heart of his academic argument— Black educational advancement at all costs. This approach set the tone for his next move after Howard.[13]

Building a Network

A byproduct of Jenkins's early career success was the expanding reach of his influence. His scholarship stirred interest in him beyond his colleagues and students at Howard. As a critical scholar in gifted education, skilled in survey research methods, he received requests to consult on or lead special projects for the federal government and several cities and states. In accepting these requests, Jenkins cultivated relationships that, in turn, enlarged his professional network. Many in this network became allies whose support he leveraged later in his career in his fight for racial equality in education and beyond.

On January 4, 1940, Fred J. Kelly, an official in the Higher Education Division of the US Office of Education, asked President Johnson at Howard to

13. Jenkins List of Publications, February 1, 1942, Jenkins Collection, Box: Personal Papers, Folder: Curriculum Vitae, MSU. Also see Biographical Sketch of Martin David Jenkins, n.d., Jenkins Collection, Box 14–14a–15, Folder 186, MSU; Jenkins solicited principals, schoolteachers, and professors for data regarding his national study of gifted Black youth. Numerous letters were sent to educators in Cincinnati, Cleveland, New York, and Chicago, among other cities. One example is Martin D. Jenkins to Leta S. Hollingworth, May 16, 1939, Jenkins Collection, Box: Ha–Pu, Folder: Ha–Hy, MSU. Hollingworth taught at Teachers College, Columbia University. On Jenkins's scholarly relationship with Hollingworth, see Ann Robinson and Pamela R. Clinkenbeard, "History of Giftedness: Perspectives from the Past Presage Modern Scholarship," in Pfeiffer, *Handbook of Giftedness in Children*, pp. 16–20. On publishing in *School and Society*, see John Dale Russell to Martin D. Jenkins, March 12, 1947, Jenkins Collection, Box: Qai–Zw, Folder: Ra–Rz, MSU. On publishing in the *Journal of Higher Education*, see R. H. Eckelberry to Martin D. Jenkins, November 9, 1945, Jenkins Collection, Box: A–G, Folder: Eb–Eu, MSU.

recommend a scholar capable of leading the federal government's Survey of the Higher Education of Negroes. In explaining the ideal scholar, Kelly described Jenkins in nearly every facet without naming him. "The job will call for knowledge of survey techniques, the formulating of questionnaires, the evaluating of measurements of student achievement, etc.," Kelly carefully told Johnson. "He must be able to maintain the good will and confidence of both races."[14]

A month later, that request for a recommendation had evolved into Jenkins accepting the invitation. Immediately, Jenkins informed Johnson that he would need half-time status as a faculty member and release from his responsibilities as director of the university's summer school program. This led to a two-year leave from Howard as he became a senior specialist in higher education for the US Office of Education; however, although he was away from Howard, his work would serve all Black colleges in his absence.[15]

In this federal role, Jenkins visited several Black colleges across the South, and his survey research earned national media coverage. By 1940, Jenkins reported that Black colleges enrolled 39,793 students. Tuskegee Institute in Alabama was the largest, with an enrollment of 1,422, followed by Howard (1,286 students), and Tennessee Agricultural & Industrial in Nashville (1,234 students). Also, nine Black colleges offered graduate-level education, but the reality was that those graduate students were largely concentrated at Howard and Atlanta University.[16]

From there, in 1943, Jenkins inserted himself into the national commentary on World War II and Black education, earning further prominence as an expert. "On the domestic front, I am especially interested in the influence of the war on education and on race relations," he wrote in a *Baltimore Afro-American* op-ed. "Negroes will be discriminated against, segregated, lynched, disfranchised in 1943—will still need vigorously to fight intolerance at home while fighting intolerance abroad." The next year, Jenkins was a featured speaker during the National Association of Deans and Registrars conference at Winston-Salem Teachers College in March 1944. There, in North Carolina where he had

14. Fred J. Kelly to Mordecai W. Johnson, January 4, 1940, Box: Ha–Pu, Folder: Johnson, MSU.

15. Martin D. Jenkins to Mordecai W. Johnson, February 14, 1940, Box: Ha–Pu, Folder: Johnson, MSU; Regarding Jenkins's formal title with the US Office of Education, see Durham, "Jenkins Succeeds Holmes"; and Jenkins (biographical clipping).

16. On visiting numerous Black colleges, see Durham, "Jenkins Succeeds Holmes"; Jenkins, "Enrollment in Institutions of Higher Education"; and "39,793 Students Enrolled in 102 Colored Colleges," *Afro*, November 1, 1941.

served as a registrar in the late 1930s, he discussed implications for curriculum development based on his national survey findings.[17]

Kelly and other federal officials considered Jenkins's survey research revolutionary. "The results reported there should do much to lift the fog that still prevails in a good many people's minds about inductions of Negroes as compared with whites," Kelly told Jenkins in September 1944. "I think the country has never faced as important a period as the one just before us in its problem of improving race relations." He closed by emphasizing that the nation needed Jenkins to fight for racial equality in education: "Men like yourself have a tremendous responsibility, and I am delighted that you approach your task through studies such as you have just now finished."[18]

By this point, Jenkins felt that his federal-level contributions were not appreciated by Howard. At the start of the 1945–46 academic year, while reflecting on his scholarly output and national voice on issues impacting Black education, Jenkins expressed his frustration. "For the past several years, I have felt that my services at the university have merited the recognition of promotion to full professor," Jenkins told President Johnson. He then listed some career highlights: forty articles published across fifteen journals, five books or monographs, extensive teaching experience and internal and external service, and numerous keynote addresses. Jenkins concluded: "I think that any objective appraisal of this statement leads naturally to the question, what must this man do to merit promotion at Howard University?"[19]

As Jenkins awaited his review for promotion, he gained more recognition. On March 19, 1946, Jenkins was one of five Black men awarded the Selective Service Medal. Specifically, he was recognized for his role as chair of the Special Research Committee of the American Teachers Association, a professional organization for Black teachers. The Selective Service System, by the authority of the US Congress, selected Jenkins because he studied why Black people failed to meet the military's literacy requirements. Jenkins's findings had been discussed among Black teachers and professors and state officials across the nation. "It is our belief that remedial measures, which have been started as a result of your study, will continue," said Colonel Campbell C. Johnson, executive assistant for the Selective Service, "and prove a most important factor in increasing the availability of young Negro men for service in the armed forces."

17. Martin D. Jenkins, "Small College Must Close," *Afro*, January 16, 1943; "Deans, Registrars to Consider War Needs of Colleges," *Afro*, March 18, 1944.

18. Fred J. Kelly to Martin D. Jenkins, September 7, 1944, Jenkins Collection, Box: Ha–Pu, Folder: Ka–Kr, MSU.

19. Martin D. Jenkins to Mordecai W. Johnson, August 14, 1945, Jenkins Collection, Box: Ha–Pu, Folder: Johnson, MSU.

Jenkins was recognized at the US Department of Labor ceremony before "a barrage of cameras."[20]

The medal presentation appeared in newspapers across the nation, and President Johnson at Howard was made aware of Jenkins's work by individuals as well. Thomasina W. Johnson, legislative representative for Alpha Kappa Alpha Sorority's Non-Partisan Council of Public Affairs, told Johnson how Jenkins had assisted the sorority in communicating with federal officials and securing Howard students as volunteer workers. "Dr. Jenkins is a most unusual person with an exceptionally brilliant mind that lends itself well to the type of unusual work that must be done in this office," she said. "Much of the success that we have had has been materially aided by the assistance of Dr. Jenkins." A week later, on April 9, 1946, Jenkins was promoted to full professor at Howard.[21]

By the time Howard trustees approved this promotion, Jenkins also had the attention of civic, political, and educational leaders in Maryland. Earlier in the year, Carl J. Murphy of Baltimore—a Howard and Harvard alumnus, a prominent Black newspaper publisher, and member of the Morgan State College trustee board—also praised Jenkins. Murphy served on Baltimore's Committee on Current Educational Problems Affecting Negroes, which secured Jenkins's services as a consultant. The committee had no resources to compensate a consultant, but Jenkins offered his services nonetheless. He analyzed student test results among Black and white high schools in Baltimore. Jenkins also helped prepare a committee report and volunteered to help defend the report before the city's Board of Education. "It has been tremendously gratifying to the committee to have had the best advice and the help from a member of the staff of Howard University and to have had it willingly without cost," Murphy wrote President Johnson at Howard. "This has been the committee's first experience with an out-of-town educator who has given so graciously of their services. We thought you ought to know about it."[22]

What appeared to be a simple letter of appreciation was actually foreshadowing Jenkins's deepening relationship with Maryland. In September 1946,

20. "Selective Service Medals Presented to 5 Leaders," *Afro*, March 30, 1946; Campbell C. Johnson to Martin D. Jenkins, February 26, 1946, Jenkins Collection, Box: Ha–Pu, Folder: Ja–Ju, MSU; Lewis B. Hershey to Martin D. Jenkins, March 1, 1946, Jenkins Collection, Box: Ha–Pu, Folder: Ha–Hy, MSU; Durham, "Jenkins Succeeds Holmes."

21. Thomasina W. Johnson to Mordecai W. Johnson, April 1, 1946, Jenkins Collection, Box: Ha–Pu, Folder: Johnson, MSU. Regarding Jenkins's promotion to full professor, see J. S. Price to Martin D. Jenkins, April 25, 1946, Jenkins Collection, Box: Ha–Pu, Folder: Pa–Pu, MSU.

22. Carl J. Murphy to Mordecai W. Johnson, January 25, 1946, Jenkins Collection, Box: Ha–Pu, Folder: Johnson, MSU.

the Maryland Commission on Higher Education hired Jenkins as a special consultant on problems of Black higher education in Maryland. He was now no longer advising at no cost. It was expected that this would not interfere with his work at Howard, but Murphy was also a member of the commission.[23]

This was another opportunity for Murphy to work with Jenkins, and the timing of his hiring as a consultant is significant. White resentment still lingered over the forced desegregation of the formerly all-white University of Maryland Law School ten years earlier. In January 1936, the Maryland Court of Appeals had ruled, in the case of *Pearson v. Murray*, that Donald G. Murray, a Black man, must be admitted to the law school. The court said, "The case, as we find it, then, is that the state has undertaken the function of education in the law, but has omitted students of one race from the only adequate provision made for it, and omitted them solely because of their color." Although only three Black students enrolled and graduated from the law school in the following decade, a record twenty Black students enrolled in the fall of 1946, and new questions were raised about the future of higher education in Maryland.[24]

On February 1, 1947, the Maryland Commission on Higher Education issued a report with recommendations to address those questions. Dubbed the Marbury Report, after commission chair William L. Marbury, the survey team was led by John Dale Russell, a professor at the University of Chicago, with Jenkins conducting "a special study of the field of Negro education." One goal was to assess Maryland's expenditures on higher education and develop a future plan for the state and its relationship with its institutions of higher education. The conflict, of course, was over the recommendations for the University of Maryland and those for the state's Black colleges.[25]

For instance, the commission recommended further expansion of the University of Maryland as long as its new programs did not duplicate those already offered at private institutions like Johns Hopkins University in Baltimore. Yet,

---

23. On Jenkins as a consultant, see John Dale Russell to Martin D. Jenkins, September 21, 1946, and John Dale Russell to To Whom It May Concern, September 21, 1946. Both letters are located in Jenkins Collection, Box: Qai–Zw, Folder: Ra–Rz, MSU. Also see "Howard Educator Named to Survey Group in Md.," *Washington Afro-American*, October 15, 1946; and Durham, "Jenkins Succeeds Holmes."

24. *Pearson v. Murray*, 169 Md. 478 (Md. 1936); Louise K. Hines, "20 Attending University of Maryland Law School: Interest in Civil Rights Responsible for Most," *Afro*, October 19, 1946.

25. Maryland Higher Education Commission's Report (hereafter cited as Marbury Report), February 1, 1947, Jenkins Collection, Box 14–14a–15, Folder 187a, MSU. For more on William L. Marbury, a Harvard law graduate, see "William L. Marbury Dead at 86; Lawyer and A Fellow of Harvard," *New York Times*, March 7, 1988.

the report treaded lightly when it came to recommendations for Morgan State. "We turn now to the thorny problem created by the long-standing practice, deeply woven into the social fabric of this state, of separation of the races," the commission stated, while acknowledging that equal education was an obligation in a democracy; however, the commission did not suggest desegregation. "While we recommend no change in the practices now being followed in this respect, we are convinced that their successful continuance depends upon the willingness and ability of the state to improve the facilities which it now offers for the higher education of Negroes." Ultimately, the commission suggested the state provide more support to Morgan State for graduate programs in education and for the activities of the other three state-supported colleges to be transferred to Morgan as well.[26]

Carl J. Murphy was infuriated by the commission's recommendation to simply defer to the state's "willingness" to improve Black colleges. The Marbury Report took a passive, hands-off stance toward blatant racism. Therefore, Murphy penned and submitted as an appendix a minority report to voice his dissent from the rest of the commission. He argued that out-of-state scholarships—a common program in southern states that funded Black residents' education in other states instead of desegregating white institutions—should be discontinued, and the University of Maryland should accept Black students in curricula "which are not offered at a state institution of higher education for colored students." Murphy argued, "It is apparent, however, that the majority of the report does not face squarely the problem of the graduate and professional education of the colored citizens of the state."[27]

The token admission of Black people to the University of Maryland Law School while the rest of the university continued growth with whites-only admissions was not sustainable, especially since Morgan State and other Black colleges were not receiving the state aid needed to develop beyond undergraduate education. "It is manifestly impossible for the state to maintain 'separate and equal' courses of study in all fields for colored and white . . . ," Murphy explained. "I believe that the state must now face this question and set its policy for the ensuing year." A month later, in March 1947, Jenkins discussed Jim Crow and education in the *Baltimore Afro-American*, which Murphy owned, and also argued that educational equality within a segregated

26. Marbury Report.

27. For Murphy's minority report, see pp. 46–48 of the Marbury Report. In 1940, the Maryland State Commission allocated $30,000 for scholarships to support Black students' study in undergraduate degree programs not offered at Morgan State or graduate programs offered in other states. Scholarships ranged from $50 to $500. For more, see "$30,000 Ready for Maryland Scholarships," *Afro*, August 10, 1940.

framework was impossible—the same point Murphy made in his minority report.[28]

Jenkins received many requests as a Howard professor, and from 1938 to 1947, he showcased his expertise while helping cities, states, and the federal government better understand the challenges facing Black education. Black presidents of Black colleges, such as Albert W. Dent at Dillard University in New Orleans, raved about his scholarship. On segregation, Dent wrote Jenkins, saying, "We ought to get away from this in America. That day will be hastened by such contributions as yours." In 1947, US president Harry S. Truman's Commission on Higher Education also requested Jenkins's survey results on Black higher education while southern state officials took interest his findings. So, too, did Washington, DC, political influencers. But of all of these relationships, nothing was more telling than the synergy he and Carl J. Murphy developed. In Murphy, Jenkins found a co-conspirator—someone equally passionate about racial equality. Their budding relationship eventually led Jenkins to Maryland for his greatest opportunity yet to shape Black education and dismantle white supremacy.[29]

The Curious Case of Maryland

On March 24, 1948, Morgan State trustees received an unexpected request from Charles H. Wesley, who, for the previous nine months, was expected to succeed Dwight O. W. Holmes as president in June 1948. However, Wesley abruptly requested release from his contract; instead of moving to Baltimore, he suddenly wanted to remain in Ohio, where he was president of the

---

28. Marbury Report. For an assessment of Maryland education in 1947, just after the Marbury report was published, see Bradley, "The Education of Negroes in Maryland"; "Jenkins Proposes 5 Basic Principles for J.C. Schools," *Afro*, March 22, 1947.

29. For examples of Black college presidents praising Jenkins's scholarship, see Albert W. Dent to Martin D. Jenkins, March 15, 1947, Jenkins Collection, Box: A–G, Folder: Da–Du, MSU; and Luther H. Foster to Martin D. Jenkins, March 13, 1947, Jenkins Collection, Box: A–G, Folder: Fa–Fur, MSU. On southern state officials using Jenkins's findings, see N. C. Newbold to Martin D. Jenkins, March 28, 1947, Jenkins Collection, Box: Ha–Pu, Folder: Ma–My, MSU. Regarding the US president Harry S. Truman's Commission on Higher Education request, see Francis J. Brown to Martin D. Jenkins, March 31, 1947, Jenkins Collection, Box: A–G, Folder: Ba–Bu, MSU. On the Washington influencers, see the letter from Agnes E. Meyer. She wrote, "Your paper on educational methods for segregated schools interests me enormously. It is always thrilling for a non-professional person to discover principles from a study of reality that coincide with conclusions of professional students." Agnes E. Meyer to Martin D. Jenkins, March 18, 1947, Jenkins Collection, Box: Ha–Pu, Folder: Ma–My, MSU.

state-supported College of Education and Industrial Arts at Wilberforce (soon renamed Central State College). Under the pressure of personal responsibility, Wesley carried with him a moral obligation—an obligation commonly accepted by Black college presidents.

While Wesley was Morgan State president-elect, unforeseen complications arose in Ohio with the North Central Association of Colleges and Secondary Schools, a regional accrediting agency. This issue was that Central State had formerly been an academic department at Wilberforce, a private Black college operated by the African Methodist Episcopal (AME) Church, and the department's separation to become its own institution raised accreditation issues. Wesley had led Wilberforce since 1942 before taking over Central State, which became a separate four-year institution, but the accreditation review depended on stable leadership. It swiftly became an inopportune time to leave a Black college vulnerable, and Wesley did not wish to leave the Morgan trustees in a difficult position without a future president; "yet, there is another desire upon me, and that is to complete the work which I have undertaken and not to leave it unfinished," he explained.[30]

Shortly after Wesley rescinded his acceptance, trustee Carl J. Murphy immediately went about the business of Morgan State. Murphy was considered to have "bankrolled" civil rights efforts in Baltimore and beyond. For instance, Thurgood Marshall, director-counsel of the NAACP Legal Defense Fund, said of his numerous desegregation court battles, "When I needed money to get lawyers, Carl was always there." Murphy also used his platform as publisher of the *Afro-American* newspaper to cover Black issues when white newspapers like the *Baltimore Sun* remained silent. He leveraged his influence, despite not being the chair of the Morgan State board, to direct his fellow trustees toward another capable educational leader: Martin D. Jenkins, who at age forty-three, accepted the Morgan State presidency on April 27, 1948.[31]

---

30. "Wesley President-Elect of Morgan for 9 Months," *Afro*, May 1, 1948. University Public Relations, "About Central State," http://www.centralstate.edu/PR/index.php?num=70 (accessed February 14, 2020).

31. On Carl J. Murphy being revered as a Black leader, see J. D. Williams, "625 Join Morgan Alumni at Testimonial for Dr. Murphy," *Afro*, April 20, 1957. Also see Jones, "Purpose, Progress, and Promise," pp. 15–16. For the quote that Carl J. Murphy "bankrolled" the Baltimore movement, see Smith, *Here Lies Jim Crow*, pp. 98–99. For more on Baltimore's desegregation, see Baum, *Brown in Baltimore*; and Sartain, *Borders of Equality*. Murphy's influence also extended beyond Baltimore. Through the *Afro-American* platform, Murphy encouraged Blacks to support the International Labor Defense, a legal advocacy group focused on civil rights. For more, see Canton, *Raymond Pace Alexander*, pp. 36–41. For the Thurgood Marshall quote, see Buni,

Because of his previous consultant work in the state, Jenkins brought an immediate benefit that Wesley did not have—an intricate understanding of Maryland's educational system at all levels. This made Morgan State especially enticing to Jenkins. In 1947, his survey research recorded Morgan's enrollment of 1,557 students as the third largest Black college in the mid-Atlantic region— Delaware, Maryland, Virginia, Washington, DC—behind only Howard University (4,502 students) and Hampton Institute (1,722 students), both private colleges. Staying in the region at a state-supported Black college would also help Jenkins maintain the federal-government relationships he had cultivated at Howard; however, the Morgan State presidency also had challenges deeply rooted in a long history of racism in the state.[32]

Maryland was a peculiar state riddled with contradictions. It was segregated although it did not secede from the Union during the Civil War. That alone made its history different from most other southern states. Yet, functionally, Maryland's white legislators acted no differently than those elsewhere in the South. The state was the worst in the nation for Black higher education, as elected officials had successfully avoided their obligation to provide a state-supported college for its Black residents, ultimately becoming the last southern state to do so. This framed Jenkins's presidency and the problems he inherited as Morgan State president.[33]

Those problems could be traced back to when Morgan State was founded as Centenary Biblical Institute by the Methodist Church in 1867. When re-named Morgan College in 1890 after Lyttleton F. Morgan, a white benefactor who served as the college's second chair of the board of trustees, the second Morrill Land-Grant Act was passed, which mandated that southern states de-segregate their white land-grant college campuses or establish a Black one. Maryland state officials, however, made an arrangement to have Morgan College academic leaders manage Princess Anne Academy—a Black secondary school already located on the rural Eastern Shore of Maryland. The plan al-lowed state officials to neither operate a Black land-grant college nor be held

---

"Murphy, Carl." On Jenkins accepting the Morgan State presidency, see Martin D. Jenkins to Morris A. Soper, April 27, 1948, Soper Collection, Box 2–5, Folder 6, MSU.

32. On Jenkins serving Maryland in multiple capacities, see "Howard Professor Succeeds Dr. Holmes: New 44-Year-Old Administrator Has Taught More Than 18 Years," *Afro*, May 1, 1948, and "Jenkins to Head Morgan," *Afro*, May 1, 1948. For 1947–48 enrollment survey data, see Jenkins, "Enrollment in Institutions of Higher Education."

33. Multiple sources note that Maryland was the last southern state to fund and operate a state-supported Black college. Examples include: Davis, "The Negro Land-Grant College," pp. 315–316; Wilson, "Predecessors of Morgan State College," p. 8; Wheatle, "'Ward of the State,'" pp. 143, 149.

accountable for disbursing the federal land-grant funds equitably to Morgan College. It was not until 1915 when the US Bureau of Education criticized the Maryland arrangement that made the private Morgan College responsible for what should have been handled by the state.[34]

Despite that critique, and even after Morgan College and state officials revisited the arrangement in 1919, it was 1935—forty-five years after the second Morrill Act (and just before the *Pearson v. Murray* ruling)—when Maryland finally agreed to operate Princess Anne Academy. In addition to state-sanctioned neglect, Morgan College had issues with discrimination similar to other private Black colleges founded by white missionary groups. Carter G. Woodson, a historian and a leading Black thinker of the time, criticized white academic leaders' racism. "Negro schools cannot go forward with such a load of inefficiency and especially when the white presidents of these institutions are often less scholarly than Negroes who have to serve under them," he wrote in his 1933 book, *The Mis-Education of the Negro*. The same year, Black leaders in Baltimore accused John O. Spencer, the white president of Morgan College since 1902, of holding the campus color line after a Black architect developed plans to construct a new campus building with Black artisans, but a white contractor was hired. Three years later, in February 1936, twenty-six students participated in a walkout after William Henry Easton, a white philosophy professor, insulted them by telling "mammy" jokes in class (and it was not his first round of insults). The culmination of racism at Black colleges left Black Marylanders ready to control their own institutions, and shortly afterward, Spencer announced his retirement.[35]

34. On Morgan State's founding, see Wilson, "Predecessors of Morgan State College," and Jones, "Purpose, Progress, and Promise." For a lengthier discussion of the relationship between the State of Maryland, Princess Anne Academy, and Morgan State, see Wheatle, "'Ward of the State,'" pp. 128–133.

35. On the *Pearson v. Murray* decision in 1936, especially in the context of what it meant for Maryland's Black colleges and the state taking over Princess Anne Academy, see Wheatle, "'Ward of the State,'" pp. 159–168. The state owed Morgan College $100,000 after the private Black college operated Princess Anne since 1890; for more, see "State May Pay Morgan College $100,000 Bill," *Afro*, December 29, 1934; "Morgan Prexy Had Color Line, Lewis Charges," *Afro*, October 21, 1933; Woodson, *The Mis-Education of the Negro*, p. 27. For more on Woodson's legacy in Black education, see Givens, "There Would Be No Lynching." Related to Woodson's assessment, Kendi wrote, "On campus, students still faced restrictive rules at segregationist white and paternalistic Black colleges in the 1930s, and most curriculums remained culturally irrelevant." For more, see Kendi, *Black Campus Movement*, p. 23. Also, for Kendi's account of early Black college student protests, see pp. 32–47, 49–62. On the racist behaviors of white presidents and faculty at Black colleges, specifically at Fisk and Hampton, see Anderson, *Education of Blacks in*

In July 1937, Dwight O. W. Holmes accepted an offer to succeed Spencer as Morgan College president—becoming the first Black person to hold the position. At the time, he was dean of the Graduate School at Howard, where he was valedictorian of the class of 1901, and held a doctorate from Columbia University. Holmes was once seriously considered for the Howard presidency and leadership posts at several other colleges and secondary schools. Perhaps most fitting, he was previously an impressive high school teacher in Baltimore. Zora Neale Hurston, the acclaimed writer, remembered Holmes as her high school teacher, saying, "There is no more dynamic teacher anywhere under any skin. He radiates newness and nerve." This was important, considering that in the same year another anti-lynching bill failed as southern congressmen filibustered, and the connection between physical and intellectual violence geared toward Black people was clear. Holmes was aware of the obstacles to Black education in Maryland and had spent fifteen years combating them as a schoolteacher by igniting learning among Baltimore Black youth. Although several white ministers were favored to succeed Spencer, an editorial in the *Baltimore Afro-American* praised the hire of Holmes, not solely because of his race, but because Morgan finally had a professional educator at the helm. "The new president, we feel, will bring Morgan a new spirit," said the editorial board; however, there were hindrances working against that new spirit.[36]

After Holmes accepted the position, it was announced that Spencer was retained to supervise the construction of a new library and stadium. Therefore, Spencer would have more than an honorific president-emeritus title. His

---

the *South*, pp. 273–274. For a lengthier account of these protests, see Wolters, *New Negro on Campus*; "Students at Morgan Strike after Insult: Resent White Teacher's Remark by Not Going to Class," *Afro*, February 19, 1936.

36. Initial news reports about hiring Dwight O. W. Holmes called him dean of education at Howard, but after being hired, coverage more accurately called him dean of the graduate school. See the following: "Dr. Holmes Offered Morgan Presidency," *Afro*, June 26, 1937; "Morgan's Good Selection," *Afro*, July 3, 1937; "Holmes Will Accept Morgan College Job," *Afro*, July 3, 1937; John Jasper, "Dr. Holmes May Accept Morgan Offer This Week," *Afro*, July 10, 1937; "Holmes Takes Morgan Bid: HU Man Accepts Job as Head of Morgan College," *Afro*, July 17, 1937. For references from when Holmes was a Baltimore teacher, see Howard E. Young, "Colored Schools in Maryland," *Afro*, September 25, 1915; and Howard E. Young, "Educational Progress of a Quarter Century," *Afro*, August 26, 1916; Hurston, *Dust Tracks on the Road*, pp. 146–148; Jenkins, "Holmes, Dwight"; "Filibuster Endangers Lynch Bill," *Afro*, October 30, 1937; "Holmes Says Jim Crow Has Made Us Too Timid," *Afro*, March 19, 1938. The autobiography of Ida B. Wells provides an exceptional first-person account of the fight to end lynching in America. For more, see Duster, *Crusade for Justice*.

activities were under the governance of the Morgan trustees instead of Holmes. Noting this second-class treatment, Holmes used his inauguration address to air strong convictions regarding whites' mistreatment of Black higher education, but from 1937 to 1948, his decade as Morgan president was marred by staggering white resistance to Black progress.[37]

In 1939, Morgan College was purchased by the state after the Maryland Commission on Higher Education of Negroes recommended the sale two years earlier. This was further stressed since Princess Anne Academy still had not developed a collegiate-level curriculum while under state control since 1935. Additionally, Morgan College had financial struggles in no small part due to the decades of trying to manage its own campus and Princess Anne. Therefore, Morgan College becoming a state-supported institution was appealing to both sides—the state needed an actual Black college and Morgan needed to remain open. The sale was controversial, however: could a state that blatantly neglected its duty to fund Black education be trusted to sufficiently fund the strongest Black institution in Maryland? Also, Morgan's success was largely of its own making, so would it maintain its own board of trustees vested in the interest of the college?[38]

The private Morgan College once had a twenty-four-person trustee board—twelve white and twelve Black members—and concern quickly arose over whether that body would become all white. The *Baltimore Afro-American* argued that an all-white board would be devastating. "It's too bad that Morgan should lose, overnight, all that it has taken sixty years to gain," an editorial assessed. Renamed to Morgan State College following the sale, the college maintained its own board, and Morris A. Soper, a white US circuit court judge and Morgan College trustee since 1916, was appointed chair of the nine-person board. The four Black members were Carl J. Murphy, publisher of

<hr>

37. "Dr. Spencer to Stay at Morgan after Dr. Holmes Takes Office," *Afro*, August 21, 1937; For details about the Holmes inauguration, see John Jasper, "Holmes's Inauguration a Brilliant Spectacle," *Afro*, November 27, 1937. Also see photos and photo captions for "Morgan President Inaugurated," *Afro*, November 27, 1937. On Holmes's strong convictions, including his critiques of Maryland's racism toward Black colleges, see Holmes, "Inaugural Address of Dwight O. W. Holmes," pp. 17–26.

38. On the Morgan sale and controversy, see the following: "Blame 3 for Morgan Sale: Mitchell Says Trustees Davis, McMechen, Bowles Could Have Averted It," *Afro*, June 10, 1939; "Morgan Sold for $200,000," *Afro*, June 10, 1939; "Morgan Is Sold for $225,000: Expect State to Take Charge About Oct. 1," *Afro*, September 23, 1939; "Delay Sale of Morgan," *Afro*, October 7, 1939. Regarding the Maryland Commission on Higher Education of Negroes, see Wilson, "Predecessors of Morgan State College," pp. 10–13. For more on Princess Anne's status, see Wheatle, "'Ward of the State,'" pp. 127–170.

Afro-American newspapers; Willard W. Allen, grand master of the Maryland
Masons and president of the Southern Life Insurance Company; Carrington L.
Davis, principal at Paul Laurence Dunbar Senior-Junior High School and
president of the American Teachers Association; and Josiah F. Henry, attorney and leader of the Monumental Elks' Lodge.[39]

Once a state-supported Black college, Morgan State faced new but familiar
challenges under two Democratic governors, Herbert O'Conor (1939–47) and
William Preston Lane Jr. (1947–51). For example, in 1940, during O'Conor's
first term, the state legislature approved a meager $30,000 for out-of-state
scholarships. Furthermore, by 1947, when Lane was in office, Morgan State's
growing enrollment was paired with inadequate facilities, insufficient staff, and
limited equipment. In April, roughly six hundred Morgan State students
marched on Annapolis, the state capital. Stretching five city blocks, the students sang the alma mater, "Fair Morgan," with placards swaying in the harbor-
stirred wind that read, "We Want an Equal Education." But the governor and
state legislators did not bend like the placards. "If I give Morgan immediately
all the money and projects for which it now asks," Lane explained, "I must do
the same thing for other institutions throughout the state, and that just can't
be done."[40]

Such difficulties characterized Holmes's presidency. Instead of investing in
Morgan State, one state official referred to the college as "a rubbish heap of
huts and shacks." Whites in Baltimore also built a brick wall along the campus
border to demonstrate their distaste for a Black college near their neighborhood. Holmes called it the "spite wall." Even the most experienced Black educator could be worn down by white resistance. Courageous, yet subdued by
racism, Holmes announced his retirement for the end of the 1947–48 academic
year. He spent his last year strategizing with Soper, trustee board chair, trying
to protect the interests of Morgan State and the state's other Black colleges—
Princess Anne as well as Coppin and Bowie, two teachers colleges—while
southern legislators proposed regional Black colleges to offer graduate and

39. On Morgan College's board having twenty-four members, see Wheatle, "'Ward of the
State,'" p. 131. For the editorial quote, see "Morgan Sold for $200,000"; "Four Named to Morgan
Board," *Afro*, November 25, 1939.

40. "$30,000 Ready for Maryland Scholarships." Historian Joy Ann Williamson-Lott offers
a comprehensive study of the transformation of southern higher education in the mid-twentieth
century. Her work succinctly explains segregation's conflict with economic advancement and
federal funding. For more, see Williamson-Lott, *Jim Crow Campus*, pp. 23–27; Another example
of southern out-of-state aid programs to maintain segregation is discussed in Pratt, *We Shall Not
Be Moved*, pp. 28–29; "600 Morgan Students March on Capitol to Demand Needed Funds for
Education," *Afro*, April 5, 1947; "Morganites See Governor," *Afro*, April 5, 1947.

professional education instead of desegregating their states' white universities. This set the stage for Martin D. Jenkins, whose first task as Holmes's successor, was to keep Morgan independent even as desegregation efforts progressed.[41]

The Fight for Black Independence

Morgan State College was in a rare position among state-supported Black colleges. In many segregated states, institutions were governed by a single all-white board responsible for every state-supported college and university. That arrangement left many southern Black colleges at the mercy of a board that prioritized white institutions, but Morgan State had its own trustees. Those advocates had direct access to the governor and legislators, but the board's existence became a point of tension as the Supreme Court continued to rule against segregation.[42]

In Maryland, the fight over Black independence came with negotiations. Black residents argued their colleges should be funded equitably if segregation was to be maintained; however, many white leaders disagreed and argued that they should govern Black campuses—a stance rooted in the white supremacist belief that whites should control all schools, segregated or desegregated. This summarized Maryland state officials' contentious relationship with Black higher education, but unlike Dwight O. W. Holmes, Jenkins began his presidency during the broader societal shift that followed World War II. School desegregation cases were beginning in multiple states. Also, with the University of Maryland Law School desegregated, NAACP lawsuits filed in the 1940s focused on the remaining segregated areas of the university. The federal courts were considering desegregation more often, and Jenkins's views on the matter were clear.[43]

41. On the racism Holmes faced and the "huts and shacks" quote, see Jones, "Purpose, Progress, and Promise," pp. 14–15. On Soper and Holmes strategizing, see Morris A. Soper to Dwight O. W. Holmes, September 22, 1947, Soper Collection, Box 2–5, Folder 7, MSU. On the regional college idea, refer to "Segregation Held: Publishers' Consultant Opposes Federal Approval of Regional Schools," *Afro*, April 3, 1948; "Principle of Regional State Graduate Colleges Opposed: AFRO Advises Governors Court Are Against Them," *Afro*, December 20, 1947; and "Regional Plan for Meharry Rapped before Senate Unit," *Afro*, March 20, 1948.

42. Scholars have characterized the South as either a monolithic region or one with varying norms in culture and ideology. In *Jim Crow Campus*, it is carefully explained that the social transformation in the South was a result of some Black colleges in the Upper South having their own boards of trustees, compared with Deep South states that commonly had a single all-white board to govern all colleges and universities. For more, see Williamson-Lott, *Jim Crow Campus*, p. 33.

43. Regarding the five school desegregation cases that later became the *Brown* decision, as well as tactics used to avoid desegregation, see Patterson, *Brown v. Board of Education*; and Bell,

In November 1946, even before starting his Morgan State presidency, Jenkins argued in the *Washington Post* that white teachers in Washington's segregated schools were teaching white children to forgo their most basic rights of democracy simply to keep Black citizens from the same rights. "This condition is one which should occasion a great deal of concern among the citizens of Washington," he said. In March 1948, Jenkins testified before the US Senate Judiciary Committee and opposed the proposed legislation to establish regional Black graduate schools instead of desegregating. "A vote for the resolution is a vote for racial segregation in education. It is our profound hope that Congress will not give its endorsement to this proposed legislation." That said, knowing well the conditions of segregation in Maryland, he saw potential at Morgan State. "I am impressed by the opportunities offered at Morgan," Jenkins said in April 1948 when accepting the job, "and I pledge you that I shall attempt to develop an outstanding educational program."[44]

Jenkins and Morris A. Soper, the white chair of the Morgan board, immediately began working to ensure that Maryland whites stayed unaware of their strategies for Morgan. Two days after Jenkins accepted the presidency, Soper informed Jenkins that news of his hire was well received in Maryland. Still in Washington, DC, Jenkins was prominently featured in an article and editorial in the white-run *Baltimore Sun*, which Soper called "a powerful influence in our state." The best part, Soper assessed, was what was not featured. "It seems to me that you were very wise in declining to discuss your future plans at Morgan," Soper told Jenkins. "Not only because you will want to become more familiar with the local situation before formulating your opinions, but also because a number of controversial questions have been received with respect to the incorporation of other institutions in the college."[45]

The questions that swirled were remnants of years past, and Soper, who had been a Morgan trustee since 1916, knew how deeply history steered the future. A year earlier, on February 1, 1947, the Marbury Report was released and its recommendations upset Carl J. Murphy. Many Maryland powerbrokers were still uninterested in investing in Princess Anne Academy and both the *Sun* and

---

Silent Covenants, especially pp. 18–19 for Bell's initial discussion of "all deliberate speed," although this is discussed throughout his book. In Maryland, the NAACP led additional attacks on University of Maryland admissions beyond the desegregation of its law school in 1936. For more, see "New Suit Filed against University of Maryland," *Afro*, September 25, 1948.

44. On Jenkins in the *Washington Post,* see Martin D. Jenkins, Letter to the Editor, "School Plebiscite," *Washington Post*, November 13, 1946; and Robert H. Estabrook to Martin D. Jenkins, November 13, 1946, Jenkins Collection, Box A–G, Folder Fa–Fur, MSU. For Jenkins's Senate testimony quote, see "Regional Plan for Meharry Rapped"; Jenkins to Soper, April 27, 1948.

45. Soper to Jenkins, April 29, 1948.

the Marbury Report favored consolidating it with Morgan. A similar idea was floated about Coppin, a Black teachers college in Baltimore. "When we get together, we can discuss these matters at length," Soper informed the media-savvy Jenkins.[46]

The two men remained in touch. In June 1948, only weeks before Holmes's final day as president, Jenkins telegrammed Soper an excerpt of what Governor Lane said during the Morgan State commencement exercises on June 2. "Quote: 'Since the college is devoted solely to the interests of the colored population, it is only reasonable that its control should remain in their hands and that they also retain the right to present the needs of the institution directly to the governor of the state.'" Lane dismissed Morgan students' earlier demands for increased funding, but he agreed that the college should stay independent. The governor's commencement statement, however, became more significant by the time Jenkins started his presidency.[47]

By the fall of 1948, University of Maryland president H. C. "Curley" Byrd and his supporters were not ceding to desegregation. Despite the law school's desegregation more than ten years earlier, the university continued to deny Black applicants admission to other graduate and professional schools and all undergraduate programs. In this vein, Byrd requested the legislative council of the Maryland Legislature remove Morgan State's independence and turn control of the college over to the University of Maryland, with its all-white board. Byrd's appeal also indirectly led to a startling realization—Morgan State had performed too well for a Black college. For the 1948–49 academic year, Morgan State enrolled 1,672 students. That was a 115-student increase from the previous year. That total also far exceeded Maryland's other state-supported Black colleges—Princess Anne (323 students), Bowie (152), and Coppin (178)—none of which had the same type of independence. Morgan State was thriving with its own board of trustees that supported the academic program that Holmes had developed and Jenkins was poised to continue. Both men were products of the uncompromising curricula of Howard and had no superstitions about the ability of Black students. As a result, Byrd's rationale for taking over Morgan State was simple: "So that segregation could be properly maintained."[48]

46. Ibid.; Marbury Report.

47. Martin D. Jenkins to Morris A. Soper, June 6 (no year on telegram), Soper Collection, Box 2–5, Folder 7, MSU.

48. On Byrd's request that Morgan be turned over to the University of Maryland's control, see "Gov. Lane Hints No Morgan Transfer at Inauguration," *Afro*, December 25, 1948. For the 1948–49 enrollment data, see Jenkins, "Enrollment in Institutions of Higher Education," p. 570.

The issue with segregation and its unequal funding was evident in the logistical issues with Jenkins's presidential inauguration. In late October 1948, less than a month before the ceremony was to occur, it was rescheduled from November 23 to December 17 because Morgan State still did not have the facilities to host it. Therefore, like Holmes in November 1937, Jenkins was inaugurated before visiting academic leaders, state officials, and other dignitaries at Frederick Douglass High School. Despite being under state control since 1939, the lack of a substantial gymnasium or auditorium was representative of Maryland's continued discrimination against Black colleges while the University of Maryland remained segregated.[49]

On December 17, 1948, many of the same state officials who were responsible for Morgan's lack of facilities made their way to Douglass High for Jenkins's inauguration. Governor Lane was present. So, too, was O'Conor, who was governor when Morgan became state-supported, but now a US senator. John Dale Russell, director of the Division of Higher Education of the US Office of Education, was also in attendance to celebrate his old colleague's new role. Byrd was also present, representing the university. As the program started, Lane promised Morgan would maintain its board. "I shall always be happy, ready, and willing to discuss with him problems of Morgan College," the governor said, offering an official welcome to Jenkins. "The door at Annapolis is open, and he shall always be welcome." Yet, John W. Davis, president of West Virginia State College, delivered assertive remarks, and used the opportunity to advocate for himself and other Black college presidents. "For the good of America," Davis said, "racial segregation must go."[50]

The remarks from Lane, Davis, and others were primers for Jenkins's inauguration address titled, "The Function of Morgan State College as a State Institution of Higher Education." He explained Morgan State's three responsibilities: develop its students, conserve and enhance knowledge, and raise the cultural level of the state and nation. "Morgan State must assume and discharge these responsibilities. To the extent that it does so, the state and nation will be richer in human resources." Jenkins then reverted to an old debate among Black educators—what Black colleges should teach. "A liberal education is these days and for this group of students is not enough," he assessed. "I shall not here take

49. "Inauguration Date of Dr. Jenkins Set," *Afro*, October 30, 1948, and "Delivering Inaugural Address," *Afro*, December 25, 1948; Douglass High School in Baltimore was important not only for its facilities but also as a site for Black intellectual life. In 1926, Carter G. Woodson delivered an address at the school during the first year of Negro History Week—the precursor to Black History Month. For more on Douglass High and broader conversation about the Black school curricula beyond the Deep South, see Givens, "There Would Be No Lynching," pp. 1462–1464.

50. "Gov. Lane Hints No Morgan Transfer."

issue with those distinguished educators who hold that this kind of education is the only legitimate kind of higher education." The college must be vocational and liberal, he said, believing the education of Black students must not be one or the other. "We intend to encourage this staff to engage in all types of scholarly activity, but especially to attack those problems which have particular relevance to the development of the state and to the adjustment of the Negro population." Therefore, Morgan State would "promote harmonious race relations" within the community.[51]

Formal purposes aside, Jenkins then discussed the root of Maryland's higher education problems—racism. The solution sat with the state's elected officials, many of whom were in attendance. And although Jenkins prefaced his following comments with "I am an educator, not a politician," the forty-four-year-old president said he could not discuss the future goals of Morgan State without addressing the clear problem of segregation. He vowed to operate the type of college Maryland wanted, "even though there be conflict with my personal views," adding that "I have always, and I shall always be opposed to the pattern of racial segregation in American life." As a scholar, Jenkins explained that research had debunked any myths that Black people were "inherently and inescapably inferior to other racial groups." Black people were acclaimed scientists like Ernest Everett Just, remarkable performers like Marian Anderson, and esteemed diplomats like Ralph Bunche.[52]

It was segregation, however, that hindered more figures like them from emerging. Black people simply needed the opportunity, and a better-funded Morgan State College would provide such opportunities. Jenkins then said Maryland must do what was best for Maryland. It must not look to Massachusetts when it had its desires to appear more liberal, or to Mississippi when seeking to validate its segregationists. "I believe that the people of the Free State of Maryland are competent to make their own decision in this matter without following the leadership of those states which, by all objective measures, are the most backward in the nation."[53]

In closing, Jenkins called for the desegregation of the University of Maryland and further investment in Morgan State. He then solicited the public to accept its role in supporting Morgan State. He asked Black Marylanders to demand the best for Morgan, and he challenged whites to accept their "moral responsibility" to hire Black professionals who were educated at Black colleges.

51. Martin D. Jenkins, "Inaugural Address," December 17, 1948, Jenkins Collection, Box: Speeches A–J, Folder: The Function of Morgan State College . . . , MSU.

52. Ibid.

53. Ibid.

Likewise, he challenged state officials to sufficiently fund Black higher education. That was the only way Morgan State could meet its goals of offering high-caliber teaching, scholarship, and community service. "We shall soon know by manifestations of your interest, by indications of your support, if this is the kind of college you want Morgan State College to be."[54]

The stirring words from Jenkins and other Black academic leaders, or even the moderate support from Governor Lane, did not sit well with Byrd. In fact, it only increased his desire to have Morgan under the University of Maryland's control. For instance, on March 8, 1949, Byrd presented a proposal to the state legislative fiscal committees that would keep the university segregated but, as a concession, invest in graduate-level education at Black colleges. That way, Black students would have access to courses similar to the university and some agricultural and industrial offerings at Princess Anne. Finally, Byrd proposed that the state continue the out-of-state aid program and prepare to participate in the regional school plan proposed by the Conference of Southern Governors. For Byrd, cost was no issue as segregation was the priority.[55]

A week later, on March 16, Soper provided Jenkins with feedback on a statement on the education of Black people in Maryland. First, Soper cautioned Jenkins not to mention his membership on the commission that produced the 1947 Marbury Report. It would look like a conflict of interest, and it would suggest that Jenkins was hired because of his poor opinion of Princess Anne. Second, Soper suggested that Jenkins add some data about the number of Black students who had received out-of-state scholarships. Finally, and perhaps most importantly, Jenkins needed to tread lightly when arguing for graduate-level programs at Morgan. Soper felt the out-of-state scholarship program, the only way Black Marylanders could earn advanced degrees, would be discontinued if Jenkins pushed too hard and too soon for graduate studies at Morgan State. "It is important that we do not furnish Dr. Byrd with ammunition," Soper advised.[56]

By the end of the month, Soper and Morgan trustees attended a closed joint meeting with the same state legislative fiscal committees and made their own proposal. The unfortunate reality was that Maryland had so drastically underfunded Black colleges that concern swirled over whether any of them would survive. Therefore, the trustees argued that continued state spending on

54. Ibid.

55. "Legislative Group Hears Pleas to Open Univ. of Md., Make Morgan Land Grant," *Afro*, April 2, 1949.

56. Morris A. Soper to Martin D. Jenkins, March 16, 1949, Soper Collection, Box 2–5, Folder 7, MSU.

Princess Anne, which remained far below any decent academic standard, would hamper the progress of Morgan State. At that rate, the state would cripple all of its Black colleges. The trustees suggested, based on the 1947 Marbury Report, that Morgan should be designated Maryland's Black land-grant college and Princess Anne a junior college with emphasis on an agricultural curriculum. Additionally, Morgan's central location in Baltimore and further development made it ideal to serve the entire state and conserve state resources.[57]

The day after the Morgan trustees went before legislative committees, Byrd had an expensive dinner with many of those same state legislators. Those men were in each other's pockets, and over a hearty meal, Byrd encouraged them to support his expansion program for Princess Anne, a branch of the university. He preferred to invest in Princess Anne because it maintained segregation under the University of Maryland's control.[58]

On April 8, 1949, only a few weeks after going before the fiscal committees, Soper updated Jenkins that the State Senate passed a resolution requesting that the governor appoint a commission composed partly of leading educators to examine the question of higher education for Black people. Soper found this encouraging and suggested that he and Jenkins gather all the information possible in advance of that commission being formed. This included information about Princess Anne's out-of-state students and faculty salaries, and Morgan State's capacity to add agricultural courses. All of this would be useful, Soper said, in influencing the commission to support Black colleges. Of course, this meant Jenkins needed to make some concessions. In the best interest of the college, he had to keep Morgan State free of controversy as state legislators held the institution's future in their hands. Plus, Governor Lane supported Morgan State's independence, and Jenkins wanted to ensure that his support continued.[59]

Therefore, on April 29, 1949, Jenkins wrote W. E. B. Du Bois, the eminent scholar, to withdraw his invitation to speak at Morgan State's upcoming June commencement services. Du Bois had appeared with Paul Robeson, the acclaimed Black actor and human rights advocate, during the recent World Peace Congress in Paris and did not distance himself from Robeson's condemnation of the United States. White Americans often tied anyone's demands for racial equality to communism, and Robeson and Du Bois were labeled as such. Rescinding the Du Bois invitation was no easy decision for Jenkins.[60]

57. "Legislative Group Hears Pleas."

58. Ibid.

59. Morris A. Soper to Martin D. Jenkins, April 8, 1949, Soper Collection, Box 2–5, Folder 7, MSU.

60. Martin D. Jenkins to W. E. B. Du Bois, April 29, 1949, Soper Collection, Box 2–5, Folder 7, MSU.

His career was guided by Du Bois's idea for liberal education. In fact, Jenkins told Du Bois he was "among the first of the great Negro scholars" and "a source of inspiration to the younger Negro scholars." But Jenkins faced a practical issue. Governor Lane would be on the platform at Morgan State's commencement, and there was no way Du Bois could appear at Morgan despite his planned speech being "The Future of the Negro State College." Furthermore, it would be Jenkins's first commencement as president. He told Du Bois, "I feel . . . that if you were to speak at Morgan State College, even on a non-political topic as you had planned, it would give the appearance of our being in sympathy with your general views."[61]

The decision was strategic because, two weeks later, Jenkins needed a favor from the governor. On May 16, 1949, he informed Governor Lane that Morgan State had been offered forty-four acres adjacent to campus at $3,000 per acre. Jenkins made it clear that he and the trustees were not getting ahead of themselves with the possibility of the state granting them an agriculture program. In fact, Jenkins said the land was not suitable for a farm, but it was Morgan's only chance to expand. The college was surrounded by residential space on all other sides, and the "spite wall" was evidence that neighborhoods figuratively and literally blocked the college's expansion. This new plot of land, however, would help Morgan State expand to eighty-seven total acres, and Jenkins wanted the state to secure this land and to do so quickly.[62]

Morgan State was at capacity, and by September, the college reached its maximum enrollment. As a result, 350 applicants were denied admission for the 1949–50 academic year. This was common at several Black colleges in the 1940s as Black veterans took advantage of the Servicemen's Readjustment Act, known as the GI Bill, and Black college enrollments increased by 25 percent in the fall of 1944 alone. Morgan was no different but did not have the physical infrastructure or space to educate more students. The upside to having its own board of trustees, however, was that those requests went directly to the

61. Jenkins to Du Bois, April 29, 1949; Jenkins also informed Soper that he rescinded the Du Bois invitation. For more, see Martin D. Jenkins to Morris A. Soper, May 3, 1949, Soper Collection, Box 2–5, Folder 6, MSU. More than a year later, *Afro* covered the decision and reported the title of Du Bois's planned speech at Morgan State. For more, see "Why Morgan Cancelled DuBois Talk," *Afro*, August 26, 1950. On Jenkins's first commencement, see "Dr. and Mrs. Martin Jenkins Are 'At Home' to Morgan State Grads," *Afro*, June 18, 1949. To further contextualize how whites linked communism and higher education desegregation efforts, the topic is discussed throughout Williamson-Lott, *Jim Crow Campus*. Also see Turner, *Sitting In and Speaking Out*, pp. 32–33.

62. Martin D. Jenkins to William P. Lane Jr., May 16, 1949, Soper Collection, Box 2–5, Folder 7, MSU.

governor, not to an all-white board and then the governor. Morgan State's independence was essential.[63]

By March 1950, Governor Lane had earmarked a record $4.8 million for Black institutions. After the pressure from Morgan State students in 1947, and the denied admission of 350 applicants to a Black college, the need to expand Black higher education was urgent. The alternative was to desegregate the University of Maryland. Therefore, before the end of the 1949–50 academic year, Governor Lane's budget passed the state legislature with $4,862,731 allocated for new buildings at six Black institutions, including a Black hospital. Morgan State received the most: $2,111,870. This was for a dining hall, the renovation of a storage room into an ROTC space, an upgrade of underground utilities, a new classroom building, a gymnasium, a women's and a men's dormitory, and other campus upgrades. In comparison, under the University of Maryland's control, Princess Anne's campus received $865,000.[64]

The $4.8 million decision was telling for two reasons. First, Morgan could promote itself better with its own board. Also, on June 5, 1950, the Supreme Court's *Sweatt v. Painter* decision was another blow to the "separate but equal" doctrine. The University of Texas had denied admission to Heman Marion Sweatt, a Black man, to its law school, and in hurried defense, the state established a Black law school in Houston. The Supreme Court found, however, that the Black law school was not equal in facilities or faculty compared with the University of Texas, thus ruling that Sweatt be admitted to the university. This challenge to yet another southern state's dual systems of higher education increased tensions in Maryland, and Governor Lane said during Morgan State's June 1950 commencement, "It is only reasonable that [Morgan State's] control should remain in their hands and that they also retain the right to present the needs of the institution directly to the governor." A week later, however, on June 17, Byrd was in the news reiterating his belief in segregation and that Morgan State should be under university control.[65]

All the while, Soper and Jenkins quietly plotted. On June 16, Jenkins shared with Soper rumors that Governor Lane's commission formed in April 1949 had a forthcoming report that would suggest Morgan keeps its own board, but rumors also indicated the governor would commission another study of

63. "Morgan State to Operate at Capacity This Term," *Afro*, September 17, 1949. On Black college enrollments post–World War II, see Kendi, *Black Campus Movement*, p. 24.

64. "Lane Provides 4 Million for New Buildings," *Afro*, March 11, 1950.

65. For an account of *Sweatt v. Painter* and the broader challenges to segregation at the University of Texas, see Goldstone, *Integrating the 40 Acres*; "Gov. Lane Lauds Morgan: Tells Grads College Rates Independence," *Afro*, June 17, 1950; "Will Attend Md. University: Appeal Plan Won't Stop Miss McCready," *Afro*, June 17, 1950.

higher education after that study. Jenkins also talked with Holmes, his predecessor, who felt white politicians were simply "passing the buck!" Nonetheless, Jenkins concluded, the forthcoming report indicated that Morgan would remain independent. "Governor Lane's statement relative to Morgan State College came at a very crucial moment," Jenkins told Soper, referencing the governor's commencement remarks, "and deterred the commission from recommending a consolidated board for Morgan and the University of Maryland."[66]

On July 12, however, Jenkins sent Soper a more sobering update. Either what he heard in June was faulty or Byrd had since influenced the commission because the forthcoming report was not as favorable to Morgan State as initially expected. It would recommend that the state form a permanent Advisory Commission on the Higher Education of Negroes. That group would determine the future of Princess Anne and investigate what courses should be offered there and at Morgan State. Afterward, the commission would be dissolved into a consolidated board.[67]

The idea was still swirling around Annapolis that the best solution to the Black colleges' problems was white control. This was the case despite Governor Lane's multiple public declarations that Morgan State should keep its own board. To further exacerbate the issue, in November 1950, Governor Lane lost his bid for reelection to the Republican, Theodore McKeldin. In recent history, the Republicans had been more favorable to Black colleges than the Democrats, but any white politician brought uncertainty for Black people. Governor Lane's looming departure left the door open for segregationists. Byrd used those two months between the election and the January 1951 inauguration to fan the flame of hate. With mounting pressure to desegregate the University of the Maryland, Byrd was even more committed to upholding segregation, and he used every opportunity to question the credibility of Morgan State.[68]

In late November, Byrd suggested Morgan State play Princess Anne (by then, renamed Maryland State College and under the university's control) in football. Morgan was a member of the Central Intercollegiate Athletic Association (CIAA), one of the nation's oldest Black athletic conferences, but the issue was that Maryland State was not an accredited college. Byrd knew that would force Jenkins to publicly explain why his college did not play against

66. Martin D. Jenkins to Morris A. Soper, June 16, 1950, Soper Collection, Box 2–5, Folder 6, MSU.

67. Martin D. Jenkins to Morris A. Soper, July 12, 1950, Soper Collection, Box 2–5, Folder 6, MSU.

68. Regarding the 1950 governor's race, see Al Sweeney, "Election Results Analyzed: Lucas', Tydings' Defeat Cause Little Sorrow," *Afro*, November 18, 1950.

unaccredited institutions, according to Morgan trustees' policy. Byrd knew unaccredited would be interpreted by the public as Maryland State was inadequate. This forced the two Black presidents—Jenkins and John Taylor Williams—to defend their institutions against each other, all courtesy of Byrd.[69]

In December 1950, Byrd suggested letting the public vote on the status of Black colleges and desegregation. He argued that only two paths existed— keep Maryland State and Morgan State at great cost to the state or admit Black people to his university. It was a perverted framing of the situation simply to stir up whites, both segregationists and fiscally conservative liberals, to maintain segregation. The Black community, of course, was keenly aware of Byrd's record. Later that month, one Black civic group stated that Byrd "has a record of callous indifference to the higher education needs of the colored people of the state." Therefore, keeping Morgan independent, "would be in line with the views of Governor Lane, Governor-elect Theodore R. McKeldin, and of the vast majority of the colored people of the state."[70]

As Governor McKeldin was sworn into office, many considered him "a racial bridge builder" who refused "to go along with the other southern governors." For example, in 1951, the University of Maryland opened its admissions to students without regard for race. The next year, in 1952, Morgan State finally opened its own gymnasium nearly five years after Jenkins was inaugurated at a local high school. But Jenkins still had concerns over state appropriations and faculty salaries, much like issues at other Black colleges. For example, in 1950, roughly three-quarters of the federal land-grant funds in Texas went to Texas A&M, with the remainder going to Prairie View A&M College, the state's Black land-grant campus. Therefore, if it took nearly two decades to get the gymnasium that Morgan needed in the 1930s, Jenkins could only imagine how long it would require the state to fund the issues that had emerged since World War II.[71]

69. "Md. State Hurls Grid at Morgan: Byrd Asserts Bears Have No Excuse," *Afro*, November 25, 1950.

70. "Dr. Byrd Fans Racial Hate: Support Referendum on JC at Maryland U," *Afro*, December 2, 1950; "Junior Association of Commerce Revises Stand on Morgan State," *Afro*, December 30, 1950.

71. On McKeldin as a "racial bridge builder," see Smith, *Here Lies Jim Crow*, p. 103. Regarding McKeldin not going along with other southern governors, see Sartain, *Borders of Equality*, pp. 150–151. On the University of Maryland opening admissions to Black undergraduates, see "Univ. of Md. Board Opens School to All," *Afro*, February 10, 1951. Regarding the new gymnasium, see "Photo Standalone 7—No Title," *Afro*, February 23, 1952; and "New Gym Was 12-Year Saga," *Afro*, February 23, 1952; Jenkins made repeated pleas for more state funding. For more see, Martin D. Jenkins to Morris A. Soper, May 29, 1951, and March 3, 1952, Soper Collection,

In the fall of 1952, Soper warned Jenkins that the University of Maryland trustees were meeting and a renewed effort to take control of Morgan State was brewing. By that point, forty-nine formerly segregated southern white colleges had desegregated, twenty-seven being private and twenty-two being state-supported. Despite this trend, Maryland segregationists were still fighting, but the elder Soper had been working to build Morgan for nearly four decades at that point, and in early 1953, he resigned as chair of the Morgan State board. His resignation was a surprise, Jenkins said, but there was an upside. Carl J. Murphy replaced Soper. Morgan State now had its first Black chair of the trustee board, but Jenkins and Murphy knew the fight for racial equality was not confined to Maryland. While fighting to keep Morgan independent, Jenkins was also strategically, and often covertly, exchanging ideas with other Black college presidents about how best to liberate Black youth across the South and the nation.[72]

Black Presidential Network in Action

NAACP attorneys are often credited as delivering the final blows to Jim Crow. But if these legal juggernauts were the winners in fights before the US Supreme Court, then Black educators were certainly the physical trainers who quietly prepared the NAACP for its greatest victories. Martin D. Jenkins was part of this tradition. Black college presidents were inclined to be part of numerous influential circles, and Jenkins was further advantaged because he was a scholar whose research focused on racial inequality and segregated schools. By the time he started as Morgan State president in 1948, Jenkins quietly utilized

---

Box 2–5, Folder 6, MSU. Jenkins also made the case for more funding during the June 1951 commencement. For more, see "Storm Causes 7,000 to Flee Morgan Exercises: Rain Dampens Graduation at Morgan State," *Afro*, June 16, 1951. Regarding data on state appropriations to Morgan State and other colleges, see Martin D. Jenkins to Morris A. Soper, March 10, 1952, Soper Collection, Box 2–5, Folder 6, MSU. In this letter, Jenkins enclosed Exhibit A–Appropriations, Exhibit B–Operating Expenses Appropriations, Exhibit C–Per Capita Appropriations, and Exhibit D–General and Special Appropriations. On faculty salaries, see Martin D. Jenkins to Russell S. Davis, May 30, 1952, Soper Collection, Box 2–5, Folder 7, MSU. On Texas land-grant funding, see Anderson, *Pursuit of Fairness*, p. 50.

72. On Soper warning of the university trustees meeting, see Morris A. Soper to Martin D. Jenkins, November 7, 1952, Soper Collection, Box 2–5, Folder 7, MSU. For the number of white colleges desegregated, see Turner, *Sitting In and Speaking Out*, p. 38. Regarding Soper's resignation as chair, see Martin D. Jenkins to Morris A. Soper, March 3, 1953, and April 1, 1953, Soper Collection, Box 2–5, Folder 6, MSU. For more on Murphy as the first Black board chair, see Jones, "Purpose, Progress, and Promise," p. 16.

networking strategies common among Black teacher associations across the South—and other key Black organizations—to advance the fight for educational opportunity. He did this while publicly battling Maryland legislators and H. C. "Curley" Byrd, president of the University of Maryland, who tried to take over governance of Morgan State College. Jenkins's efforts would prove indispensable.[73]

Before becoming president of Morgan State, Jenkins was chair of the special research committee of the American Teachers Association (ATA). Formerly the National Association of Teachers in Colored Schools, the ATA offered professional development opportunities and organization around Black teacher issues, such as unequal salaries. The organization was structured with state-level Black teacher associations focused on similar activities, and relationships between Black educators on the collegiate and secondary levels were important since several Black colleges offered limited collegiate-level courses. Therefore, Jenkins's involvement with the ATA as a college professor was not uncommon. In fact, in the 1920s, William Jasper Hale, president of the Tennessee Agricultural and Industrial State Normal School, served as ATA president. With so many Black colleges focused on teacher preparation, the work of a Black college president took place both on campus and across the South.[74]

On July 12, 1948, one of Jenkins's first public addresses as Morgan State president occurred not in Baltimore but in Nashville, Tennessee. There, he visited the Race Relations Institute at Fisk University led by President Charles S. Johnson. By the time Jenkins arrived, Johnson had established himself as a renowned sociologist. Three decades earlier, Johnson completed his bachelor of arts degree at Virginia Union, a private Black college, and shortly afterward, earned his bachelor of philosophy at the University of Chicago. Now, the Fisk Race Relations Institute, which opened in 1944, was guided by four research areas: "race and racial theories," "racial aspects of social

73. Preeminent historian Vanessa Siddle Walker offers masterful accounts of the covert organizing power of Black educators and Black teacher associations beyond the long-standing narrative that has credited the NAACP for challenging Jim Crow in education. For more, see Walker, *Lost Education of Horace Tate*; and Walker, *Hello Professor*.

74. For more about Jenkins's role in ATA, see "Selective Service Medals Presented." For a brief history of the ATA, refer to Jones-Wilson et al., *Encyclopedia of African-American Education*, p. 460. On William Jasper Hale, see "Black History Month: William J. Hale A Leader in Education," *The Tennessean*, February 6, 2014, https://www.tennessean.com/story/news/local/2014/02/06/black-history-month-william-j-hale-a-leader-in-education/5249211/ (accessed January 5, 2019). Historian Jarvis R. Givens has discussed how various people, including college presidents, took interest in and helped support the spread of Negro History Week to Black schools throughout the nation. For more, see Givens, "There Would Be No Lynching."

problems," "methods, techniques, and community planning," and "the role of personal religion in human relations."[75]

In Nashville, the meeting at Fisk was organized by the American Missionary Association and emphasized the need to end school segregation and racial and religious prejudice. In addition to Jenkins, the other speakers included Aaron J. Brumbaugh, vice president of the American Council on Education, and Edwin R. Embree, president of the Julius Rosenwald Fund, which had financed the construction of hundreds of Black schools throughout the nation. If nothing else, Jenkins's visit to the Race Relations Institute demonstrated his understanding that Black educators' scholarly inquiries were crucial in resistance to racism. This was clear from the beginning of his presidency, although it was not always broadcast in Maryland newspapers.[76]

Jenkins continued speaking before Black educators throughout the fall. On October 8, 1948, he spoke to the Maryland Teachers Association. Three weeks later, on October 28, Jenkins was in Richmond addressing the Virginia Teachers Association, this time on the topic of "Planning for Full Participation in American Life," in the 8 p.m. time slot during the association's annual convention. In that address, specifically, he called the audience's "attention to some of the things we have been doing as Negro teachers." The "we" was a testament to his active role in challenging second-class citizenship in education.[77]

75. On Jenkins's Fisk Race Relations Institute talk, see Guide to the Jenkins Collection, MSU. Regarding Charles S. Johnson's studies at the University of Chicago, Katrina M. Sanders noted that the "Ph.B. was a common degree during the early 1900s. Although referred to as Dr. Johnson, Johnson did not hold a Ph.D. In 1928, Virginia Union University awarded him an honorary Litt. D. degree." Sanders also discussed the four focal areas of the Race Relations Institute. For more, see Sanders, *"Intelligent and Effective Direction,"* pp. 31, 41, 147. Also see the work of Patrick J. Gilpin—one of the most widely published authors about Charles S. Johnson. For more, see Gilpin and White, "A Challenge to White, Southern Universities"; Gilpin, "Charles S. Johnson"; Gilpin, "Johnson and the Race Relations Institutes"; Gilpin and Gasman, *Charles S. Johnson.* On Johnson's work with southern liberals, see Dunne, "Next Steps," pp. 1–34.

76. "AMA Holds Institute on Race Relations at Fisk," *Afro,* July 24, 1948. Dozens of scholars have discussed the Rosenwald schools. For a two brief discussions of the Rosenwald Fund and Black schools, see Anderson, *Education of Blacks in the South,* pp. 152–183, and Walker, *Lost Education of Horace Tate,* pp. 40–41.

77. On Jenkins's Maryland Teachers Association talk, see Guide to the Jenkins Collection, MSU. Regarding the Virginia Teachers Association meeting, see Conference Program, October 27–30, 1948; and Martin D. Jenkins, "Planning for Full Participation in American Life," both in Jenkins Collection, Box 5–6–7, Folder 33, MSU.

In March 1949, while Jenkins and the white Morgan trustee chair, Morris A. Soper, strategized for the Maryland state legislative fiscal committees, he also visited Florida to speak before that state's Black teachers association. Later that year, in September, as Black educators quietly backed school desegregation cases, Jenkins appeared before the Eastern District Court of Virginia to testify in the *Constance Carter et al. v. School Board of Arlington County* hearing. Eleanor Taylor had filed a suit on behalf of her daughter, Constance, because there were programs offered at the segregated white Washington-Lee High School that were not available to Black students at Hoffman-Boston High School. In describing Jenkins's testimony as an expert witness, the Black press said he "lashed the separate but equal theory of education by terming it as educationally unsound." Although Eastern District judge Albert V. Bryan did not rule in favor of Carter, the decision was appealed, and on May 31, 1950, the US Court of Appeals for the Fourth Circuit reversed the ruling in favor of desegregation. It was no coincidence that Soper was one of the judges. Jenkins's network was on full display.[78]

That same spring, Jenkins made his way to Raleigh for the North Carolina Teachers Association's annual convention, hosted by Shaw University and St. Augustine's College, two private Black colleges. Again, he held a featured 8 p.m. time slot, and although he spoke his usual words before Black teachers, these conferences provided a cover for Black college presidents to meet as well. In the sea of Black principals and teachers sat Robert P. Daniel, current president of Virginia State and former longtime Shaw president. This provided an opportunity for Jenkins and Daniel, who both led state-supported Black colleges, to converse on shared issues and strategies. Those alliances, and others, would prove important.[79]

Although formal meetings of Black teacher associations were a key form of networking, Jenkins's webs of connections were many. In November 1951, Mary McLeod Bethune, a civil rights activist and former president of Bethune-Cookman College, visited Morgan State. Bethune was also active across various entities. In fact, from 1936 to 1944, she served as director of Negro Affairs

78. Regarding Jenkins's Florida Teachers Association attendance, see Guide to the Martin D. Jenkins Collection, MSU; on testifying against K–12 segregation, see Court Subpoena and Brochure Summary of Carter v. Arlington, both in Jenkins Collection, Box: Personal Papers, Folder: District Court of the US Eastern District of Virginia, MSU. Press clippings include Richard Morris, "Separate, Equal Facilities Called Educationally Unsound," *Washington Post*, September 8, 1949; "Separate, Equal Theory Hit in Va.: Dr. Jenkins Testifies in School Entry Case," *Afro*, September 17, 1949; and "Va. Equal Schools Trial Is Recessed," *Afro*, September 17, 1949.

79. Conference Program, March 30–April 1, 1950, Jenkins Collection, Box: Speeches K–R, Folder: North Carolina Teachers Association Convention, MSU.

in the National Youth Administration. By 1951, at seventy-six years old, and long aware of the trials of Black colleges, Bethune said, "I can't believe my eyes" when she arrived and observed Morgan State's growth. She was there to deliver one of the campus's weekly addresses before a packed auditorium, but before her speech, Jenkins and Bethune chatted at length in the president's home— segregation surely being among the many topics they discussed.[80]

Bethune and Jenkins, as well as Jenkins's wife, Elizabeth, also held fraternal and sorority memberships. In fact, while at Morgan State, Bethune kindly stopped to greet an undergraduate pledge of Delta Sigma Theta Sorority and signed the excited student's signature book. This was important because members of Black fraternities and sororities did not limit involvement to undergraduate students. Established Black professionals were also active members closely linked in a way that white fraternities and sororities were not. They had national, regional, and local networks. Jenkins's membership and alliances were integral to organizing Black professionals, including college presidents, around civil rights.[81]

The next month, Jenkins was in Indianapolis for Kappa Alpha Psi Fraternity's conclave. On December 28, 1951, Jenkins delivered the keynote address during the banquet, hosted by the Indianapolis Alumni Chapter and the undergraduate chapters at nearby Indiana and Purdue universities. He was a regular speaker at these national meetings. In December 1948, in Detroit, during the conclave focused on the "fraternity's responsibility to promoting and supporting civil rights and social action programs," Jenkins challenged his fraternity brothers to commit "to programs of social concerns larger than the narrow social interests of the average fraternity." Now, three years later, Jenkins did the same when he discussed the role of the fraternity.[82]

80. Lula Jones Garrett, "Mrs. Bethune Captivates Morganites: At 76, She Admits Cane Is for Swagger," *Afro*, November 3, 1951. On Bethune's political involvement, see Mary McLeod Bethune, "Full Integration—America's Newest Challenge," in Houck and Dixon, *Rhetoric, Religion, and the Civil Rights Movement*, pp. 49–50. Bethune is considered "the only Black woman president of an accredited college before 1954." For more, see Evans, *Black Women in the Ivory Tower*, p. 123.

81. Garrett, "Mrs. Bethune Captivates." Elizabeth Jenkins, a native of Gary, Indiana, and wife to Martin D. Jenkins, was a member of Alpha Kappa Alpha Sorority. For more on her, see Durham, "Jenkins Succeeds Holmes," pp. 4–7.

82. "Kappas Map Promotion and Support of Civil Rights, Social Action Fight," *Afro*, January 8, 1949; and Kappa Alpha Psi Grand Chapter Banquet speech and Banquet Program, December 28, 1951, both in Jenkins Collection, Box: Speeches K–R, Folder: The Role of the Fraternity in College Life, MSU. For more on Kappa Alpha Psi's contributions to the civil rights movement, see Parks and Layboure, "Sons of Indiana."

Jenkins also kept his connections with federal officials active when, in January 1952, he hosted US senator Hubert Humphrey (D-MN). Rumored to be under consideration for the party's nomination for president, Humphrey spoke before a thousand Morgan State students. The senator demanded stronger civil rights legislation in order to protect the nation's standing abroad. "It's time to stand up and be counted," Humphrey declared. "The war against ignorance, poverty, bigotry, and prejudice must be fought at home, and must be fought first." Jenkins warmly introduced Humphrey and was joined on the platform by Morgan trustees Ivan McDougle and Josiah F. Henry. By April 1952, Jenkins and Carl J. Murphy were named to the Maryland Olympic Fund Drive, further positioning Jenkins as a prominent influencer.[83]

In May 1952, Jenkins returned to his alma mater and former employer, Howard University, for a three-day conference on "The Courts and Racial Integration in Education." He was not one to miss an opportunity to challenge Jim Crow. Jenkins predicted the conference itself would be credited as "one of the most important milestones in our struggle for full citizenship," a nod to the fact that Howard's law school was helping develop the legal strategy behind the eventual *Brown v. Board of Education* case. Also notable was the presence of other Black college presidents, such as Dillard's Albert W. Dent and Howard's Mordecai W. Johnson, attorney and Howard law professor James M. Nabrit Jr., and editor P. L. Prattis of the Black-owned *Pittsburgh Courier*.[84]

Jenkins's public and private meetings were seemingly endless. In November 1952, at North Carolina College in Durham, President Alfonso Elder, himself a vocal supporter of civil rights, and many others listened to Jenkins deliver the Founder's Day program address. The college itself was a critical stop within Black presidential networks. For example, in October 1942, Black leaders secretly met on the campus with southern white leaders to challenge southern segregation. It was fitting that a decade later, Jenkins was invited to Durham, where his "reputation as an educator" warranted radio, television, and newspaper coverage, said Charles A. Ray, director of the North Carolina College News Bureau.[85]

83. "'The Time Is Now,' Says Humphrey: Minnesota Senator Tells Students War against Bigotry Is First," *Afro*, January 26, 1952; "Drs. Jenkins, Murphy on Olympic Fund Committee," *Afro*, April 19, 1952.

84. "Leaders Air Views on Mixed Schools: Urge Fight on All Forms of JC—North and South," *Afro*, May 3, 1952; Dark, "Role of Howard University School of Law."

85. Regarding the North Carolina College visit, see Helen G. Edmonds to Martin D. Jenkins, October 22, 1952; Charles A. Ray to Martin D. Jenkins, October 27, 1952; Martin D. Jenkins, "Tasks of the Younger Generation," November 3, 1952; and Founders Day Program, November 3, 1952, all in Jenkins Collection, Box: Speeches K–R, Folder: North Carolina College Founders

Vivian E. Cook, principal at Baltimore's Dunbar Senior-Junior High School, secured her preferred speaker when Jenkins agreed to visit for the American Education Week program. The theme was "The High School Student in a Changing Community," and Cook called it "an honor" to have him speak on November 11. Six days later, on November 17, Jenkins spoke at the annual Southern Regional Education Board meeting in New Orleans. Later that month, a *Baltimore Sun* editorial said of Jenkins's work: "Nobody can expect a Negro educator of Dr. Jenkins's caliber to put aside the long fight for improved Negro education. Nobody can expect him to forget about segregation."[86]

The *Baltimore Sun* was right in its assessment of Jenkins's stature in the field of education; however, the shortsightedness of white media, especially about segregation, should not be understated. Whites were largely occupied observing their local context, but Jenkins and other Black educators understood the "international and intercultural" implications of civil rights struggles. Whereas Jenkins visited Fisk in July 1948, Fisk president Charles S. Johnson returned Jenkins's favor in February 1953 and served as a weekly assembly speaker at Morgan State. Johnson explained to the Morgan State students that compared with whites, Black people were more global in their thinking and significantly less "materialistic." Black college presidents regularly situated segregation within an international dialogue about human rights. Howard president Mordecai W. Johnson challenged colonialism and Morehouse president Benjamin E. Mays critiqued apartheid in South Africa, just as Charles S. Johnson did before Morgan State students. Per custom, Jenkins accompanied Johnson throughout the day, exchanging ideas.[87]

Day, MSU. For more on Alfonso Elder's support of civil rights, refer to Eddie R. Cole, "Words of Action: The Speeches of President Alfonso Elder and the North Carolina Student Movement," in Danns, Purdy, and Span, *Using Past as Prologue*, pp. 141–166. On the secret meeting at North Carolina College, see Mays, *Born to Rebel*, pp. 213–218.

86. Regarding Dunbar High, see Vivian E. Cook to Martin D. Jenkins, October 14, 1952; and Martin D. Jenkins to Vivian E. Cook, October 16, 1952, both in Jenkins Collection, Box: Speeches A–J, Folder: Dunbar High School Senior Assembly, MSU. On the *Baltimore Sun* quote, see "Dr. Jenkins Accepts a Regional Position," *Baltimore Sun*, n.d., in Soper Collection, Box 2–5, Folder 7, MSU. The editorial was regarding Jenkins's role with the Southern Regional Educational Board. For more on that group, see "Martin Jenkins Asks South to Open Colleges: Southern Regional Educational Board Hears Morgan Prexy," *Afro*, November 29, 1952.

87. "Fisk Prexy Predicts New Role in World Affairs," *Afro*, February 21, 1953; On Black college presidents and internationalism, see Mordecai W. Johnson, "Emancipation Day Address," in Houck and Dixon, *Rhetoric, Religion, and the Civil Rights Movement*, pp. 26–28; Jelks, *Benjamin Elijah Mays*, pp. 195–198; Gilpin and Gasman, *Charles S. Johnson*, pp. 201–212. Also, Jacob L. Reddix, president of Jackson State from 1940 to 1967, exhibited Black educators' understanding of

His diligent efforts were noted by other Black college presidents. Stephen J. Wright, president of Bluefield State in West Virginia, commented that Jenkins had a "heavy schedule." Nonetheless, Jenkins stayed busy for justice and strategized in preparation for both an anticipated landmark Supreme Court school segregation ruling at the federal level and an unexpected uptick in direct action resistance locally. Early in 1953, Jenkins personally invited the National Newspaper Publishers Association to hold its annual convention at Morgan State. The Black media association accepted this invitation, and Morgan State trustee Carl J. Murphy's *Afro-American* newspaper would serve as the formal host. Thus, in June 1953, Black journalists from across the nation descended upon the Baltimore campus, further solidifying the Black press as an influential, longtime important ally in the fight against segregation.[88]

Later that year, in December 1953, Jenkins traveled to Memphis, Tennessee, to deliver a keynote address at the meeting of the Association of Colleges and Secondary Schools for Negroes. By this point, Black educators had watched five individual school desegregation cases—originating in South Carolina, Virginia, Kansas, Delaware, and Washington, DC—come together into a single Supreme Court case. Therefore, the leading Black experts were regularly invited to assess the implications of this case, and Jenkins found himself in Memphis on stage with an old friend. There, Johnson from Fisk spoke and offered a list of items of "urgent necessity" for Black educators, and Jenkins followed with his own address: "Next Steps in Education in the South."[89]

Jenkins first explained that he would speak "based on the assumption that the Supreme Court is going to outlaw racial segregation in education." Next, he shared his belief that there was not a monolithic South because "what is possible in race relations in Baltimore, Maryland, is not at all possible at this time in a particular county in rural Alabama." Therefore, his suggestions for how to handle desegregation would need to be amended accordingly based on educators' localities. That said, Jenkins did not believe there would be

---

foreign affairs. For more, see Reddix, *A Voice Crying in the Wilderness*, pp. 167–216. For a broader understanding of internationalism and civil rights, see Blain, *Set the World on Fire*, particularly pp. 75–103; and Gaines, *American Africans in Ghana*.

88. On Jenkins's "heavy schedule," see Stephen J. Wright to Martin D. Jenkins, November 20, 1953, Jenkins Collection, Box: Speeches A–J, Folder: Assoc. of Colleges and Secondary Schools for Negroes, MSU; "NNPA Convention Set for Baltimore: AFRO Host to Publishers at Morgan," *Afro*, February 14, 1953. For an account on the influence of the Black press, see Michaeli, *The Defender*.

89. Martin D. Jenkins, "Next Steps in Education in the South," December 3, 1953, Jenkins Collection, Box: Speeches A–J, Folder: Assoc. of Colleges and Secondary Schools for Negroes, MSU.

"radical" change after school segregation was deemed unconstitutional because housing segregation would still exist. This meant the desegregated South would see the same pattern of segregation that existed in the "schools of Harlem and the South Side of Chicago." He also addressed concerns about Black teachers losing their jobs and fears of what would happen to Black colleges, but he primarily advised Black principals and superintendents about their actions rather than their worries.[90]

Jenkins knew Black principals and college presidents faced similar pressures, and they would be asked to actively steer their supporters in the direction of continued segregation. "There is no question that this is true," Jenkins said. "It has already happened." Again, he acknowledged the variance across the South and his own advantages as a Black college president in Baltimore. "While Maryland is not as reactionary as some of the states," he said, "I don't think that an administrator anywhere has to yield to pressures which violate his integrity." Black educators needed to be courageous, and relationships with civic and social organizations were essential. The broader Black community depended on Black educators to be advocates beyond the school walls. Jenkins blamed the southern white press for stirring racist ideas while the Black press worked diligently to keep Black people informed. He then added, "Our newspapers, our social and political organizations, our improvement associations all have important roles which they cannot fully discharge without the cooperation of the Negro educators."[91]

That last point was a summary of Jenkins's efforts as a facilitator of racial equality and years of quiet work as a Black educator. Among the Black press, he regularly contributed to the *Afro-American* and, most recently, had hosted the National Newspaper Publishers Association's annual convention at Morgan State. Jenkins's research also found prominent placement in the white media. He had a rapport with *Washington Post* editor Robert H. Estabrook, and earned praise from the *Baltimore Sun* editorial board. His work with Kappa Alpha Psi fraternity and service to Alpha Kappa Alpha sorority was well documented, and he regularly spoke to Black churches throughout the mid-Atlantic region. Likewise, his service to the US Office of Education earned him federal honors, and US president Dwight Eisenhower later appointed Jenkins to the Commission on Veterans' Pensions.[92]

90. Jenkins, "Next Steps in Education." For more about segregation continuing after *Brown*, particularly how whites abandoned schools, see Baum, *Brown in Baltimore*, p. 98–99.

91. Jenkins, "Next Steps in Education."

92. On Jenkins's appointment by Eisenhower, see "Jenkins Named," *Afro*, March 12, 1955; and "Dr. Jenkins in 2nd Study of Military," *Afro*, March 19, 1955.

Most importantly, Jenkins connected all of those conversations together to serve the greater goal of racial equality. As he emphasized before the gathering of educators in Memphis, all of this was needed for Black schools and colleges to thrive after the Supreme Court's forthcoming decision. The next month, in January 1954, he repeated his Memphis prediction in the *Baltimore Afro-American*. "I believe that the decision of the Supreme Court in the five school segregation cases will be favorable to the cause of interracial progress," Jenkins wrote. "I believe that the court will outlaw segregation in public schools of the nation." He was confident in his prediction, whether due to his close proximity to the Howard-affiliated NAACP legal team or due purely to faith. In either case, he was right.[93]

On May 17, 1954, the Supreme Court's unanimous decision in *Brown v. Board of Education* deemed separate but equal education unconstitutional. Thurgood Marshall, director-counsel of the NAACP Legal Defense Fund, called it "the greatest victory we ever had." James W. Seabrook, president of Fayetteville State in North Carolina, said that despite the initial shock, the South would be stronger because of the decision. "No one would want to turn the hands of the clock back to 1862," he said. "It will be the same with respect to the present decision of the Supreme Court." Luther H. Foster, president of Tuskegee Institute in Alabama, added "the legal source of segregation is now removed." And Jenkins said, "I am gratified by the Court's decision and the fact that the verdict was unanimous." It was the legal blow to Jim Crow that Black leaders had anticipated and desired, but the realization of desegregation was another matter.[94]

Black educators had strategically networked from the local to federal level, but their success did not warrant a respite. More work lay ahead as the crumbled legal barriers only created other forms of white resistance as rubble. In Baltimore, grassroots pushback emerged as white mob activity in 1954 against the desegregation of an all-white high school. At the state level, just days before the *Brown* decision, on May 15, 1954, the racial spite of University of Maryland president H. C. "Curley" Byrd also reached full throttle. Disgruntled with previous governors' unwillingness to transfer control of Morgan State to the university and with the looming Supreme Court ruling, Byrd secured the endorsement of twenty-five leaders from eight of the state's Democratic Party

93. Martin D. Jenkins, "Selects Thurgood Marshall: Backs Republican Regime, Looks for Rights Progress," *Afro*, January 9, 1954. Benjamin E. Mays, president of Morehouse, also anticipated a favorable *Brown* ruling. See Jelks, *Benjamin Elijah Mays*, pp. 189–192.

94. Again, for more on the *Brown* decision, see Patterson, *Brown v. Board of Education*; and Bell, *Silent Covenants*. On Jenkins's and others' praise for *Brown*, see "What the Leaders Say about Court Decision," *Afro*, May 29, 1954.

clubs in his run for governor. "Dr. Byrd is the strongest candidate ever to run for governor in this state," said F. Brooke Lee, campaign manager, to a group gathered at the York Hotel in Baltimore. "Strongest" may well have been code for most dedicated white supremacist, and on June 28, 1954, Byrd won the party primary. He would face the incumbent Theodore R. McKeldin, known for his pro–civil rights stance, in the November 1954 election.[95]

Byrd's strategy focused on winning three specific Maryland counties—Prince George, Charles, and Montgomery—that bordered Washington, DC, but he naively underestimated his inability to win over even the smallest portion of Black voters, particularly Black women. While campaigning, he attended a Maryland League of Women's Clubs luncheon held at the Morgan Christian Center affiliated with Morgan State. Lillie M. Jackson, a pivotal Baltimore civil rights leader and local NAACP president, was seated with Byrd alongside other Black women leaders. This crowd offered the longtime college president and gubernatorial hopeful no easy afternoon of political promises. In fact, when the women's club president, Vivian Alleyne, introduced Byrd, a wave of murmurs and whispers greeted him from the four hundred women present.[96]

These women had not forgotten that it was Byrd who had kept the University of Maryland's other professional and graduate programs segregated, forcing the NAACP to file additional desegregation lawsuits for each program. Jenkins and Holmes remembered this as Morgan State presidents during Byrd's term as University of Maryland president since 1935. The same was true for Soper and Murphy as the Morgan trustee board chairs. And certainly this group of Black women remembered and were unwilling to cast a vote in support of Byrd as governor.[97]

This was important as the fall election approached, because Jenkins continued to secure more funding for Morgan State. In 1952, a twelve-year effort finally concluded when a thousand-seat gymnasium was opened on campus, but it did not take as long to have two new buildings set to open before the end of 1954. One would be for chemistry and physics—a testament to Jenkins's long fight for better facilities at Morgan State for the most basic forms of teaching and research—and the other would be an infirmary. This was a much-needed upgrade as Jenkins anticipated that five hundred new students would enroll that fall. This progress, however, would all but stop if Byrd was elected

95. On the Baltimore mob action, see Collier-Thomas and Franklin, *My Soul Is a Witness*, p. 13. On Byrd's endorsements, see Ed Smith, "Dems Endorse Curly Byrd," *Afro*, May 15, 1954.

96. Smith, "Dems Endorse Curly Byrd." On Black women and Byrd, see B. M. Phillips, "If You Ask Me," *Afro*, April 10, 1954. For more on Black women and civil rights struggles, see Hine and Thompson, *A Shining Thread of Hope*, pp. 266–294.

97. Phillips, "If You Ask Me."

governor. Therefore, on November 2, 1954, a pivotal election day in Maryland history, Baltimore carried its weight as the state's largest city. Byrd was defeated, with thirty-six Black precincts in Northwest Baltimore voting seven to one in favor of McKeldin over Byrd. Also notable was the election of Emory Cole, Harry Cole, and Truly Hatchett as the first Black people elected to the Maryland General Assembly.[98]

The victories were momentous and spoke to the power of voting rights—something most Black people in the Deep South did not have in the 1950s. The election results also highlighted the influence of another key component of Jenkins's network—Black women. He did not have a narrow conception of the role of women. Jenkins regularly hosted Black women leaders and spoke before Black women's groups. In some segregated cities, tensions grew between older and younger Black people about the pace of desegregation and the preference to challenge racism in the courts; however, Baltimore had a history of direct action campaigns long before many other cities, and those campaigns were led by Black women.[99]

Jackson, the Baltimore NAACP president since 1935, and Adah K. Jenkins (no relation to Martin D. Jenkins), head of the Non-Segregation Theater Committee, led a six-year effort picketing Ford's Theatre until it discontinued segregated seating in 1952. The Baltimore branch of the NAACP had three thousand members, and Jackson said the victory proved "the majority of the citizens of Baltimore believe in the Constitution of our great United States." Adah K. Jenkins called it "a victory for democracy here and elsewhere." Their efforts began as Martin D. Jenkins arrived in Baltimore as Morgan State president, so

---

98. "Morgan College to Open Two Buildings," *Afro*, August 21, 1954; "Baltimoreans Snub Dr. Byrd: Return McKeldin to Governor Post," *Afro*, November 3, 1954; "2 More Baltimore Negroes Elected to Md. Legislature," *Jet*, November 25, 1954.

99. In addition to hosting Mary McLeod Bethune in 1951, Jenkins regularly hosted other Black women leaders. For more, see "Gadabouting U.S.A.: Meet Jenkins' 'Sophronia,'" *Afro*, March 18, 1961; and "Dr. Player Says Women Star in Feminine Role in This Era," *Afro*, March 24, 1962. Historians have described the importance of the Black women's strategic organizing and networks during the Black freedom struggle. For a briefer account, see Farmer, *Remaking Black Power*, particularly pp. 22–28. For a longer account, beyond the traditional civil rights movement, see Terborg-Penn, *African American Women*. At Howard, Treva B. Lindsey wrote that President Mordecai W. Johnson "maintained a conservative understanding of black women's roles on college campuses and, more broadly, in public life." For more, see Lindsey, *Colored No More*, pp. 42–47. In comparing the Black vote in Maryland, in 1958, only 9 percent of Blacks in Alabama could vote and only 4 percent in Mississippi. For more, see Anderson, *Pursuit of Fairness*, p. 49. Atlanta is a heightened example of the tension among Black people over how best to challenge segregation. For more, see Brown-Nagin, *Courage to Dissent*.

he knew both women—Jackson as a prominent NAACP leader and Jenkins as a *Baltimore Afro-American* music critic and longtime Morgan State music instructor. Jenkins's future work challenging segregation would depend on these women and their experiences with direct action demonstrations.[100]

Black Presidents "Stand Up" for the Sit-ins

There is a direct connection between Black Baltimore youth activists, Lillie M. Jackson, and Morgan State. In June 1936, the NAACP held its annual national meeting at Sharp Street Methodist Episcopal Church. In the late 1800s, that church was one of the original locations where Morgan State held classes. Also, Jackson's daughter, Juanita, led the NAACP's Youth and College Division, and in February 1937, Morgan students were among the four hundred Black students who attended the National Negro Congress conference in Richmond with the intent to establish a Southern Negro Youth Congress. Therefore, it was not happenstance that Morgan State was where student sit-in activity emerged years before those that launched in 1960.[101]

The direct action efforts in Baltimore that started in the 1940s continued in 1955. This time, Morgan State students were the leaders, and on January 22, local media covered the students' successful sit-in demonstrations at the whites-only lunch counters of Read's Drug Stores. Ben Everinghim, vice chair of Baltimore CORE, and McQuay Kiah, assistant dean of men at Morgan State, were among those involved with the Read's sit-ins. The pressure from Morgan State students forced Read's president, Arthur Nattans Sr., to desegregate his stores.[102]

100. For a brief overview of Jackson's life, see "NAACP Leader Lillie M. Jackson Dies in Md. at 86," *Jet*, July 24, 1975. On Baltimore NAACP and conflicts between Jackson and Ella Baker, see Ransby, *Ella Baker and the Black Freedom Movement*, pp. 122–124. Regarding Adah K. Jenkins, see "Mrs. Adah Jenkins, 72, was AFRO music critic," *Afro*, May 19, 1973. On the Baltimore theater pickets, the Lillie M. Jackson and Adah K. Jenkins quotes, and the significance of the theaters as a point of protest, see "Maryland Theatre Reverts to Jim Crow: Picket Line Reactivated," *Afro*, September 17, 1949; "Md.'s Ford's Theatre Ends Separate Seating: After 6-Year Picket Line," *Afro*, February 9, 1952; and Sartain, *Borders of Equality*, pp. 64–75.

101. For more on Juanita Jackson, see Bynum, *NAACP Youth and the Fight for Black Freedom*, pp. 1–9; On Morgan and Sharp Street Methodist, see Jones, "Purpose, Progress, and Promise," p. 4–6. On the 1937 Richmond gathering, see Kelley, *Hammer and Hoe*, pp. 200–201, and Kendi, *Black Campus Movement*, p. 52; it is also notable how Baltimore students, including Morgan State students, were widely involved in the launch of Negro History Week in 1926. For more, see Givens, "There Would Be No Lynching," p. 1473.

102. "37 Baltimore Drug Stores Open Lunch Counters to All Patrons," *Afro*, January 22, 1955; and "Service for All," *Afro*, January 29, 1955.

In April 1955, the management of the segregated Northwood Theatre near the Morgan State campus requested a meeting with the students after continued demonstrations. By this point, some Johns Hopkins University students had joined in the protest. During this spring of intense student activity, Governor McKeldin called Baltimore hotel discrimination a "shame," further amplifying the chorus calling for the end of segregation. Afterward, although New York became the first state to pass an anti-discrimination in employment law in 1945, Baltimore leaders in the mid-1950s made the city the first south of the Mason-Dixon line to pass a fair employment law.[103]

In October 1955, Mamie Till, mother of Emmett Till, a fourteen-year-old who was brutally murdered in Mississippi, visited Baltimore's Bethel AME Church. Her visit and stirring account of her son's death was representative of Baltimoreans' engagement in the national fight for racial equality. The Morgan State students' actions, following the lead of Dean Kiah, earned Baltimore CORE the 1955 Achievement Award of the National Council of CORE. Similarly, Carl J. Murphy was awarded the national NAACP's 1955 Spingarn Medal, the highest honor given to a person of African descent, for his dedication to civil rights in Baltimore.[104]

Black Baltimoreans were not keen on waiting for progress and were being recognized nationally for their efforts. As Jenkins had previously stated, there was more leeway in demanding racial equality in Maryland than in the Deep South, and he and others took advantage and pushed local boundaries. Over the next few years, Jenkins continued to deploy his network following Morgan State students' direct action campaigns. In 1956, Jenkins bestowed Jackson with an honorary degree, saying "to this woman, one of the finest of this country and a first citizen of this city, our beloved country is greatly indebted." Later that year, Jenkins attended the inauguration of his friend Willa B. Player as president of Bennett College, a Black women's college in North Carolina. She became the first Black woman president of a four-year US college. Other Black presidents present—and able to celebrate Player and discuss among

103. Regarding the Northwood Theatre protests, see "Morgan Students Suspend Stand-In," *Afro*, May 7, 1955; and "Theatre Pickets Win Victory in Court: No Reason for Arrest, Says Judge," *Afro*, June 25, 1955; see also "Hotel Segregation Shameful—McKeldin," *Afro*, March 19, 1955. On the New York law in 1945, see Anderson, *Pursuit of Fairness*, p. 54. On Baltimore passing a fair employment law, see Collier-Thomas and Franklin, *My Soul Is a Witness*, p. 46; for more on the tensions between economic growth over segregation, see Williamson-Lott, *Jim Crow Campus*.

104. Mamie Till-Bradley, "I Want You to Know What They Did to My Boy," in Houck and Dixon, *Rhetoric, Religion, and the Civil Rights Movement*, pp. 131–145; "CORE Receives National Award," *Afro*, March 12, 1955. On Murphy's award, see Martin D. Jenkins to Morris A. Soper, June 23, 1955, Soper Collection, Box 2–5, Folder 6, MSU.

themselves the ongoing Baltimore demonstrations—were Harry V. Richardson of Gammon Theological Seminary; James P. Brawley of Clark College; Mordecai W. Johnson of Howard; and Frederick D. Patterson, former Tuskegee president and current head of the United Negro College Fund. Edgar Amos Love, a Methodist bishop in Baltimore, also joined this group at Player's inauguration.[105]

A few months later, in December 1956, Morgan State was the site for the conclave of Omega Psi Phi—the Black fraternity that Bishop Love co-founded in November 1911 as an undergraduate student at Howard. Morgan State was home to one of the fraternity's oldest chapters—chartered in 1923—and the 362 delegates represented twenty-nine states. Jenkins served as a speaker during that conclave, and the fraternity presented Martin Luther King Jr. with its Citizen of the Year Award as the yearlong Montgomery bus boycott ended. Furthermore, while in Baltimore, King met with Stanley Levison, Harris Wofford, and Omega Psi Phi member Bayard Rustin. Rustin later organized the 1963 March on Washington for Jobs and Freedom, Wofford became US president John F. Kennedy's internal civil rights expert, and Levison became a notable fundraiser for King's civil rights efforts. Levison was also subject to FBI wire taps as a suspected communist. Yet, this meeting was facilitated by Rustin and other Omega men's invitation to honor King (an Alpha Phi Alpha member) at Morgan State with Jenkins's approval and support.[106]

105. "Morgan Honorees: 'To This Woman . . . Our Beloved Country Is Greatly Indebted,'" *Afro*, June 16, 1956. For an in-depth account of Jackson's contributions, see Smith, *Here Lies Jim Crow*. On Willa B. Player's inauguration, see "Educators at Inauguration," *Afro*, October 27, 1956. Mary McLeod Bethune is considered to have been the first president of Bethune-Cookman College; however, that institution was not approved to offered four-year degrees until later. For more on Player as the first Black woman president of a four-year college, see "Willa Player, 94, Pioneer Black Educator," *New York Times*, April 30, 2003; and Flowers, "The Launching of the Student Sit-in Movement," p. 56.

106. "362 Omegas from 29 States at Conclave in Baltimore," *Afro*, January 5, 1957; and "Omega Award to Bus Boycott Leader," *Afro*, January 5, 1957; Omega Psi Phi has numerous contributions to the civil rights movement. For more, see Layboure and Parks, "Omega Psi Phi Fraternity and the Fight for Civil Rights." The Martin Luther King Jr. Research and Education Institute at Stanford University provides summative information about the King, Rustin, Wofford, and Levison meeting: "Wofford, Harris Llewellyn," *King Encyclopedia*, https://kinginstitute.stanford.edu/encyclopedia/wofford-harris-llewellyn (accessed January 13, 2019); "Levison, Stanley David," *King Encyclopedia*, https://kinginstitute.stanford.edu/encyclopedia/levison-stanley-david (accessed January 13, 2019); "King Addresses Omega Psi Phi," *King Encyclopedia*, https://kinginstitute.stanford.edu/encyclopedia/king-addresses-omega-psi-phi-fraternity-convention-morgan-state-college-meets-harris (accessed January 13, 2019). For more on Levison and the FBI, see Patterson, *Grand Expectations*, pp. 475–476. Patterson wrote, "No

By 1957, the presidents of Black state-supported colleges in Mississippi were under more pressure from state officials. The same year, an important meeting took place when the all-Black Association of Colleges and Schools, known as "the Association," met at the same time as the all-white Southern Association of Colleges and Schools, referred to as "the Southern Association," in Richmond. However, while Black presidents in the Deep South were restrained, Jenkins served on a panel during the Association's meeting of Black educators. This occurred as more Black students demanded an end to segregation during the remainder of the 1950s.[107]

By 1960, sit-in demonstrations were a proven technique to challenge segregation. These activities were mostly organized by local NAACP or CORE chapters during the 1950s, but on February 1, 1960, a sit-in at a whites-only F. W. Woolworth lunch counter in Greensboro by four North Carolina A&T freshmen sparked similar student demonstrations throughout the South. Bennett College students organized the ongoing sit-in effort, and it was Player who became a stalwart supporter of the student movement. Even before the lunch counter sit-ins, Player opened her campus to King in 1958 when Black leaders of Greensboro's Black high schools and North Carolina A&T would not. Bennett students participated in movie theater pickets in the 1930s and voter registration efforts in the early 1950s, and Player continued to support students after the sit-ins started, allowing students from Bennett and A&T to meet with each other. She also supported the students' cause through action when she returned her charge card to a local department store in solidarity with the students.[108]

---

evidence, however, proved that Levison had associations with communists after he had become close to King in 1956."

107. Regarding the state-supported Black colleges in Mississippi, see Williamson, *Radicalizing the Ebony Tower*, pp. 39–41. On the meeting in Richmond, see Walker, *Hello Professor*, pp. 81–109. Specifically, see pp. 81–82 and pp. 93–94 for the informal association names and Jenkins's panel appearance. In addition to demonstrating how Black college presidents discussed Black education, Walker also noted that they served as president of the Association and the American Teachers Association.

108. On the Bennett students' civil rights activity before the sit-ins, see Flowers, "Launching of the Student Sit-in Movement"; Favors, *Shelter in a Time of Storm*, pp. 70–100; Dwonna Goldstone, "Black Women in the North Carolina Civil Rights Movement," in Pitre and Glasrud, *Southern Black Women*. On King's 1958 visit and Player's voluntary return of her charge card in support of the sit-ins, see Chafe, *Civilities and Civil Rights*, pp. 80, 97. For more about Player and Bennett College, see Brown, *Belles of Liberty*, and Sanders, "Pursuing the 'Unfinished.'" Bennett was also unique as a Black women's college with a Black woman as president. At the same time, Albert E. Manley, a Black man, was president of Spelman, which did not hire a Black woman president until Johnetta B. Cole in 1987. For more, see Graham and Poulson, "Spelman College,"

As February 1960 came to a close, sit-ins had occurred at segregated lunch counters in nearly a dozen cities in North Carolina as well as other cities in Virginia, South Carolina, Florida, Tennessee, Kentucky, and Alabama, and this storm of activity stirred segregationist governors and public officials across the South. For instance, on March 3, 1960, North Carolina governor Luther Hodges wrote the president and chair of the trustee board for each state-supported institution regarding what he felt deserved their "very careful consideration," as he encouraged presidents to direct students against the sit-ins. Nevertheless, by the end of March, students in Atlanta and in cities in Texas and Louisiana soon followed. Beyond the South, several University of Wisconsin and University of California, Los Angeles, students also protested at their local Woolworth stores in solidarity with southern Black students.[109]

Ella Baker helped organize this national movement as students from across the South met for a conference on April 15–17, 1960, at Shaw University in Raleigh. At the time, Baker worked for the Southern Christian Leadership Conference (SCLC), but she remained adamant that the students remain in control of the sit-in movement. The Student Nonviolent Coordinating Committee (SNCC) emerged from the Shaw conference, which featured King as one of the speakers. Most reflective of the work of Black college presidents, however, was a private meeting held at the home of Shaw president William R. Strassner during the conference. There, civil rights leaders Baker, King, Reverend Wyatt Tee Walker, and Reverend Ralph Abernathy discussed, and even disagreed, on the next steps in the sit-in movement.[110]

---

pp. 244–245. Scholars also assert that "Without [Black women's] efforts, the modern civil rights movement very likely would not have been as successful. Or successful at all." For more, see Bruce A. Glasrud and Merline Pitre, "Introduction: Contributions of African American Women in the Modern Civil Rights Movement," in Pitre and Glasrud, *Southern Black Women*, p. 10.

109. On cities with student sit-ins by February and March 1960, see Morris, *Origins of the Civil Rights Movement*, p. 197. For the Hodges letter to presidents, see Luther Hodges to Robert H. Frazier and Warmoth T. Gibbs, March 3, 1960, Luther Hartwell Hodges Collection, North Carolina State Archives. Regarding UCLA students, see Southern California Boycott Committee flyer, n.d., University of California, Los Angeles, UCLA Students: Student Activism Materials, Box 3, Folder 13, UCLA Library Special Collections, Charles E. Young Research Library. On Wisconsin students' demonstrations, refer to Richard Bradee, "Students Picket Woolworth Store to Protest Southern Segregation: Local NAACP Criticizes Action," *Capital Times*, February 27, 1960; and Kim Willenson, "Students Here Picket Stores, Cite South," *Wisconsin State Journal*, February 28, 1960.

110. For a detailed account of Ella Baker and her role in organizing students, see Ransby, *Ella Baker*, pp. 238–247. The private meeting is discussed on pp. 242–243, and Ransby noted that

At this point, the large number of students involved, with their widespread reach, created America's first student movement against racial segregation—ignited by events in Greensboro. Player's willingness to welcome King to campus in 1958 and her active role in aiding the student sit-ins should not have come as a surprise. It was a page out of Jenkins's book. He had welcomed King to his campus in 1956. Similarly, Jenkins supported Morgan State students' sit-ins throughout the 1950s, and Player had done the same with her unique flair. As Black college campuses quieted during the summer of 1960, Jenkins was one of the college presidents most experienced at maneuvering the unprecedented wave of Black student activism. The Black presidential network was utilized once again as Black academic leaders navigated new terrain.

In October 1960, author Lerone Bennett Jr. asked readers of *Ebony* magazine to imagine that they were the president of a state-supported Black college and their all-white board ordered them to expel students who participated in the sit-ins. "You've got to act and act quickly. What to do? Expel the ringleaders and maintain rapport with the board? Defy the board and maintain rapport with the students?" For Black college presidents, however, that scenario was not hypothetical. "To be president of a college and white is no bed of roses," said Benjamin E. Mays, president of Morehouse. "To be president of a college and Black is almost a bed of thorns." George W. Gore Jr., president of Florida A&M, described the sit-in dilemma as "an extremely difficult situation." Tennessee Agricultural & Industrial President Walter S. Davis added, "There is no question about it, mass demonstrations put the college president in a tough spot." And William Trent Jr., executive director of the United Negro College Fund, surmised, "Before the sit-ins people were looking askance at all college presidents and wondering whether they were free or not."[111]

By the fall of 1960, more than one hundred students at Black colleges had been expelled or placed on probation. Rufus B. Atwood expelled twelve students at Kentucky State College; H. Councill Trenholm promised the Alabama governor and the all-white board that he would stop student demonstrators at Alabama State College; and Felton G. Clark suspended eighteen

---

"There are different versions of the meeting, and certainly differing views about whether SCLC intended to 'capture' and subordinate the emergent student movement." On Baker deciding to organize students, see Zinn, *SNCC*, pp. 32–33; and Jelks, *Benjamin Elijah Mays*, pp. 210–211. On the role of Baker's alma mater, Shaw University, in her awareness of the importance of the sit-ins, see Carson, *In Struggle*, p. 19.

111. Lerone Bennett Jr., "The Plight of Negro College Presidents: Sit-in Demonstrations and Direct Attacks on Segregation Raise Crucial Problems for Educators," *Ebony*, October 1960. For the "bed of thorns," see Mays, *Born to Rebel*, p. 196.

students at Southern University and A&M College, prompting one student to call Clark an "intellectual Uncle Tom." Marian Wright, a Spelman student, celebrated Mays as an inspiration and encourager, but described Spelman president Albert Manley as offering kind words but interested in stopping demonstrators and Atlanta University president Rufus Clement as being conservative. Howard Zinn, a white professor at Spelman and SNCC advisor, took offense that "even at some private, church-supported institutions, like Benedict and Allen Colleges in South Carolina, college administrators threatened expulsion for students who joined the sit-in movement and fired the few faculty who spoke their minds."[112]

But some faculty were more understanding and forgiving than Zinn was about the precarious position of Black college presidents. In Montgomery, Jo Ann Gibson Robinson, who taught at Alabama State College, remembered Trenholm as being supportive of civil rights. He allowed faculty members to use campus telephones and copiers for flyers during the Montgomery bus boycott that lasted from December 1955 until December 1956. In 1960, however, Alabama State students' participation in the sit-ins brought white state officials' scrutiny to campus. At that point, Robinson said, Trenholm had the "power of the presidency" removed from him by the governor and other state officials, "although he remained president in name." In Greensboro, William M. Bell, head football coach at North Carolina A&T, appreciated President Warmoth T. Gibbs's refusal to discipline students. This surprised whites, as Gibbs instead chose to consult faculty and other administrators on the

---

112. Bennett, "Negro College Presidents"; Zinn, *SNCC*, pp. 30–31. In Atlanta, the Atlanta University Center (AUC)—a consortium of six Black colleges by midcentury—presents an example of the varied stances among private Black college presidents. For more on the student perspective of the AUC presidents, see Edelman, *Lanterns*, pp. 24–36, 44–65. Black presidents' engagement with the sit-ins is one of the most frequently discussed aspects of their leadership, of which there are numerous, and often conflicting, accounts. Whereas Benjamin E. Mays is consistently celebrated as supportive of the student movement, Rufus Clement at Atlanta University has different assessments. For more revered opinions, see Jelks, *Benjamin Elijah Mays*, pp. 212–215. Jelks wrote that Clement and Mays encouraged students to write the "An Appeal for Human Rights" manifesto. Also see Daniels, *Horace T. Ward*, pp. 27–28. For a more critical assessment, see Brown-Nagin, *Courage to Dissent*, p. 151. Brown-Nagin wrote, "Rufus Clement also expressed his 'hope that there would be no more demonstrations.'" For a fairly neutral assessment of Clement, see Turner, *Sitting In and Speaking Out*, pp. 24–25, where he is described as working toward "the eventual end of segregation." There is also a general assessment that all of Atlanta's Black college presidents, including Mays, wanted to persuade students not to sit in. For more, see Lefever, *Undaunted by the Fight*, pp. 25–26.

matter. "Under great political duress, the president followed the advice of his faculty and administration," Bell said. "[L]ittle publicity has been given the fact that Dr. Gibbs, in his own quiet way, made this decision possible."[113]

It is this "quiet" work of Black presidents that is most important in understanding how these academic leaders were able to shape racial practices beyond the gaze of white state legislators, governors, and trustees. Jenkins understood that many Black presidents sacrificed their reputations and accepted public criticism without being able to explain the full breadth of how they supported desegregation. That fall, as *Ebony* and other news outlets covered Black educators, Jenkins sent a message to all Black college students, not just those at Morgan State.[114]

On September 28, 1960, Jenkins's convocation address at Morgan State demanded that students do one thing: "Stand Up." That was the title of his convocation address, and he spoke directly about the student sit-ins. Despite Morgan State's history of student participation in sit-ins well before 1960, this was the first time students' efforts were situated within the context of a national sit-in movement. It was no longer solely about Baltimore, and Jenkins directly addressed the sit-ins that had drastically changed dozens of southern cities in the last six months:

> We are witnessing in this country, and indeed throughout the world, an almost revolutionary movement against racial segregation and discrimination. This movement has many facets. Certainly one of the most interesting

---

113. For more on H. Councill Trenholm, see Robinson, *Montgomery Bus Boycott*, pp. 50–52, 167–172; and Favors, *Shelter in a Time of Storm*, pp. 101–132. Adam Fairclough's assessment is similar to Robinson's: "Those who knew both Trenholm and Alabama were less harsh in their judgements." For more, see Fairclough, *Teaching Equality*, pp. 39–41. For more on Warmoth T. Gibbs, see Bell, *Black without Malice*, pp. 145–148.

114. Several historians have discussed the challenges faced by the presidents of Black colleges during the student civil rights uprising of the early 1960s. Pertaining to private colleges, some examples include: Williamson, *Radicalizing the Ebony Tower*, pp. 97–105; Williamson-Lott, *Jim Crow Campus*, pp. 51–57; Lovett, *Civil Rights Movement in Tennessee*, pp. 127–131; Gasman, "Perceptions of Black College Presidents," pp. 844–862. Pertaining to state-supported colleges, some examples include: Williamson, *Radicalizing the Ebony Tower*, pp. 114–119; Williamson-Lott, *Jim Crow Campus*, pp. 64–71; Chafe, *Civilities and Civil Rights*, pp. 60–61, 95; Cole, "Words of Action," in Danns, Purdy, and Span, *Using Past as Prologue*, pp. 141–160; Robert Cohen, "Introduction," in Cohen and Snyder, *Rebellion in Black and White*, pp. 3–4; Joy Ann Williamson, "Black Colleges and Civil Rights: Organizing and Mobilizing in Jackson, Mississippi," in Wallenstein, *Higher Education and the Civil Rights Movement*, pp. 117–121; Sansing, *Making Haste Slowly*, pp. 144–145; Smith, *A Black Educator in the Segregated South*, pp. 149–165; Lovett, *Civil Rights Movement in Tennessee*, pp. 127–128.

of these, and one which may turn out to be of considerable long-term significance, is the so-called "sit-in" or "sit-down" developed by college students, chiefly Negro college students. . . . This is a good movement, and it has surprisingly beneficial results.

He continued by explaining the significance of the movement:

This is important, but what is more important is that this movement has brought before the people of this nation the fundamental dissatisfaction of young educated students with existing patterns of racial discrimination. . . . Too, it has brought home in vivid fashion, as nothing else ever has, the responsibility of the educated to take constructive steps toward alleviating unsatisfactory conditions in our society.

Jenkins then vowed that he would not instruct students to cease protests because "the participants are citizens who happen to be as well college students."[115]

Therefore, Jenkins demanded that Morgan State students stand up in the areas of community relations, employment, and their personal growth and development. The data were clear—Black people were displaced in society at more than segregated lunch counters. Schools were underfunded, job opportunities were limited, and community resources were scarce compared with white neighborhoods. "So you want a racially-integrated society? Stand Up," Jenkins demanded of the students. "It is your task to develop for yourself, and in the light of your abilities, qualifications, and interests, a personal philosophy which will guide your behavior as an intelligently participating member of your society." As he had done his entire career, Jenkins used rigorous research to frame discussions about the social problems facing Black people. The ability to think would serve students beyond their college years, he said, because they had a duty to take the sit-in momentum into the latter half of the century and the new millennium.[116]

This was a riveting speech, but one too dangerous for most Black college presidents to deliver, especially in the Deep South. But that did not stop Cornelius V. Troup, president of Fort Valley State College, Georgia's Black land-grant institution, from making sure his students had an opportunity to hear the same message. Black people living in Georgia's Peach County were disenfranchised, and by the mid-1950s, less than 20 percent of them were registered to vote. Also, 40 percent of the county's overall population lived in

115. Martin D. Jenkins, "Stand Up," Fall Convocation, September 28, 1960, Jenkins Collection, Box 5, Folder 15, MSU.

116. Ibid.

poverty. In this context, Troup invited Jenkins to Middle Georgia to serve as the keynote speaker for the Fort Valley State Founders' Day program. Troup was a recent president of the Association of Colleges and Secondary Schools, the same organization Jenkins had addressed in Memphis in 1953. Therefore, the two presidents were connected through the usual Black networks. That connection also provided an opportunity to quietly discuss how all Black presidents, regardless of their local context, could actively influence policies and practices in favor of desegregation.[117]

On the morning of October 10, 1960, Fort Valley State students, staff, faculty, and members of the community gathered in the campus auditorium. The processional of faculty and honored guests entered to Henry Thomas Smart's March in G, followed by an opening hymn. Next, Pastor R. S. Allison of Saint Peter AME Church provided the scripture reading and a prayer blessing the occasion. The original college charter was read and the College Choir sang "Awake the Harp." Then, student body president George Tate paid tribute to the tireless work of the late Henry Alexander Hunt, a dedicated Black educator and the school's second principal. Following another hymn, President Troup stepped forward to introduce the speaker— Martin D. Jenkins.[118]

It was Jenkins's first visit to Fort Valley State since 1941, when Horace Mann Bond was president. Therefore, his forthcoming message as an out-of-state guest may have been unknown to the Fort Valley audience, but Troup was certainly aware what his friend would share despite the state's white supremacist leaders' hatred for the sit-in demonstrations. As Jenkins stood before the auditorium, Georgia governor Ernest Vandiver had campaigned on a pro-segregation campaign, and in October 1960, Martin Luther King Jr. was arrested alongside roughly fifty others following a sit-in Atlanta. Nonetheless, Jenkins stood and delivered the same "Stand Up" speech from three weeks earlier. What Troup could not say as the president of a state-supported Black college in Georgia, Jenkins said for him. "In this time, you have a part to play

---

117. On Blacks in Peach County, see Hanks, *Struggle for Black Political Empowerment*, pp. 95–97. The operations of Black educators were so covert that earlier scholars who studied Fort Valley and Peach County have overlooked their contributions. Lawrence J. Hanks argued that "the black staff and faculty at the predominantly black Fort Valley State College and the black county school teachers offered 'no active leadership in political affairs' in Peach County during the pre-sixties era," but historian Vanessa Siddle Walker later demonstrated that was not the case. On Cornelius V. Troup and the Association of Colleges and Secondary Schools, see "Educators to Hear Integration Report," *Afro*, November 26, 1955.

118. Founders' Day Program, October 10, 1960, Jenkins Collection, Box 10–10a–11, Folder 123, MSU; and "Colleges," *Afro*, October 15, 1960.

in determining the kind of future you will have—that your children will have—that this nation will have . . . ," Jenkins professed. "I say to you—stand up!"[119]

Following this challenge to act, the College Choir sang two stirring Negro spirituals as the program neared its end:

> There is a Balm in Gilead / To make the wounded whole;
> There is a Balm in Gilead / To heal the sin-sick soul.
> Sometimes I feel discouraged / And think my work's in vain;
> But then the Holy Spirit / Revives my soul again.

Then, during the recessional, all adjourned to the campus burial ground of Henry Alexander Hunt, with the college choir and congregation joining together "We Are Climbing Jacob's Ladder" and "Soldier of the Cross." Both were favorite spirituals of Hunt, who had inherited an underresourced secondary school for Black people in 1904 that, by 1960, had grown into a college. Now, Jenkins stood alongside Troup as memorial wreaths were laid at Hunt's tomb. It took just as much courage for Troup to invite Jenkins to Fort Valley as it did for Jenkins himself to "stand up" and deliver that message. It may have been decades after Hunt's death, and neither Jenkins nor Troup were personal acquaintances of the school's early principal, but they stood there silently in an unspoken tradition. The Black educator's work was spiritual—a higher calling for Black liberation in the same vein as the spirituals that closed the Founders' Day Program.[120]

Conclusion

It was common for college presidents to be connected across multiple sectors. Holders of no other academic positions were expected to speak before churches, fraternal organizations, and women's groups, and meet with state and federal officials, faculty, staff, and students, influential donors and more. This was no different for Black college presidents. As a result, formal and informal conversations with numerous entities allowed these academic leaders to shape racial policies and practices covertly and under a cloak that hid their own influence.

119. Martin D. Jenkins, "Stand Up," Speech at Fort Valley, October 10, 1960, Jenkins Collection, Box 10–10a–11, Folder 123, MSU; Henderson, *Ernest Vandiver*. For additional information about the sit-ins in Fort Valley, see Hanks, *Struggle for Black Political Empowerment*, p. 97. On the significance of Fort Valley and Henry Alexander Hunt, see Walker, *Lost Education*, pp. 58–70. On King's arrest in Atlanta, see Brown-Nagin, *Courage to Dissent*, pp. 158–159.

120. Founders' Day Program.

Black college presidents were instrumental in disrupting southern governors' attempts to develop regional colleges for Black people instead of desegregating existing white universities. These presidents testified before federal courts regarding the shortfalls of "separate but equal" schools. They sat on federal commissions and advised US presidents at a time when the nation's international standing was criticized due to domestic racism. Furthermore, some Black academic leaders published research that challenged white scholars' inaccurate yet longstanding beliefs about Black people and education, and regularly demanded desegregation to secure more funding for Black higher education. These visible actions were paired with their invisible activities.

Black churches, fraternities, and sororities offered personal networks and connections beyond the realm of the formal positions of college presidents. Black teacher associations and other Black associations presented opportunities for backroom meetings beyond the official conference sessions. Additionally, these networks presented opportunities to organize long train rides far away from their own campuses to deliver pro-Black messages that the local Black educators could never utter aloud. Combined, these efforts further demonstrated how the greatest feats of Black educators—teachers, principals, professors, and college presidents—earned little public recognition or fanfare but influenced educational policies and practices. Yet, as Black college presidents quietly worked toward desegregation in the South, the white academic leaders of the northern urban universities were seeking publicity as they molded racial policy.

2

"We Simply Cannot Operate in Slums"

THE UNIVERSITY
AND HOUSING DISCRIMINATION

"THE OCTOPUS in the South has tentacles in the North!" That was Velma Hill's message on January 23, 1962, to nearly two hundred people gathered for a rally outside of the Administration Building at the University of Chicago. A Black activist and representative from the Congress of Racial Equality (CORE) national office in New York, Hill joined the students who had charged administrators with allowing housing discrimination in university-owned properties. Although the Black freedom struggle looked different in Chicago—where the college presidents and most students were white compared with their southern counterparts—the connection was clear to Hill: "You are part of a real movement, a real civil rights movement that is taking place here."[1]

In the early 1950s, years before University of Chicago (UChicago) students rallied against the institution's racist practices, Chancellor Lawrence A. Kimpton considered the slum conditions of the South Side a crisis. The overcrowding in the Washington Park and Woodlawn neighborhoods adjacent to the Hyde Park campus was a major concern, and several people considered crime to be a byproduct. This impeded UChicago's ability to recruit and retain faculty and students, but Kimpton also knew that similar conditions existed in

---

1. Summary of January 23, 1962, Diary of the Sit-ins, University of Chicago, Office of the President, Beadle Administration Records, Box 128, Folder 5, Special Collections Research Center, University of Chicago Library (archival collection and location hereafter cited as Beadle Records and SCRC); Robin Kaufman, "Students Sleep In," *Chicago Maroon*, January 24, 1962.

other major US cities. Therefore, by 1957, he coordinated a meeting with the presidents of Harvard University, Columbia University, the University of Pennsylvania (Penn), Yale University, and the Massachusetts Institute of Technology (MIT) and convinced them to join him in addressing their shared problem of being located in urban settings.[2]

Over the next few years, Kimpton led the way in acquiring deteriorating properties near UChicago's campus for the purpose of halting the encroaching slums and presented a model for other college presidents. Penn joined these efforts. Meanwhile, Harvard leaders looked to "re-establish friendly relations" with Cambridge, Massachusetts, while Yale administrators joined an "imaginative urban renewal program" in New Haven, Connecticut. Administrators at New York University (NYU) soon considered buying property near Washington Square, and campus officials at Temple University in Philadelphia also acquired forty acres and looked to purchase more. Eventually, sixteen universities were involved with urban renewal initiatives following Kimpton's lead, and several more would soon take part.[3]

Urban renewal, the informal name for a federal program to revitalize land use and remove what many considered slum areas, was enticing to college presidents. But the interests of these academic leaders were self-serving and perpetuated one of the nation's most prevalent civil rights issues—housing discrimination. Since the early 1900s, decades of municipal neglect and racist housing policies had resulted in decaying buildings, overcrowded apartments, and dilapidated structures in American cities, and urban renewal targeted a disproportionate number of Black communities, displacing thousands of Black residents. Racial tensions increased as college presidents took calculated actions, including lobbying federal lawmakers, to satisfy the institutional growth and tout the university's commitment to admitting Black students while also gentrifying the community. James B. Conant, Harvard president from 1933 to 1953, called the emerging issues within cities "social dynamite," and UChicago presented an acute example of the explosive fight between universities and communities, campuses versus slums.[4]

2. Fred M. Hechinger, "Campus vs. Slums: Urban Universities Join Battle for Neighborhood Renewal," *New York Times*, October 1, 1961. The 1957 meeting is also briefly discussed in Bradley, *Upending the Ivory Tower*, p. 207; and Rodin, *The University and Urban Revival*, p. 30.

3. Hechinger, "Campus vs. Slums." For a longer list of campuses, see Parsons, "Universities and Cities."

4. On Conant's use of "social dynamite," see Conant, "Social Dynamite in Our Large Cities," and Karabel, *The Chosen*, p. 314.

Restrictive Racial Covenants and Urban Renewal

For decades, white Chicagoans viciously restricted where people could live based on race and ethnicity. As veterans returned from World War I, whites made quick order of strict racial boundaries. Black people who lived near white neighborhoods suffered through the terror of home bombings, punctuated by the race riot of 1919 that resulted in more than three dozen deaths. The vehement hate became a mainstay among white supremacists for years to come, and by the late 1920s, the use of discriminatory housing policies increased drastically alongside the violence. Whites solicited signatures for racially restrictive covenants—an agreement among themselves not to rent or sell properties to nonwhites or to white landlords who would rent or sell to nonwhites.[5]

On the federal level, in 1933, President Franklin D. Roosevelt introduced the New Deal, a series of government programs aimed at helping Americans survive the Great Depression. One such program assisted homeowners with mortgages and opened the door for redlining, a practice where whites denied certain groups access to, or levied higher rates for, home loans and insurance based on neighborhoods. Additionally, if a Black family did somehow avoid physical violence and move into a white area, whites could sue those Black families for violating the restrictive covenant agreement among whites not to sell or rent to Black buyers. Combined, the housing conditions molded by local white mob violence, the state judicial system, and federal government policies rightfully earned Chicago the reputation of being the most segregated major US city. This strict enforcement of racial boundaries turned attention toward UChicago.[6]

On November 6, 1937, the editor of the *Chicago Defender*, the nation's most prominent Black newspaper, requested that Chancellor Robert M. Hutchins clarify the university's position on restrictive covenants. He responded by explaining that UChicago admitted Black students on the same terms as white students. As evidence, he pointed out that in the freshman class entering in the fall of 1937, the youngest student was a thirteen-year-old Black student. "It is the constant effort of the faculty of the university to educate men and

5. For an overview of Black migration to Chicago following World War I, see Grossman, *Land of Hope*. On white Chicagoans soliciting signatures and the 1919 race riot, see Rothstein, *The Color of Law*, pp. 105, 144. For more on the 1919 riot, see Tuttle, *Race Riot*. For more on white mob violence and housing in Chicago, see Moore, *The South Side*, pp. 40–44. For a broader discussion of US housing segregation, see Gonda, *Unjust Deeds*.

6. Rothstein, *The Color of Law*, pp. 108-109, and Moore, *The South Side*, pp. 41–42. On Chicago as the most segregated city, see Urban Renewal and the Negro in Chicago: Chicago Urban League Report, June 18, 1958, Hyde Park Historical Society Collection, Box 78, Folder 15, SCRC (collection hereafter cited as HPHS).

women to resist all sorts of prejudice and to guide their lives by the light of reason," Hutchins said. "Racial prejudice, like religious prejudice, is consistently opposed." He added that some university administrators, faculty, and trustees "advised with the authorities and actively assisted" in studying the need for adequate housing for Chicago's Black residents, but overall, Hutchins portrayed the issue as beyond his control:

> [UChicago] takes satisfaction in doing these things as a good neighbor, but it does not attempt to dictate local policies as a condition of its support. . . . One of the [neighborhood] associations to which the university belongs has defended restrictive agreements. These agreements were entered into a long time ago, and although many people doubt their social soundness, they are legal in this state and the association has the right to invoke and defend them.

Ultimately, Hutchins told the *Chicago Defender*'s far-reaching Black readership that he stood against restrictive covenants, but they were legal and UChicago would not challenge them.[7]

Hutchins's delicate dance between white neighborhood associations and Black leaders foreshadowed UChicago's approach to housing segregation over the next twenty-five years. It was representative of how academic leaders' actions spoke louder than their prepared statements against prejudice. For instance, Hutchins was hired in 1929, and throughout the 1930s and the early 1940s, UChicago spent more than $100,000 on "community interests," the bulk of which was used to protect restrictive covenants. Therefore, he was partly to blame for the housing segregation that he claimed to oppose, and by 1943, nearly two hundred neighborhood associations maintained restrictive covenants. That number increased by the end of World War II, when more than three hundred "incidents" occurred directed toward Black people, often for mere attempts to buy or rent in or near white neighborhoods. "Negroes and whites in Chicago are consciously competing for space, for jobs, for political power, and for status," assessed St. Clair Drake and Horace R. Cayton in their 1945 sociological study, *Black Metropolis*. But social changes beyond Chicago would force Hutchins and UChicago trustees to reevaluate the university's role in these matters.[8]

7. Hutchins Statement on Restrictive Covenants, November 6, 1937, Beadle Records, Box 265, Folder 1, SCRC. The *Chicago Defender* was a newspaper influential enough to warrant a response from Chancellor Hutchins. For more on its significance, see Michaeli, *The Defender*.

8. For UChicago spending totals, see Hirsch, *Making the Second Ghetto*, p. 145; Regarding the number of neighborhoods with racial covenants and postwar "incidents," see Rothstein, *Color of Law*, pp. 80, 144. See Robert Maynard Hutchins Papers finding aid at SCRC or other

In 1948, the Supreme Court's *Shelley v. Kraemer* decision found restrictive covenants unconstitutional. At the same time, the amount of white violence increased as postwar migration brought more Black southerners to Chicago and Black neighborhoods butted against longstanding racial boundaries. By 1949, on the international front, the Soviet Union successfully tested an atomic bomb. Combined, these three occurrences were detrimental to UChicago. The Supreme Court ruling meant a new method was needed ensure that Hyde Park maintained its mostly white demographics. The violence steered faculty and students away. All the while, the Cold War increased federal officials' demands on research output from universities like UChicago, where in 1942 scientists successfully conducted a controlled nuclear reaction. This required physical expansion to build new laboratories and related facilities.[9]

In 1950, the Hyde Park–Kenwood Community Conference was officially established, led mostly by idealistic whites, in hopes of curbing racial violence and developing more racially harmonious communities. But UChicago leaders and trustees knew too much was at stake to leave neighborhood decisions to local residents interested in ideals. Less than 5 percent of the residents in twelve of Hyde Park's fourteen census tracts were Black, and the only census tracts with more Black residents were those on the western border of Hyde Park adjacent to the majority Black Washington Park neighborhood. For university officials and trustees, it was imperative that Hyde Park remain majority white.[10]

In 1951, the university's role in South Side housing expanded when the UChicago trustees hired Lawrence A. Kimpton as chancellor. Raised in Kansas City, Missouri, the forty-year-old Kimpton completed his bachelor's and master's degrees from Stanford University in 1927 and 1932, respectively, and earned his doctorate in philosophy at Cornell University in 1935. He then taught at Deep Springs College in California before serving a one-year stint as dean of the University of Kansas City's College of Liberal Arts. In 1943, he was hired by UChicago as chief administrative officer for a research project related

public resources at UChicago for more on his chancellorship from 1929 to 1951; Drake and Cayton, *Black Metropolis*, p. 758.

9. *Shelley v. Kraemer*, 334 US 1. For more on the *Shelley v. Kraemer* decision, see Gonda, *Unjust Deeds*. Regarding the impact of the Cold War on higher education, expansion, and geography, see O'Mara, *Cities of Knowledge*, especially pp. 36–55. For a more expansive look at the postwar university, beyond the Cold War foci, see Schrum, *The Instrumental University*; and Roy Gibbons, "U. of C. Reveals Story of Work on Atomic Bomb: Tells of Part It Played in Development," *Chicago Tribune*, August 17, 1945.

10. On the Hyde Park–Kenwood Community Conference, see Hirsch, *Making the Second Ghetto*, pp. 140–141; Percent of Negro Population in Census Tracts, 1950, HPHS, Box 80, Folder 6, SCRC.

to the atomic bomb. From 1944 to 1946, Kimpton served as UChicago's dean of students and a philosophy professor, and in 1946, he was vice president and dean of the faculties for one year. He then returned to his alma mater to serve as Stanford's dean of students in 1947 until rehired by UChicago in 1950 as vice president of development, ultimately succeeding Hutchins as chancellor.[11]

Having led the university's external-facing development unit, Kimpton was selected to solve problems related to the shifts in neighborhood demographics. The encroachment of Black residents from west of Hyde Park had negatively impacted the university during Hutchins's last years as chancellor. As noted at the time, people living in "the South Side's Negro ghetto spilled into the area." Overcrowding in nearby Black neighborhoods impacted UChicago more than the Great Depression did, as enrollment fell to its lowest point since the 1915–16 academic year, when 1,403 total students were enrolled. By the end of the 1940s, the number of undergraduate students fell to 1,350. Hutchins's hands-off approach, as seen in his 1937 statement to the *Chicago Defender*, was no longer viable.[12]

The dismal enrollment, coupled with the Housing Act of 1949 and its appropriation of federal funds for slum clearance programs, presented new opportunities for college presidents. Thereafter, the Ford Foundation called for the development of urban universities—a call supported by academic leaders across the nation—and this was Kimpton's cue. "We must find ways to reverse the trend," the new chancellor noted. To do so, Kimpton first organized the South East Chicago Commission (SECC), with himself as head of the group, and Julian H. Levi (brother to Edward H. Levi, dean of the UChicago School of Law) as its executive director. Additionally, nearly half of the SECC's initial funds came from UChicago, which donated $15,000 to the group, and a number of faculty served it in various capacities.[13]

11. On Kimpton's background and his chancellorship, see "Biographical Note" entry for the Guide to the Lawrence A. Kimpton Papers, 1890–1978, finding aid at the SCRC; and Boyer, *The University of Chicago*, specifically pp. 321–354.

12. On the "Negro ghetto" quote and UChicago's enrollment in the late 1940s, see "The Campus Fights Back," *Newsweek*, January 4, 1960. On enrollment in 1915–16, see Wechsler, *The Qualified Student*, p. 212. Focusing on the University of Pennsylvania, historian Stefan M. Bradley briefly discussed how the Housing Act of 1949 impacted higher education. For more, see Bradley, *Upending the Ivory Tower*, p. 200.

13. On the Ford Foundation, see Haar, *The City as Campus*, p. 51. For the "reverse the trend" quote, see "The Campus Fights Back." Regarding faculty involvement with SECC and the financial support of UChicago, see Hubert L. Will to Board Members, June 7, 1952, Sol. Tax Papers, Box 5 Folder 4, SCRC; and J. McWilliams, The Contribution of the University of Chicago to the Urban Renewal Program, May 25, 1955, Beadle Records, Box 171, Folder 10, SCRC.

Kimpton's success depended on working with state and federal officials, and to his benefit, UChicago's trustees were largely the heirs to Progressive Era industrial achievements. At the turn of the century, Chicago thrived with big business in meatpacking, livestock, timber, and media enterprises, among other industries. Harold Swift, a trustee from 1914 to 1955, eventually became vice president for his father's meatpacking company. Laird Bell, trustee board chair from 1949 to 1953, was a partner at a major Chicago law firm and once president of the Chicago Council on Foreign Relations. UChicago trustees also included Marshall Field III and Marshall Field IV, the grandson and great-grandson of the retail giant Marshall Field, and publishers of the *Chicago Sun-Times*. These influential trustees controlled Chicago mainstream media and business interests as they molded local, state, and federal policies to fit the interests of the city and UChicago.[14]

For example, in 1947, the Illinois legislature created the Chicago Land Clearance Commission, which was authorized to "acquire blighted areas, raze dilapidated buildings, [and] sell land to private interests for redevelopment." But Chicago powerbrokers wanted more. Therefore, in 1952, the Citizens of Greater Chicago lobbying group proposed that the commission expand its clearance efforts, and in 1953, Julian H. Levi successfully lobbied to alter the 1941 Neighborhood Redevelopment Corporation Act. The alteration allowed UChicago to create its own redevelopment cooperation and take over properties through eminent domain.[15]

This technique was common among nonsouthern whites, who considered themselves more enlightened than white southerners. Kimpton and others did not explicitly state that their anti-slum war was anti-Black, but the land clearance commission justified slum clearance by using statistics on issues associated with Black residents, such as overcrowded neighborhoods, juvenile delinquency, and infant mortality. The commission also focused on keeping industry in the city, earning more taxes from formerly blighted areas, and slowing the population shift of white residents to the suburbs. Combined, this calmed many white residents and appeased municipal leaders. Furthermore, Cold War diplomacy and the National Defense Education Act meant Kimpton

14. The information about individual trustees was accumulated across multiple "Biographical Note" entries for finding aids at the SCRC. For a brief discussion of the influence of the UChicago trustees, see Winling, *Building the Ivory Tower*, p. 92. Regarding the differences among Chicago's white-owned newspapers, see Biondi, *The Black Revolution on Campus*, p. 92.

15. For more on the Chicago Land Clearance Commission, see "How Chicago Is Redeveloping Slum Areas," *Chicago Sun-Times*, September 28, 1952. On Julian Levi's lobbying, see Winling, *Building the Ivory Tower*, p. 93.

needed to halt the encroachment of Black neighborhoods through land acquisition for UChicago to expanded its research enterprise.[16]

Meanwhile, in early 1954, the remnants of a recent white mob riot against
a Black family that had moved into Trumbull Park Homes on the South Side
loomed prominently over UChicago. That April, Ruth McCarn, assistant dean
of students, investigated how the campus housing staff answered inquiries
about race. She found that if a local property manager had a room or apartment for rent and said they only rent to white students, the university's response was "we cannot make this notation on our records." The housing staff
would then leave it up to that manager to handle the situation should someone
other than a white student arrive seeking housing. To avoid such a situation,
the housing staff had "learned not to refer students of minority groups to certain addresses, in order to spare their sensibilities." Yet, McCarn found that
UChicago did not demand the known racist property managers to stop
discrimination.[17]

Nearly a year after McCarn's investigation, in February 1955, Levi stopped
dean of students Robert M. Strozier from having university housing staffers
inform property managers to cease discrimination. "Those of us who are closest
to this operation would be unalterably opposed to the sending of any letter,"
Levi said. "It will be a persistent source of embarrassment. At the same time,
it's really not going to solve any of the problems of the minority students
affected." The best method, Levi concluded, was for UChicago to address
Black students' housing problems individually. "Of course, this approach
doesn't give anybody a chance to make noble speeches and fancy gestures,"
Levi cynically noted. Vice President W. B. Harrell later echoed as much to
Strozier: "I do not believe that it is in the best interests of the university to
undertake to tell householders in the community what tests of eligibility they

16. On the strategic use of statistics like the Hyde Park–Kenwood mortality rate, see Carl W.
Larsen to Edward H. Levi, August 4, 1964, Beadle Records, Box 265, Folder 4, SCRC. For a
summary of how Cold War politics transformed higher education, see the argument made by
O'Mara, *Cities of Knowledge*, p. 2. For a brief overview of the impact of the Cold War and federal
funding, particularly within the context of the overall history of US higher education, see Thelin, *A History of American Higher Education*, pp. 271–274. On how domestic racism damaged the
US global reputation, see Karabel, *The Chosen*, p. 379. On urban universities: "They confronted
new technologies, Cold War politics, increased budgets for scientific research under the National Defense Education Act (NDEA), economic shifts, and new social and cultural environments." For more, see Haar, *City as Campus*, p. 51.

17. On the Trumbull Park Homes riot, see Collier-Thomas and Franklin, *My Soul Is a Witness*,
pp. 4, 7; Ruth McCarn to Robert M. Strozier, April 22, 1954, Beadle Records, Box 265, Folder 1,
SCRC.

should establish for students. . . . In my opinion, we have neither the moral nor the legal right to do so."[18]

The contradiction was that Levi and Harrell were already telling the community how housing matters should unfold through the SECC. Harrell even supported one failed proposal for an interstate highway between UChicago and the majority-Black Woodlawn community. "This drive serves two important purposes," he said. "Since we do not control the area south of 61st Street, this drive will serve as a barrier to encroachment from that direction." In these ways, the SECC, as an extension of Kimpton, dictated campus policies to the satisfaction of city officials.[19]

Three months later, on May 25, 1955, an informal report circulated among UChicago administrators that favorably assessed the university and urban renewal. "The University of Chicago has played a vital role in the Urban Renewal Program." This role was Kimpton's idea coming into fruition. In addition to the initial $15,000 donation in 1952, the university also contributed $10,000 of the SECC's $45,000 total budget in 1955. The leaders of the SECC—Levi as executive director, Elmer Donahue as vice president, and Don Blakiston as law enforcement representative—were all alumni of the university. Faculty members also served on its planning committee and offered training to block organizations while, most notably, the Marshall Field Foundation awarded the university a $100,000 grant for "community planning purposes." In summary, the report read, "[UChicago's] contributions have been and will be indispensable to [the urban renewal program's] success."[20]

Success, however, was not how Black Chicagoans described the neighborhood situation. In June 1955, Black residents marched on city hall and demanded that Mayor Richard J. Daley address the ongoing white terrorism against Black families. The pervasive violence meant that no Black people, not even the renowned gospel singer Mahalia Jackson, were exempt from being attacked if they moved into all-white neighborhoods or apartment complexes. These issues stirred whites' concerns in Hyde Park. Where most Hyde Park census tracts were still overwhelmingly white in 1950, by September 1956, the neighborhood noted significant population shifts. For instance, Black people accounted for less than 5 percent of the residents in census tract 609—located in the northwest corner of Hyde Park—in 1950. Six years later, the National

18. Julian H. Levi to Robert M. Strozier, February 17, 1955; and W. B. Harrell to Robert M. Strozier, February 22, 1955, both in Beadle Records, Box 265, Folder 1, SCRC.

19. For the Harrell quote on the interstate proposal, see Winling, *Building the Ivory Tower*, pp. 100–101; For more on proposed interstate highway, see Haar, *City as Campus*, p. 63.

20. McWilliams, The Contribution of the University of Chicago.

Opinion Research Center (NORC) at UChicago found the same census tract, divided into three city blocks, was 34.9 percent nonwhite in block 1, 89.1 percent nonwhite in block 2, and 88.7 percent nonwhite in block 3. Overall, 53 of the 142 blocks surveyed had more than 50 percent nonwhite occupants and, most notably, 67 blocks had more than 25 percent increases in the numbers of non-white residents.[21]

By February 1957, the Hyde Park–Kenwood Community Conference (HPKCC) compiled its own data about urban renewal. Referencing the NORC results, a fact sheet highlighted the need to demolish vacant stores, relieve overcrowded schools, and address the lack of space relative to the growing population. In the northwest area of Hyde Park, block groups—sets of neighbors organized by city block—asked whether groups of neighbors could buy the land after it was cleared, whether the new construction would include rental properties, and whether racial discrimination would be banned in the new housing. To the last point, HPKCC officials, in a report on "integrated housing," determined that a comprehensive anti-discrimination law was needed to halt practices that fostered overcrowding:

> It is evident that the interests of the community demand an end to segregation and the elimination of these conditions—housing congestion and slum maintenance with their attendant evils. . . . But beyond all other means, we believe that legislation prohibiting exclusion in private housing because of race, color, religion, or national origin is the most effective immediate instrument to stimulate integrated housing.

Despite this statement, however, one particular question from the block groups served as a testament to who held the real power to create change: "Where does the University of Chicago fit into the urban renewal program?"[22]

That was a fair yet complex question by February 1957. It was fair because Kimpton and the SECC were engaged in local, state, and federal decision making about urban renewal. Locally, in 1957, the Chicago City Council passed a law that banned discrimination in public housing, but that was a narrow form of relief that did not address the broader housing segregation issues. Nationally, in 1957, Kimpton had organized the presidents of Harvard, Columbia, Penn, Yale, and MIT around urban renewal efforts. Each of these men led

21. For the march on city hall and Mahalia Jackson's home being attacked, see Collier-Thomas and Franklin, *My Soul Is a Witness*, pp. 27, 46; Hyde Park–Kenwood Urban Renewal Survey, September 1956, HPHS, Box 11, Folder 14, SCRC; Percent of Negro Population, 1950.

22. Facts on the Conditions of Hyde Park, February 1957, HPHS, Box 72, Folder 27, SCRC; Key Questions Raised by Block Groups, February 7, 1952, HPHS, Box 72, Folder 27, SCRC; Integrated Housing: Its Extent and Acceptance, n.d., HPHS, Box 72, Folder 11, SCRC.

institutions that were members of the Association of American Universities (AAU), a consortium of the most influential US and Canadian research universities.[23]

Kermit C. Parsons, a professor in the Department of City and Regional Planning at Cornell University, also a founding member of the AAU, acknowledged the significance of these presidents and urban renewal. "The Association of American Universities was very active in securing passage of this legislation," Parsons assessed. "Urban universities needed more effective urban-renewal programs in their own back yards." Following that local and national activity, in January 1958, the Illinois Supreme Court ruled that UChicago could demolish four square blocks in southwest Hyde Park, an area that bordered the majority-Black Washington Park neighborhood. The court dismissed a final appeal by residents in the area and allowed plans to build housing for married students to move forward. The city approved and Mayor Daley supported the plan. This would stop the inflow of Black people, and therefore, whites—faculty, students, and others—were more likely to stay in the neighborhood; however, Kimpton's plan to demolish entire blocks was detrimental to South Side Black residents, whose housing options were already limited due to decades of racist housing policies and practices.[24]

On June 18, 1958, only a few months after the Illinois Supreme Court decision, the Chicago Urban League released a report critical of urban renewal. Titled "Urban Renewal and the Negro in Chicago," it voiced Black residents' concerns over its implementation. At the heart of the argument was Urban League president Nathaniel Oglesby Calloway's question about the contradictory nature of the urban renewal program. "It's not that we don't want slum clearance; decaying areas and outmoded streets must be rebuilt," said Calloway, who held a PhD from Iowa State and an MD from the University of Illinois, after UChicago forced him to withdraw from medical school because he was Black. "But can we, in justice, tear down people's homes when we continue to restrict their free movement into new homes? In other words, can slum clearance and the perpetuation of residential segregation live together?"[25]

---

23. On the public housing law, see Collier-Thomas and Franklin, *My Soul Is a Witness*, p. 72.

24. Parsons, "Universities and Cities," p. 205. Regarding the Illinois Supreme Court decision, see Newspaper Graphic, *Chicago Maroon*, January 31, 1958. On the city and the mayor's support, see David C. Webber, "The University of Chicago and Its Neighbors: A Case Study in Community Development," in Perry and Wiewel, *The University as Urban Developer*, p. 70.

25. Urban Renewal and the Negro in Chicago. On Calloway's educational background, including the racism he experienced at UChicago, see "Negro Medic Teaches at U. of Illinois," *Chicago Defender*, March 9, 1946. For more about Calloway within a broader conversation about Black academics, see Anderson, "Race, Meritocracy, and the American Academy," pp. 161–162.

In some cities, Black residents were on board with the idea of urban renewal, but Calloway's assessment was accurate, as the Urban League report
found a "pattern of racial segregation which Chicago now practices to an extent unmatched by any other large American city, North or South." By 1956,
two-thirds of the city's 86,000 residents displaced by urban renewal projects
were Black. The report also argued that due to restricted access to housing,
"urban renewal, because of its primary impact as presently implemented in
areas of Negro concentration, aids in this process [of displacement]." In summary, powerful city entities like UChicago were merely moving a problem
instead of fixing it, and the previous decades' worth of housing segregation
would not be solved by urban renewal without attention to Black humanity.[26]

This lack of humanity was evident in Harvard undergraduate Christopher
Jencks's take on overcrowding near Cambridge. "At the moment the cannibals
are in the form of the Boston metropolitan area, which . . . has gradually en-
croached on Cambridge," Jencks wrote in the Harvard Crimson. "The fully
matured product is visible in a slum-surrounded university like Columbia or
Chicago." Therefore, for Kimpton and other administrators, the civil rights
imperative placed before them by the Urban League and local Chicago Black
residents took a backseat. Instead, Kimpton turned toward the university's
larger goal—public relations—as UChicago soon sought publicity for helping
to save American cities from the "cannibals."[27]

Public Relations Meets Civil Rights

In January 1959, House & Home profiled the city's urban renewal program
under the headline "Chicago's Struggle to Save a High-IQ Square Mile." The
article focused on efforts to preserve the Hyde Park and Kenwood neighborhoods, and the millions of dollars involved. By that point, the city had invested

26. Urban Renewal and the Negro in Chicago. An estimated 2,500 families were displaced
over the lifespan of the Chicago urban renewal program. For more, see Haar, City as Campus,
p. 64. Historian N. D. B. Connolly argued that Miami had more promising urban renewal programs that helped Blacks secure better housing. He explained that some "believed that slum
clearance and urban renewal would hasten the 'all deliberate speed' of desegregation. Suburbia,
and all its benefits, would become available. In Miami, such logic seemed to bear out. . . . Real-
izing blacks' robust demand for better housing in 1952, white developers opened the all-black
bedroom community of Richmond Heights fifteen miles outside the city." For more, see N. D. B.
Connolly, "Sunbelt Civil Rights: Urban Renewal and the Follies of Desegregation in Greater
Miami," in Nickerson and Dochuk, Sunbelt Rising, pp. 173–174.

27. Christopher Jencks, "Harvard and Tomorrow's Community: Urban Renewal Tries to
End Danger of Local Slum Blight," Harvard Crimson, February 25, 1956.

$9.2 million into urban renewal, and the federal government agreed to provide an additional $28.5 million, making it "the biggest project of its kind the nation has yet seen." *House & Home* described a dismal situation in Hyde Park and Kenwood, which were surrounded "by the city's notorious South Side Negro ghetto, which includes some of the nation's most crowded slums." However, the mostly white neighborhoods had "not yet tipped (though by Dec. '58 it was 37% Negro), thanks to the strenuous efforts of the citizens and the university." The article praised Kimpton and other UChicago officials for saving one of the city's oldest and most established neighborhoods from an influx of low-income, mostly Black residents who would diminish property values near campus.[28]

Even before the *House & Home* feature, Kimpton's team had access to federal officials. For example, in 1954, during US president Dwight Eisenhower's first term, a group of UChicago officials met with him at the White House. Afterward, the federal government earmarked $15 million for Chicago redevelopment purposes alongside the Housing Act of 1954, which further incentivized urban renewal. Support from the Oval Office continued as Eisenhower prioritized the economy over race relations, but the recent publicity further propelled UChicago onto the national stage when it came to urban renewal.[29]

On January 26, 1959, UChicago led a national urban renewal effort back to Washington, DC. There, Levi of the SECC testified before the US Senate Banking and Currency Committee on behalf of UChicago, Penn, NYU, Baylor University, the University of Louisville, and Seattle University. Levi argued that the Senate should amend the Federal Housing Act provision that an area must be at least 51 percent residential to earn government funding for slum clearance because universities were hampered by dilapidated taverns, warehouses, and cheap hotels near residential slum areas. Levi also contended that universities' financial contributions should be included with their cities' in the federal government's formula to match every municipal dollar spent on slum clearance with up to three dollars, and that the federal government should reimburse universities for funds spent over the previous five years.[30]

Levi's argument strategically followed those of six mayors (from Los Angeles, Detroit, Cleveland, Tulsa, New York, and Philadelphia) who voiced their

28. "Urban Renewal: Chicago's Struggle to Save a High-IQ Square Mile," *House & Home*, January 1959. For a lengthier discussion on urban renewal as an effort to "save" cities, see Cohen, *Saving America's Cities.*

29. For more on the White House meeting, see Winling, *Building the Ivory Tower*, p. 95. On the Housing Act of 1954, see Rodin, *University and Urban Revival*, p. 30. Historians have consistently critiqued Eisenhower's stance on race relations. For two examples, see Anderson, *Pursuit of Fairness*, pp. 53–54; and Karabel, *The Chosen*, p. 379.

30. Thomas B. Ross, "U. of C. Leads Capitol March for More Housing," *Chicago Sun-Times*, January 27, 1959.

support of Senator Joseph S. Clark's (D-PA) urban renewal plan to offer $6 billion to American cities over a ten-year period. "Many of the proudest universities in our country are today confronted with environments of slum and blight or near slum and blight," Levi contended. "These conditions drive faculty out of the university communities and turn faculty into commuters. The consequences of this migration are vital to the future of our nation." The heart of Levi's plea was that urban renewal and higher education were needed. As Banking and Currency Committee members like Clark and Senator John F. Kennedy, both Ivy League–educated senators, were supportive of higher education, federal legislation soon passed in Levi's favor.[31]

UChicago's prominence in the national urban renewal effort proved favorable with private foundations as well. There was already the $100,000 grant from the Marshall Field Foundation, and by October 1959, Robert C. Weaver, a consultant for the Ford Foundation's Public Affairs Program, had "been giving some thought to problems of [urban] rehabilitation" and found "many facets" of the HPKCC's work of interest. He hoped to meet with representatives from that group during his next visit to Chicago.[32]

The next month, on November 1, 1959, the New York Times also called the university's efforts "the largest urban renewal project of its kind," describing a program that involved "an area of about 900 acres and costing more than $135,000,000 in city, federal, university, and private funds over a five-year period." Two months later, on January 4, 1960, Newsweek explained that the figure had grown to $195 million for the redevelopment project. "We are fighting for our lives," Kimpton said. "We simply cannot operate in slums." Now, the chancellor aimed to preserve the neighborhood "dotted with expensive Victorian brownstone homes of some of the city's wealthiest families." On February 1, US News & World Report also highlighted UChicago: "Here you can watch major surgery being performed on a city to save the life of a university," the article read. "Institutions and municipalities, concerned by the problem, are watching the Chicago operation closely. If it succeeds, they may try it themselves."[33]

31. Ross, "U. of C. Leads Capitol March"; "U. of Chicago Seeks Change in Slum Laws," Chicago Tribune, January 27, 1959; "Curb on Urban Renewal: Universities Need Housing, Too," Chicago Daily News, February 16, 1959. Regarding Senators Clark and Kennedy being favorable to higher education, see Winling, Building the Ivory Tower, p. 106.

32. Robert C. Weaver to Harry N. Gottlieb, October 20, 1959, Hyde Park–Kenwood Community Conference Records, Box 173, Folder 10, SCRC (collection hereafter cited as HPKCC).

33. Austin C. Wehrwein, "Chicago U. Spurs Renewal Project," New York Times, November 1, 1959; "The Campus Fights Back," Newsweek; "Case History: Creeping Slums vs. a University," US News & World Report, February 1, 1960.

Riding the wave of positive press from white journalists, Carl W. Larsen, director of university public relations, made a pitch to Chet Hagan of the National Broadcasting Company (NBC) in New York. In January 1960, having just seen a profile on Cuba, now led by a new prime minister, Fidel Castro, after the Cuban Revolution recently ended, Larsen had an idea for a future NBC broadcast. "It seems to me that urban renewal—the problems of our cities—would be worth a similar take-out," Larsen mused. "I would like to propose that the story of the University of Chicago's fight against blight might be a dramatic one for you to tell. We are engaged, with the aid of the city administration, in an urban renewal program that has been widely hailed as one of the most imaginative in the nation." Then, after stating that Columbia, Yale, and "other leading institutions" would also be interested, Larsen enclosed some recently published material related to urban renewal. "It provides evidence, I believe, that there is an exciting, photogenic story of significance in what is happening in and to the American city."[34]

By July 1960, Kimpton and Levi shared the spotlight in a *Chicago American* article, which explained how the city was poised to receive an additional $14.4 million in federal funds to support its urban renewal plan of "clearing out slum properties." In the article, Kimpton said that UChicago expenditures were about $7 million and, in all, about $21 million dollars were possibly available to the city and university. Levi further explained that Section 112 of the Housing Act made it possible for university urban renewal expenses to be counted toward the city's total contribution. This was a nod to the success of his January 1959 appearance before the Senate committee. With these funds, an estimated 1,250 families would need to be relocated when the next phase of urban renewal was executed. Specifically, the university would expand an entire block south of 61st Street, ranging from Cottage Grove on the west to Stony Island on the east, almost to Lake Michigan. Faculty housing, a law school, and the public administration building would be the new anchor for city blocks where many Black Chicagoans resided, but Kimpton, once again, focused on the university, not the community. "By 1964," he estimated, "the university will have one of the most valued [physical] plants devoted exclusively to higher education in America."[35]

Kimpton's bold, institution-first perspective played well for the national media, but it was a thin veil that Black people living on the South Side could

34. Carl W. Larsen to Chet Hagan, January 25, 1960, Beadle Records, Box 350, Folder 8, SCRC.

35. Walter Sutherland, "U. of C. Announces Giant Renewal Plan," *Chicago American*, July 19, 1960. Photo of UChicago's Proposed South Expansion, *Chicago Sun-Times*, July 20, 1960. On earning media praise, see Haar, *City as Campus*, p. 65. Levi is called "Slum Fighter Levi" in *Life* magazine.

easily see through. Black people were ignored by UChicago officials in the public presentation of urban renewal and interpretation of its benefits, but the *Chicago Defender* assessed that "the lily-white islands east of the University of Chicago must remain lily-white according to the dictates of Julian Levi of the South East Chicago Commission and Chancellor Lawrence Kimpton of the University of Chicago." The newspaper demanded the plan be modified because "we do not think progress should be limited to a privileged few" since relocated Black residents were "usually forced back into the Negro ghetto."[36]

Some whites in Hyde Park and Kenwood had also expressed concerns about racial discrimination but often allowed their concerns to be eased by the race-neutral statements issued by UChicago academic leaders; however, by 1960, the civil rights uprising in southern states rapidly affected race relations in Chicago. Journalists from national and major Chicago newspapers praised UChicago, but at the neighborhood level, residents grew more determined to question local housing practices. "A white family was unable to rent an apartment because they have Negro friends," opened a September 7, 1960, article in the *Hyde Park Herald*, a community newspaper. "The dateline for this story is not Little Rock, Ark., or Jackson, Miss. The dateline for this story is Hyde Park, Chicago, Ill." John Naisbitt, a Hyde Park resident, wrote this first-person narrative to explain his family's experience with housing discrimination. When Naisbitt requested a new apartment, the reference check conducted by a staffer at McKey & Poague, one of Chicago's largest real estate firms, questioned whether the Naisbitts had Black friends and were likely to invite them over to their home.[37]

Like Naisbitt, a few weeks later, Harry Gottlieb, chair of the HPKCC's board of directors, also questioned the urban renewal plan's lack of emphasis on relocation. "No urban renewal program is valid without an effective, efficient relocation program which minimizes the confusion and hardship," he stated. Another group, the Hyde Park–Kenwood Tenants and Home Owners, described the relocation efforts as "shameful trading in human misery" that "harassed" those being forced to move.[38]

Meanwhile, Kimpton and Levi started to pat themselves on the back for a decade of successful community engineering. The leaders of the UChicago team became sought-after speakers on the topic. For instance, on October 29,

36. "Urban Renewal for Whom?" *Chicago Defender*, May 26, 1958; "Charge Relocation Forces People Back into Ghetto," *Chicago Defender*, June 10, 1958.

37. John Naisbitt, "You Can't Live Here if You've Got Negro Friends," *Hyde Park Herald*, September 7, 1960.

38. "Conference to Study Relocation," *Hyde Park Herald*, October 5, 1960.

1960, Levi spoke at a conference about universities in urban settings, held at the University of Wisconsin–Milwaukee, before a gathering of white leaders such as University of Wisconsin president Conrad Elvehjem and Mayor Ben West from Nashville, Tennessee. Titled "The University and Preservation of Urban Values in Chicago," Levi explained four major urban renewal projects that Kimpton—who was set to resign at the end of 1960—had led since 1951. He detailed the private foundation grants, the clearance of dozens of acres of lands, and financial support from the federal government. He also used a portion of his speech to praise Kimpton, the architect of the university's urban renewal program. "The University of Chicago has a deep interest and a tremendous stake in our community," Levi quoted Kimpton as saying in 1952. "We are here to stay, and we are dedicated to the kind of community that is appropriate for our faculty members and our students."[39]

Yet, shortly after Levi's speech in Milwaukee, Edwin A. Rothschild, chair of the Hyde Park–Kenwood Conservation Community Council, critiqued the *Chicago Daily News* for its editorial and news coverage of urban renewal. "One would never have suspected from reading the articles alone," Rothschild said in December 1960, "that the deplorable conditions of the now-demolished slum buildings had been caused by years of exploitation and neglect by private ownership." The city's major white newspapers, whose publishers included some UChicago trustees, were not covering the community problems. Therefore, Kimpton finished his last year as chancellor largely unscathed and celebrated as having provided a blueprint for the rest of America. His successor, however, would not be as fortunate. Kimpton's resignation occurred just before the local focus on housing discrimination made its way to the UChicago Administration Building.[40]

A New Chancellor Meets an Old Problem

National events soon ignited an increase in community resistance to the South Side urban renewal program. In early 1960, sit-ins organized by students at southern Black colleges caught the nation's attention, and by the end of the year, the election of John F. Kennedy led many Americans to believe racial equality was more attainable than ever. This followed a decade of the

39. Julian H. Levi Speech, October 29, 1960, Office of Student Activities Records, Box 353, Folder 8, SCRC (collection hereafter cited as OSA); "Informed Citizens Held Urban Area's Best Aid," *Milwaukee Journal*, October 28, 1960.

40. Edwin A. Rothschild, "Raps Ex-Owners for Creating Slums," *Chicago Daily News*, December 17, 1960.

Kimpton-Levi duo ignoring local concerns, as Black residents grew frustrated while the two men overlooked the connection between the growing national civil rights movement and their plans that disproportionately displaced Black residents. This changed, however, when several UChicago alumni and students formed a coalition with local leaders. Together, the group demanded that the new chancellor confront the racial housing crisis.[41]

The transition in leadership began on December 21, 1960, when George W. Beadle, an acclaimed geneticist at the California Institute of Technology (Cal Tech) and Nobel laureate, had lunch with four prominent UChicago faculty members. Taking place in a private dining room at the university's Quadrangle Club, the lunch meeting was scheduled for one hour, but it lasted for three. When the five men finished their "heated and intense" conversation, Beadle emerged as the university's next chancellor.[42]

"The lunch clinched it," one university official said. Beadle was the type of scholar that faculty and administrators wanted to succeed Kimpton, as trustees sought someone to close the gap between the sciences and the humanities, an effect of the Cold War's emphasis on science and research, and Beadle embodied what they sought. "We concluded early that we needed a person from the scholarly world who would understand scholarship first hand," said Glen A. Lloyd, chair of the trustee board and partner at the same large law firm as former UChicago trustee Laird Bell. This meant high-profile individuals like the former Illinois governor and two-time Democratic nominee for US president Adlai E. Stevenson and US vice president Richard M. Nixon, both rumored to be considered for the job, did not meet the academic profile desired.[43]

Beadle was the ideal choice, and on January 5, 1961, only two weeks after the three-hour lunch interview, the university held a press conference announcing his appointment. Scholars at UChicago offered nearly universal approval of the hire. Napier Witt, dean of the humanities, said, "We wanted a man who had done significant research and had a broad outlook. We have that man in Dr. Beadle," adding, "We'll be better than ever." Scientists were also "jubilant." Joseph Ceithaml, a biologist, said, "Anyone who knows this man, who knows of his dedication to the finer arts, will readily testify to his interest in the totality of knowledge." Furthermore, Beadle's scholarly reputation was matched by his administrative experience. Lowell T. Coggeshall, a UChicago

41. For a brief account of the significance of Kennedy on race relations, see Patterson, *Grand Expectations*, p. 468.

42. Howard M. Ziff, "He Survived 3-Hour Test: Californian Sold Himself to 4 Top Faculty Aides," *Chicago Daily News*, January 6, 1961.

43. Ibid.

vice president, concluded that Beadle has "great administrative ability without it seeming to be obvious."[44]

The unassuming presence that Coggeshall appreciated could be attributed to Beadle's rural background. He was born in Wahoo, Nebraska, and expected to become a farmer until a high school teacher encouraged him to enroll at the University of Nebraska. There, he earned bachelor's and master's degrees in 1926 and 1927, respectively, while studying agronomy, ecology, and genetics. Beadle then attended Cornell University, where he researched cytogenetics and the origins of corn before earning his doctorate in 1931. His career in genetics then soared. First, he worked as a National Research Council Fellow at Cal Tech, followed by a brief research stint in Paris before a one-year stop at Harvard as an assistant professor of biology. In 1937, he left Harvard with a promotion to professor of biology at Stanford University, where he worked from 1937 to 1946. From there, he returned to Cal Tech as professor and chair of the division of biology. Subsequently, he received a series of honors for his research. In 1953, he received the Emil Christian Hansen Prize (Denmark) and, in 1958, the Albert Einstein Commemorative Award in Science and the Nobel Prize in physiology and medicine. He even graced the cover of the July 14, 1958, issue of *Time*.[45]

The fanfare associated with the selection of a world-renowned scientist to lead UChicago did little to change Julian H. Levi's focus on the SECC and the university's interest in urban renewal (it should be noted that Beadle named Julian's brother, Edward H. Levi, provost in 1961). In fact, two days before the new chancellor's press conference, Levi told the *Chicago American* that the SECC had spent the previous eight years combating crime in Hyde Park. "Because of the large number of young men and women students, nurses, and visitors at a half-dozen hospitals and the numerous comfortably furnished homes of professional people," the *Chicago American* reported, "it is a tempting hunting ground for robbers, rapists, burglars, and muggers."[46]

As a result, the university's police chief commanded a unit of thirty-six police officers, three university squad cars, two police dogs, and twenty-five Chicago police officers who worked on campus during their off hours. Levi admitted that only one rape and one shooting had occurred on campus that year but even that "disturbed" him. "We are never satisfied," he said. "And we

44. Arthur J. Snider, "Humanities in No Danger at University: Having Scientists as Chancellor Doesn't Worry Division's Dean," *Chicago Daily News*, January 6, 1961.

45. George Wells Beadle, an informal biography, 1981, George Wells Beadle Personal Papers, Box 31 Folder 12, SCRC (collection hereafter cited as Beadle Papers); Biography, 1981, Beadle Papers, Box 31, Folder 12, SCRC; "The Secret of Life," *Time*, July 14, 1958.

46. Sam Blair, "The Ivy Cops vs. Crime: Guard U. of C. Area," *Chicago American*, January 3, 1961.

never will be until people can walk in complete safety and our homes are entered only by those we invite." The *Chicago American* article was accompanied by a staged photo of a woman being grabbed by a larger person hiding behind a deteriorating building, and the caption read, "MUGGERS, rapists, and burglars. . . ." The crime data during this era were faulty, and future analyses suggest that crime actually decreased prior to urban renewal, but the implications of the news report were clear and served as reality: Hyde Park must rid itself of criminals and the dilapidated structures they hid in. Therefore, if Black residents were most often living in overcrowded and decrepit structures, the coded language about crime and run-down property actually meant urban renewal was about Black removal.[47]

This explains why many questions among members of the HPKCC revolved around relocation. On January 9, shortly after the *Chicago American* report, Gottlieb of the HPKCC followed up with Ozzie Badal, acting assistant director, about residents having to find new housing. Gottlieb posed the following question to Badal: "Assuming that a substantial amount of relocation activity will affect minority groups, particularly non-whites, will an adequate support of housing be available to these people without extension of open occupancy into wider areas of the city of Chicago . . . ?" His concern pointed to the obvious, and it echoed the 1958 Chicago Urban League report. Housing policies restricted where Black people could live in the city.[48]

Meanwhile, a month later, on February 10, 1961, Beadle used his last days in Southern California to attend a reception for the UChicago Alumni Club of Greater Los Angeles at the California Club. There, he explained that, despite the "beauties of Southern California," his decision to lead UChicago was easy. It was "a place of intellectual ferment." Additionally, its rich history, dating back to the "moral and financial encouragement of John D. Rockefeller," who helped establish the institution, was enticing. Previous leaders—William Rainey Harper, Robert M. Hutchins, and Lawrence A. Kimpton—also earned Beadle's praise, but it was his predecessor's urban renewal efforts that he considered most critical to the university:

47. Blair, "The Ivy Cops vs. Crime.; On the faulty crime data, see Webber, "The University of Chicago and Its Neighbors," in Perry and Wiewel, *The University as Urban Developer*, p. 69. For a historical overview of police and Black Chicago, see Balto, *Occupied Territory*. For further critique of crime statistics and the criminalization of Black people in Chicago and other US cities, see Muhammad, *The Condemnation of Blackness.*

48. Harry Gottlieb to Ozzie Badal, January 9, 1961, HPKCC, Box 173, Folder 6, SCRC. On Ozzie Badal's title and eventual role as head of relocation services for the Department of Urban Renewal, see Michal Safar, "Ozzie Badal (1927–2011)," *Hyde Park History*, a publication of the Hyde Park Historical Society, 34 (Summer 2012): 2.

Lawrence A. Kimpton made a different and equally important major contribution to the health of the university . . . partly by helping to reverse the
trend toward physical and cultural deterioration in the neighborhood. He
recognized that faculty and students will not stay, nor come, to an environment that is not decent and safe; hence, the university must continue to be
interested in the urban renewal effort on its borders.

Those borders, however, were expanding, and this is notable because one of
John F. Kennedy's first executive orders as president increased federal funds
for urban renewal. Aware of continued federal support, Beadle explained to
the California alumni that UChicago was moving its southern boundary. The
Midway Plaisance was a public park that served as the southern border of the
university along 59th Street. A block wide and a mile long, the Midway was
the divider between Hyde Park and Woodlawn. By 1960, every census tract in
Woodlawn was 40 percent or more Black, but Beadle planned to continue
Kimpton's efforts. "It will not be very long before both sides of the Midway
provide the most impressive academic façade in the world."[49]
      A few days later, Beadle was in Chicago officially leading the university, and
the fifty-seven-year-old chancellor immediately broke with UChicago customs
and traditions. For example, Beadle assumed duties in the middle of the academic year and less than two months after he was named chancellor. Additionally, in his first week on campus, he arrived at the administration building by
6:10 a.m., wrote his letters longhand, and placed his own telephone calls. Considered "unfailingly kind but a no-nonsense person," Beadle met with deans,
trustees, financial advisers, and department heads as he became acclimated to
campus. Meanwhile, Levi as SECC executive director emerged as the de facto
spokesperson for the university-involved urban renewal efforts that were increasingly contentious with South Side residents.[50]
      This tension was evident on March 14, 1961, during a hearing before the
Chicago City Council housing and planning committee. There, leaders from
the Woodlawn community attacked aspects of UChicago's south campus expansion plan as Alderman Leon M. Despres argued that the university's goals
should not supersede other development plans approved by residents.

49. Beadle speech to Los Angeles alumni, February 10, 1961, Beadle Papers, Box 1, Folder 2,
SCRC. On Woodlawn census numbers, see Percent of Negro Population in Census Tracts, 1960,
HPHS, Box 80, Folder 6, SCRC. By 1960, Woodlawn was 84 percent Black. For more, see Winling, *Building the Ivory Tower*, p. 108. On Kennedy and urban renewal funds, see Carey, *Chancellors, Commodores, and Coeds*, pp. 249–252.
      50. Richard Philbrick, "Beadle Gives U. of Ch. Life a Shaking Up," *Chicago Tribune*, Febru-
ary 27, 1961.

Despres also wanted the city council to go on record as saying it, too, wanted one single plan for the Woodlawn neighborhood, not one from the university and one from the community. In a rebuttal, Levi said the alderman's proposed amendment—one that would have the city council go on record as wanting one Woodlawn plan—jeopardized $1 million in federal funds the city hoped to receive for the south campus plan.[51]

The money, however, was not as important as the community leaders like Arthur M. Brazier having a voice in their future. Brazier, a local minister and leader of The Woodlawn Organization (TWO), which formed a few months earlier in December 1960, was steeped in an old tradition where Black ministers served as mediators between Blacks and whites. "Our community is seething in unrest," said Brazier, pastor of the Apostolic Church of God. "They want to know what is happening to them. They are worried to the point of distraction." Roughly a thousand families were slated to be relocated. Therefore, TWO feared the university's plan, tied to federal funds, would lead the city council to approve the south campus project as the unofficial Woodlawn plan. "The Woodlawn community wants to sit down as equals in the determination of the future of Woodlawn," Brazier added. "We aren't fighting the university as such, but we are fighting for Woodlawn's right to plan its own future along with the university and responsible city agencies."[52]

Levi brushed Brazier's concerns aside and also dismissed Saul Alinsky, a community organizer who, by 1961, had developed a national reputation for his work, thus efforts to bring TWO and SECC together failed. "We don't object to talking to TWO or anyone else," Levi said. "But we cannot get in the position of dealing with one group to the exclusion of others in Woodlawn." This hesitance to collaborate with the community ran counter to what urban planning experts in the early 1960s found most effective. For example, Cornell professor Kermit C. Parsons argued that "effective university area-development corporations . . . are vigorous, well-staffed, well-financed, and diversified." Levi was vigorous, but not interested in diverse views.[53]

51. Harry Swegle, "U.C. Expansion Plan Furor Heats Up: Civil Leader Julian Levi Attacks Proposed Changes," *Chicago Daily News*, March 14, 1961.

52. Swegle, "U.C. Expansion Plan Furor Heats Up." Historian Stefan M. Bradley noted other instances of Black ministers handling conflicts between Black communities and predominantly white institutions. He wrote, "Historically, black ministers acted as liaisons between black and white communities, which had typically been the case in the town of Princeton." For more, see Bradley, *Upending the Ivory Tower*, p. 46; On the south campus plan, including TWO and the number of families impacted, see Webber, "University of Chicago and Its Neighbors," in Perry and Wiewel, *The University as Urban Developer*, p. 73.

53. Swegle, "U.C. Expansion Plan Furor Heats Up." For an account from a TWO participant, see Fish, *Black Power/White Control*, particularly pp. 34–35 regarding the March 1961 city council

Nonetheless, and despite the SECC, Hyde Park and Kenwood residents presented similar concerns on April 3, 1961, when Charles R. Andrews offered a statement before the city council's judiciary and legislative committee. As a minister at First Baptist Church in Kenwood and a representative of the HPKCC board of directors, Andrews called racial segregation "the great issue of our time" and the cause of the widespread decay that city officials were so adamant about removing. Yet, the problem was not the dilapidated buildings and crime but instead the racist housing policies. "As long as racial discrimination is condoned tacitly in any area by any governmental unit, we shall be at the mercy of the slum-maker, the block buster, overcrowding, and fear—all of which maintain patterns of racial discrimination," Andrews said. "And the patterns of this segregation result in continuing urban decay." These facts, he said, warranted the need for the city council to adopt formal legislation that would stop housing discrimination in the city. Without legal means being passed and enforced, Andrews argued, slum conditions would remain. By the end of April, the Chicago City Council passed a resolution asking state legislators to pass a fair housing law, but this was merely a request. It did not impact urban renewal. The city's most powerful white leaders continued their plans throughout the spring and the summer as the new chancellor's talking points about deterioration focused on the university's triumph.[54]

On May 4, 1961, Beadle's inauguration address discussed the need to "provide education and social opportunities to people who have not had them—largely because of the color of their skins." He saw this as a matter of national importance. Yet, when updating the audience on prominent university issues, he said "the university neighborhood suffered serious deterioration, which made the community a much less desirable place in which to live than formerly, especially for students." Not that Beadle's assessment of the effects of deterioration was inaccurate. Indeed, concerns about the neighborhood had negatively impacted the reputation of the university over previous decades. But Beadle's comments about the institution's work to rebuild the South Side failed to mention the significant displacement of residents, many of whom

---

meeting. On Saul Alinsky and his relationship with TWO, see Nash, *The University and the City*, pp. 11–12; Alinsky inspired people in other cities to organize around community issues. On Alinsky's influence on Louisville, Kentucky, see K'Meyer, *Civil Rights in the Gateway to the South*, pp. 122–123. On his impact on University of Oklahoma students, see Biondi, *Black Revolution on Campus*, p. 23. His tactics were further discussed in Alinsky, *Rules for Radicals*; Parsons, "Universities and Cities," p. 216.

54. Charles R. Andrews statement, April 3, 1961, HPKCC, Box 173, Folder 6, SCRC; On the April 1961 city council resolution, see Collier-Thomas and Franklin, *My Soul Is a Witness*, p. 143.

were from the racial or ethnic backgrounds he said deserved educational and social opportunities.[55]

Instead, Beadle bragged about his predecessor's urban renewal effort. "We owe a deep debt of gratitude to Lawrence A. Kimpton for taking the lead in this enormously difficult and often discouraging undertaking," he said. "We must keep up the effort, for if we succeed, we will have established a pattern for the rest of the nation to follow. This is a noble goal for a noble university." To that point, Beadle committed to continuing Kimpton's ambitious growth enterprise. For instance, between July 1, 1946 and June 30, 1961, UChicago spent a little more than $50 million on construction projects, and following Beadle's inaugural address, university leaders sought to rekindle relationships with private foundations.[56]

In June, Carl W. Larsen, UChicago's director of public relations, told James Robillard in university development that funds from the Marshall Field Foundation grant in the late 1950s would run out soon. Therefore, proposals needed to be prepared for other private foundations to support the continuation of urban renewal plans. In July, John Kirkpatrick, vice chancellor, informed Maxwell Hahn, executive director of the Field Foundation, that "one of the major needs for which the Field Foundation grant has been used is the acquisition of threat properties in strategic locations." In the fall of 1961, Beadle continued with the same tone but that soon changed.[57]

The moment leading up to Beadle's confrontation over the university's role in housing discrimination is important because of the impact of southern student activism on nonsouthern campuses. In May 1961, University of Michigan administrators adopted a policy against landlords who discriminated, and at other nonsouthern campuses, white students, alumni, and faculty were also stirred to action. During the first week of June 1961, for example, students in Chicago organized programs with the Freedom Riders following the riders' attempt to desegregate public facilities along southern highways. The week-long events were sponsored by the UChicago chapter of the NAACP, the student government association, and Friends of New University Thought at UChicago. The Freedom Riders visited a number of Chicago churches and the

55. Beadle's inaugural address, May 4, 1961, Beadle Papers, Box 1, Folder 4, SCRC.

56. Beadle's inaugural address; University Construction List 1946–1961, n.d., Beadle Records, Box 350, Folder 9, SCRC.

57. Carl W. Larsen to James Robillard, June 20, 1961, Beadle Records, Box 351, Folder 5, SCRC; John Kirkpatrick to Maxwell Hahn, July 20, 1961, Beadle Records, Box 351, Folder 5, SCRC. In Washington, DC, and New York City, Beadle updated University of Chicago alumni about south campus and northwest Hyde Park development plans. These updates can be seen in "Notes for New York and Washington," October 1961, Beadle Papers, Box 1 Folder 7, SCRC.

Cook County Bar Association, spoke on local radio programs, and met with students from UChicago and Northwestern University. The Freedom Riders also met with TWO. From there, students and alumni became more vocal about the city's housing issues and the university.[58]

By June 1961, the Chicago Urban League reported that Black Chicagoans collectively paid $12.5 million more in apartment rent than whites and $157.6 million more than whites for home rentals or purchases. This bothered many whites associated with UChicago, such as Herman Wolf. On September 18, 1961, Wolf, a UChicago alumnus living in Hartford, Connecticut, wrote to Beadle, saying, "certain rumors have come to my attention indicating that Negroes have been discriminated against in securing housing accommodations in buildings owned by the University of Chicago." Surely, Wolf implied, Beadle must have been aware of such rumors if they had reached him in Connecticut; however, he gave the new chancellor the benefit of the doubt: "If this be true, I am sure it will be as disturbing to you as it is to me." Wolf also sent a copy of his letter to William Benton, a former US senator and onetime administrator at the university when Robert M. Hutchins was chancellor.[59]

On the same day, Julia Ashenhurst, a local resident sympathetic to the goal of eliminating housing discrimination, also wrote to university leaders. In her six-page letter to Larsen, she expressed displeasure that university administrators did not communicate with the community. "All such institutions are suffering and will continue to suffer as long as they hold such an arrogant and basically irresponsible attitude," she added, noting that she had experienced similar problems when at Harvard. "It is imperative for the administration to know and have respect for the leaders and the opinion makers of the community."[60]

By the end of October, similar concerns emerged among students despite Black students constituting less than 2 percent of UChicago's enrollment.

58. On the University of Michigan policy, see Fine, *Expanding the Frontiers of Civil Rights*, pp. 131–132. Several historians have attributed changes in white students' civil rights engagement to southern Black student activism, for example: Carson, *In Struggle*, pp. 53–54; Turner, *Sitting In and Speaking Out*, p. 80; Cohen, *Freedom's Orator*, p. 41; Meet the Freedom Riders, June 1–8, 1961, OSA, Box 23, Folder 1, SCRC.

59. On the Urban League report, see Collier-Thomas and Franklin, *My Soul Is a Witness*, p. 144; Herman Wolf to George W. Beadle, September 18, 1961, Beadle Records, Box 265, Folder 3, SCRC. It is likely that Herman Wolf heard such rumors from his son, David, a University of Chicago student. David was unable to find housing the previous spring likely because one of his desired roommates was Black. For more on David Wolf and his friends, see Winling, *Building the Ivory Tower*, p. 110.

60. Julia Ashenhurst to Carl W. Larsen, September 18, 1961, Beadle Records, Box 262, Folder 10, SCRC.

While Beadle was in Orangeburg, New York, giving an address at the dedication of the new Schwarz BioResearch plant, the All-Campus Civil Rights committee was formed on October 28, 1961. This followed the brutal October 11 beating of University of Michigan student Tom Hayden when he was in McComb, Mississippi, attempting to register Black citizens to vote. The following summer, Hayden composed the Port Huron Statement, a political manifesto for the Students for a Democratic Society. The violence against Hayden and other students who ventured south disturbed UChicago students, and the All-Campus Civil Rights committee kickoff meeting featured a talk on nonviolent direct action and voter registration. The group's purpose was "to raise funds and disseminate literature to aid the Student Non-Violent Coordinating Committee," and was open to any UChicago student. A few weeks later, on November 22, UC-NAACP dissolved its association with the national NAACP. The students then joined CORE, founded in Chicago in 1942 and considered more assertive than the NAACP, thus forming UC-CORE.[61]

Throughout November, students executed tests to determine which local rental properties discriminated against Black people. Black students would contact a rental property regarding a vacancy followed by a white person who would attempt to do the same. This was a common technique used by CORE, and the results were stark along racial lines. A month later, on December 24, Milton Davis, chair of the South Side unit of Chicago CORE, requested a meeting with Beadle. CORE was "engaged in an effort to end discrimination and segregation in the rental and sale of housing in the Chicago area," Davis explained. "We feel that one's race, color, or religion or any other such criteria should not be a barrier when housing is sought." Perhaps serendipitously, Wolf

61. On UChicago's Black enrollment, see Warner Wick to L. T. Coggeshall, September 17, 1963, Beadle Records, Box 189, Folder 3, SCRC. For context, see Biondi, *Black Revolution on Campus*, p. 81, for more about Northwestern's dismal enrollment. This book noted that, in 1965, "There were twenty-six Black students at Northwestern, twenty of whom were athletes." Despite not being segregated, midwestern universities did not enroll large numbers of Black students even when located in or near major cities with large portions of Blacks. For a firsthand account of Black students' experiences, see Hargrave, "How I Feel as a Negro at a White College." At Miami University in Ohio, Hargrave was one of twenty Black students among 3,100 students in the early 1940s. "Civil Rights Group Meets," *Chicago Maroon*, October 28, 1961; Student Organization Registration Form, Fall 1961, OSA, Box 13, Folder 14, SCRC; Beadle Comments on Science, Industry, and the Academic Life, October 28, 1961, Beadle Papers, Box 1, Folder 7, SCRC. On Tom Hayden in Mississippi, see Turner, *Sitting In and Speaking Out*, p. 129; "UC NAACP joins CORE," *Chicago Maroon*, November 22, 1961. For a brief overview of CORE and its militancy, see Ezra, "Organizations Outside the South," pp. 93–95; and Kendi, *Black Campus Movement*, p. 51.

also sent Beadle a follow-up letter about the same time. "Enclosed, my dear Chancellor, is a copy of a letter which I sent you last September and to which I have not had the courtesy of a reply," Wolf wrote, attaching his earlier inquiry about discrimination in university-owned property. "I am sure it was overlooked in your office, and I thought you would want this called to your attention." Beadle could no longer ignore the community's concern that urban renewal did not address racism in housing—an issue previously dismissed as a concern of Black residents with no formal ties to campus—but now, students, alumni, and civil rights groups demanded Beadle's attention to the university's role in the ongoing discrimination.[62]

Negotiating the Pace on Race

On January 15, 1962, Leonard M. Friedman, student government president, sent Beadle a memo in preparation for their meeting the following day. Several students and community members had filed statements with the UChicago student government that explained their experiences testing for housing discrimination. In turn, Friedman shared these notarized statements with Beadle and with each one, the racism in housing properties owned by the university became clearer. It was one thing for the university to finance restrictive covenants during the 1930s and 1940s. It was another thing when, over the years, the university acquisition of land meant that, before demolition occurred, several properties where landlords had discriminated were now owned by the university.[63]

Take the test cases from November 13, 1961, for example. At 2:15 p.m., Friedman, who was white, called Shelbourne Apartments near campus. He informed the staff that he was no longer able to rent a room he had reserved, and therefore, he inquired whether a friend could rent there. In response, Friedman was asked: "It's not a colored person, is it? If it is, there's no point in his coming down here." Twenty minutes later, Lula White, a Black UChicago student, visited the Shelbourne Apartments office. Once she requested housing, White was told there was no vacancy, but at 4 p.m., Marian Rose, a white person, visited the apartment office. She was shown a room, was provided and completed an application, and paid a deposit. "She gave me a receipt for my

62. Leonard Friedman to George W. Beadle, January 15, 1962, Beadle Records, Box 265, Folder 1, SCRC. The test case statements were enclosed in this letter to Beadle; Milton Davis to George W. Beadle, December 24, 1961, Beadle Records, Box 265, Folder 1, SCRC; Herman Wolf to George W. Beadle, January 5, 1962, Beadle Records, Box 265, Folder 3, SCRC. Benjamin E. Mays, president of Morehouse College from 1940 to 1967, also expressed his displeasure with UChicago, where he earned his doctorate, over its housing policy. For more, see Mays, *Born to Rebel*, p. 229.

63. Friedman to Beadle, January 15, 1962.

deposit," Rose's statement read, "and agreed to have the apartment redecorated and ready for occupancy by December 1, 1961." The blatant racism was not limited to the Shelbourne Apartments, as tests at the Chicago Arms Apartment, Plaisance Hotel, and University Realty Management Corporation offices yielded similar results. "These test cases, I believe, are self-explanatory, with the possible addition that all the properties in question are to the best of our knowledge owned by the University of Chicago," Friedman wrote to Beadle. "They form the basis of our complaint that the university discriminates against Negroes in the renting and leasing of a significant proportion of the housing it owns in the Hyde Park neighborhood. I hope that a solution satisfactory to all may be achieved at our meeting tomorrow."[64]

The next morning, Beadle and Friedman met. Also present were Ray E. Brown, vice president for administration; John P. Netherton, dean of students; Bruce M. Rappaport, a third-year student and chair of UC-CORE; Bernard "Bernie" Sanders, a transfer student from Brooklyn College and social activities chair of UC-CORE; and Lawrence A. Landry, a sociology doctoral student who had received his bachelors and masters at the university. Outnumbered by students, Netherton set the "ground rules" as a defensive strategy before the meeting started. The rules meant Rappaport, Sanders, and Landry could only act as advisors to Friedman. This left Friedman as the primary speaker related to the student government and UC-CORE charges that the university "bars Negroes from living in several buildings owned by the university."[65]

Beadle acknowledged there was housing discrimination in some properties, but UChicago did not plan to own those buildings permanently. He said those properties were simply acquired to prevent further deterioration. Therefore, the racial policies and practices of the previous property owners were not reversed, but "stable integration" was UChicago's goal. "But we must achieve this at a rate that is tolerable as far as all people involved are concerned," Beadle argued. "In any activity of this nature, a comparatively long period of time must be taken before a suitable solution can be reached." Beadle then asserted that UChicago was more progressive than other universities, but he felt the students did not understand what the university had done to save the neighborhood. "Tremendous amounts of money and tremendous effort has been expended in our drive to attain integration in Hyde Park," he stressed. "In this

64. Friedman to Beadle, January 15, 1962; Original Notarized Copies of Housing Statements, November 13–December 1, 1961, Beadle Records, Box 265, Folder 1, SCRC. The use of Lula White, a Black woman, as a tester is particularly insightful. For a history of Black women and their struggle to attain housing in urban areas, see Williams, *The Politics of Public Housing*.

65. Summary of January 16, 1962, Diary of the Sit-ins, Beadle Records, Box 128, Folder 5, SCRC.

practical and far from ideal world, you have to move slowly enough so that you don't lose." Otherwise, he concluded, the abrupt end to the racist practices several property owners exercised would force "another situation, such as [what] exists in Woodlawn, and the university wouldn't be here today."[66]

The students were unmoved by the university's gradualist approach. "We deplore the university's support and implementation of racial segregation in housing in the Hyde Park neighborhood," Friedman said. "It is shocking and disgraceful to see one of this nation's leading institutions of higher learning practice a policy which is almost universally considered to be totally immoral." However, Friedman's idealist perspective that segregation was "universally" disdained was not Chicago's reality. The city had well established itself using strict racial boundaries, but worse than segregation itself, Rappaport said, was the university's public relations–focused contradictions because UChicago celebrated a healthy list of Black intellectuals among its alumni, such as Carter G. Woodson, historian and founder of Black History Month; Ernest Everett Just, an accomplished biologist; and Georgiana Rose Simpson, a scholar who studied German philology. "We also cannot accept the administration's policy that takes credit for their non-discriminatory policy in academic fields and then turns around and ignores its principles when administering its off-campus housing," Rappaport explained, "refusing to take responsibility for the difference in their publicly-stated policy and their actual practice."[67]

This dichotomy was not as simple as public policy versus private actions. The situation in Woodlawn, as Beadle tried to explain, was dire. When white residents could no longer control if, or even when, Black residents moved into white neighborhoods, they moved to segregated suburban enclaves, and multiple federal policies helped perpetuate discrimination. The New Deal, Cold War initiatives, urban renewal funds, and the Interstate Highway Act of 1956 each provided incentives for whites and corporations to relocate to the suburbs. This is what happened in the Woodlawn neighborhood south of campus that, by 1962, had turned mostly Black.[68]

66. The *Chicago Maroon* offered a detailed account of the Beadle meeting with student government and UC-CORE representatives. For more, see "UC Admits Housing Segregation," *Chicago Maroon*, January 17, 1962.

67. The Friedman and Rappaport quotes opposing Beadle's stance are from "UC Admits Housing Segregation." The information about Black graduates of the University of Chicago can be found in *Integrating the Life of the Mind: African Americans at the University of Chicago, 1870–1940*, Web Exhibits, SCRC. For more on Georgiana Rose Simpson, see Evans, *Black Women in the Ivory Tower*, pp. 130–132.

68. For a comprehensive overview of the federal government and housing segregation, see Rothstein, *The Color of Law*. For a brief overview of federal policies and housing

Beadle argued that if academic leaders allowed Hyde Park to do the same as Woodlawn, UChicago would no longer exist—a nod to the fact that previous administrators once considered relocating the university to the suburbs. "We are proceeding as fast as we can to attain integration as soon as we can," he explained, emphasizing why immediate desegregation was not realistic. For Brown, whose role as the vice president made him responsible for property holdings, the situation was not even entirely within the university's control. The administrators admitted that the university owned some of these properties, but they did not have the desire to force change. "If we only intend to hold a building temporarily, we do not make any abrupt changes, which would tend to disrupt the area," Brown rationalized. "In some of the segregated buildings, the university does not ever take title, but merely provides a subsidy to the owner."[69]

The meeting ended with little resolved. The next day, January 17, writers at the UChicago's student paper *Chicago Maroon* followed the lead of Friedman and Rappaport. An editorial criticized Beadle's stance and called for an immediate change in university policy. Demanding that racist practices be banned in all property holdings, the student government, UC-CORE, and the campus newspaper rallied against Beadle. There was consensus between the administrators and students that desegregation was desired. What students debated, however, was the pace of desegregation, and Beadle felt that pace was nonnegotiable.[70]

---

segregation, see Lassiter, *The Silent Majority*, p. 10. The book details the political motives behind white flight.

69. On Beadle and Brown quotes, see "UC Admits Housing Segregation." Regarding Ray E. Brown's comment that UChicago provided owners a subsidy, shortly after the SECC was formed, in 1953–54, Julian H. Levi is said to have pressured banks to deny loans to any buyers he did not approve or those he felt were not on the same page as UChicago development. By 1959, UChicago leaders paid landlords rent in the summer so Black people could not rent from them during periods when student demand was low. For more, see Winling, *Building the Ivory Tower*, p. 104. For a broader history of banking and discriminatory housing practices, see Taylor, *Race for Profit*. On possibly relocating UChicago, see Bob Wiedrich, "How the U. of C. Fought for the City," *Chicago Tribune*, May 5, 1977. Wiedrich wrote, "In the last decade of the 19th century, the University of Chicago was offered property by a land company if it would settle in Morgan Park, then a suburb of the city." Vanderbilt University in Nashville also considered relocating prior to urban renewal. For more, see Carey, *Chancellors, Commodores, and Coeds*, p. 250.

70. For an additional reference to an editorial in the *Chicago Maroon*, see Summary of January 17, 1962, Diary of the Sit-ins, Beadle Records, Box 128, Folder 5, SCRC. Also see "UC Segregation Criticized," *Chicago Maroon*, January 17, 1962; "UC Admits Housing Segregation."

The university had invested millions of dollars since 1951, when Kimpton was hired and formed the SECC. Countless hours had been invested in marketing and promoting the university's approach as the blueprint for how higher education could save American cities. Therefore, as student resistance grew louder, university officials focused immediate attention on controlling the narrative to protect a decades-long investment instead of desegregating university properties. The day after students met with Beadle, Sy Friedman, in university public relations (no relation to Leonard M. Friedman, student government president), provided Carl W. Larsen, director of public relations, with background information about Friedman and Rappaport. The report on Friedman noted that he "was turned down at an 'un-named' eastern school and was on the waiting list at Oberlin with the University of Chicago next on his list." His high school record labeled him a "non-conformist, not radical or unstable, but occasionally tactlessly frank." At UChicago, where he enrolled in October 1958, he earned a C average his first quarter. In 1960, he failed French, and in 1961, he was late for class registration. "It appears that his extracurricular activities were more important to him than class appearance and completion of courses," the report to Larsen summarized. Conversely, Sy Friedman's report on Rappaport was positive. Rappaport, chair of UC-CORE, was "a brilliant scholar" who received a $1,200 scholarship from UChicago. His other student organizational affiliations included the former UC-NAACP as well as the University of Chicago Students for Civil Liberties. The public relations office quickly accumulated information so UChicago administrators would know who they were dealing with.[71]

Later, on the night of January 17, UC-CORE hosted an open meeting with about one hundred students in attendance. The objective was to create a protest plan in case university administrators did not immediately act to end housing discrimination. The group decided that the university must: (1) issue a public statement that the institution did not discriminate on the basis of race in renting, leasing, administering, or selling of any property owned or controlled by the university; (2) withdraw all support of any realtors who discriminated; (3) direct all personnel who administered university property to cease discrimination; and (4) appoint a board composed of administrators, faculty, and students who could hear all housing complaints. The students gave

71. Sy Friedman to Carl W. Larsen, January 17, 1962, Beadle Records, Box 128, Folder 5, SCRC. The obituary for Sy Friedman does not mention Leonard M. Friedman as a relative. For more, see "Seymour 'Sy' Friedman," *Chicago Sun-Times*, September 25, 1992. It reads, "Survivors include his wife, Ruth; two sons, Marc and Michael; a daughter, Sharon; a sister, Ethel Rath; a brother, Jerome; and four grandchildren." Leonard M. Friedman was from Scarsdale, New York.

Beadle until January 23—one week following his initial January 16 meeting with them—to meet those demands. In the meantime, the UC-CORE campus publicity and social action committees determined what action would occur if Beadle's response was unsatisfactory.[72]

The next day, January 18, Beadle issued a public statement in an attempt to demonstrate that he and the students were on the same page. "We are in complete agreement with the stated objectives of the students," the statement read. "We believe that, everything considered, we are moving toward those objectives." Furthermore, he emphasized that the university had spent decades working on the housing issues in Hyde Park that the current students were debating. "We have made very substantial progress in the past two decades," Beadle's statement continued. "We believe the University of Chicago, indeed, has assumed a position of leadership in meeting the complex problems of serving democratic ideals in a changing society." The same day, Beadle met with the Council of the University Senate to discuss the university's housing policy. However, his statement and subsequent meeting left mixed reviews among the faculty.[73]

Some faculty were understanding of Beadle, such as Sol Tax, an anthropology professor, who defended the university with a caveat. He felt the university should be criticized "for whatever share it has in this anomalous situation," but should also be praised for its involvement "in a most difficult effort to build an integrated Hyde Park–Kenwood." Similarly, Donald Meiklejohn, a philosophy professor, added, "There may well have been individual cases where I would criticize particular steps which have been taken, but Mr. Beadle's claim of progress in the past twenty years seems to me completely persuasive." Malcolm Sharp, a law professor, agreed. "While I have not agreed fully with the university's position on urban renewal," Sharp said, "I am sure that the university's purpose has been to arrest the slums for promoting stable racial integration." But Gerhard Meyer, an economics professor, was not satisfied with the university's policy. Likewise, Bert Hoselitz, a social sciences professor, said the university needed one consistent policy. "The same policy of complete racial integration that the university employs with regard to students should be maintained in all other areas, including university investments in real estate," Hoselitz argued, adding that the university should "set an example of integration" for the private landlords who discriminated.[74]

72. "CORE Meets to Plan UC Segregation Protest," *Chicago Maroon*, January 18, 1962.

73. Statement by George Wells Beadle, January 18, 1962, Beadle Records, Box 128, Folder 5, SCRC. On Beadle's meeting with the Council of the University Senate, see Summary of January 18, 1962, Diary of the Sit-ins, Beadle Records, Box 128, Folder 5, SCRC.

74. John Williams, "Faculty Mixed on Segregation," *Chicago Maroon*, January 18, 1962.

Off campus, Alderman Leon M. Despres called the university "behind the times." He found it unreasonable that UChicago would tolerate the behaviors of racists who rejected potential tenants because of their race when Beadle had an opportunity to truly save Chicago by changing university policy. He added, "Interracial use of university property under high occupancy standards could set a magnificent pattern for all Chicago to follow." Arthur M. Brazier, the local pastor and leader of TWO, went a step further and said Chicago might as well be in the South:

> The administration of the university has been trying to hide its segregation housing policies for several years. The university has been one of the most ardent supporters of restricted covenants. We think it is a disgrace for a great university in a northern city to maintain a policy of segregation in their housing. It is reminiscent of the Universities of Georgia, Alabama, and Arkansas.

This candidness from community leaders like Brazier drew the proverbial line in the sand between immediate and gradual desegregation, the community and the campus.[75]

In the background, while community leaders and some faculty lambasted university officials, Larsen worked to craft a narrative more aligned with the university's advertised policy not to discriminate based on race, and advised Brown that the university hospitals were an example worth promoting. "Nondiscriminatory attitudes of the university are reflected in the management of the university hospitals," Larsen advised. "Thirty percent of the admission to Lying-In, the hospitals' maternity wing, are Negro." Additionally, Larsen estimated that 70 percent of adults and 85 percent of children brought to the emergency rooms were Black. Inpatient and outpatient numbers reflected a nondiscriminatory Black-white ratio as well. These data were important for administrators when speaking to external audiences.[76]

Larsen then sent Lowell T. Coggeshall, vice president for biological sciences, a note on how to keep future students like Friedman from being elected student government president. Larsen said the new dean of students (Netherton officially resigned on December 5, 1961, but his replacement had not yet been appointed) should "set up some new ground rules for student activities." He suggested that these rules include that office holders be "academically qualified," similar to the rules "for athletes under the Big Ten rules." Larsen also proposed a minimum on the number of students who must vote to elect a campus-wide student leader, since only 20 percent of the student body voted

75. Ibid.
76. Carl W. Larsen to Ray Brown, January 18, 1962, Beadle Records Box 128, Folder 5, SCRC.

in the election Friedman won. "A determined effort should be made to obtain the votes of all students and a number of candidates should be offered," he suggested.[77]

Meanwhile, on January 19, Friedman and Rappaport continued the critiques. "The statement by President Beadle, in my opinion, obscures rather than clarifies the issue of discrimination in university-owned housing," Friedman said, responding to the president's statement (Beadle changed university terminology from chancellor to president by 1962). "He is clearly not in complete agreement with the students' position." Rappaport added, "President Beadle has stated that 'we are proceeding as fast as we can to attain integration,' yet the administration still refuses to reveal any facts or statistics." Furthermore, Rappaport did not lose sight of the fact that the racial issues in Hyde Park were an extension of the larger student civil rights uprising in America. "Next week, we will be visited by a member of the Student Non-violent Coordinating Committee, a group of students who are willing to give up their lives in order to rid this country of racial discrimination," he said. "As Mr. Friedman has commented, 'How can we face this student, knowing he comes here because of the great liberal tradition of the university and, at the same time, knowing the real policy of the administration?'"[78]

That last point, about UChicago students making a personal connection with their peers who were risking their lives in the South, shifted control of the narrative around South Side housing from the university to the community. UChicago's headlines for buying deteriorated property and stopping slum encroachment ended. By Friday, January 19, only three days after Beadle met with the students, the *Chicago Daily News* carried articles about the housing bias charges against the university. The same issue also featured the closing of Southern University and A&M, a Black college in Baton Rouge, Louisiana, after students there demonstrated against segregation. It was clear to a growing number of people that student demands at UChicago were not an irrational outlier, and that the university was complicit in perpetuating local racism.[79]

On Monday, January 22, Beadle issued another statement, his first since the students' demands were published on the front page of the *Chicago Maroon* on January 18. This time, Beadle elaborated over two pages, notably longer than his initial four-sentence statement the previous week. Yet, the tenor of

77. Carl W. Larsen to Lowell T. Coggeshall, January 18, 1962, Beadle Records, Box 128, Folder 5, SCRC; Netherton Press Release, December 5, 1961, Beadle Records, Box 124, Folder 7, SCRC.

78. "4 Comment on UC Segregation," *Chicago Maroon*, January 19, 1962.

79. For the *Chicago Daily News* headlines, see Summary of January 19, 1962, Diary of the Sit-ins, Beadle Records, Box 128, Folder 5, SCRC.

his message remained the same as he emphasized that the university's objectives were the same as those of the students. "The only issue on which there is arguable difference of opinion," he stated, "is the rate at which it is possible to move toward the agreed-on objective without losing more than is gained." Beadle elaborated: "Experience has proved that integration of such property does not occur spontaneously; in fact, the opposite is true. A sudden change of practice enhances the fear and distrust of present tenants, and they tend to move out." Ultimately, this second statement reiterated the talking points Beadle and Brown had stressed a week earlier when meeting with the students. Therefore, not one of the students' four demands were explicitly met. Beadle held his ground. In response to Beadle's statement, and in accordance with their plans to demonstrate if their demands were not met, UC-CORE leaders announced that they would host a civil rights rally outside the Administration Building and lead a sit-in in Beadle's office the next day. Direct action was in effect at UChicago.[80]

A Sit-in at the President's Office

By January 23, 1962, the demands made by UChicago students and community leaders had caught the attention of CORE's national office in New York, and Velma Hill of CORE made it a point to visit the campus. Having participated in the southern sit-ins and the previous summer's wade-ins to desegregate Chicago's Rainbow Beach, Hill endorsed the charges brought before UChicago during the rally held outside of the Administration Building. "Those who say be moderate and go slow are not those who live in the Negro ghetto, not those who cannot get a job," Hill told the crowd. "To those who say go slow, I say go somewhere else!"[81]

Hill's words from outside of the Administration Building echoed across rally signs that expressed a shared sentiment among those gathered: "Equal Opportunities Regardless of Race," "Urban Renewal, Not Negro Removal," and "Open Occupancy in UC Housing." Student government and UC-CORE leaders challenged Beadle to deliver more than lip service. "I reject [Beadle's] statement completely," Rappaport professed. "We are not asking [for] desegregation in the future. We are asking [for] desegregation now." Sanders said much

80. Statement by George Wells Beadle, January 22, 1962, Beadle Records, Box 128, Folder 5, SCRC; On UC-CORE's announcement to hold a rally and sit-in, see Summary of January 22, 1962, Diary of the Sit-ins, Beadle Records, Box 128, Folder 5, SCRC.

81. On the rally quotes, see Summary of January 23, 1962, Diary of the Sit-ins, Beadle Records, Box 128, Folder 5, SCRC.

the same: "We feel it is an intolerable situation when Negro and white students at the university cannot live together in university-owned apartments." He added, "Those Negroes who go to classes with us can't go to the dorms. This is an intolerable situation and has to go." Friedman was tired of Beadle's gradualist approach, and told the rally crowd: "Let's go upstairs and protest. It's a very simple point that we are making—the university has to admit and accept integration."[82]

That is when thirty-three people—twenty-nine UChicago students, two University of Wisconsin students, and two members of the South Side CORE chapter—entered the Administration Building and made their way to Beadle's fifth-floor office. The goal of the sit-in was to garner publicity and put additional pressure on the administration regarding the racist policies Black students and local Black residents faced. The demonstrators waited most of the afternoon until Beadle arrived about 3 p.m. Stepping off the elevator with a smile, he greeted the group, and the sit-in was launched.[83]

This was the first sit-in demonstration staged by CORE north of the Mason-Dixon Line, and it brought national and international media to the UChicago president's office. The students also gained the support of local unions and labor groups because working-class Black Chicagoans had long been victims of the racial restrictive covenants, and the sit-in brought attention to systemic racism in Chicago. Timuel Black, president of the Chicago chapter of Negro American Labor Council, said college students' efforts should encourage all Americans. "The southern students endured mobs, jail, and bus burning," he said. "These youngsters show almost equal courage in daring to point out how discrimination practices lie behind liberal words." Black added: "I am sure that all Negro people back these 'freedom sitters,'" and that UChicago could "hardly claim to be a liberal institution" until it addressed its housing policy. Bernard Lucas, president of Local 500 of the Packinghouse Workers of America, echoed that sentiment. "I fully support CORE in their struggle for equal housing opportunity," Lucas said. "The problem of segregated housing is one which all Chicago must attack and defeat."[84]

---

82. Summary of January 23, 1962, Diary of the Sit-ins.

83. Ibid.; Kaufman, "Students Sleep In."

84. "Winds of Change Over the Chicago Campus," *The Times* (London), February 6, 1962. Timuel Black Statement, January 23, 1962, Beadle Records, Box 128, Folder 5, SCRC; Bernard Lucas Statement, January 23, 1962, Beadle Records, Box 128, Folder 5, SCRC. Labor rights and unions were a prominent part of civil rights progress. For instance, in 1957, Martin Luther King Jr. addressed the United Packing Workers Union and encouraged union members to exercise their right to vote as a means to achieving equal rights. For more, see Collier-Thomas and Franklin, *My Soul Is a Witness*, p. 71.

Facing growing opposition, President Beadle attempted to at least appear amendable to those publicly critical of the university as the sit-in started. "I understand the question has been asked as to whether the university is willing to discuss the possibility of change in its policy as stated in today's *Maroon*," read Beadle's statement on January 23. "The answer is yes. The tradition of discussion of important issues among faculty, administration, and students is a long-standing and valuable one at the University of Chicago." Accompanying Beadle's statement, UChicago public relations staff issued a press release at 3:15 p.m., just after the sit-in started. The release tried to take advantage of some students' contempt for UC-CORE. William Klecke, wearing a sign that read "I'm for integration but not for CORE," delivered to Beadle's office a petition signed by ninety-four UChicago students and faculty. The press release noted that the petitioners opposed "the methods of the group picketing the Administration Building. He [Klecke] said the group does not represent the opinions of the student body." The petition also called tactics used by student government and UC-CORE "deplorable."[85]

Eager to show that not all students opposed Beadle, the public relations staff sent the release to Chicago's major newspapers, local television stations, and news wire services. While Sheldon Garber of the university's public relations staff handled any petition-focused media inquiries, public relations director Carl W. Larsen and his staffer, Sy Friedman, worked with the university's housing office to find examples of Black people living in "integrated buildings" in Hyde Park in an attempt to counter the negative publicity. However, their efforts did not stop the late edition newspapers from focusing on the students, as both the *Chicago American* and *Chicago Daily News* featured headlines about the sit-in.[86]

The news spread farther the next day, on January 24, by newspaper, radio, and television, including Chicago and news outlets in New York, Cincinnati, Saint Louis, Milwaukee, Minneapolis, Cleveland, and Plainfield, New Jersey. The national coverage ignited questions from previously quiet voices, like those of the twelve university chaplains who issued a joint statement. Representing the Baptists, Lutherans, Methodists, Episcopalians, and Hillel Foundation, the religious leaders said, "we are encouraged by the concern expressed by students on this campus about the inequalities which persist in our

85. George W. Beadle Statement, January 23, 1962, Beadle Records, Box 128, Folder 5, SCRC; Press Release on the Klecke petition, January 23, 1962, Beadle Records, Box 128, Folder 5, SCRC.

86. Sy Friedman to Carl W. Larsen, January 23, 1962, Beadle Records, Box 128, Folder 5, SCRC. For the actual headlines about the sit-ins, see Summary of January 23, 1962, Diary of the Sit-ins, Beadle Records, Box 128, Folder 5, SCRC.

community despite substantial improvements in the last ten years." The chaplains also recommended that a committee be formed to address the housing issue. It needed "eight members, four representing administration, faculty, and students of the university, and four representing community organizations," such as the Chicago Urban League, local churches and synagogues, and the Hyde Park–Kenwood Community Conference. These religious leaders were much later in their support than Brazier, but they sent a notable signal to the community about the moral relevance of fighting racism.[87]

Some white tenants in university-owned housing also took a moral stand. Elizabeth L. Gwynn informed the University Realty Management Office that she would not renew her lease. She copied Beadle and Larsen on her letter that read: "At the time I originally signed the lease last year, I was not aware of your apartheid policy of rentals. Had I been, I would not have signed in the first place." The sit-in was creating the onslaught the students intended, and in response, Sy Friedman spoke to Walter Kloetzli, a Lutheran leader in Chicago. Sy Friedman then consulted with Larsen regarding whether the campus would react favorably if they invited Reverend Martin Luther King to speak on campus in Rockefeller Chapel. Friedman summarized his conversation with Kloetzli: "He believes that the Rev. King's appearance will [be] conciliatory to the current sit-in situation and that it will tend to temper rousers."[88]

This mere consideration of soliciting arguably the world's most notable civil rights leader in an effort to cease a student protest demonstrates the desperation of the Beadle administration. There was seemingly nothing university officials, particularly those responsible for public relations, would not consider in an attempt to stop the sit-in. For instance, Sy Friedman noted that there had been a recent neighborhood scuffles between white girls attending University High School and Black girls at Ray Elementary School. He said Julian H. Levi, SECC executive director, and Tony Edison, chief of the university security office, "believe there may be a direct relationship between the attacks by girl students at Ray Elementary School and the CORE segregation action including the sit-ins." In their opinion, it was no coincidence that the first "assault," on Monday, January 22, occurred on the same day UC-CORE announced its intention to start the sit-in. "The reason is that many of the persons involved are in families that had access to the *Chicago Maroon* stories last

87. For a list of news outlets covering the sit-in, see Summary of January 24, 1962, Diary of the Sit-ins, Beadle Records, Box 128, Folder 5, SCRC; A Statement by Chaplains at the University, January 24, 1962, Beadle Records, Box 128, Folder 5, SCRC.

88. Elizabeth L. Gwynn to University Realty Management, January 24, 1962, Beadle Records, Box 128, Folder 5, SCRC; Sy Friedman to Carl W. Larsen, January 24, 1962, Beadle Records, Box 128, Folder 5, SCRC.

week and this week prior to the sit-ins and the attendant publicity that followed," Sy Friedman surmised in a confidential memo. SECC leaders adopted a stance similar to a broader ideology that criminalized Black youth and ultimately blamed the student newspaper, as well as elementary school–aged children, for the sit-in.[89]

While public relations staff exchanged memos on January 24, South Side CORE members, including some students, held a sit-in at the University Realty Management Office. The demonstrators demanded that Kendall Cady, general manager, place visible indicators on buildings owned by the university, immediately stop segregation, and create a new policy and provide proof of the new policy. Cady defensively refused, noting that his office would not reveal its business procedures to non-university officials. Afterward, thirteen people were arrested for refusing to leave, and Elizabeth Fattahipour, a receptionist at the office, was eventually fired because she joined the demonstrators. About the same time, Charles Bellows, a "noted Chicago attorney," was hired to represent the University Realty Management Office.[90]

Back in the Administration Building, Levi and Ray E. Brown, vice president for administration, met with the UC-CORE representatives at the Beadle office sit-in. Brown said the university would permit no more than four students to sit in at any time due to safety concerns, and they were restricted to the lobby area; however, those restrictions were ignored by the sit-in participants whose goals were to disrupt. Therefore, following an intensely active January 24, Beadle issued a three-point statement in response to the week's activities: (1) "all university-owned property is available to faculty and students . . . without any discrimination as to race, creed, or color"; (2) "the university is committed to a policy of non-discrimination in the operation of all its properties"; (3) "the university will form a faculty-student review board" that would have access to housing data. These three points were a notable step toward agreement between the students and administration. In fact, the *Chicago Maroon* reported that both sides "seemed close to agreement" regarding "methods of implementing UC's racial policies in university-owned apartment buildings." UC-CORE members, however, were not "fully satisfied" and had

89. Sy Friedman to Carl W. Larsen, January 24, 1962, Beadle Records, Box 128, Folder 5, SCRC; Regarding the criminalization of Black youth, particularly following World War II, see Suddler, *Presumed Criminal*. On whites' ideas of Black schools and its relationship to federal housing policy, see Spencer, *In the Crossfire*, pp. 53–93.

90. "Realty Sit-downers Arrested," *Chicago Maroon*, January 25, 1962; "Protesting Receptionist Dismissed from Her Job," *Chicago Maroon*, January 30, 1962. For the Bellows hire, see Summary of January 24, Diary of the Sit-ins.

a few more questions, but before a formal agreement could be reached, Beadle left campus the following day for a week-long trip to California.[91]

On January 25, the day Beadle left for California, Marvin Ceynar, chair of Chicago CORE, sent a telegram informing him of the organization's endorsement of the students' efforts. Later that day, the South Side's Plaisance Hotel, one of the locations of the November 1961 test cases, was picketed. By Friday, January 26, tensions grew thicker as the Federal Bureau of Investigation (FBI) notified university officials that the Fighting American Nationalists, a right-wing group, planned to come to campus on Saturday to "beat the daylights" out of "those sit-in kids." Measures for extra security were ordered for the Administration Building, although the white nationalists did not show. The worst that happened on Saturday was spoof flyers were distributed on campus that made jest of the protests with a fake organizational name, "Cathartic Committee of Campus Protests," and phrases like "Protest Everything at Once!"[92]

In San Francisco, Beadle was unable to escape the crisis back at UChicago when, on January 27, nearly two dozen people picketed outside of the Fairmont Hotel where he spoke to some UChicago alumni. Flyers were distributed that read, "End Segregation, Dr. Beadle!" Most of the demonstrators were students at the University of California, Berkeley. The demonstration was organized by Dorothy Datz, a former UChicago student then enrolled at Berkeley, and it was covered by the *Daily Californian* and *Chicago Maroon* student newspapers. The next morning, the *New York Times* published a detailed report of the Chicago sit-ins and posed the question: "How fast can a neighborhood in the North be integrated without impelling some whites to leave?" This was followed by a *Chicago Defender* editorial in support of the students: "The sit-in demonstration is the only intelligent, rational way of making the

---

91. On the Levi-Brown meeting with UC-CORE, see Summary of January 24, Diary of the Sit-ins; Ray E. Brown Statement, January 24, 1962, Beadle Records, Box 128, Folder 5, SCRC. On Beadle's three-point statement, see "Beadle Suggests Housing Board," *Chicago Maroon*, January 25, 1962; "CORE Dissatisfied with Beadle Offer," *Chicago Maroon*, January 26, 1962. On Beadle in California, see Summary of January 25, 1962, Diary of the Sit-ins, Beadle Records, Box 128, Folder 5, SCRC.

92. Marvin Ceynar to George W. Beadle, January 25, 1962, Beadle Records, Box 265, Folder 1, SCRC. On the Plaisance Hotel picket, see Summary of January 25, 1962, Diary of the Sit-ins, Beadle Records, Box 128, Folder 5, SCRC. On the Fighting American Nationalists threat, see Summary of January 26, 1962, and Summary of January 27, 1962, Diary of the Sit-ins, Beadle Records, Box 128, Folder 5, SCRC; "Do You Feel Oppressed" flyer, n.d., Beadle Records, Box 128, Folder 5, SCRC. There was no date on the flyer, but the Summary of January 27, 1962, noted it was distributed that day.

University of Chicago realize its moral responsibility to the surrounding community."[93]

Related to this idea of moral responsibility, on January 30, back in Chicago, the Kehilath Anshe Ma'arav Isaiah Israel Temple (KAM Temple) hosted a CORE rally. More than five hundred people heard national and local civic leaders discuss the sit-ins. This included Despres:

> They are directed against the University of Chicago real estate office, as one of the bearers of Chicago's terrible housing segregation. The CORE demonstrators are really and principally a deep protest against Chicago's housing segregation. To me, that is the clear and profound meaning of the CORE sit-ins in our community.

In addition to Despres, James Farmer, CORE national director and co-founder, told the audience that CORE was willing to discuss any questions with President Beadle or other administrators, but they were not willing to negotiate "segregation or no segregation."[94]

The next day, January 31, Farmer reiterated this message during a press conference when flanked by reporters: "The National CORE office is very much interested in the situation and pleased with the stand that the University of Chicago students are taking." A reporter asked Farmer what he would do if Beadle decided not to meet with him, and Farmer quickly replied, "We will cross that bridge when we get there." He was then asked what he would do if Beadle returned to meet with students but not the civil rights leader, and Farmer replied again: "We will cross that bridge, too." By this point, years into the Black Freedom Movement, Farmer was an expert in engaging white journalists and was not distracted by off-topic questions, even by questions about the Soviet Union and the Iron Curtain. He stayed focused on discrimination in university-owned properties and its national prominence. Commenting on Columbia University, Farmer said, "They are, if not the largest, then one of the largest real estate owners around the area." He continued, "There are still apartment houses from which Negroes appear to have been systematically

93. Summary of January 27, Diary of the Sit-ins; "End Segregation, Dr. Beadle" flyer, n.d., Beadle Records, Box 128, Folder 5, SCRC. On the *Daily Californian* coverage, see Summary of January 31, 1962, Diary of the Sit-ins, Beadle Records, Box 128, Folder 5, SCRC; "California Students Picket Beadle," *Chicago Maroon*, January 31, 1962; Austin C. Wehrwein, "Integration Bid Stirring Chicago: Picketed University Studies Effect of Housing Policy," *New York Times*, January 28, 1962; "The University of Chicago," *Chicago Defender*, January 29, 1962.

94. Leon M. Despres, "Why the Sit-ins in Our Community," January 30, 1962, Beadle Records, Box 128, Folder 5, SCRC; "CORE Head Praises UC Sit-ins," *Chicago Maroon*, January 31, 1962.

excluded. In New York, fortunately, we have fair housing laws which prohibit discrimination in private as well as public housing." Policy was the heart of the UChicago students' demands, and the sit-ins would continue until Beadle changed university policy.[95]

As support for the students increased, Levi took offense to the twelve university chaplains' statement that aligned with the sit-in goals. He called Rabbi Maurice E. Pekarsky, director of the Hillel Foundation and one of the statement's signatories, a hypocrite. Levi felt "deep humiliation" that his fellow Jewish community members had not aided the effort to stop slum activities during his years as executive director of the SECC. "Over the years the files of this office demonstrate that a significant majority of slum operators in this area are Jewish," Levi complained. "These property owners, for their private benefit and profit, have exploited the community and the Negro." For instance, dating back to the 1920s on the South Side, the rabbi of Congregation Beth Jacob solicited signatures for a restrictive covenant. He added, "Neither the Jewish community, nor its organizations, nor the Jewish Rabbinate are exceptions." Levi's jab at Pekarsky exhibited his frustrations, but it also highlighted the white liberal's contradictions. Levi had spent the previous ten years working to prevent slums from spreading on the South Side, but he had not pressed Jewish property owners regarding their part in the racial discrimination that caused the slum conditions. East Hyde Park, located closest to Lake Michigan, was once the heart of the city's Jewish community, but it was often split on race relations. Some fought for racial equality while others exploited Black people no different than other white people.[96]

95. Unofficial Farmer Press Conference Transcript, January 31, 1962, Beadle Records, Box 128, Folder 5, SCRC.

96. Julian H. Levi to Maurice E. Pekarsky, January 25, 1962, Beadle Records, Box 128, Folder 5, SCRC. Jewish Chicago residents had long discriminated against Black residents. For more on Jewish and other religious leaders, see Rothstein, *Color of Law*, p. 105. On East Hyde Park and Jewish residents, see Webber, "The University of Chicago and Its Neighbors," in Perry and Wiewel, *The University as Urban Developer*, p. 67. Historian Shana Bernstein's scholarship interrogates racial coalitions. On Jewish Americans, Bernstein wrote, "Unlike many unambiguously racialized groups like African Americans, who generally had no choice but to fight for more equality, Jews' ambiguous social and racial status between mainstream and minority confronted them with a dilemma. They wondered whether they should join forces with other minorities to address discrimination or shun civil rights activism for fear collaboration would 'lower' their status even further by association." For more, see Bernstein, "From the Southwest to the Nation: Interracial Civil Rights Activism in the Sunbelt Southwest," in Nickerson and Dochuk, *Sunbelt Rising*, p. 155. It is also notable that that white Christian segregationists regularly characterized Jews as a threat to segregation and the white race. For an example from the early 1960s, see

While Levi vented privately, he fielded questions during a press interview in Beadle's absence. What emerged in Levi's comments was a public conviction that he had not exhibited before that moment. "The students are troubled by injustice in our society, as I am, and I think all thoughtful people in this country are," Levi said. "The question in my mind is as to method. But in the long run, neither the city nor the nation can tolerate [the] depriving of anyone's rights because of their color." Yet, when asked who was responsible for Chicago's housing segregation problem and what the solution was, he did not name names or identify specific groups as he had to Pekarsky. Instead, he spread the blame widely. "I don't think there are any heroes in this business. . . . All of us approach the problem with self-announced pure hearts but those making the loudest announcements often have hands not so pure."[97]

On campus, public relations staffers did not go as far as Levi in admitting their shortcomings, but they discussed among themselves their missed opportunities to address the racial conflict in housing. Larsen sent Beadle a memo suggesting the UChicago officials emphasize all the good they have done. "Our accomplishments in making this community interracial have not been stressed adequately," he wrote. By January 29, administrators had drafted possible language for a new university rental policy, and the next day, Beadle's decision to appoint a three-man faculty committee to review the university's policies on "occupancy of its properties" made the front page of the *Chicago Maroon*. These actions were indications the university was moving toward some type of concession, and the three professors appointed to the committee—Philip Hauser, sociology; George Shultz, business; Allison Dunham, law—each lived in Hyde Park or Woodlawn; however, a snafu the day before Beadle's return from California leaked the administration's tactics.[98]

On February 1, Ray E. Brown prepared for public relations director Larsen a two-page memo about the university's real estate properties. It was his way of making sure the public relations department was on the same page while the sit-in continued in Beadle's office. The document listed a statement regularly heard in the media, such as that the university was investing in slum real estate,

---

Permaloff and Grafton, *Politics and Power in Alabama*, p. 152. Alabama highway director Sam Engelhardt is quoted as saying, "The Jew's mongrel background is undoubtedly responsible for his abysmal inferiority complex and motivates him to do everything in his power to communize, mongrelize and destroy the Great White Christian Race."

97. Levi Interview Transcript, January 26, 1962, Beadle Records, Box 128, Folder 5, SCRC.

98. Carl W. Larsen to George W. Beadle, January 25, 1962, Beadle Records, Box 128, Folder 5, SCRC. Regarding the drafted rental policy text, see Summary of January 29, 1962, Diary of the Sit-ins, Beadle Records, Box 128, Folder 5, SCRC; "Three Man Committee to Review Housing Policy," *Chicago Maroon*, January 30, 1962.

and Brown replied beneath each statement with a "fact." It was an internal document, but after Brown met to receive feedback and agreed to revisions, it was discovered that the public relations staff had mailed it to the news outlets. The public relations office was criticized, while the student newspaper ran an article calling the facts "distorted," but it was a mistake indicative of the frantic, hurried pace among university leaders. Students were being arrested, released, and arrested again during this period. National newspapers and television stations focused on the turmoil. All the while, Levi grappled with the hypocrisy recently exposed by the students' demands and sit-in. This is the situation that would welcome Beadle back to campus upon his return on February 2.[99]

Winds of Change over Chicago

On February 2, 1962, President Beadle returned from California and immediately contacted Bruce M. Rappaport, chair of UC-CORE. Beadle needed him to understand that both sides agreed that discrimination was unacceptable and stressed that it was university policy to "abolish all forms of discrimination." Beadle's only goal was to "prevent their being 'turned' from one type of segregation to another, a change not desired by CORE, the university, the community, or anyone else." Therefore, the sit-in was successful and, therefore, no longer necessary until the faculty committee rendered its report. "In organizing a student sit-in, you have abundantly demonstrated your concern," Beadle told Rappaport, and although he did not like the "emotional" sit-in, he admitted it "had its value in persuading all of us to reexamine our convictions and attitudes."[100]

This change of convictions and attitudes had become evident over the past week. Levi's comments during the press conference and his private letter to the rabbi were one example. Some local journalists changed their stances as well. For example, a February 3, 1962, editorial in the *Chicago Daily News* argued that whites must not leave neighborhoods if they wanted an integrated community. Once committed to telling the university's ambitious urban renewal story, those same news outlets now questioned UChicago's role in housing segregation. Indeed, attitudes had shifted regarding how an urban university should engage its neighboring Black community. Yet, attitudes and actions were

---

99. Ray E. Brown to Carl W. Larsen, February 1, 1962, Beadle Records, Box 128, Folder 5, SCRC; On the Brown memo leak, see Summary of February 1, 1962, Diary of the Sit-ins, Beadle Records, Box 128, Folder 5, SCRC.

100. George W. Beadle to Bruce M. Rappaport, February 2, 1962, Beadle Records, Box 128, Folder 5, SCRC.

two separate things. For Rappaport and others, university policies needed to match the new and improved attitudes that Beadle had discussed.[101]

By Sunday, February 4, the sit-in started its third week with students still steadfast in their own convictions, but campus officials decided to end the sit-in themselves. Warner Wick, the incoming dean of students (his hire would not be announced until February 6), informed Carl W. Larsen of his plan for "ejecting the demonstrators tomorrow." Wick and Beadle met to discuss said plan that afternoon and agreed to execute it the next morning. "As you will see," Wick explained, "if we are to declare war, it is important that we make clear what the war is about—the issue is not race relations or real estate policy but a misguided attempt by students to put themselves in a position to 'negotiate' with the university by creating a nuisance."[102]

Wick's plan was, first, the administration would issue a statement that withdrew permission for no more than four students to sit in (that directive had been ignored by the students since first issued on January 24). Second, all students would be asked to leave the fifth floor of the Administration Building and report to John P. Netherton's office or face suspension. There, students would be placed on probation, a condition of which prohibited them from future demonstrations. Finally, any students who remained in Beadle's office would be arrested.[103]

At 1 p.m. on February 5, the removal plan began. Beadle issued another statement that was sympathetic to the students' cause. "We would be false to our trust if we were not always ready to join with students in discussing any problem as important as that of achieving a stable interracial community in a large city," Beadle stated. But he added, "the university cannot 'negotiate' with any group of students." In closing, permission to sit in was withdrawn. Then, Ray E. Brown read his statement asking students to report to the Dean of Students office. Next, in Netherton's office, the dean of students read another statement to students about probation; however, these were performative declarations. Instead, it was Beadle's speech later that night that moved the needle toward something acceptable to UC-CORE and student government.[104]

101. On the *Chicago Daily News* editorial and its relationship to the university, see Summary of February 3, 1962, Diary of the Sit-ins, Beadle Records, Box 128, Folder 5, SCRC.

102. Warner Wick to Carl W. Larsen, February 4, 1962, Beadle Records, Box 128, Folder 5, SCRC; "Warner Wick Is Named to Dean of Students Post," *Chicago Maroon*, February 6, 1962; Beadle to Deans on Wick Hire, February 6, 1962, Beadle Records, Box 124, Folder 7, SCRC.

103. Wick to Larsen, February 4, 1962.

104. Statement by George Wells Beadle, February 5, 1962, Beadle Records, Box 264, Folder 14, SCRC. Regarding the release time of the statement, see Summary of February 5, 1962, Diary of the Sit-ins, Beadle Records, Box 128, Folder 5, SCRC; Ray E. Brown, Notice to Sit-in

That evening, about three hundred students gathered on campus for an emergency UC-CORE meeting, which Beadle also attended. "There has been a good deal of misunderstanding in the last two weeks, and I wish to try to dispel much of it as possible," he said. "No one has been punished. No one has been suspended. No one intends to suspend if this can be avoided. No one wants to." Beadle also underscored his respect and agreement "on the issue of racial equality." The students then voted to work with the university to form a commission focused on ending racial discrimination in Hyde Park, and Beadle said he would favor such a commission. The meeting ended with a student vote to suspend the sit-in.[105]

The end of the sit-in did not mean the end of tensions over racial discrimination in university-owned properties, but change was in the air. On February 6, the day following the students' vote to end the sit-in, Beadle offered short remarks before the Citizens Board at the Chicago Club. "We have all had a liberal education at the University of Chicago the past few weeks—students, faculty, and administration," he told the group. "We all ended up friends." While Beadle noted that he found the sit-in inappropriate, he also highlighted his admiration for students' "tenacity and sincerity." Back on campus, Larsen told Vice President Coggeshall that campus officials needed to "devote a bit of effort now to a positive program to inform our faculty, students, and neighbors on the problems of developing and maintaining a stable, heterogeneous community." In fact, Larsen noted that Walter Leen, university legal counsel, had proposed that a seminar series on urban renewal in major cities be sponsored by the university. Larsen's suggestions would serve two purposes. First, the seminars would slow the alumni and outside sympathizers who were flooding Beadle's office with their grievance letters over university action. Second, they would begin a public conversation about urban renewal that community members, for years, had hoped the university would join.[106]

Demonstrators, February 5, 1962, Beadle Records, Box 128, Folder 5, SCRC; John P. Netherton Statement, February 5, 1962, Beadle Records, Box 128, Folder 5, SCRC.

105. George Wells Beadle Talk with Students, February 6, 1962, Beadle Records, Box 128, Folder 5, SCRC; "CORE Halts UC Sit-ins," *Chicago Maroon*, February 6, 1962.

106. For notes about Beadle's Citizens Board talk, see Sheldon Garber to Carl W. Larsen and Sy Friedman, February 6, 1962, Beadle Records, Box 264, Folder 14, SCRC; Carl W. Larsen to Lowell T. Coggeshall, February 6, 1962, Beadle Records, Box 128, Folder 5, SCRC; President Beadle received a number of letters and telegrams from across the nation. Two examples would be alumnus Laurence R. Veysey's letter (Laurence R. Veysey to George Beadle, February 6, 1962, Beadle Records, Box 265, Folder 2, SCRC) and University of Wisconsin student Roy Woods's telegram (Roy Woods to George Beadle, February 7, 1962, Beadle Records, Box 265, Folder 3, SCRC).

On February 19, 1962, the housing report from the three-person committee of Hauser, Shultz, and Dunham was presented to Beadle. Three days later, a discussion of neighborhood problems was held at the Quadrangle Club with local and state leaders, such as State Representative Abner J. Mikva and the executive director of the Chicago Commission on Human Relations Edward Marciniak. In March, the faculty committee released its twelve-thousand-word housing report, which offered a detailed, fact-finding account of university-owned buildings and occupancy by race. For instance, south of the Midway, UChicago owned seventeen buildings, but only four had Black and white residents living together. Similar segregated trends were present across Hyde Park as well. The report also offered nearly a dozen recommendations, including the "present administrative arrangements for controlling on and off campus residential property be changed."[107]

The report helped bring closure to the sit-in and begin the process of changing university policy. Campus officials spent the week following release of the housing report settling their debts from the sit-in. Beadle was informed that the Dean of Students' office had been charged $1,950.53 by the buildings and grounds department for the additional security for the Administration Building, and the university legal counsel's office had received a $1,000 invoice for outside legal counsel. It was a small reminder that campus officials' concern over the symbolic cost of bad publicity was only one expense alongside the actual cost of the sit-in.[108]

Ultimately, on April 14, 1962, the truest goal of the student demonstrations was realized when the UChicago trustee committee on administration adopted a new statement regarding rental policy, which read: "All housing properties of the university, whether operated as commercial properties, or specifically for housing of students and faculty, are available for university students or faculty members regardless of race or creed." The trustees also addressed the deteriorating properties acquired by the university, noting that they were the only university-owned housing properties available to the general public, and that they would also eventually be "integrated" if the university decided to retain

107. Summary of February 9–March 6, 1962, Diary of the Sit-ins, Beadle Records, Box 128, Folder 5, SCRC; Abner J. Mikva to George W. Beadle, February 28, 1962, Beadle Records, Box 264, Folder 14, SCRC; George W. Beadle to Edward Marciniak, March 6, 1962, Beadle Records, Box 265, Folder 2, SCRC; Report of the Faculty Committee on Rental Policies, March 6, 1962, Beadle Records, Box 128, Folder 5, SCRC; "Housing Report Given to Beadle," *Chicago Maroon*, March 7, 1962; "Faculty Reports on Housing," *Hyde Park Herald*, March 14, 1962.

108. James E. Newman to Warner Wick, March 16, 1962; Warner Wick to George Beadle, March 19, 1962; Walter V. Leen to Ray Brown, March 19, 1962; Ray Brown to Warner Wick, March 23, 1962; all four in Beadle Records, Box 264, Folder 14, SCRC.

these buildings. A new policy was now on the record after a six-month ordeal forced Beadle to revisit the university's decades-long direct and indirect involvement with Chicago's segregation.[109]

Conclusion

The actions of UChicago academic leaders reflect the views of the broader coalition of urban college presidents regarding housing discrimination. College presidents engaged in systemic discrimination against Black people and other minoritized racial and ethnic groups. Academic leaders prepared and executed self-serving initiatives that harmed the same communities they publicly claimed to value. As racial violence resounded from the Jim Crow South, provoking thousands of Black families to migrate, college presidents endorsed similar racist tactics as the Black population increased across the Midwest, the Northeast, and the West. The generous funding of white neighborhood associations' restrictive racial covenants meant academic leaders were partially to blame for housing discrimination. Therefore, as federal policies maintained segregated cities, college presidents willingly steered the local execution of government programs while boasting that their universities, unlike segregated southern institutions, welcomed scholars regardless of race, color, or creed. Furthermore, mass media helped college presidents advance institution-serving goals and, in the case of UChicago chancellor Lawrence A. Kimpton, favor publicity over listening to community.

The University of Chicago also exemplifies college presidents' enduring disdain for student activism that confronts racism. The students' protests with South Side Black residents were an extension of the broader Black Freedom Movement, but UChicago leaders dismissed racism as a southern problem. This was another error of academic leaders who did not view students or local Black residents as equal partners in the educational enterprise. Therefore, college presidents dismissed the questions until they became too loud to ignore and then focused on the desire for students to practice civility instead of on the racist practices of the university. This became a common approach of the self-proclaimed liberal university: convince the public that the issue at hand was about anything other than racism. Yet, urban redevelopment engineering was racial at its core. By 1964, Columbia University and its president Grayson Kirk faced the charge that "in its expansion, Columbia has willfully discriminated against Negroes and Puerto Ricans." This followed the eviction of Black and Puerto Rican residents from university-owned properties in New York's

---

109. Trustee Adopted Statement, April 14, 1962, Beadle Records, Box 264, Folder 14, SCRC.

Morningside Heights. But charges aside, what these administrators said among themselves is perhaps most telling.[110]

At UChicago, while President Beadle issued race-neutral public statements, behind the scenes W. V. Morgenstern, secretary of the university, offered a more honest account. "The University has been engaged in the difficult work of saving the community and preventing its becoming another Negro slum, as so many others have," Morgenstern stated. The actions of academic leaders were explicitly about race, specifically Black people. The presidents of the leading urban universities perpetuated white supremacy, thus ignoring the social neglect that caused urban decay. This furthered the spatial violence and disenfranchisement outside of the white-enforced boundaries that Black people could not access at a time when Beadle and other college presidents could have vouched for millions of dollars to dismantle discrimination. Instead, they used the problem they helped create as a rationale for displacing rather than embracing those communities. Yet, whereas UChicago was a private institution doing public harm, the figurative and literal dismissal of Black people was also occurring in California within a state-supported university system that stifled racial advancement in the West.[111]

---

110. "Cite Columbia for Bias," *Chicago Defender*, March 14–20, 1964. For more about Columbia's expansion, see Bradley, *Harlem vs. Columbia University*.

111. W. V. Morgenstern to Avery Colt, February 5, 1962, Beadle Records, Box 265, Folder 3, SCRC. Historian Matthew D. Lassiter has argued that "racial inequality is a constant theme in American history, but the manifestations of racism are evolving and multifaceted, refracted through frameworks such as economics and geography." For more, see Lassiter, *Silent Majority*, pp. 4–7.

3

"Segregation Is Immoral"

RACE, UNIVERSITY SYSTEMS, AND BUREAUCRATIC RESISTANCE

"MY ONLY HESITANCY in the matter came out of the question as to whether I would really have the local administrative authority and flexibility to do the kind of strong and sound administrative job that quite obviously UCLA now requires." It was March 21, 1960, three days after Franklin D. Murphy accepted the chancellorship at the University of California, Los Angeles (UCLA), when he shared this concern with regent Edward W. Carter. Murphy wanted complete autonomy in his future role, but the history of the UC system presidents suggested that may not have been possible. This left Murphy uncertain about who really controlled the campus he had just agreed to lead.[1]

University of California presidents had long assessed students' activities based on what they deemed appropriate behavior rather than whether students learned about democratic processes or engaged with social issues. For instance, President Benjamin Ide Wheeler, hired in 1899, included student discipline and student government updates in his annual reports to the governor, and administrators grew more assertive from one president to the next. By World War II, student autonomy was further limited. "No individual student or student organization will be granted use of university facilities to carry on propaganda for or against a cause or movement having no direct concern with student affairs on campus," President Robert Gordon Sproul told students in November 1940. "Student organizations with outside affiliations

---

1. Franklin D. Murphy to Edward W. Carter, March 21, 1960, Franklin D. Murphy Papers, Box 4, Folder 19, UCLA Library Special Collections, Charles E. Young Research Library (collection and location hereafter cited as Murphy Papers and UCLA).

requiring promotion of specific causes or movements, therefore, should not be given official recognition by the student government."[2]

This policy resulted in student groups, such as campus chapters of the NAACP, being shunned by UC's academic leaders; however, UC presidents' ability to enforce such regulations became more complicated as access to higher education expanded dramatically after the war. The postwar university required a new organizational structure for efficiency, and in 1952, the UC system—a single university with multiple campuses located across the state—implemented a president-chancellor administrative hierarchy. This decision designated at each campus a chancellor who reported to the system president located in Berkeley. The president then led a burgeoning university system as academic leaders prioritized massive federal funding for research during the Cold War and the subsequent expansion of the knowledge industry. In turn, amid fears of communism, the president and chancellors further restricted campus activities that conflicted with the research enterprise and UC's role as the leading military contractor among US universities.[3]

This president-chancellor structure functioned with limited administrative conflict until Sproul retired in 1958 and Berkeley chancellor Clark Kerr was promoted to system president. As Kerr ascended to the presidency, he and state officials crafted the California Master Plan for Higher Education, touted as a plan that would create the premier US higher education system. This created statewide conflict as the plan outlined three college systems for the state—one for two-year colleges, another for state colleges, and a third for the University of California campuses. New concerns emerged, including many with racial implications: was this tiering higher education? Would this funnel minoritized racial and ethnic groups to the two other systems and away from the UC campuses? As state officials and residents debated the Master Plan, Murphy's immediate support of UCLA students' civil rights activities, alongside Kerr's

---

2. Robert G. Sproul Statement, November 14, 1940, University of California, Los Angeles, Office of the Chancellor–Administrative Files of Franklin D. Murphy, Box 122, Folder 246–Student Government (Kerr Directives), UCLA (collection and folder hereafter cited as Chancellor Files–Murphy and 246–Kerr Directives).

3. On the adoption of chancellors in the UC system, see Christine Lee, "A History of UC Berkeley's Chancellors," *Daily Californian*, July 4, 2017. Also see "Allen Wins Top U Post," *Daily Bruin*, December 17, 1951 (newspaper hereafter cited as *DB*); and Lou Schultz, "Chancellor Selection Evokes Approving Campus Comment," *DB*, December 18, 1951. Regarding the University of California as a university military contractor, see Murch, *Living for the City*, pp. 73–74. On the impact of the Cold War on higher education expansion, see O'Mara, *Cities of Knowledge*, pp. 36–55.

pushback, demonstrated how a large system of higher education, different from individual institutions, grappled with leaders who had different ideas on the role of higher education in society.

The Authority to Lead

Franklin D. Murphy was born on January 29, 1916, and grew up in Kansas City, Missouri, where he attended a private boys' prep school, before enrolling at the University of Kansas (KU) only forty miles from home. After graduation, he briefly studied at Germany's University of Göttingen before enrolling in the University of Pennsylvania School of Medicine—his father's alma mater. Graduating at the top of his medical school class in 1941, Murphy completed his residency at the Penn Hospital followed by a fellowship year there in cardiology. Then, in 1944, as a captain in the US Army Medical Corps, he spent two years conducting medical research for the federal government's Office of Scientific Research and Development during World War II before being discharged with the Army's Commendation Ribbon and Citation.[4]

In 1946, Murphy returned to KU as a clinical faculty member while he practiced medicine. By 1948, his knack for administrative leadership quickly elevated his status on campus despite his own reservations about his youth, and at age thirty-two, he was approached about serving as dean of the KU School of Medicine. Then, following three successful years as dean, the thirty-five-year-old Murphy was tapped by the KU regents to become chancellor beginning in 1951. Murphy immediately sought to have KU mirror the universities that he experienced at Penn and the other Ivy League institutions in the Northeast, but he did not agitate against the local social norms in Kansas to make it also mirror the cosmopolitan northeastern cities in terms of race.[5]

For example, in April 1948, the KU chapter of CORE held a sit-in demonstration at a segregated café. This involved some thirty students, a third of whom were Black, but other KU students did not rally behind their peers' effort to desegregate Lawrence, Kansas. Instead, a number of KU football players forcibly removed the demonstrators as local police watched. This occurred during Murphy's first year as medical dean and exhibited the campus ethos

4. For more about Murphy, particularly his educational background, see Davis, *The Culture Broker*, pp. 1–11. Regarding his post–medical school rise to KU chancellor, see Franklin D. Murphy, interview by Deborah L. Hickle, January 19, 1990, University of Kansas Medical Center Archives, Oral History Project; Murphy's medical career highlights were provided to Clark Kerr for an appointment on the medical faculty. For more, see Franklin D. Murphy to Clark Kerr, March 30, 1960, Murphy Papers, Box 5, Folder 3, UCLA.

5. Murphy, interview by Hinkle, January 19, 1990; Murphy to Kerr, March 30, 1960.

around race. Therefore, when he became chancellor, Murphy only made modest decisions in terms of race by welcoming prominent Black speakers to campus and opening the way to recruit Black student-athletes. Additionally, through KU's membership in the Association of American Universities, a consortium of US and Canadian research universities, Murphy developed relationships with Ivy League presidents—A. Whitney Griswold at Yale, Nathan M. Pusey at Harvard, Henry Wriston at Brown, and Harold Dodds at Princeton—as KU's national academic profile rose alongside its young star chancellor.[6]

In 1957, however, the slow rise toward a more progressive KU stalled when George Docking took office as Kansas governor. Docking's political beliefs represented the prominence of anti-intellectualism during the 1950s. Richard Hofstadter, the historian who won the 1964 Pulitzer Prize for *Anti-intellectualism in American Life*, took to task US senator Joseph R. McCarthy (R-WI) for his efforts to expose communists within the federal government and elsewhere. "Primarily it was McCarthyism which aroused the fear that the critical mind was at a ruinous discount in this country," Hofstadter argued. "Of course, intellectuals were not the only targets of McCarthy's constant detonations—he was after bigger game—but intellectuals were in the line of fire." A growing segment of elected officials catered to many Americans' fears and promoted distrust of academics perceived as sympathetic to communist views or as outright communists, and Hofstadter explained that some "university presidents" had "swelled into a national chorus of self-reproach," while other presidents were focused on developing "a university of which the football team could be proud."[7]

Docking embraced the postwar apprehension toward academia, and the governor's attacks slowly evolved from complaints about KU to personal gripes about the chancellor. For example, on February 28, 1960, Docking attacked Murphy in the *Great Bend Tribune*, a Kansas newspaper, saying that the chancellor did the state more harm than good. Docking felt that KU academics were overpaid, that higher education squandered taxpayer dollars, and that the chancellor was the ringleader for the waste. The governor criticized Murphy for his $22,000 salary, free house, car, and frequent "free junkets

6. On the KU CORE sit-in, see Taylor, *In Search of the Racial Frontier*, pp. 283–284. On the early half of Murphy's KU chancellorship and his friendship with Ivy League presidents, see Davis, *Culture Broker*, pp. 10–11.

7. On anti-intellectualism and its prominence in relation to college presidents in the 1950s, see Hofstadter, *Anti-Intellectualism in American Life*, quotes on pp. 3, 5, 301. Hofstadter added, "The universities, particularly the better-known universities, were constantly marked out as targets by right-wing critics," p. 13.

around the country." Docking continued, "He's in South America now. I think he is getting enough. We can get plenty of others as good for less."[8]

That attack was the last straw for Murphy. As chair of the Commission on Higher Education in the American Republic, Murphy was in South America in a role organized by the Carnegie Corporation at the request of the US Department of the State, but his activities as an international education leader meant little to the governor. Murphy regularly requested more state aid to grow KU into a premier research university, while Docking trimmed appropriations for what he deemed excess. "For four years, I have patiently and deliberately refused to respond to this type of attack," Murphy told Ray Evans, chair of the KU Board of Regents. "However, I am only human. My patience has come to an end. . . . I have been as patient as I think is humanly possible."[9]

By this point, Murphy's work with the Carnegie Corporation had introduced him to Clark Kerr, president of the UC system. Therefore, while Docking's attacks worsened, Kerr spent the 1959–60 academic year convincing Murphy to accept the UCLA chancellorship. "This is probably the most difficult decision Mrs. Murphy and I will ever have to make," Murphy said of his KU resignation, noting that he and Judy Murphy, a Vassar alumna, had grown up in the region and he was a KU alumnus. "Certainly, no decision in the future could ever involve as much soul-searching." Yet, on March 15, 1960, Murphy turned his attention west toward UCLA's "unlimited possibilities." He added: "Never before in history have our institutions of higher education been so crucial to our national security, to our economic, social, and cultural development." Thus, leaving KU was "at once a difficult but exciting task which I accept with enthusiasm."[10]

In Kansas, Murphy was beloved by KU regents, students, and alumni. Harry Valentine, a KU regent, said the loss of Murphy was "a major tragedy, not only to the university but to all education in Kansas." He attributed Murphy's resignation partly to the "frequent attacks made by Governor Docking."

8. For Murphy's reflections on his conflict with Docking, see Franklin D. Murphy, interview by James V. Mink, October-December 1973, UCLA Center for Oral History Research. The details of the *Great Bend Tribune* article are explained in Murphy's three-page letter to the chair of the KU Board of Regents. For more, see Franklin D. Murphy to Ray Evans, March 12, 1960, Murphy Papers, Box 3, Folder 14, UCLA.

9. Murphy to Evans, March 12, 1960.

10. Regarding the pre-UCLA Murphy and Kerr relationship, see Davis, *Culture Broker*, p. 26. On Murphy quote about the difficulty of leaving KU, see Statement of Dr. Franklin D. Murphy, n.d., Murphy Papers, Box 4, Folder 16, UCLA. On Murphy's UCLA quotes, see Franklin D. Murphy statement, March 15, 1960, Murphy Papers, Box 4, Folder 16, UCLA.

Henry A. Bubb, another KU regent, said losing Murphy was worse than the most brutal snowstorms or massive floods common to Kansas. Individual regents' reactions aside, the KU Board of Regents also passed a resolution stating that it accepted Murphy's resignation "with deep regret; and that the board unanimously [expressed] its appreciation of his superb contribution in developing with high vision and sacrificial vigor a center of sound learning for the State of Kansas and the board [wished] him continued success and happiness for himself and his family." KU students felt the same and assembled at Murphy's home when rumors swirled earlier that he was leaving, and on March 18, 1960, thousands of students crowded into KU's Hoch Auditorium for a student-organized convocation to honor him.[11]

While he was met with the cheers on campus, KU alumni flooded him with praise from afar. William S. Koester, a KU alumnus residing in Los Angeles, said, "I know my fellow Jayhawkers share my keen appreciation for the tremendous stature your leadership has given to KU all over the world during your tenure there." Clifford L. Gilles, a KU alumnus in Beverly Hills, assessed, "UCLA is very fortunate in getting such a man as you, with a background of many accomplishments and proven administrative ability to carry on the aims of one of the greatest universities in the nation." Theno F. Graves, president of the KU Alumni Association of Greater Los Angeles, added, "It is with mixed feelings that I congratulate you for at the same time I hate to see Kansas University lose such a leader." He then invited Murphy to meet with the KU alumni in Los Angeles so they could honor him. "Kansas' loss is California's gain," Graves surmised.[12]

In California, Murphy's reputation in Kansas stirred nearly universal excitement. "Committee of the regents and the faculty considered more than 100 leading American educators for this highly important post," Kerr told the *Los Angeles Times*. "Chancellor Murphy's name was enthusiastically endorsed in all quarters." Also, the *Los Angeles Examiner* noted, "Although only 44, Murphy has served as University of Kansas chancellor since 1951 and is known widely as a top university administrator." The same newspaper then dubbed

11. On Regent Valentine's quotes, see "Murphy Quits as Head of K.U.," *Clay Center Dispatch*, March 17, 1960. For Regent Bubb's take on losing Murphy, see Abrahamson, *Building Home*, p. 205; Kansas Board of Regents resolution, March 21, 1960, Murphy Papers, Box 3, Folder 14, UCLA. On KU students assembling at Murphy's home, see Davis, *Culture Broker*, pp. 21–22; Murphy Speech in Hoch Auditorium, March 18, 1960, Murphy Papers, Box 57, Folder 8, UCLA.

12. William S. Koester to Franklin D. Murphy, March 22, 1960, Murphy Papers, Box 5, Folder 3, UCLA; Clifford L. Gilles to Franklin D. Murphy, March 23, 1960, Murphy Papers, Box 4, Folder 23, UCLA; Theno F. Graves to Franklin D. Murphy, April 28, 1960, Murphy Papers, Box 4, Folder 23, UCLA.

Murphy "UCLA's youthful new chief executive." Academic leaders and state officials also received him warmly. "I want you to know that I welcome [your hire] with all my heart," said J. E. Wallace Sterling, president of Stanford University, "and will look forward to having you that much closer as a colleague and friend." Likewise, Thomas Rees (D-Los Angeles), the state assemblyman who represented UCLA's district, told Murphy that his "fine reputation" preceded him.[13]

But the national circle of confidants Murphy developed as KU chancellor warned him against accepting the UCLA chancellorship. This included Wriston and Dodds, who had recently retired as the presidents of Brown and Princeton, respectively. Murphy was also advised against the UCLA job by John Gardner, head of the Carnegie Corporation, and O. Meredith Wilson, outgoing president of the University of Oregon, who was transitioning into the presidency at the University of Minnesota. These friends, all distinguished leaders in higher education and well aware of the national landscape, considered the UCLA chancellor to be powerless. The title "chancellor" may have been the same as at KU, but UC's system required campus chancellors to report to a president, not directly to a governing board. Therefore, it was a well-known fact among college presidents that all UC decisions came from Berkeley. The job was a trap, they warned, but this intrigued Murphy even more.[14]

Murphy visited California multiple times during the 1959–60 academic year while being recruited to UCLA. He wanted assurances that he would have the authority to lead, and Kerr and UC regents promised Murphy he would have

13. Dick Turpin, "Kansan Will Become New UCLA Chancellor," *Los Angeles Times*, March 17, 1960 (newspaper hereafter cited as *LA Times*); "New UCLA Chancellor Named," *Los Angeles Examiner*, March 17, 1960; "Murphy Seeking 'Quality': New UCLA Chief Tells Philosophy," *Los Angeles Examiner*, March 17, 1960; J. E. Wallace Sterling to Franklin D. Murphy, March 23, 1960, Murphy Papers, Box 5, Folder 11, UCLA. Sterling was also deeply interested in the UC system. He believed Stanford had a responsibility to support the state-supported system despite being a private university. For more, see Lyman, *Stanford in Turmoil*, pp. 12–13; Thomas M. Rees to Franklin D. Murphy, April 12, 1960, Murphy Papers, Box 5, Folder 10, UCLA.

14. Murphy offered this summary of the advice higher education leaders provided him about the UCLA chancellorship: "In effect, they said, 'Franklin, it's an impossible job. And the reason it's impossible is (a) the chancellor is powerless, relatively. There's a strong tradition in the University of California of faculty control over the substantive issues in education on the one hand; and, administratively, the Berkeley operation runs the place. You're far away, and the north doesn't like the south anyway. There's a long history of Berkeley trying to keep UCLA down, both in administrative as well as the faculty levels, and you will not have even the administrative independence. So don't take it.'" For more, see Murphy, interview by Mink, October-December 1973.

the freedom to grow UCLA into its own premiere university out of Berkeley's shadow. Therefore, on March 18, 1960, Murphy formally accepted the chancellorship at UCLA, and he immediately wooed the Los Angeles media. Following his introductory press conference on April 18, 1960, journalists mumbled favorable remarks among themselves. "UCLA is lucky to have Murphy," one reporter said. "A solid guy," was another comment, followed by: "The kind of a leader UCLA deserves."[15]

Behind the scenes, however, Murphy reminded UC system leaders of their agreement. "I am sure you know that one of the great inducements in coming to the University of California at Los Angles is your presence in the presidency of the university," Murphy told Kerr after accepting the position. "As I told you before, you have my pledge of unswerving loyalty and support, and your pledge of the same to me was I suspect the final determinant in my decision." Three days later, Murphy wrote several UC regents individually, emphasizing that the decentralization of the UC system was the determining factor in his acceptance. He credited regent Dorothy B. Chandler's support for local authority as "one of the most persuasive factors" in his decision, and he thanked regent Edwin W. Pauley for his commitment to ensure the same. Lastly, to Donald H. McLaughlin, the chair of the board of regents when Murphy was hired, "I needed to be absolutely sure that in the reorganization of the university the adequate administrative tools, such as the necessary local authority, responsibility, and administrative flexibility, would be available."[16]

Meanwhile, Murphy's hire coincided with the California Master Plan for Higher Education being pushed through the state legislature. The plan would ultimately create three higher education systems in the state: the existing UC system, a state college system, and a two-year college system. However, there was an ongoing debate during the spring of 1960 over the merits of the plan. In January 1960, UCLA's *Daily Bruin* student journalists interrogated the negative impact the plan could have on students. The University of California

15. Franklin D. Murphy to Raymond B. Allen, April 8, 1960, Murphy Papers, Box 4, Folder 17, UCLA. For the quotes from Los Angeles journalists, see Andrew Hamilton to Franklin D. Murphy, April 22, 1960, Murphy Papers, Box 5, Folder 3, UCLA.

16. Franklin D. Murphy to Clark Kerr, March 18, 1960, Murphy Papers, Box 5, Folder 3, UCLA; Franklin D. Murphy to Dorothy B. Chandler (addressed to Mrs. Norman Chandler), March 21, 1960, Murphy Papers, Box 4, Folder 19, UCLA; Franklin D. Murphy to Edwin W. Pauley, March 21, 1960, Murphy Papers, Box 5, Folder 9, UCLA; Franklin D. Murphy to Donald H. McLaughlin, March 21, 1960, Murphy Papers, Box 5, Folder 5, UCLA. McLaughlin was chair of the board of regents from 1958 to 1960, according to biographical information accompanying the Donald H. McLaughlin papers housed at Bancroft Library, University of California, Berkeley.

accepted the top 15 percent of high school graduates in California, but that would change to 12.5 percent under the new plan. Other questions included whether UC would implement its own admissions exams alongside the College Board entrance exam, and whether transferring from a two-year college into UC would become nearly impossible. Additionally, although free tuition for California residents was a hallmark of the plan, student fees could increase significantly. In February 1960, at the state capitol in Sacramento, Assemblyman Bruce F. Allen (R-San Jose) offered the first legislative opposition to the Master Plan. In a four-page statement, Allen argued that the state legislature should not approve the plan, but if passed, he predicted, "The college door will be nailed firmly shut for many thousands of California youngsters."[17]

The criticisms of the plan actually came to fruition. By the mid-1960s, the stricter admissions criteria led to a decline in the number of Black students enrolled on some four-year campuses and funneled them to the two-year campuses, but in 1960, the critiques with regard to college access were ignored in light of UC administrators' larger goals. The University of California already led all others with the most military contracts, and Kerr later coined the term "multiversities" to capture the university's multifaceted responsibilities. This made a comprehensive higher education plan of utmost importance to UC leaders. Despite the critiques of the Master Plan, especially as it pertained to equity, McLaughlin minimized these concerns to Murphy. "The bill will undoubtedly be emphatically opposed by some groups led by a few ambitious state college presidents," McLaughlin told Murphy, "but I doubt if they will prevail."[18]

Hearing such conviction from McLaughlin, the regent chair, on April 22, 1960, Murphy told California governor Edmund "Pat" Brown that the Master Plan could make California an intellectual hub. This hub would be anchored

17. Mort Saltzman, "The Master Plan—What about the Students?" *DB*, January 6, 1960. On the state assemblyman's Master Plan critiques, see "Master Plan Attacked by Legislator Allen," *DB*, February 15, 1960; and Mort Saltzman, "Rep Views Master Plan," *DB*, February 16, 1960.

18. On the impact of the Master Plan, see Biondi, *Black Revolution on Campus*, pp. 43, 51. Biondi stated that "Black students were overwhelmingly relegated to junior colleges, the lowest rung" after the plan was implemented. Also see Murch, *Living for the City*, p. 98. Murch explained that "the plan exacerbated long-standing divisions of race and class between tiers." For a synopsis of the Master Plan and Murphy's introduction to the plan, see Davis, *Culture Broker*, pp. 26–27; Donald H. McLaughlin to Franklin D. Murphy, March 31, 1960, Murphy Papers, Box 5, Folder 5, UCLA. For a detailed overview of multi-versities, see O'Mara, *Cities of Knowledge*, especially pp. 58–94. In 1963, Clark Kerr would deliver a Harvard lecture about multi-versities. For more, see Preface to Harvard's Godkin Lectures, April 23, 1963, Clark Kerr Personal and Professional Papers, Carton 29, Folder 39, Bancroft Library, University of California, Berkeley.

by Stanford, Berkeley, and Cal Tech, and would "more than match the traditional educational supremacy of the Harvard-MIT-Yale-Columbia-Princeton axis." Murphy saw the plan, in its totality with the state and two-year colleges, as one that guaranteed "the highest quality of education" and "opportunity for all young people." To emphasize this belief, Murphy used more abrupt language when describing his hope that UCLA would become equal to the Berkeley campus. "I am sure you realize that the old super-centralized operation under former President Sproul made the position of the chancellor at UCLA an impossible one," Murphy told regent John E. Canaday. "The only way it can cease being the little brother of Berkeley and become a co-equal twin is if the institution . . . is 'given the bit.' That, I think, will be the case. At least I have staked my future on it."[19]

Murphy went into the UCLA job betting on himself. He believed he could mold UCLA into a university of distinction if it could shake being known simply as the southern branch of Berkeley. It was a commuter school with no national academic reputation and only 125 students who resided on campus, but "the tremendous and unlimited creative educational opportunities at UCLA proved to be an irresistible magnet." This phrase, "irresistible magnet," became a fixture in Murphy's description of his future home. He was drawn to Los Angeles because of its academic promise and social potential, the latter of which made UCLA students especially interested in the new chancellor. Murphy's reputation as a dynamic leader, one beloved by those at KU, was welcomed by several UCLA students just as civil rights questions took hold of the campus.[20]

Black Los Angeles, a Student Awakening, and a New Chancellor

In March 1960, when Murphy was announced as the new chancellor, southern Black students challenging segregation, alongside California's racial discrimination, inspired UCLA students to act. The student actions renewed questions about system restrictions that banned student organizing around off-campus

19. Franklin D. Murphy to Edmund C. Brown, April 22, 1960, Murphy Papers, Box 4, Folder 18, UCLA; Franklin D. Murphy to John E. Canaday, March 25, 1960, Murphy Papers, Box 4, Folder 19, UCLA.

20. On UCLA's commuter campus status, see Franklin D. Murphy to Department Chairs, March 24, 1961, Chancellor Files–Murphy, Box 1, Folder 3, UCLA. Murphy's description of the UCLA opportunity as an "irresistible magnet" was repeated throughout his personal correspondence about his chancellorship; see, e.g., Franklin D. Murphy to Theno F. Graves, May 13, 1960, Murphy Papers, Box 4, Folder 23, UCLA.

causes, but Murphy represented a notable change in tradition among UCLA administration. Robert Singleton, a Black UCLA student at the time, said the new chancellor "presented a problem" for some conservative administrators. "When Murphy accepted the position," Singleton observed, "Dean of Students Milton Hahn abruptly resigned." Those administrators perceived Murphy as a liberal who mingled with the Ivy League elites and attended invitation-only events with East Coast foundation officers and newspaper editors. But what some campus officials saw as a threat was welcomed by those UCLA students who wanted societal change. Therefore, students' emergent civil rights activities paired perfectly with the arrival of Murphy—an advocate for racial equality.[21]

The civil rights demands made by UCLA students in 1960, however, are linked to decades-long struggles for racial equality in California. Black Americans had long envisioned the West as a racial oasis. It was perceived as more tolerant of Blackness than the US South, with its legal racial segregation, and offering more opportunities than the de facto segregation in the Midwest and Northeast. At the turn of the twentieth century, the eminent scholar W. E. B. Du Bois wrote of his visit to Southern California, "There would seem to be no

21. Robert Singleton, a UCLA student in the early 1960s, said Murphy's hire "presented a problem for some of the more conservative administrators at UCLA." For more, see Singleton, "The Struggles for Racial Justice at UCLA," p. 2. For more on Dean Milton Hahn's retirement, see "Sherwood Named to New Post," *DB*, September 13, 1960. The conservative administrators' resignations should also be contextualized within a broader political ethos prominent in the West. Lisa McGirr explained that many conservative Californians did not like the federal government's "perceived allegiance" to the East Coast elites. For more, see McGirr, *Suburban Warriors*, p. 56. As previously explained in this chapter, Murphy frequently communicated with friends and colleagues at Ivy League institutions; see, e.g., Thomas E. Crooks to Franklin D. Murphy, June 1, 1960, Murphy Papers, Box 4, Folder 19, UCLA; and Felix C. Robb to Franklin D. Murphy, March 25, 1960, Murphy Papers, Box 5, Folder 10, UCLA. Regarding Murphy's access to private foundation's invitation-only events, see Carnegie Luncheon Guest List, May 4, 1960, Murphy Papers, Box 3, Folder 14, UCLA. On Murphy's relationships with *New York Times* and *Newsweek* editors, see Franklin D. Murphy to Fred M. Hechinger, May 17, 1960, Murphy Papers, Box 3, Folder 14, UCLA; and Franklin D. Murphy to Sheward Hagerty, May 17, 1960, Murphy Papers, Box 3, Folder 14, UCLA. Kurt Edward Kemper also wrote of Murphy's hire: "In their struggle against the Kerr Directives, the students found an unlikely ally in the Office of the Chancellor. It is not entirely coincidental that UCLA's larger political awakening paralleled the arrival of Franklin D. Murphy as the school's new chancellor in 1960." For more, see Kemper, "The Smell of Roses," p. 324; Perlstein, "Minds Stayed on Freedom," pp. 33–65. This chapter is an intellectual history of the ideology that guided the Black freedom struggle, specifically in the SNCC and the Black Panthers, and provides an understanding of the connection between the southern movement and California.

limit to your opportunities, your possibilities." What Du Bois explained captured the hopes and dreams that led thousands of Black people to move to Los Angeles in the early 1900s, and UCLA itself played into this perception. Before Augustus Hawkins became the first Black person from California to serve in Congress, he graduated from UCLA in 1929, where he and a group of his UCLA friends committed themselves to politics. Shortly after Hawkins graduated, UCLA's star football players—Jackie Robinson, Woody Strode, and Kenny Washington—furthered this view of California, as most desegregated universities did not have that many Black players in pivotal positions on teams during the late 1930s and early 1940s.[22]

Aside from this perception, the reality of California's racism grew evident during World War II. More than three hundred thousand Black people moved to California. In total, roughly a half a million Black people moved to western states during the war and the postwar boom. Shortages in the workforce led many factory and shipyard owners to hire Black workers, but as more Black people settled in the West, racial discrimination in urban housing markets, employment, and education became more pervasive. By the close of the decade, California had established itself as just as racist as any other state, considering Japanese internment and the Zoot Suit Riots against Mexican Americans during the 1940s.[23]

In Los Angeles, racial progress swung back and forth thereafter. During the 1950s, the NAACP emerged as the leading civil rights organization in the city as it made significant challenges to racism. A Black surgeon was appointed in the city in 1954, and during the annual American Federation of Labor (AFL) convention held in Los Angeles the same year, A. Philip Randolph introduced a resolution to ban segregation in federal public housing. Yet, by 1956, twenty-two sororities at UCLA withdrew from the Student Legislative Council (SLC)—a move that signaled their disagreement with a broader nonsouthern university movement to have white fraternities and sororities remove discriminatory clauses. Ironically, UCLA began offering Black

22. On W. E. B. Du Bois and the influx of Blacks to Los Angeles between 1900 and World War I, see Lonnie G. Bunch III, "'The Greatest State for the Negro': Jefferson L. Edmonds, Black Propagandist of the California Dream," in de Graaf, Mulroy, and Taylor, *Seeking El Dorado*, pp. 129–131. On Hawkins and UCLA friends seeking to impact politics, see Douglas Flamming, "Becoming Democrats: Liberal Politics and the African American Community in Los Angeles, 1930–1965," in de Graaf, Mulroy, and Taylor, *Seeking El Dorado*, p. 285. On the Robinson, Strode, and Washington impact on race relations, see Horne, *Fire This Time*, p. 34.

23. Regarding the data on the increase in Black California residents, see Taylor, *In Search of the Racial Frontier*, pp. 251–252, 278–279. Taylor also discussed the significance of the Japanese internment and Zoot Suit riots. On housing discrimination in Los Angeles, particularly in the years following World War II, see Sides, *L.A. City Limits*, pp. 95–130.

literature courses, making it one of the first predominantly white universities to add the topic to its curriculum. UCLA, like the broader Los Angeles area, was in a constant state of contradiction and conflict as residents approached the next gubernatorial election.[24]

In 1958, labor and employment measures were on the line as Californians made their way to the polls. For that election, Black and white working-class voters rallied behind the NAACP slogan "Keep Mississippi Out of California." The results were historic and a stark shift from the Republican-led state government of previous decades. Edmund "Pat" Brown became only the second Democratic governor of the state in that century, and both houses of the state legislature were held by Democrats for the first time since the late 1800s; however, these state-level victories did not immediately change race relations in Los Angeles. By 1960, most of Los Angeles's 334,916 Black residents were still restricted by racial practices in housing and employment. But as historian Josh Sides explained, Black youth born or raised in the city "compared their opportunities not to what blacks in other cities had, nor to the opportunities their parents had, but rather to the opportunities enjoyed by their white peers in Los Angeles." Black youth were less tolerant of and more vocal about local racial inequalities, and the stirring civil rights activities in the South sparked action among many frustrated with racism in Los Angeles.[25]

In February 1960, UCLA students took issue with racial discrimination in the Westwood neighborhood adjacent to campus. "Some 97 years after Abraham Lincoln signed a paper which led the world to call him the Great Emancipator," the *Daily Bruin* student newspaper reported, "civil rights of Negroes in Westwood are far from assured." Loren Miller, an NAACP attorney, said whites held firm to restrictive covenants that prevented Black people from residing in Westwood. In fact, Miller said, the covenants made it "difficult for a Negro to find even a cellar around here." The racism was so prevalent that

24. On the Los Angeles NAACP, see Sides, *L.A. City Limits*, p. 134. On the Black surgeon, labor resolution, and UCLA sororities, see Collier-Thomas and Franklin, *My Soul Is a Witness*, pp. 3, 13, 42.

25. On the NAACP slogan and cross-racial alliance, see Robert O. Self, "'Negro Leadership and Negro Money'": African American Political Organizing in Oakland before the Panthers," in Theoharis and Woodard, *Freedom North*, p. 108. On Democrats gaining control of state government, see Flamming, "Becoming Democrats," in de Graaf, Mulroy, and Taylor, *Seeking El Dorado*, p. 297. On the number of Black residents in Los Angeles, see Taylor, *In Search of the Racial Frontier*, pp. 286–287; Sides, *L.A. City Limits*, p. 172. Regarding the housing discrimination, see "Los Angeles CORE Stages Housing Sit-in," *Chicago Defender*, March 12, 1962; and "Monterey Highlands Pickets Protest Realty Bias: Council to Back Pickets," *Los Angeles Sentinel*, March 8, 1962 (newspaper hereafter cited as *LA Sentinel*).

Black taxi drivers were not dispatched to certain parts of Los Angeles. UCLA's associate dean of students Byron H. Atkinson agreed that the outlook for housing Black students was grim. "It was impossible for a Negro to room here in 1930," Atkinson said. "It is almost impossible now, except in state-provided housing or rooms provided by the University Cooperative Housing Association." He said the challenge facing UCLA administrators was proving discrimination existed because the local property owners were savvy enough to never admit race was an issue.[26]

The coverage in the *Daily Bruin* was a fairly local concern, but by the end of the month, UCLA students started to contextualize their concerns within the larger movement. On February 27, 1960, dozens of Black college students in Nashville, Tennessee, were arrested for peaceful sit-in demonstrations at segregated lunch counters. A white mob assaulted the Black students before police jailed the demonstrators. Two days later, Berkeley students demonstrated—like those at other nonsouthern universities—in an act of solidarity, and were urged to send telegrams of support to Diane Nash, a Fisk University student and Nashville sit-in leader.[27]

The SLC at UCLA then passed a resolution condemning police actions in Nashville, but that raised questions that concerned UC students. The Kerr Directives, informally named after President Clark Kerr, were updated UC regulations that specified that students and student organizations could neither affiliate with political or religious groups nor take a position on any "off-campus political, religious, economic, international, or other issues of the time." But events in the South pushed UCLA students to challenge these regulations, so the SLC considered its resolution academic in nature, a move used to circumvent the directives.[28]

On March 15, 1960, UCLA students launched the Los Angeles–area student pickets at F. W. Woolworth locations, the same company southern Black

26. Marty Kasindorf, "The Emancipator Hasn't Won Yet," *DB*, February 12, 1960. For more about Westwood within the broader conversation about US housing segregation, see Rothstein, *Color of Law*, p. 81. On racism and Black taxi drivers, see Horne, *Fire This Time*, pp. 35–36.

27. Chuck Rossie, "Students Protest Arrest of Nashville 'Strikers,'" *DB*, March 1, 1960.

28. Alan Rothstein, "SLC Attacks Police Action in Nashville," *DB*, March 3, 1960. On the Kerr Directives, see three separate documents: Regulation on Student Government, Regulation on Use of University Facilities, and Regulation on Student Organizations, October 22, 1959; all located in Chancellor Files–Murphy, Box 122, Folder 246–Kerr Directives, UCLA. Several historians have attributed changes in white students' civil rights engagement to southern Black student activism. For specific examples, see Carson, *In Struggle*, pp. 53–54; Turner, *Sitting In and Speaking Out*, p. 80; and Cohen, *Freedom's Orator*, p. 41. Cohen added that "Berkeley student politics was a strange amalgam of freedom and repression in the early 1960s," noting that the repression came from Kerr. For more, see ibid., p. 75.

students regularly targeted for segregated lunch counter sit-ins. Led by Jesse Morris, a UCLA senior and chair of the Southern California Boycott committee, UCLA and Santa Monica City College students picketed the Santa Monica Woolworth store. Two days later, on March 17, Los Angeles State College students demonstrated at the downtown Woolworth store. The students encouraged others to boycott Woolworth stores until its national headquarters implemented a national policy against segregation. The three student co-chairs—Dave Axelrod and Robert Farrell of UCLA and Walter Davis of LA State—wanted Los Angeles residents to "help in our fight for universal equality." By March 26, seventeen Woolworth and S. H. Kress stores in Los Angeles were being picketed by students from UCLA, LA State, the University of Southern California, and Los Angeles City College. Their demonstrations across the city were supported by CORE and the NAACP.[29]

The UC students' support of the southern sit-ins reignited the debate over the Kerr Directives. In January 1960, system administrators loosened their interpretation of the directives, allowing students to engage in activities related to off-campus issues, but the active support of the sit-ins forced them to retreat on their looser interpretations. By April 1960, the *Daily Californian* editor in Berkeley was "appalled" that UC academic leaders determined that the National Student Association (NSA) was unable to take a stance on off-campus issues. The NSA, a national student organization that universities joined as members, had a history of encouraging student bodies to aid movements over international issues, such as those in Algeria and South Africa. Yet, when it came to actively encouraging US students to aid the southern student movement, the directives were strictly interpreted to include the NSA. This perplexed the Berkeley students who, in May 1960, captured the nation's attention for disrupting a House Un-American Activities Committee (HUAC) meeting in downtown San Francisco.[30]

29. For information regarding the March 15 and March 17 boycott plans, see Southern California Boycott Committee flyer, n.d., UCLA Students: Student Activism Materials, Box 3, Folder 13, UCLA. The quote from the three co-chairs is from "L.A. College Students Join Picket Lines," *LA Sentinel*, March 17, 1960. On the students having the support of CORE and NAACP, see "17 Chain Stores Picketed by Sympathizers of Negro Sitdowns," *LA Times*, March 27, 1960. On Jesse Morris's student status, see "Students to Picket Local Stores," *DB*, March 14, 1960. He was a senior economics major at UCLA.

30. The tension between the Kerr Directives and UC participation in civil rights demonstrations unfolded in the student press. See, e.g., "No Courage," *Daily Californian*, April 4, 1960; "Kerr Directives," *Daily Californian*, April 4, 1960; "Boycotts from Both Sides," *DB*, March 16, 1960; "How about Some Ideals," *DB*, March 16, 1960. On the significance of the NSA in the South, see Turner, *Sitting In and Speaking Out*, pp. 119–123. On Berkeley students and the HUAC meeting, see Murch, *Living for the City*, p. 73. Robert Cohen also noted that Mario Savio, the

The tensions between students and state officials, including UC system leaders, was telling of the conservative nature of many Californians who did not want their state-supported universities engaged in political and social issues. Among the opinion pages of the student newspapers, from Berkeley to Los Angeles, students were split on whether they were doing too little to advance civil rights or were doing too much. As for Murphy, upon his arrival, he agreed that UCLA was not doing enough.

Slow to see racial progress in Kansas, a state Murphy had known since childhood, he used his last month as KU chancellor to leave Kansas residents with his hopes for the future. On June 6, 1960, in Murphy's farewell speech during the KU commencement exercise, he told the graduates that in addressing the "crucial issues of our time," they must accept "the obligation to assist [their] fellow man, to insist that all of us are God's creatures, regardless of race or creed, and as such the possessors of the right to equality of opportunity." As a man of faith, Murphy preached the importance of equal rights for all people, and this message resounded far beyond the state boundaries of Kansas. The next month, and only a few days after Murphy's official UCLA start date of July 1, 1960, civil rights advocacy gained momentum when US senator John F. Kennedy, who would campaign in support of a stronger civil rights bill, secured the Democratic nomination for president during the party's national convention held in Los Angeles.[31]

In September 1960, Murphy's first series of public remarks set the tone for his chancellorship. On September 19, he told the *Daily Bruin* that UCLA was destined to establish its own reputation and campus culture. Its new identity would be different from when UCLA was merely an extension campus to Berkeley, and Murphy was not one to become a symbolic leader. "I think there is gradually growing an awareness that a singular university—the University of California—just doesn't exist anymore," he told the *Daily Bruin*. "The single university is becoming a 'system' . . . in which there are institutions which are developing their own particular flavor, emphasis, and traditions."[32]

---

leader of the Free Speech Movement, considered attending UCLA, but the Berkeley students' HUAC meeting disruption nudged him to choose that UC campus instead. For more, see Cohen, *Freedom's Orator*, p. 39.

31. Farewell to the Graduates, June 6, 1960, Murphy Papers, Box 3, Folder 11, UCLA. John F. Kennedy was later elected US president in November 1960, and asked Murphy to serve on his education advisory council. For more, see Davis, *Culture Broker*, pp. 45, 49.

32. For the singular university quote, see Mort Saltzman, "Murphy Tells Plans for UCLA Distinction," *DB*, September 19, 1960. Murphy emphasized his goal to make UCLA one of the ten most distinctive universities in the world.

Two days later, on September 21, Murphy acted on this belief and started a new tradition—the student convocation. It was scheduled before his inauguration as the new chancellor, and he canceled classes for the ceremony. Murphy's "State of the University" address, the first ever from a UCLA chancellor, reiterated his belief in the campus as a separate entity from Berkeley and signaled that students came first. This created quite a positive buzz among the UCLA students. "The chancellor has already shown his interest in and respect for the student body by calling this convocation," said Russ Serber, director of rallies and assemblies, who encouraged students to attend the event. Then, before some 2,500 students gathered outdoors in the 100-degree heat, Murphy offered an ambitious look toward the future. He emphasized a future UCLA with more residential students, an international academic reputation, and students who would function independently. "The American university student is primarily a responsible, mature human being," he stressed to the student body. "We believe that the student should be given the opportunity to manage his own affairs."[33]

On September 23, before Murphy delivered his morning inauguration address, he had already made another monumental decision on behalf of the students. The university administration agreed to recognize the campus NAACP chapter as an on-campus student organization. Since 1955, students in the NAACP had repeatedly been denied recognition as a student group by UCLA academic leaders, but under Murphy's leadership, the administration immediately reversed course. Bruin NAACP could now use campus facilities for meetings, debates, and rallies. Previous administrators opposed this because of the NAACP's partisan activities, but Murphy felt otherwise. This was no small decision within the UC system that, for decades, held policies that banned student or student group activities affiliated with national groups. In fact, the *Los Angeles Times* dedicated coverage to UCLA's decision to grant the NAACP on-campus recognition after the five-year battle. Robert Singleton, Bruin NAACP president and a graduate student in economics, said the group's purpose was the "abolition of discrimination against all minorities, in all its spectrum of forms, from de jure to de facto."[34]

Murphy welcomed Singleton's goal, and during his inaugural address only hours after news of the NAACP's recognition spread across campus, a small

33. On the student convocation being the first of its type, see "Chancellor Addresses Student Body Sept. 21," *DB*, September 13, 1960; and "Murphy Speaks, Class Dismissed," *DB*, September 20, 1960. Regarding Murphy's quote on student independence, see Nancy Knaus, "Chancellor Lauds UCLA Past, Points to Future," *DB*, September 22, 1960.

34. Judy Hare, "NAACP Gains Campus Status," *DB*, September 23, 1960; "NAACP Given On-Campus OK at UCLA," *LA Times*, October 30, 1960.

portion of his remarks focused on the question of freedom. To Murphy, a question representative of the social issues of the day was whether all Americans could find their own opportunities, or whether some were regulated by "arbitrary man-made" rules. "In short," he asked, "is he free or is he not free?" Considering that, Murphy pressed onward in his first academic term as UCLA chancellor as a defender of students' rights as citizens. In fact, in October 1960, Murphy defended student journalists against claims from Patrick J. Hillings, chair of the Los Angeles County Republican Central Committee, that the *Daily Bruin* used smear tactics against US vice president Richard Nixon, who was campaigning for the US presidency against Kennedy. Murphy stood behind the students, and gave them license to engage off-campus issues, with Bruin NAACP members as the most active of them all.[35]

Throughout the fall of 1960, Bruin NAACP organized a food drive, held civil rights lectures and rallies, and challenged local housing discrimination. First, the group launched the "Feed Haywood County" project. The goal was to collect food across Los Angeles and ship the items to rural West Tennessee, where white creditors, landowners, and merchants were starving Black sharecroppers for registering to vote. This project did not occur by happenstance, as Murphy, on November 22, underscored to students the importance of service. "It is our obligation, and perhaps our privilege, to be concerned about the welfare of our neighbors," he emphasized. The Bruin NAACP lecture speakers included Ulysses Prince, a southern sit-in participant and former CORE field secretary; Adam Clayton Powell, a US Representative (D-NY); UCLA professors Robert Bone, Councill S. Taylor, and Harold M. Hyman; and notably, Richard Haley, a former professor fired by Florida A&M, a state-supported Black college, for aiding the sit-ins.[36]

35. Inaugural Address, September 23, 1960, University of California, Los Angeles, Murphy Papers, Box 57, Folder 10, UCLA; "Murphy Says DB Editorial Answered Hillings Amply," *DB*, October 24, 1960.

36. "Anti-Boycott Project Begins," *DB*, October 10, 1960; "NAACP to Pack Food for Tennessee Project," *DB*, November 23, 1960; "Chancellor Stresses Need for Community Service," *DB*, November 23, 1960. Regarding the speaker series, see "Prince Speaks at NAACP Rally Wednesday Noon," *DB*, October 25, 1960; "Rip Sit-in 'News Blackout,'" *DB*, October 27, 1960; "Rep Powell Campaign Talk at Noon Today," *DB*, October 27, 1960; "Fired Prof Haley Speaks in 3rd Civil Rights Talk," *DB*, December 8, 1960. For more on Haley losing his job, see White, *Blood, Sweat, and Tears*, pp. 123–128; and Rabby, *The Pain and the Promise*, pp. 121; "Bone Views Founding of NAACP in Noon Speech," *DB*, November 17, 1960; Joyce Hosokawa, "Hyman—Civil Rights," *DB*, December 2, 1960; Joyce Hosokawa, "Taylor Slams

By late fall, however, Murphy's support of some students' newfound emphasis on civil rights on the UCLA campus was met with significant resistance from a segment of the student body. On November 29, *Daily Bruin* feature editor Pete Hacsi kicked off a debate over the merits of UCLA administrators' Bruin NAACP recognition. Hacsi said he sympathized with Black southerners; however, he felt Californians were carelessly interested in an issue they knew little about occurring two thousand miles away. To him, those in California, which he called "a liberal stronghold," often acted simply to display their righteousness. In sum, Hacsi felt the Bruin NAACP was overzealous. "We give full support to the university's recognition of the NAACP here," he wrote. "We hope they use their potential without alienating support from would-be liberal university minds." Hacsi felt civil rights efforts should be gradual and more considerate of potential white supporters' feelings, and in a letter to the editor, another writer issued a "challenge to the NAACP" asking, "Is forced integration any more democratic than forced segregation?"[37]

The callous nature of the moderate UCLA students was met with equal assertiveness from Bruin NAACP members and supporters. Barbara Campbell, in a response to Hacsi's commentary, said his writing fit "the armchair sympathizer's attitudes." She added: "I think your timely article pointed up every absurdity in the argument of those individuals who lend verbal agreement to any controversy but who, under no circumstances, would allow himself to become personally involved." The same day, Bernard Hilberman, a Bruin NAACP member, wrote, "As for his complaint that some UCLA civil rights leaders are too emotional, I am thankful that some people do get incensed when they see their fellow man mistreated," Hilberman wrote. "Yes, even 2,000 miles away." Similarly, Kenny Jordan and Marsha Rotkin coauthored a letter that pointed to Hacsi's contradictory complaint. "Thousands and billions of dollars are sent overseas for relief purposes, but not a penny for

Attitudes that Maintain Segregated Areas," *DB*, December 16, 1960. Among the three professors named here, Taylor was a leading Black scholar. For more on Taylor's influence, see Marable, "Black Studies and the Racial Mountain," p. 32; and Brown, *Fighting for US*, p. 13. This is notable considering how few Black faculty worked at predominantly white institutions in the early 1960s. According to Ibram X. Kendi, "two of the 'sanctuaries' for black professors were UChicago and UCLA, with no more than six." For more, see Kendi, *Black Campus Movement*, p. 27.

37. Pete Hacsi, "Tread Softly," *DB*, November 29, 1960; Bob Walter, "To NAACP: A Challenge," *DB*, December 1, 1960.

a starving Negro American baby," they wrote. "Doesn't charity begin at home? Mr. Hacsi, don't you care?"[38]

This last question—does charity begin at home—was an underlying theme to Bruin NAACP's efforts during Murphy's first months as chancellor. It also stretched back to February 1960, when NAACP attorney Loren Miller criticized Westwood housing discrimination. Therefore, as people questioned students' southern support, Bruin NAACP turned its attention squarely to UCLA and Westwood, and on December 7, 1960, the student group asked the SLC to address racism in Westwood. In addition to their focus on housing discrimination, Black and white student teams tested six local barber shops and found that barbers discriminated against Black students.[39]

Afterward, Bruin NAACP demanded action from the student council and secured support from the UCLA American Civil Liberties Union (ACLU), Westwood Young Democrats, and Platform, a left-leaning student political party. The Bruin Young Republicans declined to support, citing their purpose to increase interest in the Republican Party, not participate in "bi-partisan activity in the field of civil rights." Nevertheless, the SLC unanimously passed a resolution in support of Bruin NAACP. To work around the Kerr Directives, this time, the resolution was noted to have been passed by individuals in the SLC, not the SLC itself, and established a committee to investigate potential "action on non-discriminatory policy."[40]

On January 4, 1961, upon students' return from winter recess, the SLC moved forward with its support by proposing that a chancellor's committee be formed to address Westwood discrimination. After lengthy discussion, the SLC voted unanimously to recommend that Murphy form the committee that would be led by his office. Murphy supported this. Vice chancellor Foster H. Sherwood and associate dean of students Byron H. Atkinson also favored the proposed committee, which signaled a notable first six months of Murphy's chancellorship. Bruin NAACP had swiftly moved from being denied recognition to the impetus for a chancellor-led committee on racial discrimination. As historian Gerald Horne later explained, "Despite their support through taxes, blacks were largely absent from the University of California, and those few enrolled at UCLA often faced an alienating and hostile atmosphere." This was the reality that ran counter to Murphy's image of Los Angeles before he

38. Barbara Campbell, "NAACP Editorial a Biting Satire," *DB*, November 30, 1960; Bernard Hilberman, "Can't Be Too Fast," *DB*, November 30, 1960; Kenny Jordan and Marsha Rotkin, "Facts—for the Uninformed," *DB*, December 1, 1960.

39. Alan Rothstein, "NAACP Requests Action from SLC," *DB*, December 7, 1960.

40. George Nicholson, "SLC Air Sharp Attack at Village Discrimination," *DB*, December 8, 1960; Rothstein, "NAACP Requests."

arrived, and students' request that he address racism on and near campus was significant as UCLA and the UC system faced growing conflict over students' civil rights activities.[41]

UC Administrators' Conflict Goes Public

"Segregation is immoral," said Murphy, in April 1961, "and all university activities dealing with discrimination will be geared toward its end." This statement officially launched the chancellor's committee on discrimination. Murphy personally appointed each of the committee's two students and three professors, and the group adopted three objectives. First, the committee would make sure discrimination did not occur on campus. Second, it aimed to investigate campus fraternities and sororities for discriminatory clauses in their charters. Finally, it would examine off-campus businesses in relation to discrimination. "We plan to be friendly but firm," Murphy said of the committee's approach. "By explaining the problem, we hope there will be complete cooperation." However, Murphy's desired "friendly but firm" approach to quietly end discrimination faced a challenge. The growing external interest in the reports of discrimination at UCLA heightened system administrators' attentiveness to students' long-time complaints about off-campus racism.[42]

On April 7, the *Wall Street Journal* assessed the challenges academic leaders faced when striving to make their universities internationally renowned.

41. "SLC Ponders Discrimination in Westwood," *DB*, January 4, 1961; Alan Rothstein, "Discrimination Acted Upon," *DB*, January 5, 1961; Horne, *Fire This Time*, p. 229. Years after Gerald Horne's assessment of UCLA, Ana-Christina Ramón and Darnell Hunt reached a similar conclusion: "Beneath the veneer of UCLA's proud legacy of black achievement were the realities of a pre-Civil Rights Act America—token blacks admitted largely because of their athletic prowess and unacceptable levels of segregation and alienation on campus." For more, see Ana-Christina Ramón and Darnell Hunt, "Reclaiming UCLA: The Education Crisis in Black Los Angeles," in Ramón and Hunt, *Black Los Angeles*, p. 384. Because of the limited number of Black students, it is important to note that the UC student organizations that took up civil rights causes largely consisted of white students. For more, see Crowe, *Prophets of Rage*, pp. 123–124. Within an institutional history of UCLA, it is noted that Murphy eventually opened barbershops on campus due to some Westwood barbers' refusal to serve Black students. For more, see Dundjerski, *UCLA*, p. 159.

42. Bob Seigel, "FDM's Comm Begins Anti-Discrim Work," *DB*, April 18, 1961. For more about Murphy's committee selections, see Charles E. Young to Joel Wachs, February 2, 1961, Chancellor Files–Murphy, Box 49, Folder 8–Chancellor's Administrative Committees, 1961–62, UCLA. (The title of the folder is included because the folders are not numbered; however, it is the eighth folder in this particular box. This number-title format is used when applicable hereafter.)

UCLA enrolled a number of students from other countries, but the slight against American institutions was the racism those students experienced. "In playing host to African students, as well as to Asian youths, American schools find racial discrimination is a major problem," read the front-page article. "African students at the University of California at Los Angeles complain they're refused haircuts in Westwood, the community surrounding the school." UCLA and its local problems were exposed to a national audience.[43]

Three days later, on April 10, Bob Siegel, a *Daily Bruin* feature writer, said discrimination tainted international students' perception of the United States. He had hoped the months of student newspaper coverage prior to the *Wall Street Journal* article would have nudged white business owners in Westwood to "take the hint" without "naming names," but now the nation was aware of racism at UCLA. Siegel argued, referencing the street that separated the UCLA campus to the north from the Westwood community to the south, that "We'd hate to have history remember Westwood as a community where the 'Mason-Dixon Line' ran down Le Conte Avenue."[44]

Joseph A. Steinborn, in reaction to Siegel's article, felt compelled to act. He likened the inaction of UCLA students toward racial injustice to that of the Germans' failure to challenge anti-Jewish sentiment. "With a little organized effort, the students of UCLA could accomplish a great deal towards overcoming injustices towards minority groups," Steinborn wrote in the *Daily Bruin*. Therefore, Le Conte Avenue would not become a figurative Mason-Dixon Line if enough students boycotted and picketed against racial discrimination. He added: "I would be proud to participate in such organized action."[45]

Murphy and Kerr responded to students' call to action with a shared message when it came to student organizing because many who feared communism often characterized civil rights demonstrations as communist activity. In June 1961, the two academic leaders replied to a State Senate Un-American

---

43. Stewart A. Toy, "Effort to Win Friends by Importing Foreign Students Hits Snags: Africans Irked by Racial Bias; Schools Say Some Visitors Are Ill-Prepared, Clannish," *Wall Street Journal*, April 7, 1961. The *Wall Street Journal* quote was also used in Bob Siegel's editorial. For more, see Bob Siegel, "The Hairline," *DB*, April 10, 1961. Because of the racial and ethnic diversity, scholars have credited racial progress in California to cross-racial alliances. For more, see Shana Bernstein, "From the Southwest to the Nation: Interracial Civil Rights Activism in the Sunbelt Southwest," in Nickerson and Dochuk, *Sunbelt Rising*, pp. 141–163; Daniel Martinez HoSang, "Racial Liberalism and the Rise of the Sunbelt West: The Defeat of Fair Housing on the 1964 California Ballot," in Nickerson and Dochuk, *Sunbelt Rising*, p. 191; Flamming, "Becoming Democrats," in de Graaf, Mulroy, and Taylor, *Seeking El Dorado*, p. 299.

44. Siegel, "The Hairline."

45. Joseph A. Steinborn, "Overcoming Injustices," *DB*, April 12, 1961.

Activities subcommittee report that warned that communist activities would "plague California campuses in the near future." In tandem, the chancellor and president dismissed the perceived threats. Kerr added, "The Senate subcommittee and the university are in agreement that the primary goal at the university is to promote the search for truth rather than to indoctrinate students." This suggested that Murphy and Kerr were on the same page regarding UCLA activities. Yet, privately, they could not have been farther from agreement.[46]

Murphy had been perturbed since his arrival after Kerr, as system president, made no effort to plan an inauguration ceremony for him as the new UCLA chancellor. After Murphy inquired, it was agreed upon that Murphy would coordinate his own ceremony and UC officials from Berkeley would host a formal luncheon in Los Angeles; however, the luncheon was "absolutely disastrous," with attendees having no assigned seating and other miscues. This damaged the image Murphy sought to develop for UCLA before his distinguished guests. As the first year continued, Murphy learned that Kerr also required the UCLA chancellor's secretary to report to the system president whenever Kerr came to Los Angeles for business. Murphy saw this as creating the potential for the secretary to be more of a spy monitoring him than an assistant. He was also disgruntled when he realized that UCLA telephone operators answered calls by saying "University of California." Murphy immediately changed that, to the disagreement of UC officials, to "UCLA."[47]

These issues dovetailed with Clark Kerr being featured on the cover of an October 1960 issue of *Time* magazine which presented the Master Plan but made no mention of UCLA. Additionally, Kerr attempted to implement a rule that no campus chancellor could speak to a UC regent without the system president's permission. Of all things, this infuriated Murphy the most since he was promised autonomy to lead UCLA. Murphy asked Kerr, "Do you merely want me to say that I'm a housekeeper?" as he took offense to Kerr's micromanagement and the

---

46. "Any Radical Groups at UCLA Are Unofficial: Murphy, President Kerr of UC Reply to State Senate Subcommittee Report," *LA Times*, June 13, 1961. Related to the questions Kerr and Murphy fielded from elected officials, college presidents received correspondence from several citizens who felt civil rights activities were the ploy of communists. This was found throughout the course of the research for this book across the nation, not just in the South. Two examples are E. L. Cross to the University of Alabama Trustees, December 3, 1962, J. Jefferson Bennett Papers, Box 4, Location 088–102, Folder: Segregation (1956–1962 and Mel Meyer), University of Alabama, W. S. Hoole Special Collections Library; and Jno C. Batte to Robert F. Goheen, October 1, 1963, Office of the President Records: Robert F. Goheen Subgroup, Box 425, Folder 3, Princeton University Archives, Department of Rare Books and Special Collections, Princeton University Library.

47. Regarding the conflicts between Murphy and Kerr, see Murphy, interview by Mink, October–December 1973.

other UC chancellors' silence on such matters. For example, Edward Strong, chancellor of the Berkeley campus, did not have his own stationary and instead sent correspondence with Kerr's name printed on it.[48]

As these issues simmered privately, the Freedom Rides drew hundreds of people to the South to challenge segregated facilities along public highways. Bus stations became civil rights battlegrounds as hundreds were jailed or beaten by white supremacists. In May 1961, in Anniston, Alabama, a bus was firebombed and a white mob held the bus doors closed with the intent of having the riders burn to death. Similar violence was inflicted on Freedom Riders in Birmingham. This increased pressure on US president John F. Kennedy to deliver on the civil rights promises of his campaign.[49]

Los Angeles residents and college students soon headed south to join the Freedom Rides. Local Black churches in the Los Angeles area raised money for the riders prior to their departure, knowing the outcome, at best, would be jail. In fact, following a July 12, 1961, sendoff gathering at Second Baptist Church, the *Los Angeles Times* predicted the "Likely Jailing" of the twelve Los Angeles riders—eight white and four Black—upon their arrival. That group included Mike Wolfson, an incoming UCLA freshman, and Marilyn Eisenberg, a sophomore at Berkeley. Two weeks later, on July 28, Robert Singleton, Bruin NAACP president, and other UCLA students departed for Jackson, Mississippi. That group was sponsored by CORE. Within two days, fifteen Freedom Riders, ten white and five Black, were arrested. Nine of the fifteen were UCLA students, bringing the overall total of arrested Freedom Riders to almost three hundred.[50]

In August, UCLA student Steve McNichols and three other white men departed for Houston to join the Freedom Riders in that city. Upon arriving

---

48. Murphy, interview by Mink, October–December 1973. For more on the conflicts between Kerr, Murphy, and other UC chancellors, see Dundjerski, *UCLA*, pp. 144–146, 164; Cohen, *Freedom's Orator*, p. 79; Rorabaugh, *Berkeley at War*, p. 13.

49. On the Alabama violence, see "Integrationist Group Continuing Trip after Brutal Beatings Here," *Birmingham News*, May 15, 1961; and "'Freedom' Bus Target of Anniston Bomb," *Birmingham News*, May 15, 1961. On the broader significance of the Freedom Rides, see Carson, *In Struggle*, pp. 37–38; and Zinn, *SNCC*, pp. 40–41. On the impact of the Freedom Rides on federal policies, see Ransby, *Ella Baker*, pp. 265–267; and Patterson, *Grand Expectations*, p. 470. For two comprehensive histories of the Freedom Rides, see Catsam, *Freedom's Main Line*, and Arsenault, *Freedom Riders*. See Arsenault, pp. 384–385, for a brief discussion on the UCLA riders.

50. Regarding Los Angeles Freedom Riders, see "12 L.A. 'Riders' Off for South, Likely Jailing," *LA Times*, July 13, 1961; "UCLA Produces Freedom Riders," *DB*, July 18, 1961. On the UCLA student arrests, see "Freedom Riders from UCLA Crowding Jails," *LA Sentinel*, August 3, 1961. Notably, in May 1961, James Farmer, co-founder of CORE, visited the UCLA campus regarding the Freedom Rides. For more, see Dundjerski, *UCLA*, p. 159.

at Union Station in Houston, the four riders were arrested, jailed, and beaten throughout the night by other inmates. "When we arrived at the cell, one of the prisoners got up and asked if we were the 'nigger lovers' from L.A.," McNichols recounted. "When we told him who we were, several other prisoners joined in and helped inflict the beating." Aside from those students working for civil rights in the South, starting on August 20, seven UCLA students attended the ten-day NSA conference held in Madison, Wisconsin. As seen during the lunch counter sit-ins, civil rights advocacy was among the issues NSA leaders adopted, and the national conference allowed student delegates to coordinate efforts.[51]

The entire time, UC administrators were aware that their students were being arrested during the Freedom Rides; however, the arrests in the South were punctuated by the tragic deaths of two UCLA students, Bob Siegel and Al Barouh, who died in an airplane crash outside of Chicago on September 1, 1961, while returning from the NSA conference. Siegel was a *Daily Bruin* editorial board member, and Barouh was president of UCLA's NSA chapter. Barouh was also one of the nine UCLA students arrested in Mississippi at the end of July and had been released on bail in time to attend the NSA conference. The two student deaths, alongside the brutal treatment of the jailed student Freedom Riders, prompted UC system administrators to further tighten university policy on off-campus activities. In so doing, they exposed the conflict between the views of the system leaders in Berkeley and those of Murphy at UCLA.[52]

On July 31, 1961, two UCLA student leaders—Steve Weiner and Kathleen Lenihan—called on Murphy and Kerr to act on behalf of the nine students arrested in Mississippi. The arrested group included Singleton, a member of the chancellor's committee on discrimination. "We believe it necessary and proper that members of the university community protest these arrests," Weiner and Lenihan told Murphy. The two students planned to send telegrams to Mississippi governor Ross Barnett and US attorney general Robert F. Kennedy, urging both men to release the jailed students, and they wanted Murphy to authorize use of his name as signatory on the telegrams.[53]

51. Al Rothstein, "Rider Describes Brutality," *DB*, September 18, 1961; "Seven Bruins Head East in August for NSA Conference at Wisconsin," *DB*, June 16, 1961.

52. "Two UCLA Students among Plane Dead," *LA Times*, September 2, 1961. For more on the national implications of Barouh's and Siegel's deaths, see Nina Turner to Gordon C. Carey, September 21, 1961; Gordon C. Carey to Nina Turner, December 6, 1961; both in Congress on Racial Equality Collection–Series 5, Box 51, Folder 2, Wisconsin Historical Society.

53. Steve Weiner and Kathleen Lenihan to Franklin D. Murphy, July 31, 1961, Chancellor Files–Murphy, Box 122, Folder 246–Freedom Riders, UCLA.

By this point, however, UC administrators took a stronger hold of the principles of the system's longtime commitment to distance itself from off-campus issues. Harry R. Wellman, vice president of the UC system, intervened quickly. "[President Kerr's] name should not be used as signatory to the protest telegram," Wellman informed students on August 4. "Faculty and students are, of course, free to sign such telegrams so long as they do so in their individual capacities. Campus mail should not be used for soliciting signatures." Five days later, on August 9, Murphy informed the students that he was willing to speak with them personally about their request, but based on Wellman's response, he could not accommodate them. "I cannot authorize my name as signatory to the protest telegrams in spite of my personal sympathy for our students who were arrested in Jackson," Murphy explained.[54]

This conflict between Murphy's belief in racial equality and his professional role within the university system became more pronounced because the conflict was as much about the UC regents as it was him and Kerr. Some regents disagreed with Kerr's micromanagement. For instance, UC regents developed interests within geographical camps, and those in Southern California had enormous influence and desire to develop Los Angeles into an urban cultural center since it had long been perceived as a sleepy western town. This included Edward W. Carter, a retail giant who was president of the Broadway Stores; Dorothy B. Chandler, whose family owned the *Los Angeles Times* and the Times Mirror Company; Edwin W. Pauley, a successful oil executive; and John E. Canaday, an executive for the Lockheed Aircraft Corporation—one of the leading manufacturers that employed Black people during World War II.[55]

These southern regents were committed to supporting Murphy, whom they considered the strong administrator needed to build UCLA into the prominent university that the city deserved. They wanted the university to become more engaged with the Los Angeles community, and previous chancellors had been ineffective in challenging Berkeley officials' limitations on UCLA. Furthermore, as Murphy entered the 1961–62 academic year, he and those

54. H. R. Wellman to Steve Weiner, August 4, 1961, Chancellor Files–Murphy, Box 122, Folder 246–Freedom Riders, UCLA; Franklin D. Murphy to Steve Weiner, August 9, 1961, Chancellor Files–Murphy, Box 122, Folder 246–Freedom Riders, UCLA.

55. To further emphasize that the regents supported Murphy, instead of quitting due to lack of autonomy, he vowed to wait until the regents fired him over his spats with Kerr. Because of his close social relationship with the southern regents, however, Murphy knew this would not happen. For more, see Murphy, interview by Mink, October-December 1973. On the southern regents' interest in hiring Murphy, see Davis, *Culture Broker*, pp. 27–34. On Lockheed employing Black workers, see Taylor, *In Search of the Racial Frontier*, pp. 260–261.

southern regents had become social friends. As a result, Murphy could negotiate for a more independent UCLA without regent interference.[56]

Meanwhile, Murphy's hardline stances about UCLA ebbed and flowed. For example, on September 8, 1961, he retreated on a talking point he had emphasized since his arrival in July 1960. In a letter to Al Rothstein, *Daily Bruin* editor, the chancellor took issue with a quote the newspaper attributed to him: "I think there is gradually growing an awareness that a singular university—the University of California—just doesn't exist anymore." This quote had appeared in the *Daily Bruin* on multiple occasions since Murphy's arrival as chancellor, one of the most prominent uses being in the September 19, 1960, issue. However, a year later, Murphy penned a three-page letter explaining that the quote "does not reflect my views at all." He continued: "A singular University of California does exist, both de jure as well as de facto. It has its governing body and its statewide officers. UCLA is part of this singular University of California. I regard this as important and necessary, both in the best interests of the State of California as well as UCLA." Most notably, aside from the effort to explain to Rothstein, Murphy also shared his letter with Kerr and some of UC regents, each blind copy unknown to the other.[57]

Murphy, in his clarification letter, appeared to be on the same page as Kerr, who shortly afterward issued a new policy aimed to prevent the use of the UC name and facilities by "special interest groups." On September 18, the *Daily Bruin* called the policy "explosive," as it focused on students and student groups taking stands on off-campus issues and limited the student government's ability to "claim to represent the university and the students." The state constitution, according to Kerr's statement, determined that the university should be "entirely independent of all political and sectarian influence and kept free therefrom in the appointment of its regents and in the administration of its affairs." Issued almost simultaneously with the Los Angeles Freedom Riders, including some UCLA students, making headlines for discussing their experiences in the South, Kerr's policy stood in direct response to students' off-campus civil rights activities. Therefore, although Murphy used his September 18 faculty and staff convocation to, once again, emphasize system decentralization, Kerr sent a clear message regarding where the single university stood regarding civil rights activities across all UC campuses.[58]

56. Murphy, interview by Mink, October-December 1973; Davis, *Culture Broker*.

57. Franklin D. Murphy to Al Rothstein, September 8, 1961, Chancellor Files–Murphy, Box 107, Folder 190–Statements and Articles by Dr. Murphy–1961, UCLA.

58. Regarding the Kerr policy, see Dini Seigel, "Kerr Limits Group Recognition: New Policies Define Use of Name, Facility," *DB*, September 18, 1961. For news coverage of the Freedom Riders' return to Los Angeles, see "Freedom Riders to Be Heard in Santa Monica," *LA Sentinel*,

By September 22, it became clearer that the tighter university policy on student activities was connected to broader conservative pressures in California, and UC system leaders in Berkeley catered to them. In 1960, conservatives started the John Birch Society, and California became its leading state with more than three hundred chapters. Therefore, days after Kerr's new policy was issued, a bill designed to outlaw racial discrimination in the sale or renting of properties was defeated in the state house. Governor Edmund "Pat" Brown, a Democrat, called the vote a "major disappointment," as the rampant housing discrimination in California failed to be remedied during the 1961 state legislative session. Similarly, UCLA Freedom Riders also found themselves shunned by the university upon their return while released on bail. In early October, although more than two hundred people attended a campus discussion about the Freedom Rides, the *Daily Bruin* explained that "since the beginning of this semester, University President Clark Kerr has declared that organizations dealing with the segregation problem must operate from off campus. Thus, they would have no affiliation with the university."[59]

The next month, on November 2, it was reported that Kerr continued to emphasize his distaste for what he considered radical behavior. In a talk before the California Junior College Association, he said college campuses were experiencing an increase in activity from the radical left and radical right, with California seeing the highest uptick in such behavior. Then, on November 3, Kerr delivered a keynote address during a California Club banquet held at the Bel-Air Hotel, where, again, he stressed his belief that questionable activity was more active. "People are scared and worried," he explained to the Southern California audience. "They lose their rationality. Slogans and stereotypes do not make for the best democracy." To Kerr, the marches, rallies, and boycotts leaned on emotions, but careful consideration was needed to implement actual change.[60]

September 14, 1961; "Meeting Hears Freedom Riders in Santa Monica," *LA Sentinel*, September 21, 1961; and Rothstein, "Rider Describes Brutality." For Murphy's convocation remarks, see Art Harris, "University Must Not Lose Itself," *DB*, September 19, 1961.

59. Regarding Governor Brown's "disappointment" quote, see "Racial Housing Bill Fails," *DB*, September 22, 1961. California residents had a history of intense debate over anti-discrimination bills, especially with regard to housing. For more, see HoSang, "Racial Liberalism," in Nickerson and Dochuk, *Sunbelt Rising*, pp. 188–213. On the John Birch Society, alongside a lengthier discussion about conservativism in California, see McGirr, *Suburban Warriors*, pp. 54–110. Scholars have discussed California's conservativism across a variety of issues in the early 1960s. For one example relevant to this paragraph, see Lassiter, *Silent Majority*, pp. 16, 304; "Freedom Rider Tells Experience," *DB*, October 3, 1961; Les Ostrow, "Freedom Ride Described as Brutal Beating," *DB*, October 4, 1961.

60. "'Radical Upswing' Kerr Tells JCs," *DB*, November 2, 1961; Shirley Folmer, "Kerr Keynotes Controversy," *DB*, November 7, 1961.

This opinion is unsurprising, considering that in May 1960 dozens of Berkeley students were arrested in San Francisco for demonstrating against the HUAC meeting. Civil rights demonstrations were one of numerous sources of pressure Kerr attempted to manage. But Governor Brown, in a November 3 talk at UCLA, shared a different opinion before four thousand people. The governor said a "fearful minority" threatened American democracy. "They are frightened—and in their fear they want to deny us our most basic and fundamental rights." Brown then urged UCLA students and faculty to aggressively protect their democratic rights.[61]

By this point, the conflicting messages being sent by state leaders—Kerr, Brown, and Murphy—left students confused. Months earlier, Steve Weiner had attempted to get Kerr and Murphy to sign telegrams opposing the arrest of the student Freedom Riders. Now, after hearing the governor's address, he did not know what to think. "I'm beginning to wonder whether Pat Brown and Clark Kerr believe the same things," Weiner said. "Fortunately, Brown's actions speak louder than his words." *Daily Bruin* editorial editor Harry Shearer, however, criticized Brown for praising Kerr. He said Brown championed Kerr's noble words but ignored the Kerr directives. Shearer argued that the governor "failed to point out the glaring discrepancy between the president's shiny phrases and his dismaying attempt to placate political pressure from the state's radical right." In defense of Kerr, on November 17, Murphy privately wrote Shearer about his editorial and attempted to explain that the university policies were more lenient than those of previous system administrations; however, the damage was done, and the state-level inconsistent messaging had already trickled down to the UCLA student body.[62]

On November 15, 1961, the largest controversy of the academic year began when students started a petition requesting that the Associated Students UCLA (ASUCLA) issue a $5,000 loan to five UCLA Freedom Riders who still needed financial assistance regarding their criminal charges in Mississippi. The student riders were required to return to Mississippi in March 1962 for a court appearance, and each needed to make a $1,000 bail payment. The

61. Dini Seigel, "Brown Praises Educated Man: Crowd Packs Union," *DB*, November 6, 1961. Regarding the House Un-American Activities Committee meeting riot, see "UCB HUAC Rioter Acquitted: Jury Decrees Verdict on SF HUAC Riot," *DB*, May 4, 1961. On the San Francisco HUAC meeting and key players and the tensions between the political right and left, see McGirr, *Suburban Warriors*, p. 57.

62. For Weiner's opinion on the Brown-Kerr conflict, see "Reaction to the Speech: Murphy Praises Governor," *DB*, November 6, 1961; Harry Shearer, "The Speech & Reality," *DB*, November 6, 1961; Franklin D. Murphy to Harry Shearer, November 17, 1961, University of California, Chancellor Files–Murphy, Box 122, Folder 246–Student Government (Kerr Directives), UCLA.

dilemma was that Mississippi bail bondsmen would lose their licenses if they issued money to the Freedom Riders, and the Mississippi courts required the students make cash payments. Therefore, the petition was sympathetic to the students' financial hardship and wanted ASUCLA funds used so the students could remain in school.[63]

By November 30, however, some UCLA students pushed back and argued that student government funds should not be used for off-campus student-involved civil rights activities. Soon, there were two petitions circulating on campus, one for and the other against a "Freedom Loan," with thousands of signatures on each. Then, on December 13, the opposing petitions went before the SLC, which voted to send the Freedom Loan recommendation to a special election. The election would determine whether the loan request should go before the Board of Control, ASUCLA's financial governing body.[64]

As the fall 1961 term concluded, elected officials received letters containing varying opinions on whether a state-supported campus should even consider allowing students to vote on the use of funds for a civil rights cause. Similarly, the *Los Angeles Times* saw the election as offering insight into the position of the university: for or against the Freedom Riders. Murphy's greatest challenge in advocating for civil rights unfolded with Californians focused squarely on him. UC leaders' conflicting views drew more attention to an already difficult moment, and Murphy closed 1961 in a situation that placed his professional obligations and personal views on Black freedom before the entire state.[65]

A Vote for Freedom and More

On January 3, 1962, the SLC scheduled February 14 and 15 for the student vote to send the Freedom Loan decision to the Board of Control. While students prepared for the election, Murphy and other UCLA administrators discussed

63. For more on the loan petition, see Les Ostrov, "Petition Requests $5000 Assistance," *DB*, November 28, 1961. Regarding a detailed account of the Freedom Loan situation, see Dave Lawton, "Petition Vote Next Week," *DB*, February 5, 1962.

64. For conservative students' challenge to the petition, see Chuck Rose and Chuck Burleigh, "Freedom Riders & Bail," *DB*, November 30, 1961; "Two Petitions Gain Support, Wait for SLC," *DB*, December 8, 1961; Les Ostrov, "Council Calls for $5,000 Loan Vote: SLC Nixes Proposal, Puts Question to Vote," *DB*, December 14, 1962.

65. Norman Dash, "Vote Slated on Freedom Rider Loan: UCLA Students to Use $5,000 for Bail if Granted," *LA Times*, December 24, 1961. On state-level elected officials receiving letters about the loan vote, see Ewing Hass to James H. Corley, December 30, 1961, Chancellor Files–Murphy, Box 122, Folder 246–Freedom Riders, UCLA. Also see Gustav A. Amberg to Thomas Kuchel, December 1961, Chancellor Files–Murphy, Box 122, Folder 246–Freedom Riders, UCLA.

the potential implications of the loan. Judy Lembcke of the ASUCLA saw the student loan vote as directly linked to the Kerr Directives and asked Murphy a series of questions before a potential decision came before the Board of Control. Lembcke wanted the chancellor's opinion on whether the loan would serve as an endorsement of Freedom Rides, whether it would violate the UC directive on student government, and whether on- or off-campus distinctions mattered. Furthermore, since the Board of Control was composed mostly of nonstudents, if students voted to send the decision to the board, did the board members answer to Kerr or to Murphy? Lembcke's questions were common and reasonable considering the public contradictions between the two academic leaders; however, the answers remained unclear to UCLA administrators.[66]

Between December 13, 1961, when the SLC decided to send the loan to the campus-wide vote, and January 11, 1962, administrators sent questions up and down the UCLA leadership hierarchy. On December 13, Royce L. Hamilton, ASUCLA business manager, informed William C. Ackerman, ASUCLA executive director, that the loan might violate ASUCLA's tax-exempt status. According to the federal tax code, Hamilton said, none of a tax-exempt organization's net earnings could be used to influence legislation or the affairs of a political office. "I believe that before any such loan commitments are entered into by the Board of Control," Hamilton advised, "this area should be thoroughly explored in order that the tax exempt status of the ASUCLA would not be jeopardized." On January 4, Ackerman then turned to Charles E. Young, special assistant to the chancellor, with the same questions about the legal position of UCLA. In turn, on January 9, Young asked Thomas J. Cunningham, UC system-wide vice president and general counsel, for his "opinion regarding the legality of the proposed loan."[67]

Finally, on January 11, 1962, Cunningham answered the question that UCLA officials had discussed for a month. In his legal opinion, the $5,000 loan was too insignificant an amount to consider "carrying on of propaganda [as] a substantial part of the activities of ASUCLA." In essence, for ASUCLA to

66. "Council to Set Date for Loan Referendum," DB, January 3, 1962; "Freedom Loan Election Date Determined," DB, January 4, 1962; Judy Lembcke to Franklin D. Murphy, December 13, 1961, Chancellor Files–Murphy, Box 122, Folder 246–Freedom Riders, UCLA.

67. Royce L. Hamilton to William C. Ackerman, December 13, 1961, Chancellor Files–Murphy, Box 122, Folder 246–Freedom Riders, UCLA; William C. Ackerman to Charles E. Young, January 4, 1962, Chancellor Files–Murphy, Box 122, Folder 246–Freedom Riders, UCLA; Charles E. Young to Thomas J. Cunningham, January 9, 1962, Chancellor Files–Murphy, Box 122, Folder 246–Freedom Riders, UCLA; Thomas J. Cunningham to Charles E. Young, January 11, 1962, Chancellor Files–Murphy, Box 122, Folder 246–Freedom Riders, UCLA.

serve a campus with thousands of students, the loan amount was trivial as it pertained to the tax-exempt status of the UCLA student government. Of course, Cunningham was careful to explain that his legal opinion should not be taken as a recommendation. "It may well be that you will decide, from a policy standpoint, that it would not be prudent to accede to the request which has been made because of the public relations factors necessarily involved," he said. However, "patently, the loans would have no bearing on legislation. Nor would they involve ASUCLA in any campaign on behalf of any candidate for public office."[68]

With the legality question addressed, Murphy's opinion focused on the public relations aspect of the loan request. The chancellor would have preferred the petition sponsors to have requested the loan directly from the Board of Control instead of the SLC, which sent it to a campus-wide vote. Despite this, Murphy and the Dean of Students Office, under Byron H. Atkinson, would permit the loan if it were made to individual students instead of to a student organization. Also, the board was a "financial watchdog" over the ASUCLA and, thus, not subject to the strict on-campus or off-campus directives pertinent to the student government. These combined facts made Murphy confident that "under these circumstances, there is no implied endorsement of the Freedom Riders, although I am sure many people would find an implied endorsement."[69]

Indeed, when the polls opened on February 14, UCLA became the home of the first student referendum on any campus regarding the Freedom Riders, thus the implications went beyond a mere vote. "The eyes of the state and, indeed, the entire United States" were focused on the election, surmised the *Daily Bruin* that morning. The editorial board's observation aligned with Murphy's earlier statement that he wished students had sought the loan directly from the board instead of through a public vote. Nevertheless, the election was now underway. The student newspaper endorsed the loan and supported the riders, "not only in their attempt to continue to their education but in their stand for full implementation in all areas of this country of equal treatment before the law." The ASUCLA funds were out of Murphy's hands, but in a subtle move, he silently signaled his own endorsement of the freedom loan.[70]

68. Cunningham to Young, January 11, 1962.

69. Franklin D. Murphy to Judy Lembcke, December 27, 1961, Chancellor Files–Murphy, Box 122, Folder 246–Freedom Riders, UCLA.

70. For the quote on the eyes of the state and nation being focused on UCLA, see Steve Weiner, "Loan Vote Begins Today," *DB*, February 14, 1962. Regarding the *DB*'s endorsement, see "Yes on the Riders," *DB*, February 14, 1962.

A week before the vote, Murphy announced that he would release a new policy on athletic teams' competing against segregated southern universities. Students had pressured Murphy to adopt a stronger stance on segregation following a December 1961 basketball tournament in Houston, Texas, where Black UCLA players were harassed during the first game. The three Black players did not play in the second game. Ultimately, the SLC recommended that UCLA athletes not participate in future athletic contests where racial discrimination was present in opponents' facilities. This recommendation echoed some students' threat in the fall of 1961 to boycott the Rose Bowl if the University of Alabama was invited to play against UCLA, but the University of Minnesota received the actual invitation.[71]

A week later, on February 14, in the middle of the two-day election, Murphy released a formal statement of policy on athletic discrimination. As students voted by the thousands, the chancellor shared that UC now withheld systemwide participation against institutions that could not provide assurance that racial segregation would not be allowed. This included segregation in athletic contest participation, housing, and admissions and seating for fans. Therefore, without explicitly stating his opinion on the Freedom Rides, Murphy's timing spoke volumes about his stance on off-campus racism.[72]

The next day, on February 15, the polls closed as UCLA tallied its largest turnout for a student referendum in school history. In the end, 2,086 students voted in favor of sending the loan request to the Board of Control while 1,435 opposed. The loan decision would go before the board at its next meeting on March 8. Over the next three weeks, three views circulated on campus. Although more than 3,500 students voted, there was a question about the nearly 9,000 nonvoters (by 1962, UCLA's total enrollment exceeded 20,000, inclusive of graduate students). The first view suggested that those who did not vote did not care if the loan was granted. Second, conservative students argued the students who did not vote should be counted as opponents since they did not actively vote for the loan. Finally, most people assumed nonvoters included students on both sides. That last opinion gave the Board of Control the greatest flexibility in its own vote.[73]

71. Les Ostrov, "FDM to Set Athletic Policy on Segregation," DB, February 6, 1962; "New Discrimination Code Stated," DB, February 15, 1962. On the potential Rose Bowl boycott, see Kemper, "The Smell of Roses."

72. "New Discrimination Code Stated."

73. "UCLA Votes on Freedom Rider Loan Dispute," LA Times, February 15, 1962; "Freedom Rider Loan Voted by UCLA Students," LA Times, February 18, 1962; Les Ostrov, "Voters Approve Loan: Measure Given 60% Support; 3,532 Vote," DB, February 16, 1962; Dave Lawton, "Freedom Ride Loan Decision from BOC Within 3 Weeks," DB, February 19, 1962. On UCLA's

On March 8, the nine-member board met to determine its stance on the Freedom Loan. The group was comprised of four students and five nonstudents. Of the four students, three were undergraduates and one was a graduate student. The other members were a faculty representative, an alumni representative, and three university administrators: dean of men Adolph Brugger, university business manager Paul Hannum, and ASUCLA executive director William C. Ackerman. Ackerman was a nonvoting member, which left the decision to the eight other members, and an appeal could be made only to Murphy, who had the final decision as the chief campus officer.[74]

As the board assembled, the meeting room was filled with onlookers and television news cameras. Durward Poynter, the graduate student representative, argued that it would be "a sham" if the board rejected the loan despite the student body's vote. Gerry Corrigan, an undergraduate representative, joined Poynter in supporting the loan, arguing that $5,000 was a trivial amount when the ASUCLA had $200,000 in its general fund. Another undergraduate representative, Lindsay Nielson, opposed the loan because so few students had voted compared with the size of the student body. Each of the four nonstudents voted against the loan, with Nielson being the only student to oppose the loan while the three other students voted in favor of it. In the end, the short but heated discussion ended as the board refused the loan by a 5–3 vote.[75]

Over the next week, a number of student groups appealed to Murphy. On March 9, immediately following the board's vote, Platform telegrammed Murphy and Edwin W. Pauley, then chair of the board of regents, its appeal. On March 14, several hundred students attended a rally organized by an ad hoc committee of UCLA law students. At the time, Murphy was away in South America, but to ensure that the chancellor heard their complaints, the rally leaders urged the audience to return on the morning of March 16 to coincide with Murphy's return to campus. Thus, two days later, about two hundred students gathered outside of the Administration Building awaiting Murphy. Before the protesting students, the chancellor reaffirmed the board's decision:

> I support the decision of the Board of Control on the clear and logical grounds which it and Vice Chancellor Foster Sherwood have stated. To do otherwise would be to create a precedent without limit or bounds. I wish

---

1962 enrollment, see UCLA History: Timeline, UCLA Alumni, https://alumni.ucla.edu/ucla-history/ucla-history-timeline/ (accessed March 8, 2019).

74. For the details about the Board of Control, see "Freedom Loan Comes Before BOC Today," *DB*, March 8, 1962.

75. Dave Lawton, "BOC Refuses $5000 Freedom Rider Loan," *DB*, March 9, 1962.

to re-emphasize that our decision in supporting the position of the Board of Control carries absolutely no implication concerning our attitude toward the action of those students who are seeking to achieve social justice for all Americans.

Murphy then met privately with a handful of the rally leaders, and although his decision remained unchanged, he considered the meeting "a friendly and useful interchange."[76]

Accepting the students' appeal would have meant overturning the vote of the three UCLA administrators on the board, thus Murphy supported the board's decision. But the students left that meeting with a recommendation that the Freedom Riders could apply to the UCLA Loan Office for financial assistance. He advised the students that office's former $600 maximum loan limit was now $1,000 since chancellors had the authority to make campus-level loan exceptions as needed. Mostly notably, Murphy made a personal financial contribution of an undisclosed amount to the Student Loan Fund to increase the amount available to the Freedom Riders. Then, also on March 16, Murphy informed Kerr of the student loan vote and board decision that "flared up" while he was in South America and said he hoped "the matter is now relatively closed," although he did not mention his personal contribution to the Student Loan Fund. This concluded one of Murphy's greatest challenges as UCLA chancellor, a position confined by the university system hierarchy.[77]

Conclusion

The administrative challenges in the UC system were symptomatic of the unprecedented midcentury growth of US higher education, and academic leaders' commitment to the conservative ideology that had long guided state politics. This allowed them to overlook the connections between the postwar

76. "Appeal BOC Loan Decision to Chancellor," *DB*, March 9, 1962; "Hundreds Join in Anti-BOC Protest," *DB*, March 15, 1962; Dave Lawton, "FDM Rejects Appeal: Riders Told to Apply for University Funds," *DB*, March 19, 1962; Franklin D. Murphy Statement, March 16, 1962, Chancellor Files–Murphy, Box 122, Folder 246–Freedom Riders, UCLA.

77. On Murphy's personal loan, see Lawton, "FDM Rejects Appeal." In December 1959, Clark Kerr informed campus chancellors that eligibility for student loans had been revised. Among the four revisions, one was "the maximum amount of single loans allowed to a single individual from $600 to $1,000." For more, see Clark Kerr to Chief Campus Officers, December 3, 1959, Chancellor Files–Murphy, Box 37, Folder 1–Student Loan Funds, 1959–1964, UCLA; Clark Kerr to Chief Campus Officers, April 15, 1960, Chancellor Files–Murphy, Box 37, Folder 1–Student Loan Funds, 1959–1964, UCLA; Franklin D. Murphy to Clark Kerr, March 16, 1962, Chancellor Files–Murphy, Box 122, Folder 246–Freedom Riders, UCLA.

economy and migration and how racial tensions transcended regional boundaries and descended upon California. Administrators of the UC system prepared for increased numbers of students and prioritized administrative structures and efficiency without creating mechanisms to account for the dramatic
societal shifts on their campuses. This lack of foresight allowed the student
restrictions on off-campus activities to conflict increasingly with administrative priorities of expanding institutional capacities to accommodate more
research and students.

Therefore, the Black citizens who migrated west from the Jim Crow South
during the 1930s and 1940s developed into frustrated residents as white Californians also adhered to racial segregation. By the late 1950s, the political right's
concerns about communism opposed the left's civil rights concerns on UC campuses, and the paternalistic directives that banned organizing for off-campus
causes agitated students. A series of decisions made by UC system administrators demonstrated how neutral stances on the Black Freedom Movement
impacted public perception of the role of higher education in society.

The conflicts between UC president Clark Kerr and UCLA chancellor
Franklin D. Murphy also exhibit the pitfalls of symbolic administrative hires.
Murphy sought the autonomy to mold UCLA into a university he deemed
equal in standing to the Berkeley campus. This meant ending racial discrimination on campus and in the surrounding neighborhoods; however, he reported
to UC system administrators who demanded more moderate appeals to challenging racial discrimination. Therefore, although Murphy was a student-
centered administrator, the complex organizational structure of the university
did not allow a campus chancellor to outpace the system. As a result, anti-
racist initiatives at UCLA were as much about higher education's illiberalism
as they were about civil rights.

Although the Freedom Rider loans were contested, examining the Black
Freedom Movement against the backdrop of academic leaders' actions conveys
a clearer understanding of college presidents' role within their local community. Murphy's efforts to challenge local housing discrimination, barbers' refusal
to serve Black students, and campus sororities' bias were recognized by Black
Los Angeles. In February 1962, just days before the student loan vote, Murphy
served as the keynote speaker at a commemoration of the founding of the First
African Methodist Episcopal Church, the oldest Black church in Los Angeles,
and delivered a speech titled "Los Angeles, Its Image and Its Reality." Established in 1872, Pastor H. H. Brookins and his congregation listened intently
as Chancellor Murphy praised the members of the historic Black church for
their civic achievements and contributions to Los Angeles. In April 1962, a
month after the Board of Control's controversial Freedom Loan decision,
Franklin and Judy Murphy were honored by the Los Angeles Alumnae

Chapter of Delta Sigma Theta Sorority, a prominent Black sorority, before more than 1,500 guests at the Los Angeles Wilfandel Club. "We believe we are honoring a great man," said Jerolean Sneed, president of the alumnae chapter.[78]

These events and others demonstrate that despite Murphy's challenges within the UC system, his efforts did not go unnoticed by those most affected by racism in Los Angeles. He believed eliminating discrimination was essential to elevating the prominence of UCLA—something the southern regents desired from the new chancellor. In the end, however, as the nation considered the California Master Plan for Higher Education the prototype for public higher education, academic leaders accepted a pivotal role in university systems that stifled racial progress through bureaucratic resistance—a model that would be later replicated by other states—and Murphy was not the only chancellor challenged by the lack of autonomy to lead a state-supported university.[79]

78. "First AME Praised by UCLA Chancellor," *LA Sentinel*, February 15, 1962. The First AME Church was significant to the California civil rights efforts. Historian Gerald Horne wrote of First AME, "The turmoil of the civil rights movement in the Deep South also had reverberations in LA. As in the South, pastors like the Reverend H. H. Brookins played a crucial role." For more, see Horne, *Fire This Time*, p. 46. Regarding First AME being the first Black-organized church in Los Angeles, see Campbell, *Making Black Los Angeles*, p. 54; and Stanford, *African Americans in Los Angeles*, p. 25. Additionally, as of October 2018, First AME Los Angeles also refers to itself as "the oldest church founded by African Americans in the City of Angels" on its website, famechurch.org. On Delta Sigma Theta honoring the Murphys, see "1500 Attend Delta Fete for UCLA Head," *LA Sentinel*, April 19, 1962, and "Sorority Fetes UCLA Head, Wife at College," *LA Sentinel*, April 5, 1962.

79. Scholars who focus on the late 1960s have pointed assessments of the Master Plan. Noliwe M. Rooks wrote, "In 1960, 12 percent of the students at San Francisco State College were African American. By 1968, Black enrollment had dropped to 3 percent, in part as a result of the military draft into the war in Vietnam, and in part as a result of a system of 'tracking' Black and poor students into schools for vocational education, as opposed to the liberal arts." For more, see Rooks, *White Money/Black Power*, p. 36.

4

"The University Has Become a Pawn"

THE FIGHT FOR AUTONOMY
AT A PUBLIC UNIVERSITY

"IN MY HUMBLE opinion, if it were possible to give one person credit for the advances made by the university since 1946, that man would have to be you." Richard M. Allen felt compelled to share this with John Davis Williams, chancellor of the University of Mississippi. The previous night, June 25, 1962, Williams visited Allen and other Sunflower County Alumni Association members in Indianola, a small town in the heart of the Mississippi Delta. The chancellor provided updates about the academic progress being made on the campus, located 110 miles northeast of them, and Allen was especially "impressed" by Williams's talk. He was proud of his alma mater's growth, but in the summer of 1962, none of that mattered. Most Mississippians were interested in only one aspect of the university—segregation. In Allen's assessment, the "tremendous strides" of the university had hardly raised an eyebrow for anyone outside of his modest office at the Cooper and Allen law firm. Thus, he wrote Williams the next day with disappointment: "I regret that more people are not aware."[1]

In the Deep South, Williams and the other presidents of the segregated white state-supported universities understood what Allen had just realized. Their universities were monuments to a southern heritage, and white residents tied their segregationist beliefs to these institutions designed to train the next generation of the southern genteel. Therefore, academic content rivaled social

1. Richard M. Allen to John Davis Williams, June 26, 1962, J. D. Williams Collection, Box 6, Folder 8, University of Mississippi, Archives and Special Collections (collection and location hereafter cited as JDW and UM).

behavior in importance, and college presidents were expected to ensure that southern universities did not deviate from their sacred missions. Yet, demands for racial equality grew louder after World War II, and federal officials were forced to address said demands as the nation's international standing weakened due to its failed domestic policies for addressing racial inequality. American racism was a global topic, and by the mid-twentieth century, white universities in states that anchored the old Confederacy were the focal point of tensions between advocates for state rights and proponents for stronger federal civil rights enforcement.

There, the free exchange of ideas was contested. White supremacist public officials and the broader southern white citizenry were unwilling to allow intellectual arguments for desegregation or interracial interactions to occur on college campuses. Faculty who espoused views in favor of desegregation were targeted and labeled communists. This infringed on academic freedom, but it was representative of a history of southern academic leaders lacking the autonomy to lead their universities. Federal dollars and academic accreditation agencies, however, required southern universities to function independent of state influence.

This independence was critical to successful desegregation, whether voluntary or court ordered, and southern white college presidents played an integral role in securing institutional autonomy from public officials. The autonomy was needed to protect faculty, university accreditation, and frankly, college presidents' own careers. That tension was most pronounced at the University of Mississippi (Ole Miss), where residents had largely dismissed Williams's role as chancellor before 1962; however, following a campus race riot over the admission of James Meredith, a Black student, Williams emerged as an important voice that influenced racial practices among college presidents across the nation. In turn, this shaped how academic leaders understood and engaged the relationship between campus racism and administrative autonomy.

First a Southerner, Then a Chancellor

In February 1946, immediately following World War II, the all-white board of trustees overseeing Mississippi colleges and universities sought a new chancellor for the state's flagship university—Ole Miss. This was a pivotal point of reflection on the past with an eye toward the future, and perhaps no state grappled with the link between past and future more than Mississippi. This was the task facing the Mississippi Board of Institutions of Higher Learning. Despite achieving what many considered progress, Alfred Benjamin Butts, Ole Miss chancellor from 1935 to 1946, was not reappointed by the board during its January 1946 meeting. Butts and the board members developed conflicting philosophies over the role of a "state university" as a "center of service to the people of Mississippi as a whole." In fact, H. M. Ivy, a board member and superintendent of the Meridian Public Schools, considered Butts's views "contrary to that necessary" for the further development of Ole Miss.[2]

The firing provided Ivy and the other board members the opportunity to sketch their ideal chancellor. First, he should be younger than fifty-five years old. Next, the chancellor needed to believe that a state-supported university "holds an obligation" to connect with every aspect of the state. This meant Ole Miss should be the institution that elected officials, industrial and agricultural leaders, and others turned to "for advice and cooperation." Therefore, a necessary skill would be the ability to "work cooperatively with others." The chancellor also needed to be resourceful. Furthermore, the man should have an established reputation beyond his current place of employment. Although the trustees did not specify that the ideal candidate should be an academic or have experience in higher education, they did stipulate, perhaps most importantly, that: "We prefer a southern man. A Mississippian would be preferred but is not essential."[3]

The need to be a southerner was as important as any other characteristic an Ole Miss chancellor might possess. The board wanted an individual accustomed to the southern way of life and who could ensure that Black people, and white women for that matter, knew their place in society. Ole Miss was a bastion for upholding those sacred social traditions, but it had difficulty finding the ideal candidate because the relationship between past public officials and academic leaders had drawn criticism throughout academia. By the time trustees sought the next chancellor, the cross-regional question was whether Ole Miss could gain autonomy from public officials while also continuing its traditional role in the state.[4]

History was driving the trustees' decision about the future, and Ole Miss and state politics were linked. During Reconstruction, in September 1870, Ole Miss chancellor John N. Waddel said the university "never, for a moment, conceived it possible or proper that a Negro should be admitted to its classes,

2. H. M. Ivy to Henry H. Hill, February 8, 1946, JDW, Box 6, Folder 2, UM. For more on the Butts dismissal, see Sansing, *Making Haste Slowly*, p. 131. For more on H. M. Ivy's views on desegregation, see Anderson, "The Case of Mississippi," pp. 306–307.

3. Ivy to Hill, February 8, 1946.

4. This chapter builds upon previous histories of Mississippi higher education. In particular, historians David G. Sansing and Joy Williamson-Lott had provided book-length accounts about the state's institutions of higher learning. For more, see Sansing, *Making Haste Slowly*, and Williamson, *Radicalizing the Ebony Tower*. For a conversation about how Mississippi fit within the broader southern higher education landscape, see Williamson-Lott, *Jim Crow Campus*.

graduated with its honors, or presented with its diplomas." By the 1890s, the governor served on the Ole Miss board of trustees, meaning university leaders were "drawn into political contests and could be dismissed if they had supported the losing candidate." In 1910, educators successfully lobbied state legislators to restructure governing boards and barred elected officials from serving as trustees, but this was merely a change in semantics. The actual influence of officials over the affairs of the state's colleges and universities remained intact, and the on- and off-again chancellorship of Alfred Hume is an example. In 1924, Hume was a politically motivated hire selected by a new governor, Henry Whitfield, in a vindictive move against the previous chancellor, who had not supported Whitfield. Hume emphasized moral and Christian development over academic or athletic success to signal Ole Miss's commitment to transmitting whites' ideals to the next generation, but this did not bode well for the university's status beyond Mississippi.[5]

The outside assessments of Ole Miss were also hurtful. It was one thing to neglect Mississippi's Black colleges. For example, the Mississippi legislature refused to match the General Education Board's pledge of $100,000 toward new buildings at Alcorn, the state's Black land-grant college, in March 1926. But the same type of neglect was also directed toward Ole Miss. By 1927, nonsouthern evaluators considered the quality of the university's curriculum, facilities, and faculty to be below national standards, and the law school lost its accreditation the same year.[6]

Furthermore, in 1928, Theodore Bilbo was elected governor a second time (his first term was 1916–1920) and immediately entered into a multiyear fight with Hume. Bilbo wanted to relocate Ole Miss to Jackson, the state capital, but Hume opposed the idea and successfully convinced state legislators against the move. Bilbo desired to build up the faculty and facilities to make the university more progressive and on par with nationally recognized universities, although that was not to be confused with a desire for desegregation. Meanwhile, Hume held steadfast to his commitment to character

5. For the "never, for a moment" quote, see John N. Waddel to R. S. Hudson, September 28, 1870, JDW, Box 6, Folder 4, UM. For more context on Chancellor Waddell's quote, see Anderson, "The Case of Mississippi," p. 296. For a detailed account of Mississippi higher education from 1890 to 1928, see Sansing, *Making Haste Slowly*, pp. 68–90; see p. 99 for more about Hume's focus on moral development over athletic or academic success. For a briefer account and the "drawn into political contests" quote, see Cohadas, *The Band Played Dixie*, pp. 22, 27.

6. On Mississippi officials not funding Alcorn, see Anderson, "The Case of Mississippi," p. 298. In 1927, Michael V. O'Shea led a University of Wisconsin research team to evaluate the state's education system. For more on the subsequent O'Shea Report and law school accreditation, see Sansing, *Making Haste Slowly*, pp. 89–98; and Cohadas, *The Band Played Dixie*, pp. 22, 27.

development as Ole Miss's main focus. From 1928 to 1930, Bilbo attempted to have the board fire Hume multiple times because he did not like the direction of the university, eventually succeeding on his third attempt in June 1930. In the process, although the two men held drastically different views regarding the direction of the university, neither did much to help Ole Miss, as the medical school found itself on probation and enrollment declined by about four hundred students during the two-year Bilbo-Hume spat.[7]

The most telling aspect of the failing Ole Miss was that the best way out of the conundrum was the same as the way the university's leaders and board had entered it. In 1930, the Southern Education Association suspended Ole Miss and three other state-supported white institutions due to political interference, notably not impacting Alcorn because the association did not accredit Black colleges at the time. The association blamed Ole Miss administrators, those appointed by Bilbo to replace Hume, for the situation. Two years later, the state's colleges and universities were reorganized under one board with ten trustees. This was a critical step toward regaining accreditation. Also, one key member of the association's evaluators was Hume's friend, and in December 1932, the Southern Education Association offered to reinstate Ole Miss if all individuals fired by Bilbo were rehired. Hume was back as chancellor thanks to the same political influence that led to his firing, and Ole Miss proceeded as usual from there.[8]

By 1937, roughly 90 percent of the state's attorneys were Ole Miss alumni, and seven years later, as World War II neared its end, another amendment to the state constitution was passed with the hope of preventing a future Bilbo-Hume type conflict. This time, state legislators reordered the governing board again in an attempt to keep politics out of university affairs. But as Russell H. Barrett, an Ole Miss political science professor in the 1960s, assessed, "The chancellor knows that he really does not run the university, and this weakness constantly endangers its prestige in the academic world."[9]

---

7. On the Bilbo-Hume tensions, see Sansing, *Making Haste Slowly*, pp. 91–110. On page 96, Sansing explained, "Although Bilbo's reorganization plan was well conceived . . . it was overwhelmed by the emotional reaction to his proposal to move the university. Consequently, the plan itself was never considered on its merits." For more on Bilbo-Hume, see Cohadas, *The Band Played Dixie*, pp. 22–28.

8. On the four white colleges losing accreditation in 1930, see Sansing, *Making Haste Slowly*, p. 109. Regarding the accreditation loss not impacting Alcorn, see Anderson, "The Case of Mississippi," p. 300. On the accreditation scenario and Hume's friend being an evaluator, see Cohadas, *The Band Played Dixie*, pp. 29–32.

9. Regarding the percentage of state attorneys and the state constitutional amendment, see Cohadas, *The Band Played Dixie*, pp. 38, 42. On both state constitutional amendment and the

White Mississippians were more interested in their university being good for them than in Ole Miss being a good university. This explains why H. M. Ivy was so adamant about preferring a Mississippian, or a southerner at a minimum, as the next Ole Miss chancellor. The Mississippi way of life had to be maintained, and Ole Miss was a critical entity in ensuring that this was accomplished. Yet, the university also had an image problem. It lagged behind other white southern colleges in academic rigor and reputation even in a region that was considered academically inferior to other regions. Additionally, the embarrassment of the Bilbo-Hume debacle still lingered. Therefore, the trustees may have wanted a southerner, but they needed an administrator skilled in communications. Ivy sent his call for recommendations out across the South to other trusted white educators and leaders, and in 1946, one name consistently returned as a top choice—John Davis Williams.[10]

At the time, Williams was president of Marshall College, a state-supported college in Huntington, West Virginia. Born in 1902 in Newport, Kentucky, a town on the Ohio River across from Cincinnati, he attended public schools throughout his childhood. Williams then earned a bachelor's degree in business and education administration at the University of Kentucky (UK) in 1926 and stayed in Kentucky for most of his adult life, working in the public schools as a teacher and principal at several schools. He even served as school superintendent in Falmouth, Kentucky. Along the way, he earned his master's degree from UK in 1930 and his doctorate in education from Teachers College, Columbia University in 1940. He was a southerner, albeit not a Mississippian, and an experienced administrator.[11]

Williams had been president of Marshall since 1942 and was only in his early forties when people recommended him for the Ole Miss chancellorship.

"chancellor knows" quote, see Barrett, *Integration at Ole Miss*, pp. 23–24. Former US Senator Trent Lott attended Ole Miss. He later noted that, in the 1950s, all state officials, including governors, were Ole Miss graduates. For more, see Turner, *Sitting In and Speaking Out*, p. 107.

10. The national perception of education at southern white colleges is evident across multiple sources. At the University of Alabama, a student editorial took offense to *Time* magazine's description of the football and fraternity culture. See "'Country Club' Image," *Crimson White*, December 13, 1962. At the University of Mississippi, Chancellor John Davis Williams wrote the editor of *Life* magazine following its article titled, "Beauty to Spare." Williams thanked the editor for the article featuring back-to-back Miss America winners, both of whom were Ole Miss students when selected, but emphasized that the university was "primarily interested in serving the major purposes of an educational institution." For more, see John Davis Williams to Henry R. Luce, September 1, 1961, JDW, Box 6, Folder 5, UM.

11. Biographical Data–Chancellor J. D. Williams, October 20, 1954, JDW, Box 14, Folder 1, UM.

Henry H. Hill, president of Peabody College for Teachers in Nashville, considered Williams "unusually successful" at Marshall with its roughly two thousand students. His reputation prior to that, Hill said, was also notable. In 1934, during the Great Depression, he was the superintendent of education for the Tennessee Valley Authority in the Norris Dam area in East Tennessee. From 1935 to 1942, Williams was a professor of education at UK, where he also served as director of the university's training school, and he took a sabbatical from during the 1941–42 academic year and consulted for the American Council on Education (ACE) Committee on Teacher Education. He continued his relationship with ACE, serving on its executive committee after he became Marshall's president. "He is very good on public relations," Hill added.[12]

Williams met the preferred qualifications of the board, but his commitment to segregation was questionable. For example, as Marshall president, he permitted measured interactions across race. In fact, in 1945, one of his most notable decisions was allowing Marshall to participate in an ACE program on intergroup relations. Fewer than ten colleges nationally participated in the program, which brought conversations about interacting across racial difference to the Huntington community. Of course, such activities would not be permitted at Ole Miss or any other state-supported college in Mississippi, and surely Williams must have understood as much. Therefore, Williams entered an Ole Miss in need of a chancellor who could strengthen its academic reputation while also appeasing officials' longstanding desires that the university remain pure in its teachings. An old battle over autonomy would ensue with a new chancellor.[13]

An Unusual Chancellorship

When John Davis Williams was inaugurated as Ole Miss chancellor, he was aware of state officials' history of interference with how the university functioned. White Mississippians wanted students to preserve social norms as much as they achieved proficiency in any academic subject area. The concept of academic freedom was, at best, narrowly interpreted, if one believed in it at

12. For the specific dates of positions held, see Biographical Data, October 20, 1954; Henry H. Hill to H. M. Ivy, February 12, 1946, JDW, Box 6, Folder 2, UM.

13. On the ACE committee on intergroup relations, see Eagles, *The Price of Defiance*, p. 26–28. Eagles concluded the following about Williams, upon accepting the Ole Miss job: "His attitudes and experiences regarding race would certainly have concerned the trustees, but his explanations must have reassured them that he would not agitate the racial status quo and satisfied them that he was safe." For more on Williams at Marshall, see Sarah Hendrickson, "The Integration of Marshall University," Carter G. Woodson Project, https://www.marshall.edu/woodson-dev/the-integration-of-marshall-university/ (accessed May 14, 2020).

all. For instance, former chancellor Alfred Hume, as a devout Christian, said, "It goes without saying that anything tending toward atheistic teaching will never be tolerated by me." As a conduit between the state and the university, the Ole Miss chancellor long held a similar stance on teaching. But Williams wanted to support academic freedom for faculty, and if the university were to expand its academic reputation, he hoped white Mississippians would soon understand the value of intellectual growth. Therefore, for his inauguration in the fall of 1946, he strategically had his friend Herman Lee Donovan, president of the University of Kentucky, deliver an address on the topic of academic freedom.[14]

As an out-of-state guest, Donovan told the audience members that they could not "control or interfere with what takes place in the classrooms and laboratories" of Ole Miss or UK if they wanted those universities to "redound to the glory of the state and the promotion of the welfare of society." Donovan essentially said neither Mississippians nor any other southerners should expect statewide economic advancement and prosperity if academic leaders were constantly stifled by elected officials. For example, in 1946, state pressure led Mississippi State administrators to cancel a football game against the University of Nevada because their opponent had Black players. Therefore, Williams should be credited for his passive attempt to lay the groundwork for his chancellorship. He could not be direct about such a sensitive matter, and he would need state legislators to pass generous budgets to aid the growth of Ole Miss; however, the calculated speech by Donovan did little to alter reality. For the next fifteen years, Williams found success in growing the physical infrastructure of Ole Miss but also repeatedly had his authority overridden by meddling state officials.[15]

After World War II, Black veterans returned to the United States with heightened awareness of their rights after serving abroad fighting for democracy. In Mississippi, conditions were especially brutal and inconsistent with the freedoms touted by federal officials. More than 80 percent of Black men worked as sharecroppers or in some other form of labor for white farmers. This provoked T.R.M. Howard, a Black doctor and civil rights activist, to tell audiences during a national speaking tour that, "I'm from what is considered the 'Iron Curtain state of Mississippi,'" and Black people demanded that curtain

14. On Hume's narrow view of academic freedom, see Sansing, *Making Haste Slowly*, p. 100. On both Hume's view of academic freedom and Donovan speaking at Ole Miss, see Cohadas, *The Band Played Dixie*, pp. 25, 42.

15. Cohadas, *The Band Played Dixie*, p. 42. On the canceled game, see Dittmer, *Local People*, p. 20.

be raised. These demands from Black people may have been largely overlooked by an oblivious Ole Miss student body, but state officials worked diligently to uphold white supremacy and protect the minds of white undergraduates.[16]

This coincided with the first attempt to desegregate Ole Miss. It was unsuccessful due to the Black applicant's undergraduate degree being from an unaccredited institution, but although rejected on a technicality, this attempt to enroll was telling of the changing landscape facing segregationists. An invitation for the university to join the National Student Association, a group known for its liberal leanings, was declined by Ole Miss academic officials in January 1948. Although its presence was limited in the South, the NSA eventually established campus chapters in every southern state except Mississippi. Meanwhile, in the summer of 1948, many southern delegates walked out of the Democratic National Convention as the party rallied behind stronger civil rights policies. About the same time, some Ole Miss professors remained quiet regarding politics because of fear of retribution and being accused of being a communist in the late 1940s. This was the case despite the American Association of University Professors (AAUP) adopting a Statement of the Principles on Academic Freedom and Tenure in 1940. The ability to pursue ideas and new knowledge was not a reality at Ole Miss. Williams's hopes to foster an environment where the free exchange of ideas prospered were doused by segregationist leaders.[17]

Williams's challenges were a byproduct of the personal beliefs of the board members and state officials. In 1951, H. M. Ivy, as a board member and

16. On Black veterans returning home from war expecting rights, see Silver, *The Closed Society*, p. 83. For more on the number of Blacks in agriculture-oriented jobs, see Dittmer, *Local People*, p. 19. On October 2, 1955, only months after the gruesome death of Emmett Till, T.R.M. Howard spoke at Sharp Street Methodist Church in Baltimore before 2,500 people. He discussed the "Iron Curtain" in Maryland and elsewhere in the nation. For more, see T.R.M. Howard, "Terror Reigns in Mississippi," in Houck and Dixon, *Rhetoric, Religion, and the Civil Rights Movement*, pp. 116–131.

17. On the Dixiecrats, see Silver, *The Closed Society*, p. 84. For more on the Dixiecrats, see Dittmer, *Local People*, pp. 27–28. Regarding the first denied Black applicant to Ole Miss, see Barrett, *Integration at Ole Miss*, p. 25. On Ole Miss declining the NSA invitation and faculty being investigated for communism, see Cohadas, *The Band Played Dixie*, pp. 34, 49. Regarding all southern states having NSA chapters except Mississippi, see NSA Institutional Membership List, August 9, 1961, Office of Student Activities Records, Box 23, Folder 3, Special Collections Research Center, University of Chicago Library. For a brief synopsis of the AAUP Statement in 1940, see Whittington, *Speak Freely*, pp. 141–142. A notable example of southern professors being branded as communist is the case of Georgia governor Eugene Talmadge. In 1941, Talmadge dismissed ten University of Georgia employees for what Matthew D. Lassiter called "New Deal liberalism." For more on the Georgia case, see Lassiter, *Silent Majority*, p. 56; and Turner, *Sitting In and Speaking Out*, p. 33.

superintendent of Meridian schools, told a public forum of 175 whites that Mississippi's schools would remain segregated for another twenty-five years. Three years later, after the Supreme Court's *Brown v. Board of Education* ruling, a decision that outlawed segregated schools, US senator James O. Eastland from Mississippi said, "I know southern people will not surrender their dual school system and their racial heritage at the command of this crowd of racial politicians in judicial robes." As proof of this sentiment, in 1952, there were slightly more than 20,000 Black voters in Mississippi, but violent intimidation tactics used by Citizens' Councils dwindled that number to around 8,000 by 1958—a year when only 9 percent of Black residents in Alabama could vote, but Mississippi was worse with only 4 percent. The white press also fanned hatred's flame, calling the *Brown* decision a "black day of tragedy," and in 1956, state legislators generously funded the establishment of the State Sovereignty Commission as a "watchdog" group to protect segregation and investigate any suspicious activities that endangered their way of life. Two years later, in case desegregation occurred, a plan was proposed to give the governor the authority to abolish schools, including colleges.[18]

Throughout the 1950s, as statewide policies were passed to protect segregation, public officials also paid particular attention to higher education. Just before Ivy predicted a long future for school segregation, the Supreme Court's *Sweatt v. Painter* decision in June 1950 offered a different forecast. The University of Texas in Austin denied Heman Marion Sweatt, a Black man, admission to its law school. As an alternative, the state established a Black law school in Houston, but the High Court ruled that the Black law school was not equal in terms of its facilities or faculty. Therefore, "separate but equal" meant separate facilities based on race must also be equal in terms caliber and experience of faculty members, and Sweatt was admitted to the University of Texas. By 1952, forty-nine once-segregated white colleges had desegregated, but Mississippi was one of the last holdouts. Despite public officials' desires, Williams and

18. "Gives Jim Crow 25 Years to Live," *Jet*, November 8, 1951. For the Eastland quote, the plan to abolish schools, and State Sovereignty Commission, see Barrett, *Integration at Ole Miss*, pp. 22, 26, 28. On the white press and number of Black voters, see Silver, *The Closed Society*, p. 90. For the "black day of tragedy" quote, see Cohadas, *The Band Played Dixie*, p. 39. On the Alabama and Mississippi Black voter percentages, see Anderson, *Pursuit of Fairness*, p. 49. In cross-checking voter percentages with US Census Records for Mississippi from 1960, there were 915,743 "Negro" residents. Therefore, the single-digit percentage of eligible voters is accurate. For more, see table 15 of the 1960 US Census Report for Mississippi.

other Ole Miss officials knew any future Black applicants could not be denied admission due to race.[19]

Racist southern public officials' attempted interference with the exchange of ideas at state-supported colleges was not unique to Mississippi. Segregationists across the South made overtures to college presidents and chancellors about what should be taught, who should speak on campus, and what research should be published. Even the presidents at private southern universities struggled to convince trustees to support intellectual expansion as trustees tied this all to communism. What was distinctive in Mississippi was their effectiveness. Following the *Sweatt* decision, Albin Krebs, an Ole Miss senior, sympathized with Black people in an editorial and argued that southern universities should obey the courts and admit Black students. The backlash was swift as one state official accused Krebs of being influenced by communists. It was a common ploy by segregationists to link civil rights and communism whenever dissent against the dominant social order arose on southern campuses. As a result, Krebs found no in-state journalism jobs, later moving to New York for his career. In 1953 and 1954, respectively, Charles Dubra and Medgar Evers applied to the Ole Miss law school, but neither filed legal action after the university did not immediately admit them. The ultimate decision was in the board members' hands, not those of the law faculty or Williams as chancellor.[20]

The tactics to maintain segregation were numerous. White state officials used Black colleges as bargaining tools. For example, in the summer of 1954, Governor Hugh White met with seven Black leaders, all men, including Alcorn president J. D. Boyd and Mississippi Vocational College president J. H. White. He tried to convince them that if Black residents accepted segregation, the state would invest millions into Black education, but the attempt eventually failed. Later in 1954, for white campuses, the board determined that letters of recommendation from alumni were needed for admission—a move that made it nearly impossible for a future Black applicant to be admitted.[21]

19. For a detailed account of *Sweatt v. Painter* and the broader challenges of desegregating the University of Texas, see Goldstone, *Integrating the 40 Acres*. On Ole Miss officials watching the *Sweatt* decision, see Barrett, *Integration at Ole Miss*, p. 25. On the number of desegregated southern white institutions by 1952, see Turner, *Sitting In and Speaking Out*, p. 38. Even when some colleges did desegregate, historian R. Scott Baker has noted that white academic leaders wanted to keep the number of Blacks admitted to a minimum. For more, see Baker, *Paradoxes of Desegregation*, p. 134.

20. Regarding the struggles of presidents of white private universities, see Kean, *Desegregating Private Higher Education in the South*. On Krebs, see Cohadas, *The Band Played Dixie*, pp. 35–38. On Dubra and Evers, see Barrett, *Integration at Ole Miss*, pp. 25–26.

21. On Governor Hugh White's meeting with Black leaders, see Dittmer, *Local People*, pp. 38–40. On the letters of recommendation requirement, see Barrett, *Integration at Ole Miss*, p. 26.

The next year, in 1955, the same year fourteen-year-old Emmett Till was murdered in Mississippi, garnering national headlines, the board passed a policy to screen all campus speakers. The Ole Miss chapter of the AAUP, the State Council of the AAUP, and the Campus Senate of Ole Miss passed resolutions condemning such a policy, which was antithetical to academic freedom and to protecting the university from being influenced by political pressure. Nonetheless, the policy was implemented. In the spring of 1956, Williams rescinded a campus speaking invitation to Alvin Kershaw, an Ohio minister who championed desegregation, after the governor and others retreated on supporting the chancellor's initial decision to welcome the speaker.[22]

The Kershaw episode would impact Williams's future efforts to ease clashes between public officials and campus ideas. By 1958, attacks on students and faculty turned toward Williams. The mere concept of the Krebs editorial in 1950, the two Black applicants in 1953 and 1954, and Kershaw's original invitation to campus led two Ole Miss graduates to criticize the chancellor. Under Williams, they assessed that Ole Miss was not moving with the same urgency to maintain segregation as the segregationist state officials, white Citizens' Councils, and the Sovereignty Commission. Williams was accused of letting the campus go awry in teaching communist-inspired beliefs that hailed desegregation as viable.[23]

In 1960, Ross Barnett's inauguration as governor proved to be the perfect culmination of the Citizens' Councils' grassroots desires and state officials' efforts to control Ole Miss. Barnett was committed to segregation, and he would become Williams's very own Theodore Bilbo; however, in November 1960, Senator John F. Kennedy (D-MA) was elected US president. This set the stage for a clash between Barnett and Kennedy, with Williams caught in the crossfire, but as historian Frank Lambert surmised, "Barnett knew his audience. For Mississippians, race was not just an important political issue, it was the paramount issue."[24]

Regarding Boyd at Alcorn and White at Mississippi Vocational, see Williamson, *Radicalizing the Ebony Tower*, pp. 117–123.

22. On the Kershaw episode, see Cohadas, *The Band Played Dixie*, pp. 44–48. For more on Kershaw and the Ole Miss speakers policy, see Williamson-Lott, *Jim Crow Campus*, pp. 40–42. On the Emmett Till murder and its reach, see Mamie Till-Bradley, "I Want You to Know What They Did to My Boy," in Houck and Dixon, *Rhetoric, Religion, and the Civil Rights Movement*, pp. 131–145.

23. Cohadas, *The Band Played Dixie*, pp. 48–49.

24. On Barnett's election being the Citizens' Council goal, see Barrett, *Integration at Ole Miss*, p. 28; Lambert, *Battle of Ole Miss*, p. 98.

The Chancellor "Preserving the Precious Heritage"

Chancellor Williams amassed an extraordinary record of developing the infrastructure of Ole Miss through the 1950s and early 1960s. The university's main campus in Oxford and its medical center in Jackson morphed into something white Mississippians could brag about. Two decades earlier, Ole Miss had lost its accreditation due to political interference, inadequate facilities, and poorly credentialed faculty, many of them without doctorates. By the start of the 1960s, however, the building program was booming. In Oxford, Williams ushered in 13.8 million dollars' worth of new academic, residential, and auxiliary buildings, totaling a million new square feet on campus. In Jackson, the medical center gained 14.7 million dollars' worth of new construction, for nearly 700,000 new square feet.[25]

That growth was not uncommon nationally as the Cold War and anti-communist sentiment nudged federal and state officials to allocate more funds to universities for scientific expansion to combat the Soviets. As a result, Ole Miss had been awarded twenty-four National Defense Act Fellowships and a contract from the Atomic Energy Commission for nuclear research, and Hinds County officials in Jackson had plans to build Ole Miss a million-dollar research facility. Williams was unwavering in demanding that state legislators support the university fiscally. Yet, Williams stepped aside when state legislators attacked the idea of desegregation.[26]

By 1961, Williams still did not vocally champion segregation, nor did he call for desegregation. Despite having lived in Mississippi for the past fifteen years, he was well aware of the changing landscape of once-segregated universities. In fact, both of his alma maters had enrolled Black students before 1950. In 1949, the University of Kentucky became one of the first southern universities to admit a Black student, and Teachers College, Columbia University, had long enrolled some Black graduate students. These facts, alongside his liberal-leaning actions at Marshall, likely guided his decision to remain silent on the issue of

25. Building Program Summary, 1963, JDW, Box 6, Folder 5, UM.

26. On the Cold War and higher education, see O'Mara, *Cities of Knowledge*. On nuclear and defense research at Ole Miss, see J. D. Williams, The Achievement of Greatness Speech, Sunflower County Alumni Association, June 25, 1962, JDW, Box 11, Folder 5, UM. Peter Wallenstein has explained the federal pressure at Mississippi State, with president Dean W. Colvard "understanding by 1965 that the institution's continued receipt of federal funding would be in grave jeopardy if it continued to exclude all African Americans." For more, see Peter Wallenstein, "Black Southerners and NonBlack Universities: The Process of Desegregating Southern Higher Education, 1935–1965," in Wallenstein, *Higher Education and the Civil Rights Movement*, p. 19. For a regional assessment of the federal pressure on white administrators, see Williamson-Lott, *Jim Crow Campus*.

desegregation. The federal courts had already determined educational segregation to be unconstitutional, but most white Mississippians had no interest in the courts. This quickly changed, however, as Williams soon faced his greatest challenge—the first serious attempt to desegregate Ole Miss.[27]

On January 21, 1961, the day after President Kennedy was inaugurated, James Meredith requested an application from Ole Miss registrar Robert B. Ellis. Meredith received the standard generic response sent to potential applicants that encouraged him to apply—the same thing Ellis would say to any prospective student. But upon submitting his application, Meredith added a letter. "I sincerely hope that your attitude toward me as a potential member of your student body reflects the attitude of the school and that it will not change upon learning that I am not a white applicant," he informed Ellis. "I am an American-Mississippi-Negro citizen." Meredith then informed Ellis that he had not submitted the required six alumni references because he was Black. In exchange, he submitted the names of Black people who could speak to his character. "Except for the requirement mentioned above, my application is complete."[28]

Meredith was immediately informed that spring admissions were closed, and that prompted him to seek the legal advice of attorneys with the NAACP Legal Defense Fund. Over the next three months, from February until May, Ole Miss officials followed the trustees' mandate and stalled in rendering a formal decision on Meredith's application while the board adopted new and revised old admissions policies. Williams's silence, however, did not sit well with many white Mississippians who had no patience for anything less than the chancellor pronouncing that Ole Miss would remain a segregated university.[29]

27. For a contemporary account of the University of Kentucky's desegregation, see Linda B. Blackford, "University of Kentucky Names Residence Hall after School's First Black Student," *Lexington Herald-Leader*, May 8, 2015. Teachers College, Columbia University, was a destination for numerous Black educators in the South looking to obtain graduate-level training during segregation. Two examples pertinent to this book are Alfonso Elder and Francis Atkins. Elder was president of North Carolina College in Durham from 1948 to 1963, and Atkins was president of Winston-Salem State from 1938 to 1961. Both leaders were vocally supportive of students' civil rights protests in the early 1960s. Both also earned their master's degrees at Teachers College, Columbia University, in 1924. Biographical information for both Elder and Atkins are in the author's possession.

28. On Meredith requesting an application, see Lambert, *Battle of Ole Miss*, pp. 89–92. For the full Meredith letter, see Barrett, *Integration at Ole Miss*, p. 39. Meredith's note about his race has also been called "a historic postscript." For more, see Sansing, *Making Haste Slowly*, p. 158.

29. On the delay from February to May 1961, see Barrett, *Integration at Ole Miss*, pp. 40–44. David G. Sansing wrote, "Mississippi's white power structure, in consort with the board of

For example, W. M. Drake of Church Hill, Mississippi, down in the south-western corner of the state, was more than two hundred miles away and was not even an Ole Miss alumnus, but he was deeply disturbed by the events unfolding at the university. On March 14, 1961, Drake wrote to Williams that he was particularly "astonished and deeply grieved" that US Supreme Court Justice Thomas C. Clark had been an "invited and honored guest" at Ole Miss. To Drake, Clark was a traitor, and his vote in the unanimous *Brown* decision in 1954 was the worst kind of offense to Mississippi. That court's ruling and related decisions against segregation were "a continuous insult to the State of Mississippi, whose constitution and statutes it seeks to trample down."[30]

A week later, Williams's response to Drake captured the overarching theme of his fifteen-year tenure as Ole Miss chancellor. He explained that Clark had been invited to campus by law students, and that he found it important—as any good university leader should—to allow students to "make such contacts" with individuals who offered varying perspectives. Williams felt that it would be easy to deny Clark's visit, but it would be just as easy for those same law students to leave the state in disappointment and work elsewhere. Therefore, the visiting judge's full day and evening on campus was a delight for the Ole Miss students, and several other "distinguished Mississippians" made their way to campus to hear him. In fact, one person who had first objected to the visit told Williams afterward that the students had done a good job in inviting the Supreme Court justice. Therefore, Williams said, Drake should not worry about Clark despite the attempts to desegregate Ole Miss. "They have all been successfully resisted with the cooperation of our state officials," the chancellor said, adding that "I am sure that we are both dedicated to the maintenance of the laws and the traditions of our state."[31]

Drake was not pleased, however. "It is clear that our ideas about the Constitution of the United States and the duties of a Supreme Court Justice are very far apart," Drake responded. He then laid out his issues with Williams and any others who did not have absolute disdain for Black people and anyone who sympathized with equal rights. "I hope no well-raised young Mississippi lawyer will ever be in close contact with Justice Clark, whom I regard as thoroughly dishonest." Complete segregation was the only acceptable way to live

---

trustees and university officials, employed a strategy of delay, deception, and duplicity in the hope of dissuading James Meredith from breaking the barrier of race and color at Mississippi's first, oldest, and proudest university." For more, see Sansing, *Making Haste Slowly*, p. 159.

30. A series of letters between Williams and W. M. Drake from Church Hill, Mississippi, exhibit the pressures Williams faced when it came to segregation at Ole Miss. For more, see W. M. Drake to/from J. D. Williams, March-April 1961, JDW, Box 6, Folder 4, UM.

31. Drake to/from Williams correspondence, March-April 1961.

in Mississippi, with school segregation being the most sacred form of racial separation, and Drake felt Clark wanted to violate white children. In Jefferson County, where Church Hill was located, Drake said there were ten times as many Black children than white ones. "All [of] the white children are legitimate, a great many of the black ones are illegitimate," he pleaded with the chancellor. "I refuse to believe that if you were close to this reality you could be indifferent."[32]

That last sentence accusing Williams of being "indifferent" to desegregation forced the chancellor to offer a rare, hardline segregationist stance. "I am unable to understand why you would consider me to be indifferent to the integration problem, as is implied." Williams then offered a well-thought list of his efforts to keep Ole Miss segregated. He explained that athletic teams had refused to play desegregated teams. There had also been five attempts to desegregate the university, and "five times the attempts have failed." Williams said he and other university administrators believed in "the traditions of the State of Mississippi" and had defended them "not merely with words but with action."[33]

The chancellor was perturbed. For years, despite all he had accomplished in building up Ole Miss, his reputation was that he was either too weak on defending segregation or too passive to confront state officials who would not offer him the autonomy as chancellor. No one was willing to give Williams due credit. "This is the university, which under my administration, has been tried and tried again and has stood firm and uncompromising on every occasion," he explained to Drake. "This, I respectfully submit, is not indifference.... I regret the Supreme Court's decision on integration.... I am for preserving the precious heritage which is ours." Then, he closed his April 11, 1961, letter: "Thank you for the opportunity to express myself frankly in this letter."[34]

Meredith's initial request for an application had come three months before this, and Williams simply had not expressed himself. He was under the constraints of the board until they advised him and Ellis on how to proceed. Then, on May 25, 1961, Ellis denied Meredith admission, citing his previous college credits earned at Jackson State, an unaccredited Black college, and his letters of recommendation as insufficient. Less than a week later, on May 31, Meredith and a team of NAACP attorneys filed a complaint against the board, Williams, Ellis, and Dean Arthur B. Lewis. The *Meredith v. Fair* trial was lengthy, lasting from May 1961 until September 1962. In fact, Ole Miss professor

32. Ibid.
33. Ibid.
34. Ibid.

Russell H. Barrett said of the court proceedings, "The length of this case may be a tribute to the thoroughness with which both relevant and meaningless issues are considered, but it is also a standing indictment of the failure of our legal system to protect an individual's rights with reasonable speed." This was true enough, but the case was also an indictment of the chancellor's lack of power and authority at the university.[35]

Given these circumstances, Williams attempted to let his perspective be known during the trial. For example, in late May 1961, he visited Atlanta to deliver a commencement address at the Georgia State College of Business. The speech focused on integrity and ethics in business, but it was sprinkled with messages pertinent to the unfolding events at Ole Miss. Were Williams's formal concessions as chancellor the same as his personal convictions? That had been a question dating back to his hire in 1946 after his Marshall College presidency facilitated interracial interactions in West Virginia. He advised Georgia State graduates to avoid being placed in the same predicament. "You cannot keep your public and private morality in separate, mutually inviolate compartments," Williams said. "If you want to live with self-respect, and lie down at night with a quiet conscience, dismiss from your minds forever the idea that you can have one code of decency for the office and another for your private life." He then briefly noted that freedom of speech and freedom of the ballot were "a foundation stone of our country." His message was delivered to the future business leaders of Georgia, but for who else was it equally relevant?[36]

On one hand, it could be interpreted that Williams simply echoed what he had written to Drake a month before. It was federal-level leaders like Supreme Court Justice Clark who were two-faced, bringing their smiles to Ole Miss and then, in turn, voting for desegregation. On the other hand, perhaps his speech was equally relevant to Mississippi segregationists. With the Meredith case beginning, the midcentury fight for racial equality was situated within the broader issue of southern whites' moral barometer, allowing them to tout Christian ideals but viciously make proclamations of whites being superior to Black citizens. In fact, Meredith himself recalled that Williams, on the first day of the court hearing, "was the only one of the group to act in any way as if we were human." Williams, unlike the other Ole Miss officials and attorneys, acknowledged Meredith's humanity with a slight nod of his head as they passed. Therefore, as the trial began, Williams had made it clear that he was committed

---

35. Barrett, *Integration at Ole Miss*, pp. 38, 44.

36. J. D. Williams, Self-Reverence, Self-Knowledge, Self-Control, Georgia State Commencement, May 28, 1961, JDW, Box 11, Folder 2, UM.

to "preserving the precious heritage." It simply remained unclear if Williams meant Mississippi's heritage of hatred or the US Constitution's professed belief that "all men are created equal."[37]

A Voice Emerges from the Riot

When the Meredith case began, college presidents across the nation followed with interest because the outcome would have a ripple effect on how other institutions' trustees and public officials interacted with academic leaders regarding Black students. Understanding those implications, on June 8, 1961, Walter S. Newman, president of Virginia Polytechnic Institute, sent his friend an encouraging note. "Dear J.D.," he wrote. "I have been thinking about you and the federal court disturbance and certainly wish you all the luck in the world." Newman was deeply attentive to how the court proceedings in Mississippi would unfold, and frankly, all Williams could do was watch as well.[38]

Mississippi had its share of racial unrest as the trial spanned the majority of 1961 and 1962. In the summer of 1961, more than three hundred Freedom Riders were arrested in Jackson and many were sent to Mississippi's notorious Parchman Farm, the state penitentiary. But unlike Alabama, where white mob violence awaited the riders' attempt to desegregate public highway facilities, a *Detroit Free Press* column noted that "Jackson has acted as though it couldn't care less." There, officials arrested the Freedom Riders not for violating segregation but for "breach of the peace" when refusing to obey authorities' orders. The lack of violence let many people say the disturbance was handled "quietly." Yet, racists could not restrain themselves for long. In October 1961, the brutal beating of college students, including University of Michigan student Tom Hayden, in McComb, Mississippi, brought more attention to the state's vicious racism and the Meredith trial.[39]

On February 10, 1962, the Mississippi Board of Institutions of Higher Learning moved to adopt what they termed "findings of fact and order" regarding Meredith. The trustees investigated and concluded that Ellis acted

---

37. Meredith, *Three Years in Mississippi*, p. 272.

38. Walter S. Newman to John Davis Williams, June 8, 1961, JDW, Box 6, Folder 4, UM.

39. On the number of Freedom Riders arrested, see Patterson, *Grand Expectations*, p. 470. On the broader significance of the Freedom Rides, see Carson, *In Struggle*, pp. 37–38; and Zinn, *SNCC*, pp. 40–41. On the impact of the Freedom Rides on federal policies, see Ransby, *Ella Baker*, pp. 265–267. On the violence in McComb, see Turner, *Sitting In and Speaking Out*, p. 129; Judd Arnett, "Jackson Shrugs Off Integration Hubbub: Riders' Jailed Quietly," *Detroit Free Press*, June 4, 1961. This column ended with a brief mention of James Meredith's recent lawsuit brought before the US District Court.

"correctly and properly" as registrar when he denied Meredith's application. It was not Meredith's race, the board determined, that resulted in his denial. "Any application of any race [in] similar conditions would have been and should have been denied admission in similar fashion." As a result, Ellis's decision was "hereby ratified, approved, and confirmed as being in full and proper accord" with the board's rules and regulations. As for the ongoing court battle, the board issued one more directive: "Said registrar and said chancellor of the University of Mississippi are hereby ordered and directed not to admit said Meredith." The meeting minutes were then immediately sent to Williams and Ellis.[40]

The next month, in March 1962, law professor William P. Murphy resigned from Ole Miss. Years earlier, Murphy was attacked for his belief that Mississippians should obey the *Brown* decision. Following the board's decision to not admit Meredith, Murphy's resignation was a reminder of the chancellor's failure to defend the professor in the name of academic freedom and overall lack of authority. Although Williams did not advocate for desegregation and racial equality, the lack of academic freedom was worsening the university's reputation. As a result, he attempted to combat this trend in his discussions with Ole Miss alumni.[41]

For example, on June 25, 1962, he visited the Mississippi Delta to speak before the Sunflower County Alumni Association in Indianola. He explained that some universities were great through generous gifts upon their founding, such as the University of Chicago, while others, like Duke University, had greatness thrust upon them by donors. Ole Miss, on the other hand, "must achieve greatness," and to accomplish this, three characteristics were essential: knowledge, a dedication to the pursuit of knowledge, and free inquiry. "You cannot take scholars who have dedicated their lives to the pursuit of knowledge and then set up walls they are forbidden to look beyond—not if you want to be a great university," he added.[42]

Williams called for scholars to have the freedom to explore controversial ideas, but his voice never emerged strongly enough to sway board members, most alumni, or public officials. Even the fact that this speech was delivered in Sunflower County was telling. Civil rights leader Fannie Lou Hamer had called the county home to the "ruralest of the ruralest and poorest of the poorest," and by 1955, the Citizens' Council had effectively removed all Black people

40. Board of Trustee Minutes, February 10, 1962, Board of Trustee Reports and Minutes, Box 12, UM (collection hereafter cited as Board Reports).

41. On the Murphy controversy, see Barrett, *Integration at Ole Miss*, pp. 76–77; and Cohadas, *The Band Played Dixie*, pp. 38–41, 51.

42. Williams, The Achievement of Greatness Speech.

from the county's registered voter list. In a county that was overwhelmingly Black, the council made sure of the following: "Members of the white minority made decisions for the majority, and anyone who dared to question their authority would be crushed." It was that same sentiment that kept Ole Miss segregated and Williams unknown to most Mississippians besides Ole Miss alumni and others connected to the university. Their authority figure was Governor Ross Barnett.[43]

On August 15, 1962, what little autonomy Williams did have through the summer of 1962 was formally removed by the board as the case neared its end. The board met and moved to withdraw all "prerogatives, powers, duties, responsibilities, and authority" from "every official of the University of Mississippi" as it pertained to Meredith's admission. All future decisions were "reserved exclusively" for the board, and Williams was left to facilitate how the campus reacted. Therefore, on September 11, Williams and dean of students L. L. Love met with the campus fraternities and encouraged peace among the undergraduates. Then, three days later, the US District Court issued a permanent injunction ordering that Meredith be admitted, and on September 15, Williams spoke at the opening faculty meeting and said the university must avoid any closures or violence. But when journalists asked Williams questions about Meredith, he had no authority to update the public on the possibility of Ole Miss desegregating. "We have no official statement to make at this time," he said. "Major decisions concerning policy for all the state institutions of higher learning are made by the Board of Trustees."[44]

Then, on September 20, trustee and Hattiesburg attorney M. M. Roberts, frustrated with the federal court decision, moved that the board invest all authority in Governor Barnett regarding the order to admit Meredith. In a secret ballot, the trustees agreed with a 9-1-1 vote (yes-no-abstain), and then turned over to Barnett the "full rights, power, authority, and discretion for such

43. Lee, *For Freedom's Sake*, p. 2. Lee's book provides a comprehensive overview of Fannie Lou Hamer and the struggle for racial equality in Mississippi. On Sunflower County and Black voters, see Barrett, *Integration at Ole Miss*, p. 27. For the "crushed" quote, see Moye, *Let the People Decide*, p. 66. On John Davis Williams not being known by Mississippi residents, see Eagles, *Price of Defiance*, p. 139.

44. On the board's removal of authority from all Ole Miss officials, see Board of Trustee Minutes, August 15, 1962, Board Reports, Box 12, UM; US District Court Order Granting Permanent Injunction, September 14, 1962, George Street Collection, Box 17, Folder–Meredith Crisis (Sept. 1962), UM (collection hereafter cited as Street Collection). For Williams's deference to the board, see "No Statement on Meredith," *Mississippian*, September 18, 1962. On Williams meeting with fraternities and speaking before the faculty, see Barrett, *Integration at Ole Miss*, pp. 92, 99.

course of action as the governor shall deem legal, fit, and proper in the premises." Immediately, the governor issued an executive directive to Meredith. "Pursuant to the authority vested in me under the Constitution and the laws of the State of Mississippi, . . ." the order read, signed by the governor and notarized by Mississippi secretary of state Heber Ladner, "you, James H. Meredith, are hereby refused admission as a student to the University of Mississippi." Barnett closed, "Take due notice thereof and govern yourself accordingly."[45]

Over the next week, Barnett and Lieutenant Governor Paul Johnson denied the federal troop-escorted Meredith's attempt to enroll three times. In the process, Williams, Dean Arthur B. Lewis, and the registrar, Robert B. Ellis, were ordered to appear in court for not adhering to federal laws. After increased federal pressure, on September 25, the board reversed course and revoked the authority given to Barnett, but that decision was too late as racial tensions mounted. By September 27, Barnett had stoked local white supremacists, while others traveled to Ole Miss from across the South to praise the governor. Even a joint legislative committee of legislators, not the chancellor or faculty, released a report that identified nine reasons Meredith was denied admission. By this point, Barnett was greeted with cheers of "We want Ross" as he and Johnson waited on campus during one of their denials to Meredith, and rumors swirled that if Ole Miss closed, all other state universities would be closed—all decisions out of Williams's control.[46]

By sundown on Sunday, September 30, when word spread of Meredith's quiet registration away from journalists and television cameras, a white mob of roughly two thousand gathered. Bricks, bottles, firebombs, and gunfire cut through campus over the next eight hours. By sunrise, two men—Paul Guihard, a European journalist, and Ray Gunter, an Oxford resident—were killed in the melee, dozens of US Marshals were injured, and ninety-three people had

---

45. Board of Trustees, September 20, 1962, Board Reports, Box 12, UM; Barnett proclamation and Ladner notarization, September 20, 1962, James Howard Meredith Collection, Box 2, UM.

46. For information about each of the three denied attempts, see (first attempt) Barnett proclamation; (second attempt) Sidna Brower, "Barnett Defies Court Injunction," *Mississippian*, September 26, 1962; (third attempt) Sidna Brower, "Lt. Governor Stands Firm: Meredith Rejected Again," *Mississippian*, September 27, 1962. On Williams and other Ole Miss officials being ordered to appear in federal court, refer to "Bulletin," *Mississippian*, September 21, 1962. For the joint legislative committee report, see "Report on Meredith: Lack of Qualifications Cited," *Mississippian*, October 1, 1962. On the board's decision after court pressure to revoke authority from Barnett, see "Chancellor under Board Instruction," *Mississippian*, September 26, 1962; and E. R. Jobe, Trustees Statement on Court Injunction, September 25, 1962, Street Collection, Box 17, Folder–Meredith Crisis (Sept. 1962), UM; Brower, "Crowd Cheers Barnett," *Mississippian*, September 28, 1962.

been apprehended and questioned. The riot marred the university's image before an international audience as radio and television outlets broadcast from Oxford.[47]

Academia was also watching. In particular, the Southern Association of Colleges and Schools (SACS), an accrediting body, took notice of the instability of the university's academic environment and launched an investigation. In fact, SACS decided to review all Mississippi state-supported colleges and universities, since the trustees and governor used Ole Miss for political influence. This left Ole Miss in a precarious position, but it presented an opportunity for Williams. For the first time in his sixteen-year chancellorship, he was tasked with leading the university's conversation on academic freedom. It just so happened that it was racial violence that presented him with the greatest opportunity to assert his voice. For the remainder of the 1962–63 academic year, Williams needed to exhibit control over the university while he carefully crafted a narrative that would lead toward recovery.[48]

Chancellor Issues Statewide Plea for Peace

On Monday, October 1, 1962, the morning after the riot, an editorial in the *Mississippian* student newspaper summarized Chancellor Williams's predicament. "This is a battle between the State of Mississippi and the United States government. The university is caught in the middle." The public did not blame Williams for the violence. Instead, some white clergy condemned the violence and blamed the broader white citizenry that remained silent as segregationists spewed hateful rhetoric. Yet, regardless of the blame, the responsibility for Ole Miss's survival and recovery fell squarely on Williams.[49]

That morning, hundreds of federal troops on campus served as the backdrop to this challenge as they placed roadblocks at each entrance to campus

47. Several primary sources were consulted to describe the riots. For this paragraph, see Confrontation by Dates, n.d., Street Collection, Box 17, Folder–Meredith Crisis (Oct. 1962), UM; Jan Humber, "Death, Injuries from Campus Rioting," *Mississippian*, October 1, 1962; Sidna Brower, "Troops Surround Ole Miss," *Mississippian*, October 2, 1962. Several historians have rehashed the lead-up to the violent clash at the University of Mississippi on September 30, 1962. For a detailed daily, and sometimes hourly, account of the days before September 30, see Doyle, *An American Insurrection*, pp. 67–117.

48. Trustees were immediately updated on accreditation regarding SACS within weeks of the riot. For more, see Board of Trustees, October 18, 1962, Board Reports, Box 12, UM.

49. "Violence Will Not Help," *Mississippian*, October 1, 1962. On white clergy blaming white silence, see Murphey C. Wilds, Day of Repentance sermon, October 7, 1962, Murphey Wilds Collection, Folder 1.3–Day of Repentance Sermon and Program, UM.

and searched vehicles for weapons. By that point, approximately two hundred people had been arrested related to the riots, thirty of whom were apprehended for weapons possession. These included a number of Ole Miss students as well. Now, the troops organized a tent city on campus in front of the Lyceum, and additional troops camped out off campus near the local airport. Before the riot, US attorney general Robert F. Kennedy expressed concern directly to Williams about potential violence. Now, Edwin Guthman, press secretary for the attorney general, said of the troops' presence on campus, "We have only one purpose in being here and that is to see that the orders of the federal government are obeyed." For Williams, the federal troops on campus could prevent additional white mob violence, but their presence also reminded segregationists of the federal government's intervention and stoked more white supremacist anger.[50]

Therefore, on October 1, Chancellor Williams made a plea to the student body. "Ole Miss is a great university," he said. "Your conduct at this time can make it greater. The finest service you may render Ole Miss is to help keep the university operating." He then instructed students who lived on campus to stay on campus, and he advised them not to congregate in groups and to avoid demonstrations of any kind. Finally, the chancellor asked students to report any suspicious activity to campus police. Likewise, the same day, dean of students L. L. Love issued a statement encouraging the students to read the student newspaper and listen to the campus radio station for administrative updates. In fact, every fifteen minutes, the radio station repeated a recording from Williams about restoring campus to its regular operations. Love told the students, "For your protection, and that of this university, there will probably be about 100 highway patrolmen stationed on campus at our request to properly deal with any outside person or groups who come here to cause trouble. They are not here to resist the federal government."[51]

In addition to issuing statements emphasizing peace, Williams also met with the faculty on October 1 and underscored the importance of peace for maintaining the university's accreditation. If Ole Miss continued its regular

50. "Troops Conduct Auto Searches, Make Arrests," *Mississippian*, October 2, 1962. For a list of Ole Miss students detained during riots, see George Street Memorandum, October 2, 1962, Street Collection, Box 17, Folder–Meredith Crisis (Oct. 1962), UM. For the Edwin Guthman quote, see "Officials Speak: Marshals to Stay," *Mississippian*, October 1, 1962. For more on the Williams–Robert Kennedy conversation, see Cohadas, *The Band Played Dixie*, pp. 90–91.

51. "Chancellor Issues Plea," *Mississippian*, October 1, 1962; "Dean L. L. Love Addresses Students," *Mississippian*, October 1, 1962. For Williams's radio statement and the frequency with which it aired, see Chancellor Williams Statement for Radio Broadcast, October 1, 1962, Street Collection, Box 17, Folder–Meredith Crisis (Nov. 20–30, 1962), UM.

academic schedule without another violent interruption, he believed SACS would not revoke the institution's accreditation. Williams also explained that the federal court ruling that no one could interfere with Meredith's enrollment was worded broadly enough to also include students and faculty. There was a clause, "and all persons acting in concert," that meant anyone could jeopardize the good standing of the university. That said, he told the faculty that he believed all Mississippi colleges and universities, not just Ole Miss, would remain in good standing as long as academic leaders made the final decisions about campus activities, and everyone on campus had a responsibility to maintain peace.[52]

By Meredith's second day as a student, he said, "I think I am being treated fine under the conditions." This short but significant opinion was useful for Williams, and he used it to demonstrate that the campus was stable. On October 3, he issued another statement saying, "I am able to announce to parents, students, and faculty that the safety of those on campus and in Oxford is now assured, provided they abide by the normal regulations." Several Ole Miss faculty members, however, were not ready to move forward or concede that campus was back to normal.[53]

That evening, members of the campus AAUP chapter met and voted to issue a four-point resolution. The first point was critical of university leaders. "While it is obvious that errors of judgment were made by those in authority on the university campus on Sunday, September 30," read the resolution, "we have evidence that the attempt of men in prominent positions to place all the blame for the riot on the United States marshals is not only unfair and reprehensible, but is almost completely false. We encourage an investigation by the proper authorities." The faculty also blamed some of the Mississippi press for its "distortion of the facts," challenged all Mississippi residents to obey "the law of the land," and condemned any campus "riots, weapons, and agitators." Over the next week, the resolution was published in several newspapers, and by October 9, fifty-four professors had signed the statement that argued against Mississippians who attributed the riot to US Marshals.[54]

52. "Faculty Members Hear Chancellor on Vital Points," *Mississippian*, October 2, 1962.

53. "Meredith Gives Views on Treatment So Far," *Mississippian*, October 3, 1962; "Chancellor's Statement," *Mississippian*, October 3, 1962.

54. "Profs Sign Statement on Recent Happenings," *Mississippian*, October 9, 1962. For more on the initial AAUP meeting, see Barrett, *Integration at Ole Miss*, pp. 179–181. The AAUP was influential even at private white universities. For example, at Duke University, the AAUP chapter passed a resolution that denounced segregation. For more, see Kean, *Desegregating Private Higher Education*, pp. 142–143.

As faculty members called for accountability, university officials implemented proactive measures that were not in place prior to Meredith's arrival.
For instance, it was not uncommon for students to possess guns. There was no
university policy that prevented it, but circumstances required a change. "It
has become absolutely necessary to insist that students dispose of all firearms
they may have in their possession," said Love, the dean of students, in an October 9 notice to the campus. Students residing on campus had to comply by
October 11 at 6 p.m. "The consequences will be very serious for any student
discovered with firearms after the time mentioned above. I regret the necessity
of sending this notice."[55]

The notice indirectly acknowledged what the Ole Miss AAUP members
argued—there were numerous errors in judgment on the part of university
officials, thus Williams worked to get key parties to agree on the route toward
recovery. On October 10, Williams, Governor Barnett, and three state senators
drafted a statement to be broadcast as a campus announcement, but only the
chancellor's voice was used—a nod to the need for the chancellor to appear
to be in charge at the university. Williams advised students to "take due notice
of the statements made by the governor and to live up to the fine traditions of
our state as a peace-loving, law abiding people." The following day, a similar
statement was repeated every two hours on area radio broadcasts.[56]

Almost immediately, some students voiced their support for the chancellor.
The *Mississippian* editor Sidna Brower wrote, "It is sad, indeed, when supposedly
educated people must be reminded that rioting and violence do not help any
cause but bring humiliation to all concerned," as the entire student newspaper
staff later issued its formal support for Williams's calls for peace. Likewise, on
October 12, two honor societies—the Mortar Board and Omicron Delta
Kappa—passed a joint resolution that encouraged students to "desist from acts
which, not only achieve no worthwhile purpose, but also adversely reflect on the
integrity and character of our university and its students." The resolution blatantly
explained the students' disagreement with the 1954 *Brown v. Board of Education*
decision, but the two societies' members put peace before violent resistance.[57]

---

55. L. L. Love to Residents of the Village, October 9, 1962, Street Collection, Box 17, Folder–
Meredith Crisis (Nov. 20–30, 1962), UM.

56. Chancellor Williams Statement in Support of Governor, October 10, 1962, Street Collection, Box 17, Folder–Meredith Crisis (Nov. 20–30, 1962), UM; Chancellor Williams Statement for Radio Broadcast, October 11, 1962, Street Collection, Box 17, Folder–Meredith Crisis
(Nov. 20–30, 1962), UM.

57. Sidna Brower, "Editor's Comment," *Mississippian*, October 10, 1962; "Mississippian Staff
Supports Statements," *Mississippian*, October 16, 1962; Joint Resolution of Mortar Board and ODK,
October 12, 1962, Street Collection, Box 17, Folder–Meredith Crisis (Nov. 20–30, 1962), UM.

The next day, on October 13, Love said, "The administration recognizes and expresses its gratitude to the vast majority of students who have conducted themselves in a responsible and mature manner." Three days later, on October 16, Mississippi attorney general Joe T. Patterson spoke on campus to Ole Miss law students, but he eased away from the rigid segregationist statements that the governor had used leading up to the riot. "My only purpose in being here is the sincere hope that I may be able to make some contribution to the purpose for which this university was established 114 years ago—the educating of young men and women," Patterson said. Similarly, on October 18, the university's Academic Council issued a formal statement expressing regret for the riot. It commended the faculty, staff, and students for helping restore Ole Miss to its regular schedule and reaffirmed its support for the chancellor. Yet, despite campus and state officials' shared message of peace, remnants of violence remained on campus, and questions about whether Ole Miss could maintain its usual academic schedule still loomed.[58]

On October 18, the trustees discussed a telegram in which Henry King Stanford, president of SACS, warned that all Mississippi colleges and universities might lose accreditation "unless assurances were given that unwarranted procedures and political interferences of the State of Mississippi would be discontinued." A week later, Governor Barnett sent Stanford a telegram promising that all higher education decisions and related responsibilities were in the hands of academic leaders. "It is not my wish or purpose to accept or assume any of these prerogatives," the governor said. The same day, Provost Charles F. Haywood confirmed that there would be no change to the 1962–63 academic calendar. "It is the consensus of the members of the Academic Council that it will not be necessary to extend the calendar for this semester," said Haywood, attempting to convey that Ole Miss was unscathed by the riot. State officials understood that unaccredited colleges and universities would lead to economic ruin, a problem even more pronounced in the South, but that meant little to the individual segregationist.[59]

58. For Love's statement of gratitude to the students, see L. L. Love Notice to Students, n.d., Street Collection, Box 17, Folder–Meredith Crisis (Oct. 1962), UM; and "Dean's Statement," *Mississippian*, October 16, 1962. Regarding Joe T. Patterson's visit, see Danny Roy, "Official Answers," *Mississippian*, October 16, 1962; and "Strong Remarks Made by Attorney General," *Mississippian*, October 17, 1962. For the full Academic Council statement, see "Academic Statement," *Mississippian*, October 18, 1962.

59. Board of Trustees, October 18, 1962; Ross Barnett to Henry King Stanford, October 25, 1962, Street Collection, Box 17, Folder–Meredith Crisis (Oct. 1962), UM; "Council Says, 'No Extension' on Calendar," *Mississippian*, October 25, 1962.

On October 29, despite the pleas for peace, a white mob gathered outside of Meredith's dormitory shouting and throwing firecrackers. The sound of the occasional firecracker was common at nightfall since Meredith had enrolled, but stronger and more powerful cherry bombs were used this time. Explosions rocked the campus, and another group added to the chaos by shooting fireworks from behind another nearby dormitory. Federal troops guarded Meredith's residence but did not engage the mob. On the inside, Love and Binford Nash, director of men's housing, talked to residents until the mob eventually dispersed. The violence continued over the next days. This worried Williams, who confided in Robert A. Herring, Jr., chair of the engineering department, that "much has been done to present to the public the concept that the university has indeed returned to normal." Yet, despite Williams's efforts, the violent resistance to Meredith only amplified national media outlets' coverage of events on campus.[60]

As accreditation warnings were issued alongside continued mob violence, the *New York Times* published a detailed report critical of the Ole Miss student body. "Virtually all 4,638 white students at the University of Mississippi exist in an isolation more profound than that which they impose on the one Negro student, James H. Meredith," read the late October 1962 article. Ole Miss students were described as "uninformed and little interested in events and opinions in the rest of the nation and the world." The students were considered closed-minded, guided by narrow segregationist beliefs. "There are many reports that even a smile or a nod in [Meredith's] direction has resulted in a student's being punched or cursed." Published in the Sunday edition, commonly the most-read issue per week, the *New York Times* report forced Williams to become more vocal about his perception of the campus. Throughout the remainder of the fall, Chancellor Williams would use two major speaking events to reframe the public perception of Mississippi and ultimately save the university's accreditation.[61]

Telling "Another Mississippi Story"

Editor Sidna Brower of the *Mississippian* issued a challenge to the university administrators. "While the rest of the United States is concerned with Berlin, Cuba, and India," Brower wrote on October 31, "some antagonists on the Ole

60. Ed Williams, "Mob Demonstrates at Meredith's Dorm," *Mississippian*, October 31, 1962; Information on the Riots of October 29–31, n.d., Street Collection, Box 17, Folder–Meredith Crisis (Nov. 1–19, 1962), UM; John Davis Williams to Robert A. Herring Jr., October 30, 1962, Street Collection, Box 17, Folder–Meredith Crisis (Oct. 1962), UM.

61. Thomas Buckley, "U. of Mississippi Found 'Isolated,'" *New York Times*, October 21, 1962.

Miss campus persist in keeping their university in the headlines with bad publicity." For her, the *New York Times* report about Ole Miss had some validity.
Voicing disapproval over desegregation and using violence were drastically
different, so Brower asked why, one month after the riot, academic leaders had
not implemented their "get tough policy." Williams and Love had issued a
series of statements that condemned violence, but few students had been expelled for their continued actions. "There are some of us students who are still
proud of the University of Mississippi and do not care for such degrading actions," Brower argued. "Why then is the 'get tough policy' not enforced and a
few of the rabble-rousers removed so that we can consider matters of more
importance than the actions of a few immature weaklings who have nothing
more to do than 'play war.'"[62]

Brower made it clear that Williams needed to guide Ole Miss students,
faculty, and the general public toward a better understanding of the last month.
His statements and radio broadcasts asking for peace did not resolve the fact
that Meredith was still enrolled. Meanwhile, segregationists were trying to
reconcile what it meant to be a Mississippian in the face of another defeat from
the federal government. As those concerns swirled among white people, that
night, Williams was back in the Mississippi Delta speaking in Greenville,
where he spoke to the Lions and Kiwanis Clubs and Ole Miss Alumni of
Washington County about the riot and subsequent turmoil.

In his talk, titled "Another Mississippi Story," Williams openly reflected on
the events of September 30 and wondered "whether another chancellor had
ever had cause to feel such bitterness and anguish." Academic leaders were not
trained for "riot, lawlessness, destruction, murder" while being covered "by
every media of communication that exists." He felt useless as state officials
used Ole Miss as the battleground for a larger fight between southern states
and the federal government. "The university has become a pawn in a combat
between powerful political forces," Williams assessed. "With little consultation

62. Sidna Brower, "UM 'Get Tough Policy' Appears Lost in Crowd," *Mississippian*, October 31, 1962. Shortly after Brower's column, a group of students met and approved a resolution
supporting the university's "Get Tough Policy." The resolution urged Ole Miss leaders to expel
students convicted of disruptive activities. For more on that resolution, see "Start Petition:
Students React," *Mississippian*, November 2, 1962. Regarding the arrested students, several were
apprehended by federal authorities but not prosecuted; however, Chancellor Williams was
informed which students were arrested. For a list of student names and specific charges, see
Nicholas B. Katzenbach to John Davis Williams, October 10, 1962, Street Collection, Box 17,
Folder–Meredith Crisis (Oct. 1962), UM; and Norbert A. Schlei to L. L. Love, October 16, 1962,
Street Collection, Box 17, Folder–Meredith Crisis (Oct. 1962), UM.

with administrative officers, without giving adequate notice, the effective control of the university was taken out of our hands."[63]

Yet, Williams found inspiration in the same Confederate figures that lifelong white Mississippians revered and, thus, situated his talk within the context of a noted Mississippi Confederate hero—Lucius Quintus Cincinnatus Lamar. He explained how Lamar resigned as a professor from Ole Miss to "help establish and then to serve the Confederacy." However, upon Lamar's defeated return, "he became one of our greatest teachers and one of the most loved." The lesson in Lamar's life was that he held no bitterness. Following the Civil War, Lamar issued a charge to Mississippians: be loyal to America, not the former Confederacy. "I have needed such an example," Williams confessed before the Greenville audience. "Today is the last day in the month of October 1962. I shall never, as long as I live, forget the first day of this month."[64]

Williams then utilized a common southern narrative that people actually lived together in harmony during segregation. Southern whites regularly said this in rebuttal to outsiders who challenged segregation. The narrative also indirectly blamed federal officials, not segregationists, for stirring violence by interfering with local norms, thus Williams praised the university's Black employees. "I have been especially moved by the loyalty of our colored workers," he told the Greenville alumni, noting that the majority of them returned to work only days after the riot. "We have always had particularly fine relations with our Negro staff members. They have been friends as well as workers. Students have come back to the campus in later years no more interested in revisiting their professors than seeing Bondy Webb again at the cafeteria, or Calvin Lott, or Dean Hefley's right-hand man, Bishop Harvey, or some other colored friend."[65]

In his reframing of the Mississippi narrative, Williams ignored the reality that Ole Miss offered employment in a state that systematically limited Black economic advancement. Instead, he portrayed Black staff as loyal to Ole Miss instead of simply being in need of a job. The irony in Williams's characterization is that the first Black students at formerly segregated colleges found solace in those Black staff members' presence. Nonetheless, Williams said, it was the white students who were most harmed by the tragic violence, and he concluded by focusing on the responsibility of Ole Miss to all students. "We cannot shortchange them, we cannot betray their faith, by giving them a third-rate

---

63. John Davis Williams, Speech to Lions and Kiwanis, October 31, 1962, JDW, Box 11, Folder 7, UM.

64. Ibid. For more on Lamar, see Sansing, *Making Haste Slowly*, p. 58.

65. Speech to Lions and Kiwanis.

education," Williams said. "Ole Miss graduates must have at least an equal chance at the starters' gate with those who graduate from our nation's best state universities." It was the part about the best universities that was uncertain. He admitted, considering accreditation questions, "A deeper question presses upon us: Shall we continue to have a real university, or only the outward husk and mere appearance of a university?"[66]

The following afternoon, on November 1, Williams called all the men students except Meredith to Fulton Chapel. He wanted to guarantee that the next month did not start the way October ended. "I have asked for this opportunity to meet with you for the purpose of discussion of what is today the university's most serious problem," he said. "That problem is the maintenance of peaceful and orderly conditions on campus." The "normal campus life" had dissipated, and Williams said the sounds of exploding tear gas shells, shattering glass, detonating cherry bombs, and vulgarities had become the new normal. He then reiterated what he said in Greenville about the university's responsibility. "The university has a solemn obligation to you. That obligation is to see that your education is not further disrupted by that small minority of the student body which has persisted in creating disorder on the campus." That said, Williams felt it would be shameful if Ole Miss, one of six charter members of SACS, lost its accreditation due to its inability to maintain a stable environment. "The threat posed by the recent disturbances is not just to our accreditation but also to the very survival of the university."[67]

The potential that the university could no longer exist was a point Williams had not emphasized the previous night when speaking to alumni in Greenville, but he found this necessary to share with the students. The previous day, Brower had called out administrators for not taking their "get tough policy" seriously, and afterward, evidence against roughly ten students had been collected and serious conduct violations were being pursued against them. Williams, therefore, no longer focused on simply asking students to stay peaceful for peace's sake. He now vowed to expel students who jeopardized the status of the university.[68]

---

66. Ibid. As Clemson's first Black student, Harvey B. Gantt said there were enough Black people at Clemson that he was never alone. Those Black people had serviced the university since Clemson opened, and they beamed with pride at his admission because they could now envision their own family there. For more, see Harvey B. Gantt, "Voices from the Civil Rights Movement in South Carolina," in Moore and Burton, *Toward the Meeting of the Waters*, p. 358.

67. Chancellor's Statement to Students, November 1, 1962, JDW, Box 11, Folder 6, UM.

68. Ibid.; "Chancellor Speaks Firmly: Men Hear Talk Promising Action," *Mississippian*, November 2, 1962.

This upset segregationists who felt Williams infringed on their right to protest against Meredith. "It is my opinion that if the university officials would give their word not to take any action upon any students who peacefully pickets," read one letter to the editor, "the noise and loud demonstrations would stop. Then, a true atmosphere of academic freedom could be maintained." However, that argument was disingenuous, and Williams knew peaceful resistance was not white supremacists' option of choice. "My responsibility is clear," Williams told the chapel audience. "It is to preserve the university, to maintain its accreditation, and to see that it continues to serve you as the best institution in the state. I am prepared to take whatever steps are necessary to fulfill this responsibility."[69]

Meanwhile, a segment of the student population took it upon themselves to do what was necessary to protect their university. On October 31, when the chancellor was in Greenville, roughly seventy students met to compose a resolution they planned to present to him. The following night, after Williams's talk in Fulton Chapel, a larger group of students gathered to approve the resolution. The students wanted to protect the university's accreditation and decrease the likelihood of losing faculty. "We do further urge the university administration to expel those students apprehended and convicted by duly constituted authorities and pledge our active support to those same authorities," the resolution read. The students demanded persecution of violent offenders despite the counterargument that, if SACS was worried about an academic atmosphere, the association needed to investigate why university officials frowned upon the students who peacefully protested against Meredith.[70]

Per the students' resolution, on November 1, the dean of students referred a student to the student judicial council for "possession, distribution, and explosion of fireworks." On October 29, Associated Student Body (ASB) president Gray Jackson and ASB executive assistant Tom Cleveland caught Ed Fleming throwing eggs at military officers. The two student body leaders let Fleming off with a warning advising him to stop throwing eggs. However, on October 30, Fleming was caught giving fireworks to other students. Jackson and Cleveland took matters into their own hands by reporting the violations that landed Fleming before the judicial council. This demonstrated that some white students—like Williams—wanted to protect the institution and its

---

69. Chancellor's Statement to Students; John Allen, Letter to the Editor, *Mississippian*, November 1, 1962. Historian Jeffery A. Turner assessed, "No state and no institution better demonstrated the costs of massive resistance to academic freedom than Mississippi and its flagship school, the University of Mississippi." For more, see Turner, *Sitting In and Speaking Out*, p. 82.

70. "Students React: Start Petition," *Mississippian*, November 2, 1962.

reputation more than they wanted to protect the most violent forms of white supremacy.[71]

Throughout November, alumni celebrated Williams before the SACS meeting on November 28 in Dallas, where accreditation officials would decide Ole Miss's status. On November 9, Williams delivered a State of the University address to the Board of Directors of the Alumni Association and the University Development Committee. He called journalists' characterization of university administrators as weak "most unfair and most irresponsible." Williams also said that weaker universities would have crumbled under similar circumstances, but Ole Miss was stronger and its survival was a tribute to "its loyal and devoted alumni and friends." Afterward, the board of directors of the Alumni Association passed a resolution praising the chancellor. The alumni board vowed to lend "their support and assistance in his efforts to make the university an institution of excellence and prominence in the educational world." The alumni offered public praise and so, too, did Williams's fellow college presidents.[72]

On November 7, A. D. Holt, president of the University of Tennessee, read the Greenville speech in the Memphis daily newspaper, the *Commercial Appeal*, which printed it in its entirety. "I can never tell you how much I appreciate your beautiful analysis of the situation at Ole Miss," Holt said. "Certainly, any person with an ounce of loyalty to your institution or an iota of interest in public higher education will applaud your statement." On November 19, John T. Caldwell, president of North Carolina State College, called the speech "splendid." He added, "This kind of speech widely circulated will help at least put in perspective the role and attitudes of the administration and students of the university." The same day, Horace B. Brown, vice president for business and finance at the University of Oklahoma, also commended Williams, saying, "I am sure that all of the thinking people and true leaders of the state stand 100% behind you." And Oliver S. Willham, president of Oklahoma State University declared, "We are all backing [Williams]."[73]

Two days later, on November 21, Oliver C. Carmichael sent empathetic regards considering that he was president of the University of Alabama in 1956, when a white mob violently ravaged the campus in protest of Autherine Lucy's

71. L. L. Love to Jack Lynch, November 1, 1962, Street Collection, Box 17, Folder–Meredith Crisis (Nov. 1–19, 1962), UM.

72. State of the University speech, November 9, 1962, JDW, Box 11, Folder 7, UM; "Praise Chancellor: Alumni Elect Officials," *Mississippian*, November 13, 1962.

73. Horace B. Brown to John Davis Williams, November 19, 1962, JDW, Box 6, Folder 8, UM; A. D. Holt to John Davis Williams, November 7, 1962; John T. Caldwell to Charles D. Fair, November 19, 1962; Oliver S. Willham to Charles D. Fair, November 19, 1962; all three letters in Street Collection, Box 17, Folder–Meredith Crisis (Nov. 1–19, 1962), UM.

enrollment as the first Black student. "I was moved by the sincerity and eloquence of my good friend, J. D. Williams, whose sufferings in the ordeal of
October 1 I could well understand," Carmichael told Charles D. Fair, chair of
the state board of trustees. Also, from New York City, John H. Fischer, president
of Teachers College, Columbia University, told Williams he first felt sympathy
since the Ole Miss episode reminded him of the 1954 violence in Baltimore
against desegregating that city's public schools. Yet, Fischer also felt a sense of
pride "in the exemplary behavior and leadership of one of our alumni."[74]

These declarations of encouragement from administrators across the nation
carried more weight than simple gestures of support. Some college presidents
led or served on committees for SACS. For instance, in the early 1960s,
Harry H. Ransom, chancellor of the University of Texas, was the chair of the
Commission on Colleges for SACS. In fact, each of SACS's 388 member institutions had a vote regarding the association's recommendation regarding Ole
Miss's accreditation. Therefore, it was advantageous for Ole Miss that Fair, as
a trustee, sent copies of Williams's speech and a favorable editorial in the *Commercial Appeal* to university leaders across the region.[75]

Doak S. Campbell, president of Florida State University from 1941 to 1957,
was one of the dozens who received Fair's package. On November 21, Campbell told Fair the widespread circulation of those materials provided the public
with a fair assessment of the Ole Miss situation. "Many of us, of course, are
greatly concerned over the difficulties under which the university has been
operating," Campbell said. "We are also concerned 'bout actions that may be
taken in the meeting in Dallas. We sincerely hope that educators generally will
give every possible assistance in keeping the university in a position to operate
without undue adverse influences." Former and current college presidents
wanted Ole Miss to maintain its accreditation because desegregation was an
issue most white academic leaders were unprepared to address. Now, with
"Another Mississippi Story" told and shared widely, Williams and other Ole
Miss supporters waited to see if the reframed narrative regarding the university
was enough to demonstrate his full authority and save accreditation.[76]

74. Oliver C. Carmichael to Charles D. Fair, November 21, 1962; John H. Fischer to John
Davis Williams, November 21, 1962; both in Street Collection, Box 17, Folder–Meredith Crisis
(Nov. 20–30, 1962), UM.

75. For a sample of Harry H. Ransom's duties for SACS, see Harry H. Ransom to George
Wallace, May 1963, Frank A. Rose Papers, Box 6, Location 084–079, Folder: Integration Plans,
University of Alabama, W. S. Hoole Special Collections Library. Regarding the reference to
each member institution having a vote, see "Association Deliberates on Mississippi Decision,"
Mississippian, November 28, 1962.

76. Doak S. Campbell to Charles D. Fair, November 21, 1962, Street Collection, Box 17,
Folder–Meredith Crisis (Nov. 20–30, 1962), UM.

Making Mississippi's Story America's Story

On November 28, 1962, SACS's College Delegate Assembly gathered at the Baker Hotel in Dallas, Texas. Segregation was one of the most prominent topics before the white southern academic leaders during the four-day meeting. In fact, as chair of the SACS Commission on Colleges, Harry H. Ransom appealed to his contemporaries that southern institutions needed to rid themselves of segregation or accept being left behind. This was a direct nod to federal funding requirements and general competitiveness against a national cohort of institutions. The South's most recent example of this was Ole Miss, whose accreditation status ruling neared almost two months after the campus riot that left two people dead and dozens of others injured.[77]

The *Mississippian* characterized the meeting as the university being on trial. "The major issue of accreditation is whether or not Governor Barnett and the Board of Trustees violated association rules in connection with action before the admission of Meredith to the university," the student newspaper concluded. Other issues working against Ole Miss were the potential violence against any students who were friendly to Meredith, the pressure placed on the *Mississippian* editor Sidna Brower for her critical editorials, and state legislators' demands that some Ole Miss faculty be fired.[78]

Yet, following the closed-door meeting in Dallas, the association recommended that Ole Miss and Mississippi's other colleges and universities be placed under "continued and careful observation." It also considered the state's institutions to have "extraordinary status" among its membership, with the understanding that reevaluation would occur at the association's next regular meeting, or as needed. In short, the state's higher education institutions' accreditation remained intact, and Williams needed to ensure that Ole Miss continued to function without political influence. This was important to Mississippi and other southern academic leaders. Therefore, Ransom told reporters following the meeting: "We will do anything to help Chancellor Williams if the need ever arises again."[79]

Immediately, on November 28, Williams shared the news with the Ole Miss faculty. SACS commended the trustees, faculty, and academic leaders for their "acts and attitudes" regarding their vow to protect the university. SACS also added four areas it would observe in the future: the intentional weakening of

77. On Harry Huntt Ransom at the SACS meeting, see Gribben, *Harry Huntt Ransom*, pp. 158–161.

78. "Association Deliberates," *Mississippian*.

79. "Commission Gives UM 'Extraordinary Status,'" *Mississippian*, November 29, 1962. For the Ransom quote, Gribben, *Harry Huntt Ransom*, p. 161.

the trustee board; any "encroachment" by external groups to limit the academic freedom of the faculty, administrators, or students; the manipulation of state appropriations as a "punitive measure" against institutions; and any failure of administrators to maintain an environment favorable to learning. From Memphis, on November 30, the *Commercial Appeal* labeled the SACS decision "a vote of confidence" in the Ole Miss faculty and administrators and "a warning" to Mississippi's elected officials. The editorial board also credited the integrity of leaders like Williams and the majority of the Ole Miss student body, alongside engaged alumni, for the preservation of accreditation. "Despite the violence and bloodshed which accompanied Meredith's arrival at Ole Miss, the university and its sister institutions have stood above the fray and have survived," the editorial read.[80]

For Williams, however, the tempered response from SACS and continued praise from regional newspapers did not fully vindicate Ole Miss. The same *Commercial Appeal* editorial also nodded to the looming questions beyond the South: who was at fault for the Ole Miss riot? Regarding SACS's favorable decision, the editorial said, "Undoubtedly, some consideration also was given to the inflammatory actions of the federal government in the Mississippi situation." From New Orleans, on December 22, the *Times-Picayune* echoed that sentiment in its praise of Williams and others, noting, "Despite the interruption of campus routine, caused by the collision of federal and state political power, university officials now feel that classroom activities are back on schedule." As both editorial boards indicated, with its accreditation status unharmed, the emerging issue was what national narrative would emerge about Ole Miss.[81]

In the South, several other universities remained segregated, and by 1963, which side accepted blame was significant for those southern institutions with pending desegregation decisions. Mississippi officials would argue to the rest of America that federal force caused the riot, and federal officials would counter by explaining that they were forced to use troops due to Mississippians' defiance. "The next skirmish between Mississippi and the federal government is expected to find salesmanship the chief weapon on both sides," wrote William B. Street, a Memphis-based journalist, on December 16, 1962. At about

80. John Davis Williams to the Ole Miss Faculty, November 28, 1962, Street Collection, Box 17, Folder–Meredith Crisis (Nov. 20–30, 1962), UM; "Commission Gives UM"; "Vote of Confidence," *Commercial Appeal*, November 30, 1962.

81. "Vote of Confidence," *Commercial Appeal*; "Ole Miss in Good Academic Order," *Times-Picayune*, December 22, 1962.

the same time, Williams was presented with an opportunity to tell the Ole Miss story on a national stage.[82]

In November, Williams was invited to San Francisco to speak before the Commonwealth Club of California. Founded in 1903, the club's two-part purpose was to provide a forum to discuss and debate ideas and interrogate state, national, and international problems. As of November 1962, roughly three thousand notable individuals had spoken before the Commonwealth Club during the organization's nearly sixty-year existence. This included US presidents Dwight D. Eisenhower, William Howard Taft, and Woodrow Wilson; civil rights leaders such as Roy Wilkins, executive director of the NAACP; Supreme Court Justice Earl Warren; and academic leaders such as Benjamin Ide Wheeler, president of the University of California at the turn of the century, among several foreign dignitaries. The Commonwealth Club wanted Williams to discuss "The University and Integration," which would be recorded for broadcast. This invitation presented him with an opportunity to share the Mississippi story before a national audience, specifically a credible group that had hosted a distinguished list of global leaders. The two sides agreed on February 21, 1963, as the date for Williams's California visit.[83]

The spring visit with the Commonwealth Club became a looming priority for Williams and the state trustees despite the numerous minor flare-ups that could jeopardize accreditation. Following his Greenville and Fulton Chapel speeches, as well as his State of the University talk, Williams admitted that the media was a concern. On campus, the Student Senate reprimanded Sidna Brower, editor of the *Mississippian*, for what it deemed irresponsible leadership of the student newspaper. Ole Miss faculty responded, nearly unanimously, by passing a resolution supporting Brower. Likewise, news of the riot and subsequent smaller violent demonstrations were spread by the media. In fact, on New Year's Eve in 1962, *Look*—a national magazine—published an article that said Barnett and Kennedy attempted to broker a deal for a staged Meredith enrollment where the governor was forced aside by federal officials. The Mississippi story was being told but from a variety of perspectives. "The problem, however, is a two-edged sword," Williams said of the media.[84]

82. William B. Street, "Ole Miss Battle of Words Beginning," *Commercial Appeal*, December 16, 1962.

83. For the Commonwealth Club invitation and information about that group, see Stuart R. Ward to John Davis Williams, November 21, 1962, JDW, Box 7, Folder 4, UM. Regarding the agreement to broadcast the talk, see Stuart R. Ward to John Davis Williams, December 11, 1962, JDW, Box 7, Folder 4, UM.

84. On the Student Senate and Sidna Brower, see John Corlew, "Decision on Editor Will Come Tonight," *Mississippian*, December 4, 1962; John Corlew, "Senate Reprimands Editor,"

On January 7, 1963, Meredith announced during a press conference that he would not enroll for the spring term. This also stirred more media attention, and it caused the chancellor to meet with Meredith for the first time. Williams then banned unauthorized press from campus, which angered journalism faculty in particular, but three weeks later, Williams announced to the campus that Meredith would, indeed, remain enrolled. All the while, in January, some students were finally suspended for their participation in the fall's violent demonstrations and provost Charles F. Haywood resigned, requiring the midyear hiring of his replacement. Despite these events, Williams stayed focused on his upcoming talk in California.[85]

By February 15, a week before the Commonwealth Club address, Williams had fully drafted his address, and he and other Ole Miss officials combed through each line in preparation for taking the Mississippi story national. Additionally, Williams requested background data regarding other controversies in higher education. For instance, the 1950 University of California loyalty oath that required faculty to subscribe to a formal pledge not to adopt radical beliefs was of particular interest to Williams. Notably, these controversies were from nonsouthern states.[86]

Mississippian, December 6, 1962; "Text of Resolution," *Mississippian*, December 6, 1962; "Faculty Takes Action: Commends Editor," *Mississippian*, December 7, 1962. Regarding the "two-edged sword" comment, see John Davis Williams to Mrs. Walter Robert Jones, November 16, 1962, Street Collection, Box 17, Folder–Meredith Crisis (Nov. 1–19, 1962), UM; George B. Leonard, T. George Harris, and Christopher S. Wren, "How A Secret Deal Prevented a Massacre at Ole Miss," *Look*, December 31, 1962. Frank Lambert concluded that "Barnett was a staunch segregationist, but he did not want to destroy the university or plunge the state into a second civil war," thus he worked to broker a desegregation deal with President Kennedy. For more, see Lambert, *Battle of Ole Miss*, p. 107.

85. On Meredith's plan to not re-enroll, see James Meredith Statement, January 7, 1963, Street Collection, Box 17, Folder–Meredith Civil Rights Correspondence (1963), UM; and "Meredith Says He Will Leave," *Mississippian*, January 8, 1963. Meredith said he had not seen Chancellor Williams at any point during the fall of 1962 term. His announced decision not to enroll for the spring of 1963 prompted a meeting with Williams. For more, see Meredith, *Three Years in Mississippi*, pp. 272–273; Regarding the announcement that Meredith would remained enrolled, see John Davis Williams, Memorandum to Campus, January 30, 1963, JDW, Box 11, Folder 6, UM. Some scholars credit Williams, in part, for Meredith's decision to re-enroll. For more, see Eagles, *Price of Defiance*, pp. 398–399; John Davis Williams to Faculty, Staff, and Students, January 31, 1963; and Journalism Faculty Statement, February 6, 1963, Street Collection, Box 18, Folder–Meredith Civil Rights Correspondence (1963), UM; "Student Held in Disturbance Is Suspended," *Mississippian*, January 15, 1963; "Board Names Noyes Provost," *Mississippian*, February 5, 1963.

86. Regarding the information gathered for the California speech, see A. J. Peet to John Davis Williams, February 15, 1963, JDW, Box 11, Folder 10, UM.

The same day, Charles E. Noyes, the new provost, provided Williams with feedback on his latest draft of the speech. "Revisions make a considerable improvement over the original version," Noyes told Williams. "However, I feel that the last section, the most important of all, somehow lacks a little weight. I am wondering if just a little more repetition of the central idea might not make the closing paragraphs more effective." From there, Williams put the final touches on the speech, which he also shared with Charles D. Fair, chair of the board of trustees. "It is an excellent statement," Fair told Williams. "I wish I could hear it delivered by you."[87]

On February 21, 1963, about 250 people attended the Commonwealth Club luncheon at downtown San Francisco's Sheraton-Palace Hotel to hear Williams. He started his talk by offering the club members, guests and radio and newspaper reporters "a swift recapitulation of the more salient facts" about the Meredith case. He explained that Ole Miss and the other state colleges and universities were governed by the Mississippi Board of Institutions of Higher Learning, and the board members were against admitting Meredith since, before September 1962, no segregated white institution in the state had admitted Black students. Yet, the political battle between state and federal officials left board members facing a prison sentence for violating state law if they admitted Meredith or facing federal contempt of court charges if they did not admit him. Trapped between both sides, the board used a provision under the Mississippi State Constitution that allowed it to delegate its authority to the governor. That decision, Williams said, was the last step toward "a bloody riot which provided a Roman holiday for newspaper readers and television viewers, and which gave our university its unenviable notoriety."[88]

Williams felt it was paramount that the California audience, and by default the nation, understand the context that ignited the riot. "No doubt here in California, 2,000 miles away, you have asked, 'Why did it happen? How could it have happened?'" To segregationists, he explained, the forced enrollment of Meredith conjured up the terrible memories of the Civil War. "The Civil War is not so far away from us in Mississippi .... A defeated and pillaged people do not easily forget," he added. "Jealousy and a certain distrust of the federal government exists throughout this country. It is an established fact of political life in Mississippi and in the rest of the Deep South." The "southern way of life," Williams said, and its separation of races is "a fact of existence." As evidence of

87. Charles E. Noyes to John Davis Williams, February 15, 1963, JDW, Box 11, Folder 10, UM; Charles D. Fair to John Davis Williams, February 15, 1963, JDW, Box 6, Folder 9, UM.

88. For the number of people in attendance, see "Traumatic Doings at Ole Miss," *San Francisco Chronicle*, February 22, 1963; The University and Integration Speech, February 21, 1963, JDW, Box 11, Folder 10, UM.

this, there had been no serious progress with school desegregation in Mississippi nearly ten years after the *Brown* decision. Therefore, he told the San Francisco audience, "A practical politician in the Deep South would no more advocate school integration than a candidate for mayor in your city would run on a platform advocating earthquakes."[89]

Williams used that statement to shift the conversation from the mishaps of Mississippians to the mistakes made by Americans who did not live in the South. The race riots on September 30, 1962, had as much to do with Californians as they did Mississippians. In fact, Williams suggested the nation should actually credit Ole Miss for the peaceful January 1963 desegregation of Clemson College in South Carolina (although it is notable that the white press villainized Meredith as an adult who had served in the military, in contrast to Harvey B. Gantt at Clemson, where media noted that he was of traditional college age). The chancellor then shared other examples of social and political influences on higher education, each pulled from the information his staff had gathered a week earlier. "May I say in closing that this struggle is not ours alone, but yours too," he said, emphasizing that Ole Miss was a national tragedy. "America is one nation. What hurts a part, hurts the whole. The South today is the nation's frontier, a rich land, still unexploited. The South has a tradition and a culture that America cannot afford to lose."[90]

Afterward, Williams fielded questions from the audience, leaving them delighted by his attention, and he also gave interviews to seven radio stations. His performance, said Stuart Ward, executive secretary for the Commonwealth Club, was "truly superlative," and his speech was "thoughtful and informative." The next day, the *San Francisco Chronicle*, the city's major daily newspaper, covered the chancellor's address. The same was the case for smaller newspapers throughout California, such as the *Santa Ana Register* in Orange County outside of Los Angeles. Back in the Deep South, the *Birmingham News* editorial board quoted Williams's take on Ole Miss's loss of prestige, faculty, and students. Then, the editorial referenced the University of Alabama's anticipated desegregation: "The wise man will see advice in that. Though Chancellor Williams spoke in California, his words fit Alabama ears."[91]

89. University and Integration Speech.

90. Ibid. On Clemson's peaceful enrollment of Harvey B. Gantt, see Eisiminger, *Integration with Dignity*, pp. 2–3. On the media comparisons between Meredith and Gantt, see M. Ron Cox, Jr., "'Integration with [Relative] Dignity': The Desegregation of Clemson College and George McMillan's Article at Forty," in Moore and Burton, *Toward the Meeting of the Waters*, pp. 282–283.

91. Stuart R. Ward to John Davis Williams, February 27, 1963, JDW, Box 6, Folder 11, UM; "Traumatic Doings at Ole Miss"; "No Real Sign of Integration Says Chancellor," *Santa Ana Register*, February 22, 1963; "What Ole Miss Lost, Taught," *Birmingham News*, February 22, 1963.

Additionally, Williams telling the Mississippi story resonated with presidents and chancellors across the country. Herman B Wells of Indiana University said he read the speech with great interest. E. Wilson Lyon of Pomona College in Los Angeles County told Williams that he handled "the subject ably and with dignity." Franklin D. Murphy, chancellor of the University of California, Los Angeles, wrote Williams saying, "I hasten to tell you that I think you handled a very difficult job with remarkable candor and integrity and, therefore, most effectively." Meanwhile, I. D. Weeks at the University of South Dakota felt Williams should be congratulated for how he handled "an extremely difficult and explosive situation. I have often wondered what I would have done under similar circumstances."[92]

Over the next few months, Ole Miss officials heard from national media outlets as well. On March 8, Thomas W. Moore, vice president in charge of the American Broadcasting Company, wrote Williams directly:

> It is an extremely effective address, and the first clear concise account from the Ole Miss point of view which I have read. I have taken the liberty of sending it to a few of my associates because it explains as I have been unable to do, the extreme pressures that Ole Miss underwent in a most difficult situation. You refer to the fact that Clemson learned a great deal from Ole Miss's misfortune. I hope also that Ole Miss learned a great deal, and I am sure they have.

Later, in mid-April, William R. McAndrew, executive vice president of the National Broadcasting Company, wrote Fair, and John Fischer at *Harper's* magazine indicated that he followed the chancellor's California visit "with the greatest interest." Fischer then inquired whether any other US magazine or newspaper had published the address in its entirety. The combined responses demonstrate the effectiveness of Ole Miss officials' three-pronged effort to craft a narrative about the academic stability of the university. In the end, Williams established his authority as chancellor of Ole Miss, and at the same time, he modeled how the presidents of other white institutions could reframe a public narrative around campus racial violence—a practice that would be used through the remainder of the decade as more racial unrest unfolded on college campuses.[93]

---

92. Herman B Wells to Charles D. Fair, April 9, 1963, JDW, Box 6, Folder 12, UM; E. Wilson Lyon to John Davis Williams, March 6, 1963, JDW, Box 6, Folder 11, UM; Franklin D. Murphy to John Davis Williams, April 10, 1963, JDW, Box 6, Folder 12, UM; I. D. Weeks to John Davis Williams, April 9, 1963, JDW, Box 6, Folder 12, UM.

93. Thomas W. Moore to John Davis Williams, March 8, 1963, JDW, Box 6, Folder 11, UM; William R. McAndrew to Charles D. Fair, April 16, 1963, JDW, Box 7, Folder 1, UM; John Fischer to Charles D. Fair, April 15, 1963, JDW, Box 7, Folder 1, UM.

Conclusion

In May 1963, Ole Miss closed the academic year with its accreditation intact, and in June, the federal troops—roughly three hundred of them—were removed from campus after they had spent the entire 1962–63 academic year stationed on campus. By August, James H. Meredith graduated and participated in summer commencement services. There was widespread critique of who or what entities were to blame for the riot over Meredith's enrollment, and Williams was also blamed due to his inaction while Governor Barnett and President Kennedy debated desegregation.[94]

At best, Williams was a white moderate during that time. He did not challenge Mississippi's segregationist leaders despite past liberal-leaning, cross-racial actions in West Virginia during the 1940s. As a result, he took no side. In fact, in February 1961, only weeks after Meredith applied to Ole Miss, Williams confided as much to a longtime friend from West Virginia. "We are having our problems with segregation," he told J. B. Shouse, who lived in Huntington near Marshall College. "It is interesting to observe the social, economic, and spiritual forces at work. I am trying to maintain an objective position, for I believe that is my first responsibility to the students and faculty." His objectivity, however, did nothing to prepare the campus for the violent clash that occurred a year and a half later.[95]

In October 1962, for the first time at Ole Miss, Williams inserted his voice as the leader when it came to the race-related actions of the university. The potential loss of accreditation clarified that desegregation and academic freedom were intertwined and that Williams needed to exhibit the authority to lead the university. Social networks were used strategically by Williams to challenge students and local residents to reframe what it meant to be a Mississippian and to recraft the national narrative around white southern resistance. In Mississippi, Williams eventually earned the ear and support of the state's most prominent bankers, newspaper publishers, and clergy members, and academic leaders of other southern institutions offered their understanding of the desegregation dilemma. This proved to be critically important when the

---

94. In May 1963, Ole Miss received an accreditation update. For more, see "SACS Statement on Accreditation," *Mississippian*, May 14, 1963; and "Accreditation Agency Says . . . ," *Mississippian*, May 14, 1963; "300 Troops Removed from UM Campus," *Mississippian*, June 12, 1963. For details about Meredith and the security presence at the August 1963 commencement exercises, see Doyle, *American Insurrection*, p. 294.

95. John Davis Williams to J. B. Shouse, February 9, 1961, JDW, Box 6, Folder 3, UM.

academic stability of the university was questioned, threatening its accreditation status.[96]

The manner in which Ole Miss officials approached recovery from the riot resonated with college presidents across America. The sociopolitical context of the Black Freedom Movement transformed academic leadership, and the new demands on the presidency transcended regional boundaries. Ole Miss was the focal point in this case, but racial unrest was possible on any college campus, and academic leaders were sympathetic to the trials in Mississippi. Presidents were also keenly interested in how a university recovered from such an incident if they were unable to prevent it in the first place. Most apropos among these letters of interest to Williams was one from Henry Schmitz, president emeritus of the University of Washington. Although geographically distant from Mississippi, Schmitz complimented Williams for the "sane, logical, and convincing analysis" he offered in San Francisco. "I know from first-hand experience the heartaches and difficulties that confront an educational administration in a situation such as you confronted," Schmitz advised. "That all important factor, I believe, is being able to live with oneself after the crisis is over."[97]

The extent to which white college presidents from varying institutional types and regions cheered on Williams should not be understated. Although a riot was the catalyst for change, his post-riot actions emphasized the need for college presidents—not state officials—to lead state-supported universities, and influenced how presidents across the nation considered framing their campus racial policies. The campus race riot and accreditation pressures demonstrated that autonomy had become more necessary for effective campus leadership than in any other period in the history of American colleges and universities. Williams may not have been known by Mississippians before desegregation, but his efforts after the crisis exhibited the critical role of college presidents in handling complex issues of race and academic freedom—and nowhere were academic leaders more interested than next door in Alabama.

96. A group of Mississippi bankers agreed with the San Francisco speech. For more, see Will Lewis to John Davis Williams, February 22, 1963, JDW, Box 6, Folder 9, UM. Regarding southern journalists' support, the executive editor of the *Clarion-Ledger* also commended Williams. In fact, Williams was encouraged to "throw away that old script" after the Commonwealth Club speech. For more, Purser Hewitt to John Davis Williams, February 22, 1963, JDW, Box 6, Folder 10, UM. Regarding the clergy, see Mark K. Lytle to John Davis Williams, February 22, 1963, JDW, Box 6, Folder 10, UM.

97. Henry Schmitz to John Davis Williams, April 10, 1963, JDW, Box 6, Folder 12, UM.

5

"The More Violent and Adamant"

ANTICIPATING AND PREVENTING
WHITE RESISTANCE

"FRANK ANTHONY ROSE has been preparing for the University of Alabama's desegregation crisis ever since he became its president in September 1957," reported *The New York Times* on June 11, 1963. "This has made him a middleman between the federal government and Gov. George C. Wallace." This report was published only hours before Wallace's infamous stand in the schoolhouse door to deny two Black students—Vivian Malone and James Hood—admission to the University of Alabama (UA). The newspaper account also came just months after a race riot over desegregation at the University of Mississippi in September 1962; however, events were unfolding differently in Alabama. Journalists had hardly mentioned the chancellor prior to desegregation in Mississippi, but press coverage about the potential desegregation of UA framed Rose as a central figure.[1]

By June 1963, reporters from national and international news outlets had followed the Deep South desegregation question from Mississippi to Alabama—the last state where the most prominent white state-supported university remained segregated. Rose faced what Chancellor John Davis Williams at Ole Miss had already confronted: easing tensions over supporting academic freedom but not Black equality, fending off recalcitrant white legislators over control of their universities, appealing to alumni for support, and working to prevent violence. Yet, the two academic leaders adopted different

---

1. "Middleman in Alabama," *New York Times*, June 11, 1963. This article presents a unique contrast to news coverage about the University of Mississippi leading up to its September 1962 desegregation. For example, across multiple *New York Times* articles from June 1961 through September 1962, Chancellor John Davis Williams is repeatedly mentioned as one of three campus officials charged with contempt of court for denying James Meredith admission, but he is not framed as a key decision maker regarding higher education desegregation in Mississippi.

approaches that demonstrate that the southern white college presidency was nuanced and varied even between border states Alabama and Mississippi.

In the Deep South, white resistance to university desegregation was rigorous. In addition to the 1962 race riot at Ole Miss, in January 1961, violence erupted at the University of Georgia after two Black students, Charlayne Hunter and Hamilton Holmes, enrolled by court order. Also, in February 1956, before Rose was hired, white mob violence spread across the UA campus after Autherine Lucy enrolled by court order, but she was enrolled less than a week—ultimately keeping the university segregated. Compared with these previous white supremacist uprisings, by 1963, however, Rose at Alabama was working proactively to prevent violence. His strategies were unlike what journalists had previously observed of the presidents of segregated white institutions in the Deep South, and provides insights into presidents' anticipation and prevention of racial violence. Thus, as the *New York Times* report concluded, Rose "fits the perfect image for a successful college president. It is a model of organization and self-discipline."[2]

A New President and a Changing Alabama

UA officials pondered the race issue as early as the 1940s following successful legal challenges to segregated colleges and universities elsewhere in the South. In January 1936, the Maryland Court of Appeals ruled that Donald Murray, a Black man initially denied admission because of his race, should be admitted to study law at the segregated University of Maryland because the state did not provide a Black state-supported law school. In December 1938, the Supreme Court's *Missouri ex rel. Gaines v. Canada* ruling in favor of Lloyd Gaines, a Black applicant to the University of Missouri Law School, signaled a changing landscape in the South. These two cases focused on Upper South states but influenced white administrators in the Deep South. For instance, in November 1949, A. B. Moore, dean of the UA graduate school, knew most southern Black colleges did not offer graduate-level degrees or research opportunities. Therefore, Moore anticipated that some Black people would "expect Negroes to be admitted to state universities, as has been done in three states."[3]

2. Ibid.

3. On the Maryland case, see "Education in Maryland Shows Progress but Struggles Ahead: University of Maryland Case Stands Out as Most Important Achievement," *Baltimore Afro-American*, January 11, 1936. For more about the Supreme Court's *Missouri ex rel. Gaines v. Canada* decision, see Endersby and Horner, *Lloyd Gaines and the Fight to End Segregation*; A. B. Moore to John R. McLure, November 17, 1949, Frank A. Rose Papers, Box 6, Location 084–079, Folder:

As expected, a court order eventually forced UA academic leaders to admit Autherine Lucy, and on Friday, February 3, 1956, she became the university's first Black student. The first day of enrollment for the twenty-six-year-old graduate of Miles College, a private Black college near Birmingham, was considered uneventful; however, UA students and local white residents protested her enrollment and, that weekend, turned violent. A cross burning on University Avenue attracted a large crowd before a mob gathered near the student union. The white mob attacked passing cars, threw fireworks, and rocked a Greyhound bus attempting to leave Tuscaloosa. It then moved to UA president Oliver C. Carmichael's home, where fireworks were thrown at him when he attempted to address the impromptu assembly of racists.[4]

Lucy blamed UA officials for allowing the violence to occur, and trustees used her assessment to expel her from the university for "outrageous, false, and baseless accusations." Over the next year, Ku Klux Klan violence against Black residents in town was prominent, and twenty-five UA professors resigned over the Lucy situation. The violence captured national headlines, stigmatizing both the university and Carmichael. He resigned in 1957.[5]

In the search to replace Carmichael, UA trustees initially wanted John Davis Williams, the chancellor at Ole Miss, which had never had a Black student enroll; however, Williams—then in his mid-fifties and having been a college president or chancellor since 1942—declined and suggested UA hire a younger leader. The trustees took Williams's advice and turned their attention toward Rose, a promising young academic leader in Kentucky. Born in October 1920, in Meridian, Mississippi, the thirty-seven-year-old Rose graduated from

---

Integration Plans, University of Alabama, W. S. Hoole Special Collections Library. Moore's letter did not specify whether he meant undergraduate- or graduate-level admission, nor did he name the three southern states he referenced (collection and location hereafter cited as Rose Papers and UA).

4. Madison Davis, "First Negro's Entrance Sets Off Chain Reaction; Adams Called into Court," *Crimson White*, February 7, 1956 (newspaper hereafter cited as *CW*); "Events at Bama Being Publicized to Far Extremes," *CW*, February 7, 1956.

5. Regarding the university's expulsion of Lucy, see Anthony Lewis, "A New Racial Era: U.S. Policy Changed Basically Since Autherine Lucy Entered Alabama U.," *New York Times*, June 13, 1963; and Claude Sitton, "Alabamans Act to Bar Violence at University," *New York Times*, November 24, 1962. On Klan violence and the resignation of UA professors, see Collier-Thomas and Franklin, *My Soul Is a Witness*, pp. 51, 59. Historian Jeffrey A. Turner noted that the violent events at Alabama, Ole Miss, and Georgia "were not typical developments" in desegregating southern institutions, but were "revealing. The intrusion of serious racial politics forced students to consider the future of segregation." For more see, Turner, *Sitting In and Speaking Out*, pp. 40–41.

Meridian High School in 1939. He then attended Transylvania College in Lexington, Kentucky. In 1942, he earned his first degree from Transylvania, and in 1946, he earned a bachelor of divinity from the seminary also located at Transylvania. Briefly, in 1950, he completed some graduate-level studies in philosophy at the University of London, but he spent most of his post-undergraduate years working at Transylvania College, as chair of the philosophy department and dean of admissions.[6]

In 1951, he was named president of Transylvania College and developed a reputation as an institution builder. His tenure as president included a successful campaign to raise $4 million to eliminate the small college's debt. He was also credited for the building of a new library, gymnasium, and women's residence hall. Additionally, enrollment doubled during his presidency, and he nearly doubled the annual salary for Transylvania faculty. His success caught the attention of the National Junior Chamber of Commerce (known as the Jaycees), which, in 1954, named him one of the nation's ten most outstanding young men, and Rose was selected in 1957 as UA's next president.[7]

A number of distinguished guests welcomed Rose to Tuscaloosa, as evident from his April 9, 1958, inauguration ceremony. Governor James E. Folsom brought greetings on behalf of the State of Alabama. President Ralph Draughon from Alabama Polytechnic Institute and President Henry King Stanford from Birmingham Southern College did the same on behalf of Alabama's state-supported and private colleges, respectively. Then, Colgate W. Darden, president of the University of Virginia, delivered the inaugural address. After the dignitaries from across the South left campus, university trustees quickly moved to solidify Rose's presidency with one final item—a doctorate.[8]

Carmichael, his predecessor, fit the profile of an accomplished scholar and college president. He had earned a master's from UA, attended Oxford University as a Rhodes Scholar, and served as chancellor of Vanderbilt University and president of the Carnegie Foundation for the Advancement of Teaching before returning to UA as president; Rose, however, had not earned a doctorate or a master's degree, although he did have honorary degrees from the

6. Regarding John D. Williams declining the UA presidency, see Faulkner, "Frank A. Rose," p. 108; Biographical Data–Frank Anthony Rose, July 23, 1957, Rose Papers, Box 7, Location 089–102, Folder: Rose Biographical Data, UA; and Biographical Data–Dr. Frank A. Rose, 1959, Rose Papers, Box 7, Location 089–102, Folder: Rose Biographical Data, UA.

7. Biographical Data–Frank Anthony Rose; Biographical Data–Dr. Frank A. Rose.

8. Inauguration Program, April 9, 1958, Rose Papers, Box 5, Location 086–103, Folder: Inauguration of Dr. Frank A. Rose, UA.

University of Cincinnati and Lynchburg College. Therefore, in June 1958, UA awarded Rose with an honorary doctorate and proceeded to refer to him as "Dr. Rose." He was hired with more than academic prowess in mind.[9]

In 1958, the university only received $1.3 million in outside support. Therefore, Rose needed to fundraise. He was also expected to rebuild a failing football program, and, in his first year, he hired Paul "Bear" Bryant as head coach. Most importantly, he needed to exercise the diplomacy required to discuss desegregation in Alabama, but the 1958 gubernatorial race brought significant changes that would impact that discussion.[10]

By 1958, the Big Mule—a political alliance of industrial and agricultural leaders—had controlled state government since the turn of the century. Powerful interest groups dictated the priorities of the state, and industrialists were not interested in racial equality. No elected officials represented the interests of disenfranchised Black residents, since only 9 percent of them could vote. Educational attainment in the state also consistently fell behind the national average, and rural Greene and Hale counties, both of which bordered Tuscaloosa County, were among the nation's lowest in average income. The Big Mule had profited from these dismal conditions for years; however, the governor's race shifted the interests of Alabamians as segregation rose in prominence, and as political scientists Anne Permaloff and Carl Grafton explained, "The campaigns of that year set the pattern for many elections to come as race openly became a major issue."[11]

The contested race featured three main candidates—George C. Wallace, John M. Patterson, and Jimmy Faulkner. As the current state attorney general, Patterson emerged victorious because he successfully tied up the NAACP in a legal battle over whether it could operate in Alabama. Although the organization was not banned, the fight was notable considering the NAACP's successful legal challenges to segregation across the nation, and Patterson leveraged his role to appeal to white voters that he was the best candidate. As governor,

9. On Rose's academic credentials, including honorary degrees, see Biographical Data–Dr. Frank A. Rose, 1959. For more about Oliver C. Carmichael, see "Education: Goodbye to 'Bama," *Time*, November 19, 1956.

10. In 1958, the University of Alabama brought in $1.3 million in outside support. By 1969, as Rose concluded his presidency, the university had received $33 million in outside support. For more, see Barbara Thomas and Harold Kennedy, "Dr. Rose Leaves Educational Legacy," *Birmingham News*, March 9, 1969.

11. On the Big Mule alliance, see Frederick, *Stand Up for Alabama*, p. 2. On the Big Mule and other state dynamics, see Permaloff and Grafton, *Politics and Power in Alabama*, pp. 1, 3, 28, 31, 69. On the percentage of Black Alabamians who could vote in 1958, see Anderson, *Pursuit of Fairness*, p. 49.

Patterson leaned toward the usual lobbyist groups, such as the Alabama Education Association, that had long controlled state politics. For example, Rose was part of a group of educators that, in 1958–59, lobbied Patterson to increase state appropriations for education, but the new governor tied his agreement to increase education funding to a request that he have the authority to close the state's schools if forced to desegregate.[12]

In February 1960, white state officials' preemptive tactics to maintain segregation were met by direct-action campaigns. In Montgomery, the state capital, Alabama State College students joined the broader Black college student sit-in movement at whites-only lunch counters. Patterson demanded that H. Councill Trenholm, president of Alabama State, halt the sit-ins. There was also surveillance of Alabama State faculty suspected of assisting the students. Eventually, nine students were expelled, and Patterson's interference in campus affairs caused the American Association of University Professors to condemn his actions; however, the governor deemed his action necessary "to prevent bloodshed in the city. If we ever bow to the threat of a mob, we are on our way out and they'll get more arrogant every day." Although many people understood Trenholm's predicament, on March 2, 1960, roughly one thousand Alabama State students voted to boycott classes until the expelled students were reinstated.[13]

Although UA's main campus was segregated and located one hundred miles northwest of Montgomery, Rose felt the impact in Tuscaloosa because, on March 22, six Black students sought admission to UA's Montgomery Center while they boycotted Alabama State. Over the next two weeks, between March 22 and April 4, Rose and his assistant J. Jefferson Bennett communicated with the press and state officials about the applicants. Rose's office issued a press release to the *Tuscaloosa News*, the *Birmingham News*, and the Birmingham offices of the Associated Press and United Press International. The six applications were "being individually examined," according to the press release. The issue soon went away as the six Alabama State students' issue was with their campus, not UA's Montgomery Center, but if Carmichael was

12. Permaloff and Grafton, *Politics and Power*, pp. 70–73, 96–97.

13. For a brief overview of the Alabama State College expulsions, see Permaloff and Grafton, *Politics and Power*, pp. 140–141, 149–150; and "ASU Students Expelled for 1960 Sit-in Reinstated," *Associated Press*, February 26, 2010. The Alabama State expulsions also galvanized white students in the Midwest, West, and Northeast. For more and Patterson's "threat of a mob" quote, see "Nine Negro Students Out," *Daily Bruin*, March 3, 1960. For perspectives sympathetic to Trenholm and his civil rights efforts, see Robinson, *Montgomery Bus Boycott*, pp. 167–172; Fairclough, *Teaching Equality*, pp. 39–41; and Favors, *Shelter in a Time of Storm*, pp. 101–132.

criticized for not being proactive, Rose overcommunicated to stay ahead of the press.[14]

Following the Montgomery issue, on April 4, Rose personally thanked Patterson for his cooperation with the university's "recent problem in Montgomery." The problem, Rose admitted, had been given "a great deal of time and study and [UA's approach] has been successful to date. If you have any suggestions or counsel to give to this approach, I would be most happy to receive it." Rose had desegregation on his mind, but he gave no indication that he wanted Black students at the university.[15]

In January 1961, less than one year after the Montgomery problem, violence erupted at the University of Georgia after two Black students, Charlayne Hunter and Hamilton Holmes, enrolled following a court order. Reminiscent of events in Alabama in 1956, angry Georgia students and Klan members rioted. Afterward, the *Atlanta Journal* predicted that if Georgia state officials continued resisting desegregation, the university might lose its accreditation, top faculty would depart for other institutions, and the state would become less attractive to industry. This prompted Marvin B. Perry, president of the Georgia alumni society, to send a memo begging graduates to help set the record straight about the university. All of this and more had Rose's attention.[16]

Knowing the Georgia scenario, Rose delayed desegregating the campus until after Alabama's 1962 gubernatorial race, which further illustrated how southern states varied politically. At Transylvania, Rose had seen the University of Kentucky enroll its first Black student in 1949 and its first Black undergraduates in 1954. Also, North Carolina voters had recently elected Terry Sanford governor, replacing Luther H. Hodges, who had instructed the president of each state-supported college to halt students' lunch counter sit-ins in March 1960. Sanford adopted a more liberal philosophy and advocated for desegregation in North Carolina, and Rose hoped the same—a more liberal governor—was possible in Alabama. Until then, Black students were denied admission.[17]

14. President's Office Press Release Memorandum, n.d., Rose Papers, Box 6, Location 084–079, Folder: Integration Plans, UA.

15. Frank A. Rose to John Patterson, April 4, 1960, Rose Papers, Box 6, Location 084–079, Folder: Integration Plans, UA.

16. For more about the University of Georgia riots, see Daniels, *Horace T. Ward*, pp. 150–155; and Pratt, *We Shall Not Be Moved*, pp. 103–106; Marvin B. Perry to Georgia alumni, January 17, 1961, Rose Papers, Box 6, Location 084–079, Folder: Integration Plans, UA; "The University's Crisis," *Atlanta Journal*, January 22, 1961. For more about the Klan activity and violence garnering Rose's attention, see Clark, *The Schoolhouse Door*, pp. 148–149.

17. Linda B. Blackford, "University of Kentucky Names Residence Hall after School's First Black Student," *Lexington Herald-Leader*, May 8, 2015; Luther Hodges to Robert H. Frazier and

Two months later, on March 17, 1961, David L. Darden, assistant dean of admissions, instructed Fred Whiddon, director of the UA Mobile Center, to deny admission to Vivian Malone, a Black woman. At the time, Malone was a full-time student at Alabama A&M, the state's Black land-grant college. Darden explained that she was midway through her current coursework and could not enroll. "Will you be kind enough to notify the applicant that her application is not being processed, and therefore, she will not be allowed to begin work during the coming quarter at the Mobile Center," Darden told Whiddon. In 1962, Darden gave a similar directive regarding Harold Alonza Franklin's application to the UA Law School because his previous college coursework came from an unaccredited Black college. This rationale was commonly employed at segregated white institutions because Black applicants typically had previously attended Black colleges, most of which were not approved by the South's white accreditation agency.[18]

In June 1962, the Democratic primary was the default governor's election in Alabama. Rose backed the moderate Democrat Ryan deGraffenried, but George C. Wallace dominated the primary (and subsequent runoff election) while running on a strict segregationist platform. He won fifty-seven of the state's sixty-seven counties. White Alabamians voted for segregation, which was against the state's economic interests, and Bennett immediately recognized Wallace's election as a clear problem for UA. He knew Wallace. In the late 1930s, Bennett and Wallace had arrived on the same train to Tuscaloosa as freshmen. Wallace was from rural Bullock County and remained at UA through the completion of law school. As a student, Wallace did not have the financial means to participate in the influential fraternity and social scene, but twenty-five years later, he stood as a state leader with a promise to maintain segregation. On the other hand, Rose was hired to ensure that the Alabama campus did not have a repeat of 1956.[19]

Warmoth T. Gibbs, March 3, 1960, Luther Hartwell Hodges Collection, North Carolina State Archives, Raleigh, North Carolina.

18. David L. Darden to Fred Whiddon, March 17, 1961, Rose Papers, Box 6, Location 084–079, Folder: Integration Plans, UA; David L. Darden to M. Leigh Harrison, July 26, 1962, Rose Papers, Box 6, Location 084–079, Folder: Integration Plans, UA.

19. For a reference to Rose supporting Wallace's gubernatorial opponent, see "Middleman in Alabama"; On the 1962 gubernatorial election results, see Permaloff and Grafton, *Politics and Power*, pp. 156–162. For more about Wallace's childhood and time as a UA student, see Frederick, *Stand Up for Alabama*, pp. 7, 11. The *Huntsville Times* argued it was critical to think nationally to attract industry in selecting a governor. For more, see pp. 24–25. Regarding Bennett and Wallace on the same train as freshman, see Hollars, *Opening the Doors*, p. 101.

Seeing the potential for future conflict, Bennett wrote Wallace a congratulatory note. Cordially, Wallace replied: "I certainly appreciate your letter and your congratulations. I am looking forward to renewing our acquaintance and working with you during the coming four years toward building a greater University of Alabama and State of Alabama in general." The question for Rose and Bennett was how this renewed acquaintance would unfold. The answer could be seen in Mississippi.[20]

From Alabama to Mississippi and Back Again

In the fall of 1962, UA enrolled around eight thousand students in Tuscaloosa and an additional six thousand students at extension centers. The university was growing, but white residents' opinions on desegregation remained consistent. The all-but-official election of George C. Wallace also reinforced those beliefs. With a new governor expected in January, there were many unknowns about UA desegregation, as the Autherine Lucy episode persisted in recent memory; however, Mississippi governor Ross Barnett's defiance of a federal court order to desegregate Ole Miss in September 1962 moved up Rose's timeline to earnestly prepare UA for the same.[21]

On September 20, 1962, Barnett issued Meredith an executive order denying his admission to Ole Miss. James Meredith's admission, Barnett stated, "would lead to a breach of the peace and be contrary to the administrative procedures and regulations of the University of Mississippi and the laws of the State of Mississippi." On the same day, the *Montgomery Advertiser* observed that Barnett's actions were familiar. "Events in Mississippi remind Alabama that it was six years ago that Autherine Lucy, the Negro student, attended classes for three days at the University of Alabama," the newspaper stated. "You can admire Gov. Barnett's sacrificial defiance, but it has not yet been made clear what it will accomplish beyond demonstrating once again that federal power is supreme." Indeed, on September 30, the governor's resistance was overridden by federal authorities to enroll Meredith, and as Barnett predicted, peace was breached as violence erupted on campus. The riots left two people dead, and dozens of the US Marshals on campus injured. The public immediately turned its attention to Alabama.[22]

20. J. Jefferson Bennett to George C. Wallace, May 30, 1962; and George C. Wallace to J. Jefferson Bennett, June 19, 1962; both in J. Jefferson Bennett Papers, Box 25, Location 088–109, Folder: Wallace, UA (collection hereafter cited as Bennett Papers). The two men also discussed arriving on the same train to Tuscaloosa their freshman year.

21. On UA's overall enrollment in 1962, see Tilford, *Turning the Tide*, p. 8.

22. Ross Barnett to James Meredith, September 20, 1962, James Howard Meredith Collection, Box 2, University of Mississippi, J. D. Williams Library, Archives and Special Collections;

Before the riot, the *Crimson White* student newspaper at UA published an editorial in favor of Meredith's enrollment at Ole Miss. "We lost something American in Oxford this week," the newspaper said after Barnett denied Meredith enrollment, "and every American citizen is the less for it." The editorial stirred white supremacists. Tuscaloosa was the national headquarters for the United Klans of America of the Knights of the Ku Klux Klan, and during the September 30 riot at Ole Miss, Melvin M. Meyer, editor of the *Crimson White*, received a death threat via an anonymous telephone call. He was told he would be left "in a pine box" if he did not leave Tuscaloosa within twenty-four hours. Two nights later, a cross was burned in front of the Zeta Beta Tau fraternity house, where Meyer resided. Rose hired private detectives to protect Meyer. "This institution has the duty to protect every student from harassment or being subjected to any experience that might tend to place him in any danger," Rose said. "The threatening phone calls led us to the conclusion that such action was warranted in this incident."[23]

On October 4, a pep rally was scheduled as rumors circulated that a demonstration similar to the Ole Miss violence would occur at UA. Rose and other administrators considered canceling the event, but the university's football team was undefeated at the time. In fact, the Crimson Tide were the defending national champions. Therefore, the pep rally was not canceled, and instead, administrators met with student leaders and asked them to use their influence to stop any potential trouble. Carleton Butler, the university band director, was also instructed to have the band drown out any noise suspected of being a demonstration, and the dean of men's staff patrolled campus all week with "an unusually large" number of university, city, and state patrolmen. During the rally itself, head football coach Paul "Bear" Bryant spoke to the campus. Bryant was not initially scheduled to speak, but Rose understood his influence could

---

"When Badges Are Banged Together," *Montgomery Advertiser*, September 20, 1962; For more about the aftermath of the Ole Miss riots, see Eagles, *Price of Defiance*, pp. 377–378; and Doyle, *American Insurrection*, pp. 280–281.

23. For the *CW* editorial, see "A Bell Rang . . . ," *CW*, September 27, 1962. Regarding the violent reaction to the *CW* editorial, see Sitton, "Alabamans Act to Bar Violence." On the Klan as it related to the University of Alabama and desegregation, see Gaillard, *Cradle of Freedom*, pp. 37–42. For more on the Klan and Alabama politics, see Frederick, *Stand Up for Alabama*, p. 3. The Klan varied in its scope and organization from county to county. For a detailed overview of the variations of the KKK, particularly in the early 1960s, see David Cunningham, "Shades of Anti-Civil Rights Violence," in Ownby, *The Civil Rights Movement in Mississippi*, pp. 180–203. Regarding private security, President Rose preferred that the precaution be unpublicized, but a *Birmingham News* report in November led Rose to confirm that the university had hired detectives to protect Meyer. For more, see "Rose Says Editor Guard Report True," *Birmingham News*, November 14, 1962.

calm a restless crowd. Bryant emphasized "togetherness" and "oneness." Rose then told the crowd to "maintain the spirit that has brought prestige to this institution" instead of rioting. Rose's successful efforts saw the rally end with no demonstration during or after the event.[24]

Three weeks later, on October 24, 1962, the university received a preliminary application from a prospective Black student. Hubert Mate, dean of admissions, declined to release the name of the applicant, but the lone application was significant. It was the first of three anticipated from Black students. This round of applicants represented the first significant attempt to desegregate the university since the Autherine Lucy fiasco in 1956. Therefore, on the same day the application was received, John Blackburn, dean of men, hosted a question-and-answer session in Palmer Hall. The receipt of a Black person's completed application put Blackburn and others on alert. "There will not be another Oxford here," Blackburn stressed to the students. "This is your university. Law and order will be maintained."[25]

The next week, on October 30, Rose delivered his State of the University address. "It is in such a confused world that our universities are called to serve," the president emphasized. For Rose, "the times are too serious and education too expensive" for the university to use its resources on anything other than academic achievement. This was especially pertinent considering Mississippi

24. Hank Black, "Riot Rumors Cause Needless Alarm at Foster Pep Rally Last Monday," *CW*, October 11, 1962. It should also be noted that the UA football team was having an undefeated season, and by November 1962, the defending national champions were on a 25-game streak without a loss as it welcomed the University of Miami to campus. For more, see "Mira and Hurricanes Are Great: Tide Greater?" *CW*, November 8, 1962. On the broader culture of UA football, see Tilford, *Turning the Tide*, p. 1. Tilford said the university "possessed a well-deserved reputation as one of the South's leading party schools." An additional element to championship football was the negative impact of being a segregated university. Some sports writers, particularly those not in the Deep South, critiqued UA for not playing against "integrated teams." For more, see Craig Knowles, "Washington Post Attacks Alabama: Segregation Policy Knocked," *CW*, November 1, 1962.

25. Regarding the October 24 receipt of a Black person's application, the *CW* noted it was the first attempt of Black people to enroll at Alabama since Autherine Lucy; however, that account ignored the March 1960 attempt of Black students from Alabama State College at the UA Montgomery Center. Therefore, it is more accurate to say the October 24 application was likely the first submitted for admission to the university's main campus in Tuscaloosa. For more, see Don Chapin, "Group to Examine, Evaluate the Lone Negro Application," *CW*, October 25, 1962. Also, a later report in the *New York Times* noted that the October 24 applicant was the first to submit a completed application. Previously, since Autherine Lucy in 1956, "a number of Negro students have applied for admissions to the university but none of the applications has been completed." For more on this, see Sitton, "Alabamans Act to Bar Violence"; "Blackburn Discusses Oxford, Evaluation, at Palmer Meet," *CW*, November 1, 1962.

leaders' failure to prevent violence and subsequent efforts to recover Ole Miss from physical and social ruin. "I am fully aware that there are some serious questions on your mind about the immediate future," he told the audience. "First, let me say, I do not know when we will be faced with the problem of enrolling a Negro student. Each semester we have several Negro students, along with hundreds of other students, to begin making [an] application; but we have not had one to complete [their] registration since 1956." However, it was anticipated that the previous week's application and two others would be completed by the close of the fall semester.[26]

That said, Rose intended to keep the university open if desegregation occurred. "I want to assure you that there is no thought on the part of the Board of Trustees either to close the university or to meet any crisis facing it in such a manner as to compromise the intellectual integrity of this institution," he said. "The University of Alabama cannot go through another crisis such as occurred in 1956 or happened at the University of Mississippi a few weeks ago." Rose believed administrators had a clear responsibility: "The university must never be made the place for troops, mobs, or national news media seeking sensation." However, the media attention and threat of violence already existed.[27]

For instance, in October 1962, the *Wall Street Journal* used the aftermath of Mississippi to focus on the ensuing university desegregation questions in Alabama and South Carolina. "While segregationist sentiments are overwhelmingly dominant in both states," the report stated, "talks with politicians, business leaders, and other residents suggest Alabama is likely to prove the more violent and adamant in its opposition to integration." The brutal treatment of the Freedom Riders by white Alabamians in 1961 partly caused this prediction. At the time, Patterson said of the riders: "When you go somewhere seeking trouble, you usually find it. I lay full blame on the agitators who come in here for the express purpose of stirring up just such a thing." Now, in 1962, Governor-elect George C. Wallace signaled even more resistance than his predecessor. "If a federal judge orders me to place a Negro student in a white school, I would refuse to do so," Wallace said. "They'll have to arrest me. And when they put their filthy hands on the governor of a sovereign state, it'll wake this country up. We're going to create headlines here. We Anglo-Saxon folks don't like to be pushed around."[28]

26. State of the University address, October 30, 1962, Bennett Papers, Box 17, Location 088–106, Folder: Rose Reports and Speeches, UA.

27. State of the University; "'No Thought' of Closing UA, Dr. Rose Says," *CW*, November 1, 1962.

28. Joseph W. Sullivan, "After Mississippi: Two Holdout States Brace for Showdowns on School Segregation," *Wall Street Journal*, October 10, 1962. On the Patterson Freedom Rider quote, see Permaloff and Grafton, *Politics and Power*, p. 141.

Those potential headlines were what Rose feared, as he explained in the State of the University address, but the headlines themselves were only a portion of his concerns. It was the behavior of local citizens, not just the elected officials, that also worried Rose, but there was hope. The *Wall Street Journal* assessed that white moderates in Alabama "may speak up more quickly if disorder threatens than did their counterparts in Mississippi." Black residents' boycott of businesses in nearby Birmingham caught white business leaders' attention and suggested that money, more than race, might answer the desegregation question; however, the news report closed by stating the obvious: "The lengths to which Alabama and South Carolina whites are prepared to go to defend segregation should not be underestimated."[29]

One day following the State of the University address, Rose started to secure support to curb violence in Alabama. Robert K. Bell, an attorney in Huntsville, commended Rose "for the very able" approach and said several others in northern Alabama felt the same. "I can say without reservation that I have never seen such problems coped with in such an efficient and wise manner as you and your staff have accomplished." On November 1, E. M. Friend Jr., an Alabama alumnus and attorney in Birmingham, shared similar sentiments. "It is unthinkable that we should have a repetition of what took place at the University of Mississippi," Friend told Rose. "I realize, however, that the governor of the state of Alabama will be in a position to affect the situation, without regard to what you, the Board of Trustees, and other officials at the university may wish to do. The only purpose of this letter is to tell you that I, and many of my friends, deeply appreciate what you are doing for the university."[30]

On November 2, the support Rose received from Bell and Friend was echoed indirectly by other sources. In Memphis, the *Commercial Appeal* published an editorial sympathetic to the college presidents of white segregated universities. The newspaper praised Ole Miss chancellor John Davis Williams for his leadership after the riot on campus and considered the university a victim of a political battle. "[Ole Miss] had a crisis thrust upon it without adequate warning that saw the institution removed from the control of its administrative organization." Despite this, Williams stayed true to leading the university, and the editorial applauded him for it. "The manner in which he carried

29. Sullivan, "After Mississippi."

30. Robert K. Bell to Frank A. Rose, October 31, 1962; and E. M. Friend Jr. to Frank A. Rose, November 1, 1962 both letters in Rose Papers, Box 6, Location 084–079, Folder: Integration Plans, UA.

out his assignment has earned him a high measure of acclaim for the courage, eloquence, and realism he displayed."[31]

Five days later, on November 7, Sidna Brower, editor of the Ole Miss student newspaper, spoke at UA during a luncheon for Omicron Delta Kappa, a senior men's honor society. "Approximately, only 200 students were not ready to give in," Brower said, emphasizing that the majority of Ole Miss students accepted Meredith's admission. Hearing this from an Ole Miss student bolstered Rose and Blackburn's pleas for students to remain peaceful, but nothing was more significant than the support of the UA Board of Trustees. On November 9, 1962, the trustees met in regular open session, where board members declared their "determination to do whatever necessary to prevent violence, riot, or disorder on the campus." The trustees' unanimous resolution was the first of its kind, and Rose used this to launch a statewide campaign against violence at the university.[32]

A Resolution to Prevent Violence

The November 1962 resolution adopted by UA trustees was significant. In addition to joining a chorus of support, it demonstrated how even segregationists in positions of influence, in contrast to the average white citizen, saw violence as a losing proposition. For example, Gessner T. McCorvey, president pro tem of the board, was a segregationist responsible for the Lucy expulsion. He was also a Dixiecrat, one of the southern democrats who rebelled against the national party in 1948 over civil rights. Yet, he proposed the trustees' resolution, and his support for peace warranted attention.[33]

On November 12, the Birmingham News said, "The State of Alabama is well served by this trustee pronouncement, which is a reaffirmation of reason and logic in handling university affairs." The newspaper added, "The mob will not

31. "Williams Earns Acclaim," *Commercial Appeal*, November 2, 1962. The *Commercial Appeal* editorial is also important because Memphis State enrolled Black students without violence four years prior to Ole Miss. This is evidence that it was the symbolic nature of the major state-supported southern universities that drew the most desegregation attention. For more, see Sorrells, *The Exciting Years*, p. 75.

32. "Brower Speaks on Mississippi at ODK Meet," *CW*, November 8, 1962; "U of A Alumni Add Support to Law, Order on Campus," *Montgomery Advertiser*, November 11, 1962.

33. On McCorvey being a segregationist yet proposing the trustee resolution, see Sitton, "Alabamans Act to Bar Violence." Regarding McCorvey's role in the Lucy expulsion, see McCorvey and UA Trustees, n.d., *Encyclopedia of Alabama*, http://www.encyclopediaofalabama .org/article/m-8228 (accessed March 2, 2018). On McCorvey as a Dixiecrat, see Permaloff and Grafton, *Politics and Power*, p. 112.

rule if it is the people's will that it be barred from the outset." On the same day, a *Birmingham Post-Herald* editorial argued, "The board and President Frank Rose deserve the thanks of every citizen for their firm action." The media praise was enough to prompt Rose to request an internal scrapbook of the press clippings in case he needed them in court, a reminder that UA was still under the Lucy case's court order to desegregate. This was also important considering Governor-elect Wallace's public statements.[34]

As the board passed its resolution on November 10, Wallace told the *Crimson White*, "If there is anyone who doesn't want another Oxford incident, [it is US] President [John F.] Kennedy." Wallace then downplayed the "law and order" resolution of the trustees. "Some people say that a person's stand for law and order is an implication that that person is against George Wallace, and that is not true," the governor-elect stated. Wallace then said McCorvey was one of his biggest supporters. Yet, while Wallace blurred the lines of where people stood on segregation, others were clearer. The same day, George LeMaistre, president of the City National Bank of Tuscaloosa, told the Tuscaloosa Civitan Club about the economic impact of violence. He encouraged them to accept the court rulings and said that no resident, Wallace included, was above the law. "What happened in Mississippi does not have to happen again," LeMaistre said, before receiving a standing ovation. "It would be tragic to think we learned nothing from the first incident." Also on November 10, the UA Alumni Council, which represented more than sixty thousand alumni, issued its support to the trustees' peace resolution.[35]

On November 14, Rose presided over a university-wide faculty meeting before more than six hundred faculty members and administrators in Morgan Hall. The faculty in attendance voted to adopt a statement prepared by the campus AAUP chapter, which read, in part, "We, the faculty of the University

34. "Trustees Say—University: Law, Order," *Birmingham News*, November 12, 1962; "Forthright Statement of Policy," *Birmingham Post-Herald*, November 12, 1962; Regarding the scrapbook, see Memo to W. V. Brown, n.d., Rose Papers, Box 4, Location 092–009, Folder: Newspaper Clippings, UA.

35. Regarding the Wallace quotes, see Buddy Cornett, "Kennedy Last One to Want Another Oxford—Says Wallace," *CW*, November 15, 1962; Ian Haney-Lopez wrote, "By the mid-1960s, 'law and order' had become a surrogate expression for concern about the civil rights movement." For more, see Haney-Lopez, *Dog Whistle Politics*, p. 24. For the LeMaistre speech, see Sitton, "Alabamans Act to Bar Violence." Related to LeMaistre's argument, historians Joy Ann Williamson-Lott and Melissa Kean have provided excellent overviews of the economic ramifications of segregation and its impact on higher education. For more, see Williamson-Lott, *Jim Crow Campus*; Kean, *Desegregating Private Higher Education*; "U of A Alumni Add Support to Law, Order on Campus," *Montgomery Advertiser*, November 11, 1962.

of Alabama, hereby affirm these truths: . . . that it is the duty and purpose of the faculty to teach all students enrolled at this institution," and "that learning can flourish only in a peaceful atmosphere free from the threat of violence." The faculty also commended Rose for his effort to maintain peace on campus, and newspapers across the state covered the statement.[36]

The next day, a *Crimson White* editorial board argued for peace while recalling the May 1961 Freedom Rides. Whereas some Alabamians violently attacked the Freedom Riders' efforts to desegregate public highway facilities, Mississippians avoided public violence. "Mississippi learned much from Alabama regarding the 'Freedom Riders,'" the editorial read. "Alabama mishandled the whole problem. We succeeded only in focusing the national spotlight on the smoldering ruins of a Greyhound bus in Anniston, and on a crowded bus station in Birmingham. Mississippi escaped that national spotlight." Therefore, UA desegregation presented an opportunity to reverse course and learn from Mississippi, and local groups took heed.[37]

Earl Brandon, a local doctor, informed the UA trustees that the Tuscaloosa County Medical Society had passed a resolution on November 15. The society, as "an organization whose chief concern is the health and welfare of the people," commended the trustees for their stand against violence. By November 19, Alto V. Lee III, president of the UA National Alumni Association, mailed the president of each alumni club a copy of the UA trustees' November 9 resolution and the alumni council's November 10 resolution. "We hope the club presidents will bring this statement and resolution to the attention of their alumni club," Lee stated. "Please notify the alumni office if your club adopts any similar resolutions." Soon after, individual alumni clubs passed resolutions as well. So, too, did the Tuscaloosa Rotary Club.[38]

36. Press Release on Alabama Faculty Resolution, November 14, 1962, Rose Papers, Box 4, Location 092–009, Folder: Newspaper Clippings, UA; "UA Faculty Joins in 'Order' Appeal," *Birmingham Post-Herald*, November 15, 1962; Don Chapin, "UA Faculty Joins Groups Asking 'Law and Order,'" *CW*, November 15, 1962. For more about the Morgan Hall meeting, see Tilford, *Turning the Tide*, pp. 3–5.

37. "A Mature Movement," *CW*, November 15, 1962. For an example of Mississippi and positive publicity over the Freedom Riders, see Judd Arnett, "Jackson Shrugs Off Integration Hubbub: Riders Jailed Quietly," *Detroit Free Press*, June 4, 1961.

38. Earl Brandon to Board of Trustees, November 15, 1962; Alto V. Lee III to Alumni Club Presidents and Members, November 19, 1962. For an example of local alumni club resolutions, see Frank A. Rose to John F. Proctor, November 29, 1962; regarding the rotary club resolution, see Frank A. Rose to William Cassell Stewart, November 26, 1962; all in Rose Papers, Box 6, Location 084–079, Folder: Integration Statements, UA.

By December, the Student Government Association Student Legislature unanimously agreed to issue its own "law and order" resolution in support of Rose and the UA trustees. The same stamp of approval came from the southern part of the state when the Methodist ministers of the Mobile District of the Alabama-Florida Conference commended Rose for his approach. The ministers' statement, in particular, was important given that white ministers regularly preached the gospel of segregation in churches. Nonetheless, they issued their support for peace. This even prompted the *New York Times* to say UA administrators were "acting with admirable resolution" to ensure that the campus would not be marred by the same rioting that occurred at Ole Miss.[39]

As white Alabamians anticipated another attempt at university desegregation, on November 24, 1962, Reverend Wyatt Tee Walker, a prominent Black pastor and leader in the Southern Christian Leadership Conference (SCLC), announced that two more Black people planned to apply to UA in addition to the preliminary application received on October 24. Walker vowed that the SCLC would assist the students and the NAACP if court action was needed to admit the three applicants. Three days later, on November 27, Vivian Malone identified herself as an applicant to UA. In March 1961, David L. Darden, assistant dean of admissions, had instructed Fred Whiddon to deny her admission to the Mobile Center. Now, Malone sought enrollment on the Tuscaloosa campus. At the time, Malone was a junior at Alabama A&M, but she now had the backing of the NAACP Legal Defense Fund, according to J. L. LeFlore, a Black civil rights leader in Mobile. Malone's rationale was simple: "I hope to enter personnel management or a related line after graduation and need the courses offered at the university." By November 29, it was confirmed that three applications from prospective Black students had been submitted to UA, and those applications and Rose's push for peace stirred a sizable amount of pushback among segregationists.[40]

39. Bill Plott, "'Law–Order' Motion Okayed by Legislature," *CW*, December 6, 1962. Regarding the ministers, see W. Earl Dubois and Billy D. Gaither to Frank A. Rose and Gessner T. McCorvey, December 10, 1962, Box 5, Location 084–079, Folder: D–General Correspondence, UA (General Correspondence folders hereafter cited as Correspondence). For more on the "anti-black and anti-federal government" sermons of white ministers, see Frederick, *Stand Up for Alabama*, p. 29. For the "acting with admirable resolution" quote, see "Alabama's Counsel of Reason," *New York Times*, November 26, 1962.

40. For Walker's assessment, see Sitton, "Alabamans Act to Bar Violence"; Regarding Malone, see "Girl among 3 Negroes Seeking U of A Entry: 'Good Student' at Alabama A&M Wants to Transfer to University," *Birmingham Post Herald*, November 27, 1962; "Negro Co-Ed to Seek Entry This Spring," *CW*, November 29, 1962.

In Montgomery, on November 21, a letter to the editor voiced disdain for the numerous "law and order" resolutions. "These remonstrations imply that Gov. Ross Barnett of Mississippi encouraged defiance of law, with the results that rioting occurred at the University of Mississippi when the Negro Meredith was enrolled," the letter read in the *Montgomery Advertiser*. "Quite the contrary. It was Gov. Barnett who obeyed the law and his oath to enforce the constitutions of Mississippi and of the United States." Echoing that sentiment, the small-town *Andalusia Star-News* newspaper said, "In Mississippi, there were no mobs and no shooting until the federals mounted bayonets and took over at Oxford. . . . The federals ignited the mob action at the University of Mississippi."[41]

That said, on November 24, Governor-elect Wallace told the *New York Times*, "I am going to pose some constitutional questions in Alabama that have not been posed so far." Three days later, Wallace was in Jackson, Mississippi, where he spoke before a joint session of the Mississippi State Legislature. There, he vowed to use Barnett's tactics when it came time for him to confront desegregation at UA. Wallace then promised that any federal directive to enroll Black students must be directed toward him. "This, in essence, I believe, was your governor's intention," Wallace told Mississippi's all-white legislature. "But he was denied the right to peacefully test by due process what he considered to be an usurpation of power by federal authority." The peace resolutions had not curbed his commitment to segregation.[42]

What was not mentioned in the news coverage about the joint legislative session in Mississippi was that, at the same time, the academic leaders of white southern institutions were in Dallas for a four-day meeting of the Southern Association of Colleges and Schools. There, Harry Huntt Ransom, chancellor of the University of Texas and chair of the Commission on Colleges for SACS, warned his colleagues that segregation was a detriment to garnering academic prestige nationally. Also, due to Barnett's interference with Ole Miss admissions, SACS delegates placed all of Mississippi state-supported institutions under observation before determining their accreditation status. Seeing

41. "On the School Door," letter to the editor, *Montgomery Advertiser*, November 21, 1962. On November 25, 1962, the *Montgomery Advertiser* published editorials from smaller newspapers in the state. The opinions varied, some for and against the trustees' resolution for law and order. In particular, "Wrong Target," the *Andalusia Star-News*, stated that the federal government ignited the mob action at Ole Miss.

42. Regarding Wallace's constitutional questions, see Sitton, "Alabamans Act to Bar Violence." For more about Wallace speaking in Mississippi, see "Will Use Barnett Methods at Capstone, Says Wallace: Wants to Be in 'Middle' of Mix Action," *Tuscaloosa News*, November 28, 1962.

firsthand how violence and a meddling racist governor could harm a university, on November 30, 1962, Rose decided to close UA transfer admissions. This meant the three Black applicants could not enroll in the spring.[43]

Constance Baker Motley, an attorney for the NAACP, said the organization planned to fight the decision, but legal action would likely take weeks, if not months, into the spring term. Rose did not reply to Motley's plans, but afterward, he was critiqued. "All of the work that went into the planning and preparations now seems to have been futile," one professor told the *Crimson White*. Another faculty member added, "The reputation of the university will suffer due to this action." On December 10, the *Detroit Free Press* ran a wire story about the UA decision under the headline, "Alabama U. Surrenders to Racists." The university's reputation, once positive due to the resolutions, was shaken. Wallace was credited as "the new element" that altered UA officials' plans to maintain peace, and Rose was seen as cowering under political pressure. "Last week, university President Frank Rose quietly surrendered," the *Detroit Free Press* concluded. Then, on December 14, the Louisville *Courier-Journal* recanted its earlier support of Rose. The Kentucky editorial board felt its confidence in Rose was "misplaced." It continued: "He has now surrendered to the bellowings of Governor-elect George Wallace, a dead-end segregationist who declares he will take Alabama down the same dangerous road that Ross Barnett took Mississippi."[44]

Indeed, Rose's efforts to prevent violence, his support of Wallace's gubernatorial opponent Ryan deGraffenried, and the university's need for state support put him in a peculiar position. Rose would have preferred a governor like North Carolina's Terry Sanford, who challenged segregation and staunchly supported higher education. In fact, only days before Wallace's January 1963 inaugural ceremonies, Rose wrote Sanford. "It is most heartening to all of us to find men of your abilities and interests serving as governor of one our great states," Rose told the North Carolina governor. "We will always remain indebted to you for your leadership." However, white Alabamians elected Wallace, and Rose needed to be courteous, if not outright cordial, to the new governor.[45]

43. On the SACS meeting in Dallas, see Gribben, *Harry Huntt Ransom*, pp. 158–161; and "Association Deliberates on Mississippi Decision," *Mississippian*, November 28, 1962; Don Chapin, "NAACP to Fight University Closing of Spring Registration," *CW*, December 6, 1962.

44. Chapin, "NAACP to Fight"; "Alabama U. Surrenders to Racists," *Detroit Free Press*, December 10, 1962. For more on Louisville's *Courier-Journal*, see "Kentucky Paper Off Its Rocker," *Birmingham News*, December 18, 1962.

45. Frank A. Rose to Terry Sanford, January 9, 1963, Rose Papers, Box 7, Location 084–080, Folder: S–Correspondence, UA.

Therefore, when invited to the Wallace inauguration, Rose replied, "We are looking forward to being present on this great occasion, and we appreciate deeply your remembering us." Then, on January 14, 1963, Wallace delivered a historic inaugural address, written by a Klan member who also served as the new governor's advisor, and perhaps most notable was Wallace's challenge to federal officials in Washington, DC:

> Let us rise to the call of freedom-loving blood that is in us and send our answer to the tyranny that clanks its chains upon the South. In the name of the greatest people that have ever trod this earth, I draw the line in the dust and toss the gauntlet before the feet of tyranny and I say: segregation now, segregation tomorrow, segregation forever.

The *Birmingham News* described the address as "a militant pledge to preserve southern customs and a call for other sections of the country to join the South in the fight." Rose's campaign for peace and Wallace's promise met head-to-head. Rose was present for the inaugural ceremonies, and he saw the challenge before him, prompting a personal dilemma: finish the job he was hired to do or seek a college presidency elsewhere.[46]

Fight or Flight: A Personal Conflict over Desegregation

As George C. Wallace was sworn into office, Frank A. Rose reevaluated his five years as UA president. *Time* magazine had recently covered the UA football and fraternity culture, dubbing the university the "Country Club of the South," while the *Crimson White* noted that the possibility of admitting three Black students was the top campus story of 1962. Raising UA's academic profile and peaceful desegregation, if ever forced on them, were the trustees' main reason for hiring Rose. Yet, with the exception of hiring a winning football coach, he had had limited success. Rose was at a crossroads. He repeatedly admitted that Wallace "will create some serious problems for us," but he had also grown tired of civil rights leaders' push to admit Black students. "We have not received much help from the Negro leadership due to their impatience," Rose confided

---

46. Frank A. Rose to John Pemberton, January 10, 1963, Rose Papers, Box 7, Location 084–080, Folder: P–Correspondence, UA; "Text of Wallace's Inaugural Address," *Birmingham News*, January 14, 1963. On the Wallace inauguration speech, see Frederick, *Stand Up for Alabama*, pp. 33–34. Frederick also characterized Alabama in 1963: "Beset by staggering poverty, a prevailing sentiment of anti-intellectualism, and decades of ineffective, inattentive, or just plain incompetent governance, Alabamians had come to accept comparative inferiority and underdog status as a byproduct of their culture." For more, see p. 26.

in a friend. The personal question was whether he would stay at UA to confront those problems.[47]

On January 18, 1963, less than a week after Wallace's inaugural address, Rose contemplated leaving UA. Professionally, Wallace tightened regulations on state employees, including the use of state vehicles to attend UA football games, and the state's education budget was dismal—a constant critique that Rose publicly offered. Wallace's initial actions illustrated what historian Richard Hofstadter described as the prevalence of anti-intellectualism during this era. Conservative state officials attacked colleges and universities while vowing to be looking out for the common citizen, not overpaid academics. Personally, Rose missed living in Kentucky, which he called "one of the most wonderful places in the country to live." This made his presidency even more difficult. "This job is a tough one, particularly in view of the many problems facing the people," Rose told Frank Kraus, a friend in Bardstown, Kentucky, near Transylvania, "but the splendid responses that are beginning to be made to our leadership are encouraging. I have worked hard." Rose was conflicted: "It would be most difficult for me to explain why I would leave at this time. However, I am giving it serious thought."[48]

By February, Rose's uncertainty became public. For instance, he was away from campus an average of two days per week due to speechmaking. Therefore, it was odd that on February 8, Rose declined an invitation to speak in Macon, Georgia, for a Thanksgiving program nine months in advance. His rationale was the pending desegregation crisis, and the need to stay near campus during

---

47. "'Country Club' Image," *CW*, December 13, 1962; "Negro Applications Top News Items of Old Year," *CW*, January 10, 1963. Rose stated in several letters throughout the first half of 1963 that Governor Wallace would cause issues for the university and desegregation. For one example, see Frank A. Rose to Rhodes Thompson Jr., March 26, 1963, Rose Papers, Box 8, Location 084–080, Folder: T–Correspondence, UA. For the quote on Black leaders' "impatience," see Frank A. Rose to Mrs. James F. Chandler (the former Sara Kay Burner), April 9, 1963, Rose Papers, Box 5, Location 084–079, Folder: C–Correspondence, UA. This letter to Chandler exhibits Rose's personal views on desegregation. Despite his efforts to maintain peace, he was at best a gradualist when it came to admitting Black students. Relatedly, as an example of white paternalism, white academic leaders often felt they should be responsible for the pace of Black advancement. For more, see Kean, *Desegregating Private Higher Education*, p. 5. In reference to white presidents, Kean wrote, "The pace and scope of racial change, these men argued, must rest on the judgment of the education white establishment."

48. On Wallace, state spending, and Rose's critiques, see Frederick, *Stand Up for Alabama*, pp. 38, 49. On anti-intellectualism, see Hofstadter, *Anti-Intellectualism in American Life*; Frank A. Rose to Frank Kraus, January 18, 1963, Rose Papers, Box 6, Location 084–079, Folder: K–Correspondence, UA.

"our period of great crisis for the University of Alabama." Therefore, he was not accepting speaking engagements during the fall semester. However, the excuse about staying near during the crisis held little weight because news about his potential departure for the presidency at the University of Kentucky was swirling by that point. In reality, he did not accept speaking engagements because he was not sure if he would stay at UA, and everybody knew it.[49]

In fact, on February 8, Stephanie Maxwell, a friend in Birmingham sent Rose well wishes on his new job. "I am sorry to hear of your departure from the university," Maxwell wrote, certain that Rose was headed to Kentucky. "I want to extend to you our deep sense of personal loss and regrettably a great loss to the university and the state of Alabama." The next day, on February 9, Sim Wyatt, of Lexington, Kentucky, called the UA situation a "tough mess," and told Rose that "a number of the University of Kentucky alumni told me that they wanted you to be president here, and all were working hard to that end." Wyatt enclosed newspaper clippings from the *Louisville Times*.[50]

On February 12, Rose replied to both Maxwell and Wyatt, hoping to halt the speculation. To Maxwell, he explained, "I am wrestling with this decision and letters like yours are most encouraging for us to remain here." Rose, however, did not acknowledge Wyatt's reference to the Kentucky courtship. Instead, he focused on the enclosed press clippings. "I can assure you that there was an error in the report as presented in the *Louisville Times*," Rose told Wyatt. "Governor Wallace specifically stated they would not close any schools in Alabama because of integration." Rose added that he was encouraged. "We have a long way to go, but it is looking much better."[51]

By February 14, Rose had been able to slow the rumblings about the Kentucky presidency, and he told the *Crimson White* that he had given no serious consideration to the Kentucky position. Although Rose lied to the student journalists, the rumors provided an opportunity for the UA community to assess his presidency. An editorial argued that UA had achieved "enormous progress" under Rose, and he was credited with enhancing the institution's academics. "Our university has come a long way," the student editors concluded. "In

49. On Rose being a frequent public speaker, see "Middleman in Alabama." Regarding Rose not accepting fall 1963 speaking engagements, see Frank A. Rose to Charles O. McAfee, Sr., February 8, 1963, Rose Papers, Box 6, Location 084–079, Folder: Mc–Correspondence, UA.

50. Stephanie Maxwell to Frank A. Rose, February 8, 1963, Frank A. Rose Papers, Box 6, Location 084–079, Folder: M–Correspondence, UA; Sim Wyatt to Frank A. Rose, February 9, 1963, Frank A. Rose Papers, Box 8, Location 084–080, Folder: W–Correspondence, UA.

51. Frank A. Rose to Stephanie Maxwell, February 12, 1963, Rose Papers, Box 6, Location 084–079, Folder: M–Correspondence, UA; Frank A. Rose to Sim Wyatt, February 12, 1963, Rose Papers, Box 8, Location 084–080, Folder: W–Correspondence, UA.

upcoming years, we will be faced with some of our sternest tests. It is to be hoped that our university, under Dr. Rose, can pass through this time with dignity."[52]

The *Crimson White*'s hope for Rose to lead UA into its upcoming tests was not taken lightly. He still felt a responsibility to the university, students, and staff. Charley Scott, at the University of Michigan Center for the Study of Higher Education, had accepted a position at UA's Huntsville Center, and he did not hesitate to share his feelings about the Kentucky rumors. On February 18, Scott asked Rose to recommend John Myers, a Michigan Fellow in University Administration, for the Kentucky job instead. He added, "I am counting on your having removed your name [from the Kentucky presidency pool] as your presence was one of my considerations in accepting the position at Huntsville." Individually, Scott's letter was a fair concern from a future employee, but in the bigger picture, Rose understood what his departure would mean to UA. By the end of February, a number of faculty were leaving the university at the close of the spring semester. Low salaries and "substandard teaching conditions" were the main causes. Alabama ranked the lowest among sixteen southern states in faculty pay, and by the end of the spring term, thirty-two faculty were not returning. Rose, too, was poised to abandon UA, but the challenges before him also presented an opportunity.[53]

In early March, the *Louisville Courier-Journal* and *Lexington Herald* reported that Rose had declined the Kentucky presidency, and Julian Riffe, a friend in Danville, Kentucky, was pleased with the decision. Riffe felt Kentucky had its own issues and the challenge in Alabama was actually in Rose's favor. "From my observation, you are not only doing a terrific job where you are," Riffe said. "You seemingly have a very strong and loyal board (which is most unusual). All of these things, plus the fact you are the moving spirit in what is probably

52. "U. of K. Offer Not Being Considered Seriously by Rose," *CW*, February 14, 1963; "Years of Progress," *CW*, February 14, 1963.

53. Charley Scott to Frank A. Rose, February 18, 1963, Rose Papers, Box 7, Location 084–080, Folder: S–Correspondence, UA. There was also a notable debate over the duplication of academic programs. In 1958, UA trustees voted to open a permanent center in Huntsville, and Alabama A&M, a state-supported Black college, was already located near Huntsville. For more, see Permaloff and Grafton, *Politics and Power*, p. 182; Lonnie Falk, "Low Salaries, Poor Conditions Cause Exodus of Many Profs," *CW*, February 28, 1963; "Thirty-two Faculty Members Will Not Return Next Semester," *CW*, May 16, 1963. Rose spoke before business leaders and state legislators about low faculty salaries. He said, "Alabama will continue to remain one of the poorest states in the nation until we provide the leadership for tomorrow." For more, see "Rose Stresses Need for Leadership at Tuscaloosa Meet," *CW*, February 28, 1963.

the greatest development that has ever been attempted in the State of Alabama, and one that will be of great good to the entire South."[54]

Riffe saw an opportunity for Rose to implement change across the South, and Rose agreed. "I think you have summed up pretty well my reason for not returning to Kentucky," Rose said. "I assure you it was a difficult decision during the last ten days, but I could not leave here without accomplishing the big program that is before us and is bound to come with the crisis." Rose had also been in communication with US president John F. Kennedy, who was instrumental in his decision to remain at UA. "I had a long talk with the president, and he assured me that he would stand behind my leadership and insisted that I remain at the University of Alabama," Rose said. "However, I am getting little cooperation from the governor, but with the board of trustees that I have and the alumni support, I am not greatly concerned."[55]

The two-month ordeal over the Kentucky job helped Rose clarify his vision at UA. It was as much a personal conflict as it was professional. This brief but significant consideration of another job underscored the complexity of desegregation and weight of segregation on the lives of presidents. Rose had to reconcile whether he was personally committed to the task ahead, but President Kennedy helped ease that internal conflict. The two men were both in Miami on January 1, 1963, when the Crimson Tide football team defeated the Sooners from the University of Oklahoma in the Orange Bowl. Then, two months later, Rose and Kennedy once again took a shared interest in UA. Now, with promised support from Kennedy and the backing of his trustees, Rose turned his attention back to UA. He was ready to attempt peaceful desegregation despite Governor Wallace.[56]

54. Julian Riffe to Frank A. Rose, March 6, 1963, Rose Papers, Box 7, Location 084–080, Folder: R–Correspondence, UA.

55. Frank A. Rose to Julian Riffe, March 5, 1963, Rose Papers, Box 7, Location 084–080, Folder: R–Correspondence, UA. Please note the date on Rose's letter is a typing error. The body of the letter acknowledged receipt of Riffe's letter on March 6, 1963, but he then dated his own letter March 5. It should also be noted that few people were aware of Rose's relationship with the Kennedy Administration. On April 1, 1963, Charley Scott in Michigan shared that someone had recently mentioned the details of Rose's meeting at the White House the previous fall. Rose replied: "I am sure there must be a few people who know of my Washington conversations, but I hope that there aren't many. I do appreciate your telling me about this as I can put a stop to it." For more about this conversation, see Charley Scott to Frank A. Rose, April 1, 1963, Rose Papers, Box 7, Location 084–080, Folder: S–Correspondence, UA; and Frank A. Rose to Charley Scott, April 10, 1963, Rose Papers, Box 7, Location 084–080, Folder: S–Correspondence, UA. For further elaboration on UA officials and Kennedy, see Clark, *Schoolhouse Door*, p. 207.

56. On Kennedy attending the Orange Bowl, see Charles Land, "Tide Rolls Over Sooners, Namath, Jordan Shine," *Tuscaloosa News*, January 2, 1963.

Consulting Other College Presidents

On January 28, 1963, only two weeks after Governor Wallace vowed to maintain segregation during his inaugural address, Clemson College in South Carolina peacefully enrolled Harvey B. Gantt as its first Black student—three months after the violence at Ole Miss and two years after the University of Georgia turmoil. Yet, unlike its Deep South counterparts, Clemson had no US Marshals assigned to it to maintain the peace, and there was no violence against Gantt. The gunfire and mob violence that rocked some other segregated white state-supported institutions in the Deep South never emerged at Clemson. One news outlet labeled the deed "integration with dignity," and Clemson became a model of peaceful desegregation. Afterward, Rose received letters from across the nation suggesting he lead UA in the same manner that President Robert C. Edwards led Clemson.[57]

On February 28, Albert S. Polk Jr. wrote Rose from Silver Spring, Maryland, about UA. Polk worked at the Applied Physics Laboratory at Johns Hopkins University and asked Rose for an update on affairs at UA as Polk weighed options for one of his children that was starting college in the fall of 1963. Rose responded with an optimistic yet uncertain answer. "I wish it were easy to answer your question regarding our coming crisis," Rose said, citing Wallace's plan to "come to the campus" as the wildcard in determining whether desegregation would occur peacefully. Therefore, he sent Polk "regret" that he was unable to "give you more assurances." However, Rose noted, "You may be sure that the administration and faculty of the University of Alabama . . . will exert force at our command to handle our problem as quietly as Clemson."[58]

Similarly, on April 22, Paul S. Sanders, UA class of 1939, wrote Rose from Amherst, Massachusetts. "May I say that I feel very deeply that the university must accept qualified Negro students," he said. "I should hope the world will not be called upon to witness a repetition of past mistakes in this regard. Let there be instead, at least, a repetition of what took place at Georgia Tech and at Clemson." Sanders closed saying, "I shall be bitterly disappointed if my Alma Mater again gives cause for its public execration." Again, Clemson was considered the model, and once more, Rose offered the same calculated response to Sanders as he had to Polk: "you may be certain that we will do everything we can to preserve the integrity of the institution." But unknown

---

57. For the "integration with dignity" quote, see Eisiminger, *Integration with Dignity*, p. 2.

58. Albert S. Polk, Jr. to Frank A. Rose, February 28, 1963; and Frank A. Rose to Albert S. Polk, Jr., March 4, 1963; both in Rose Papers, Box 7, Location 084–080, Folder: P–Correspondence, UA.

to Polk and Sanders, Rose was already in conversation with President Edwards at Clemson.[59]

On March 29, 1963, Rose and Edwards had a telephone conversation about techniques to ensure that desegregation occurred peacefully. Edwards warmly received Rose's questions. Of note, Edwards had not advocated for desegregation when Gantt first applied in 1961, but he used the additional time during the court appeal to quietly coordinate an influential group of state leaders to develop a plan. Edwards gained the support of Edgar Brown, state senator and chair of the Clemson board of trustees; Ernest Hollings, governor of South Carolina; and Charlie Daniel, an influential businessman in the construction industry. Edwards also threatened to resign as Clemson president if he did not get their support before that group started working to shape public opinion across the state. On campus, Edwards dispatched Clemson public relations director Joe Sherman to Mississippi to study the mistakes at Ole Miss, and academic leaders stayed in regular contact with Gantt and his legal team. "We kept each other informed of what was happening and why it was happening," Edwards said. "I am sure that the reason we succeeded and did not have the problems that might have occurred was the fact that everybody knew everything they needed to know as it occurred."[60]

These tips and others were valuable for Rose, but the two men agreed that a face-to-face meeting was also necessary between UA and Clemson representatives. Rose followed Clemson's model and gathered a group of UA's most influential supporters to fly to South Carolina to chat with Edwards. The group included George LeMaistre, whom Rose called "one of Alabama's outstanding attorneys." In November 1962, as president of City National Bank of Tuscaloosa, LeMaistre had warned Tuscaloosa residents about the economic backlash to violence. Next, there was Harry Pritchett, president of Pritchett-Moore Realty and Insurance. He was also chair of the Tuscaloosa school board and vice president of the UA National Alumni Council. The third member of the UA delegation was Jack Warner, one of the state's leading industrialists and president of the Alabama State Chamber of Commerce, who owned the Gulf States Paper Corporation. Rose said the three men would also select a fourth person "of the same stature" to accompany them to Clemson. "You may feel perfectly free to discuss anything about this issue and problem that you wish

59. Paul S. Sanders to Frank A. Rose, April 22, 1963; and Frank A. Rose to Paul S. Sanders, April 30, 1963; both in Rose Papers, Box 7, Location 084–080, Folder: S–Correspondence, UA.

60. On the telephone call between the two presidents, see Frank A. Rose to Robert C. Edwards, March 29, 1963, Rose Papers, Box 5, Location 084–079, Folder: E–Correspondence, UA. For the details about Edwards's strategy and his not advocating for Gantt in 1961, see Eisiminger, *Integration with Dignity*, pp. 3, 56.

as we are all very close," Rose told Edwards. "They are extremely hopeful with hundreds of other leading citizens of this state to get the governor to assume the right posture and handle our problem as well as you have yours."[61]

On April 1, Edwards generously followed up with Rose after their telephone call. He was "delighted" to host the Alabama group. "We shall be glad to give the gentlemen all the information we have relating to our recent experience and hope it will prove of value to the responsible leadership in Alabama," Edwards assured Rose. "I am sure your leaders are as anxious as we were to avoid incidents that could mar the image of our educational institutions and the public image of our sovereign states."[62]

Two days later, on April 3, the Alabama group flew to Anderson, South Carolina. They were met by Clemson officials at the airport, at 10 a.m., to discuss peaceful desegregation techniques. The four men returned with a plan they could execute at UA. Afterward, Rose told Edwards that he was "damn delighted that you are so generous with your time as to see my friends from Alabama and to give them counsel on our impending problem. I will always remain indebted to you for this."[63]

Rose himself did not travel to Clemson with the group, but the private meeting in South Carolina was his doing. He understood that college presidents needed to have a hands-on role—regardless of whether they were for or against segregation—as they positioned businessmen and state officials to handle the public aspects of higher education desegregation. Rose knew that UA could not afford to have a repeat of 1956 or the previous fall's events at Ole Miss, and when the small group returned from Clemson, they returned with a plan that would help the university desegregate peacefully.

The Plan: Lights, Cameras, but No Action

On April 15, 1963, a motion was filed in the US District Court against Hubert E. Mate, UA dean of admissions. This formally initiated what Rose and others had anticipated all spring—the enrollment of Black students. Over the next month, court decisions favored the admission of Vivian Malone, James A. Hood, and Dave M. McGlathery. On May 16, Judge H. Hobart Grooms ruled that the university was still bound by the Autherine Lucy court order, and five

61. Rose to Edwards, March 29, 1963.

62. Robert C. Edwards to Frank A. Rose, April 1, 1963, Box 5, Rose Papers, Location 084–079, Folder: E–Correspondence, UA.

63. Frank A. Rose to Robert C. Edwards, April 3, 1963, Box 5, Location 084–079, Folder: E–Correspondence, UA.

days later, he ordered Mate to demonstrate why he should not be charged with contempt of court for failure to comply with the 1955 injunction. To determine this, Mate was given the opportunity to proceed with admitting the three students for the summer session starting June 10, 1963 (McGlathery would enroll at UA's Huntsville Center).[64]

In Alabama, however, a court decision in favor of racial equality never meant that white citizens accepted the judicial ruling. In fact, on May 3, 1963, Americans watched Birmingham law enforcement officers use police dogs and high-powered water hoses on children participating in a peaceful civil rights march. The images soon circulated around the world. Therefore, Rose's activities leading up to June 1963 were critical.[65]

All spring, Rose was exceedingly nice to the governor. Wallace made it clear he would not entertain the idea of Black students enrolling at UA. Since Rose had his own issues with desegregation, having complained to an acquaintance that he believed Black civil rights leaders wanted to move too quickly, it was not difficult for Rose to offer a friendly hand to Wallace, considering that the two men were not total opposites when it came to racial equality.[66]

For example, on March 29, the same day of his telephone conversation with Clemson's president, Rose sent Wallace warm wishes after hearing that the governor's daughter, Bobbie, had undergone a serious medical procedure. Rose expressed his "deepest and most profound hope that it will not be long before she will be fully recovered and feeling much better." He also offered the university's medical center if the Wallace family needed any additional services. Then, unrelated to Bobbie's health, Rose used the moment to praise Wallace. "Again, allow me to express my appreciation for the splendid leadership you are giving our state and the seriousness of the legislature which is evident in all of their meetings," he told the governor. "It is most encouraging."[67]

In April, Rose hosted Wallace during the annual Governor's Day ceremony on campus; and in May, Wallace thanked Rose for the invitation to attend A-Day, the annual spring festival that welcomed alumni back to campus and featured the spring football game. In fact, on May 11, during A-Day weekend, Rose praised Wallace's education plan, which would increase state

64. Chronology of Legal Actions in US District Court, n.d., Rose Papers, Box 6, Location 084–079, Folder: Integration Plans, UA; Ted Bryant, "Court Says Dean Bound by Order," *Birmingham Post-Herald*, May 17, 1963.

65. "Police Use Water, Dogs on Marchers," *Birmingham Post-Herald*, May 4, 1963.

66. For the Rose quote about Black leaders, refer, again, to Rose to Chandler (the former Sara Kay Burner), April 9, 1963.

67. Frank A. Rose to George C. Wallace, March 29, 1963, Rose Papers, Box 8, Location 084–080, Folder: Wallace, Gov. George C., UA.

appropriations to UA. It would help Rose retain faculty, which was a pressing issue, and recruit more professors to accommodate the growing enrollment. In fact, in 1962, UA officials had to "turn away" roughly 1,500 students due to lack of space. Therefore, when addressing a group of alumni, Rose called Wallace's plan a "breakthrough" for the state.[68]

Next up for Rose was communicating a plan to local police, students, alumni, faculty and staff, and the media. By May 16, Rose and Bill Marable, the local police chief, were in regular contact about a plan for desegregation. Marable said the local police force aimed to maintain order but were trained to handle riots. The next week, on May 24, university officials coordinated a meeting at the Hotel Stafford. In attendance were leaders from the Tuscaloosa police department, the county sheriff's department, and the state highway patrol, as well as university officials.[69]

For the student body, J. Jefferson Bennett (by this point, his title had changed from special assistant to administrative vice president), and John Blackburn, the dean of men, met in Paty Hall to address students' segregation questions. On May 13, Sarah L. Healy, the dean of women, did the same with a separate group of students. Maintaining peace was the primary concern expressed by the administrators, and any students involved in riots would be suspended. Students were also encouraged not to travel to Birmingham. Likewise, on May 29, vice president for student affairs C. T. Sharpton told summer session students that peaceful desegregation depended on their cooperation. He then provided step-by-step procedures for summer registration. "We will rely upon each student to cooperate with the above measures and use good judgement and discretion in fulfilling [your] responsibilities as a University of Alabama student," Sharpton said.[70]

Rose facilitated similar messages to alumni, faculty, and staff. In late May, Rose was in the nation's capital, where he addressed the Washington, DC, chapter of the UA Alumni Association and emphasized the need to protect

68. Frank A. Rose to George C. Wallace, May 1, 1963, Rose Papers, Box 8, Location 084–080, Folder: Wallace, Gov. George C., UA; George C. Wallace to Frank A. Rose, May 9, 1963, Frank A. Rose Papers, Box 8, Location 084–080, Folder: Wallace, Gov. George C., UA. For more on Governor's Day in 1963, see Tilford, *Turning the Tide*, p. 23; Jack Hopper, "Alumni Visit UA Campus, Hear Dr. Rose, Bryant," *Birmingham News*, May 12, 1963.

69. "Marable Gives View on Police Activity if UA Integrated," *CW*, May 16, 1963; Security Meeting Minutes, May 24, 1963, Rose Papers, Box 6, Location 084–079, Folder: Integration Plans, UA.

70. "Bennett, Healy Questioned on Integration Recently," *CW*, May 16, 1963; C. T. Sharpton to Student Body, May 29, 1963, Rose Papers, Box 6, Location 084–079, Folder: Integration Plans, UA.

the academic integrity of the university. Back on campus, on May 23, Rose notified all deans and department heads about the May 21 court ruling and said that Black students would enroll during the summer session. He then stated that employee identification cards would be needed for access to campus. The next week, on May 31, Rose thanked faculty and staff for their confidence in the trustees' decision to admit Black students. He then explained the security measures in place to maintain peace. Starting June 8, the campus was closed to automobile traffic, and Rose asked that employees be dropped off on campus that day. "I know you will understand the necessity for following instructions of law enforcement officers gracefully," he said. "You should report any untoward incident involving those officers to your dean or director in order for the university administration to mediate any misunderstandings."[71]

By June 1, 1963, it was time to enact the final aspect of Rose's plan. He had to manage the international press pool that descended on the campus. On June 2, Wallace himself had used his appearance on *Meet the Press*, a nationally televised news broadcast, to his advantage, and Rose knew this could also be done to the advantage of the university. Ed Brown, director of the University News Bureau, took the lead on the "mechanics" and prepared a twelve-point plan for "what should be said and when and how." The initial and most important point was that if campus remained peaceful, that alone would be a significant story. Therefore, Brown advised senior administrators to have Rose emphasize the same points he made a few days earlier in Washington, DC. Brown also provided a day-by-day press release schedule starting June 3 and continuing through June 10, the day the summer session would begin. The university converted the old *Tuscaloosa News* building into the University News Center to accommodate the out-of-town media. Relatedly, Bennett adhered to Clemson's suggestion to meet with the Black students prior to enrollment to ensure that they were well aware of the university's plan.[72]

71. For more about Rose's speech in Washington, DC, see "Wisdom in Alabama," *Evening Star*, May 27, 1963. In Earl H. Tilford's history of UA during the 1960s, he mentioned that Rose, Bennett, Kennedy, and Robert F. Kennedy had a meeting while the UA officials were in Washington, DC. There, Rose advised the Kennedys to federalize Alabama's national guard instead of sending in federal troops. For more, see Tilford, *Turning the Tide*, pp. 26–28; Frank A. Rose memorandum, May 23, 1963, Rose Papers, Box 6, Location 084–079, Folder: Integration Plans, UA; Frank A. Rose memorandum, May 31, 1963, Rose Papers, Box 6, Location 084–079, Folder: Integration Plans, UA. On closing the campus to automobile traffic, see W. E. Pickens Jr. to Faculty and Staff, June 4, 1963, Rose Papers, Box 6, Location 084–079, Folder: Integration Plans, UA.

72. On Wallace's *Meet the Press* appearance, see Permaloff and Grafton, *Politics and Power in Alabama*, p. 199; Ed Brown to Alex S. Pow, June 1, 1963; Alex S. Pow, vice president for institutional development, shared Brown's press procedure with Rose and Bennett on Monday, June 3. For

Leading up to the summer session, any last-minute resistance from the trustees or administrators to the court ruling would result in jail time for contempt of court for anyone who prevented Malone or Hood from registering in Tuscaloosa. Therefore, the board of trustees issued a public statement that directed the admissions staff "to notify the two Negro applicants who have been found qualified of their admission to the university . . . for the sessions which begin June 10, 1963." Any violent resistance to desegregation would potentially also cost UA its accreditation. In May, Harry Huntt Ransom, University of Texas chancellor and chair of the Commission on Colleges for SACS, sent Governor Wallace the following telegram:

> News media consistently report your intention to intervene and set aside a decision of the board of trustees and administration of the University of Alabama to admit qualified applicants to the university.

It continued:

> If this information is correct, we hope you will consider the fact that such interference with the duly constituted authorities of the University of Alabama threatens the good name of all state-supported higher education in Alabama, violates standards of the Southern Association of Colleges and Schools, and would require investigation and possible action by the Commission on Colleges.

The ramifications were clear, but Wallace-led tensions between the university and the average white Alabamian remained despite national pressure to admit Black students.[73]

On June 8, a Ku Klux Klan rally was held near Tuscaloosa, where more than three thousand spectators gathered in the name of maintaining segregation. "Many of the spectators were women and small children," the *Birmingham News* reported. "A gigantic cross, about 60-feet tall with 40-foot arms, enwrapped in burlap bags, was ignited to kick-off the rally." The next night, on June 9, another

---

more, see Alex S. Pow to Frank A. Rose and J. Jefferson Bennett, June 3, 1963; regarding the old *Tuscaloosa News* building, see Frank A. Rose to C. C. Randall, June 7, 1963, all in Rose Papers, Box 6, Location 084–079, Folder: Integration Plans, UA. On J. Jefferson Bennett's meeting with Vivian Malone, James Hood, and David M. McGlathery, see Hollars, *Opening the Doors*, pp. 62–63.

73. Trustee Board Statement on Federal Court Order, n.d., Rose Papers, Box 8, Location 084–080, Folder: Board of Trustees Meeting, UA; Harry H. Ransom to George C. Wallace, May 1963, Rose Papers, Box 6, Location 084–079, Folder: Integration Plans, UA. For more context, Ransom was by no means pushing for integration, but he was practical. He had his own issues when he was a vice president at UT-Austin when it came to housing and/or educational facilities. For more, see Goldstone, *Integrating the 40 Acres*, pp. 36–55.

rally occurred near Tuscaloosa. This time, about 1,500 "cheering segregation-ists" gathered. Grand Dragon Robert Shelton told the crowd that Governor Wallace had a "mandate from the people to stand up for Alabama, and he will do this." Shelton's confidence in Wallace is important because the Klansman had been linked to Governor Patterson as well. The Klan had access to the state officials, and these rallies were more than public confessions of white suprema-cist hatred toward Black people. Many people came to town armed for a race riot. In fact, on June 8, six men from neighboring Jefferson County were ar-rested outside of campus with an arsenal of weapons. As of late June 10, there had been fifteen whites arrested near Tuscaloosa for weapons possession.[74]

Meanwhile, on June 9, as the Klan presence gathered outside of Tuscaloosa, more than two hundred news reporters gathered for a 2 p.m. press conference on campus. In a prepared statement, Rose laid out a detailed overview of the university's accomplishments and its reach across the state, noting that it was critical that the institution stay at the forefront of everyone's concerns over desegregation. "I am confident that no thinking person in Alabama wants any-thing destroyed at the university." Rose continued:

> The people fully realize that learning can take place only within the security of law and order, and while a large majority of the people of Alabama regret the integration that has been ordered upon them, they have no desire to see their school closed nor their universities destroyed.

Rose added, "A great university is the most precious possession we have. It holds the answer to all of the questions we are asking and promises solutions to all of the problems we face."[75]

After the prepared remarks, reporters questioned Rose for fifteen minutes, but the president excelled at answering them. Some questions sought sensa-tionalism. Others asked leading questions that attempted to position Rose against federal and state officials. But Rose avoided the media pitfalls. He did not comment on whether Wallace was making a smart move by defying the court ruling. Rose also said, "I don't care to comment on that," when asked how he personally felt about desegregation. "I am the president of the univer-sity, and it has been ordered to integrate by a court order and the board of

74. Tom Lankford, "Jefferson Men Arrested with Weapons Near U of A," *Birmingham News*, June 9, 1963; "500 Guardsmen, 800 Troopers on Alert in Tense Tuscaloosa: Sent to UA by Governor," *Birmingham Post Herald*, June 10, 1963; "6 Men Arrested with Weapons," *Tuscaloosa News*, June 9, 1963; Robert Shelton, as a Klan leader, had long been closely tied to the governor's office. For more, see Frederick, *Stand Up for Alabama*, p. 27.

75. Press Conference remarks, June 9, 1963, Rose Papers, Box 6, Location 084–079, Folder: Integration Plans, UA.

trustees and I will obey the order," Rose said. "I don't care to discuss my personal philosophy at this time."[76]

Later that night, during a statewide radio and television broadcast, Wallace hinted that he might be jailed when he attempted to block Black students from entering UA. "Stay at home," the governor said. "We don't want or need unauthorized people at the university. I have kept the faith. You keep the peace." On the next day, June 10, more media organizations registered at the University News Center in anticipation of Malone and Hood enrolling. The total number rose to more than three hundred journalists (and as many as 400 were in Tuscaloosa to cover the actual desegregation on June 11).[77]

That evening, at 8 p.m., the UA trustees met in the boardroom of the Administration Building, and Wallace was present as an ex officio member of the board. All trustees were present except Thomas D. Russell of Alexander City, who was out of the country. Also present were Rose, Bennett, and Alex S. Pow, vice president for institutional development. The discussion focused more on semantics than on actual preparation for violence. Despite President Kennedy's request that the governor not visit campus to interfere, Wallace told the board that his presence in Tuscaloosa was necessary to maintain law and order. He informed the trustees and administrators that he planned to block the admission of the Black students, but he also explained what steps he had taken to prevent any violence. In response, Rose told the board about the measures he had prepared to make sure the university and state law enforcement agencies cooperated. Wallace then left the trustee meeting early for other appointments, but before leaving, he thanked the board and Rose for their support. The board then adopted a resolution that read, in part, that the board declared that the "presence of Governor Wallace is necessary to preserve peace and order." The meeting was then dismissed until morning.[78]

76. Multiple sources were used to re-create the press conference: On leading or sensationalized questions, see "Weight of Crisis Tells on Dr. Rose," *Birmingham News*, June 10, 1963. This article also has Rose's "don't care to comment" quote. On whether Wallace was acting wisely, see James Bennett, "Rose Says Security Force Is Necessary and Adequate," *Birmingham Post-Herald*, June 10, 1963. For the quote about personal philosophy, see Mickey Logue, "Rose Says Wallace Should Be Present," *Birmingham News*, June 10, 1963.

77. "Wallace Calls for Calm at University," *Birmingham Post-Herald*, June 10, 1963; Bill Shamblin, "Over 300 Newsmen to Get Red-Carpet Treatment by UA," *CW*, June 9, 1963. On the estimated 400 journalists by June 11, see Hollars, *Opening the Doors*, p. 81.

78. Trustee Meeting Minutes, June 10, 1963, Rose Papers, Box 7, Location 084–080, Folder: Board of Trustees Correspondence, UA.

On June 11 at 9:30 a.m., the board reconvened on campus at the President's Mansion—built in 1841 and still including the living quarters for enslaved Black people under UA's first presidents. Now, Gessner T. McCorvey, president pro tem, presided over a meeting in a building symbolic of the university's past racism. Rose presented a report regarding the pending enrollment of two Black students, Vivian Malone and James A. Hood, to the Tuscaloosa campus. The board discussed a request from journalists to photograph the Black students once they were in their assigned dormitory rooms. The board objected to the request and unanimously voted it down. The request, however, was telling of their expected outcome for the day. Regardless of the governor, the trustees knew the Black students would enroll, and they remained at the President's Mansion to consult Rose as needed during their registration.[79]

By afternoon, the two students were enrolled. Governor Wallace did stand in the schoolhouse door to block Malone and Hood from registering, but it was merely symbolic. Wallace eventually stepped aside as Alabama National Guardsmen were federalized, requiring local men to follow Kennedy Administration orders. Unlike at Ole Miss in September 1962 or UA in February 1956, there was no violence. At 3:33 p.m., Wallace sent Kennedy a telegram stating that "through the use of federal troops, you assumed full responsibility for the presence of Negro students and for preserving peace and order on the campus of the University of the Alabama." At 4 p.m., the trustees dismissed their meeting at the President's Mansion.[80]

Rose's plan worked, and that evening, Kennedy appeared on national radio and television broadcasts. "I hope that every American, regardless of where he lives, will stop and examine his conscience about this and other related incidents," Kennedy told the nation. "When Americans are sent to Vietnam or West Berlin, we do not ask for whites only. It ought to be possible, therefore, for American students of any color to attend any public institution they select

79. Trustee Meeting Minutes, June 10, 1963; Kyarra Harris, "Strange Alabama: The Past of the President's Mansion Still Not Acknowledged on Campus Tours," *CW*, October 19, 2016.

80. "Classes Started, UA Quiet," *Tuscaloosa News*, June 12, 1963. On the behind-the-scenes dynamics of Rose and Wallace's stand in the schoolhouse door, see McWhorter, *Carry Me Home*, pp. 437–447. For more on the day UA was desegregated, see Gaillard, *Cradle of Freedom*, pp. 163–178. It should be noted that the only reference to President Frank Rose is his description as "the charismatic, dark-haired president who had taken the job in 1958, and who after resolute struggle against integration, now seemed ready to accept the inevitable." For more, see p. 170; George C. Wallace to John F. Kennedy, June 12, 1963, Rose Papers, Box 6, Location 084–079, Folder: Integration Plans, UA; Trustee Meeting Minutes, June 10, 1963.

without having to be backed up by troops." Kennedy used peaceful desegregation at UA, under Rose's leadership, to advance a civil rights bill.[81]

"As hard as university officials worked, they exercised no meaningful control," E. Culpepper Clark wrote in *The Schoolhouse Door: Segregation's Last
Stand at the University of Alabama*. "By laboring behind the scenes with the
Kennedys and by holding the sheet music while business leaders orchestrated
pressure on Wallace, university officials helped. In reality, they were stage
hands while Wallace produced and directed that play." This assessment fits the
narrative Wallace sought, but this summation does not accurately describe
Frank A. Rose. He was more than a stage hand, and his activities demonstrated
the significant, yet often quiet, role that college presidents played in influencing racial policies and procedures. The resolutions that alumni chapters, civic
organizations, and the trustees adopted were initiated due to Rose. Likewise,
business leaders' pressure was critical to helping white Alabamians put economic benefits before segregation, but Rose coordinated the pivotal Clemson
visit. He was the director.[82]

Conclusion

Frank A. Rose's decisions were informed by lessons from other academic leaders, and Clemson provided a model for how to achieve this. At Ole Miss,
Chancellor John Davis Williams never communicated with James Meredith
about the university's plans around desegregation, and Clemson president
Robert C. Edwards found this to be one of the most notable errors that led to
violence in Mississippi. With this in mind, J. Jefferson Bennett, special assistant to Rose, executed one of the most pivotal aspects of the UA plan by communicating directly with the Black students before they were admitted. The
Rose-Bennett duo frequently communicated with all stakeholders and learned
from the mistakes and successes of other academic leaders. This was imperative to Rose's success.

Equally notable is what can be learned about college presidents and racial
practices by what paths Rose did not take. Southern governors learned quickly
that the termination of college presidents, faculty, and students would result
in censure from national organizations like the AAUP or SACS, the regional
accreditation agency. Therefore, a change in college presidents, voluntary or
not, would destabilize the institutions as state officials and trustees considered
desegregation. At Clemson, Edwards's threat to resign if he did not have the

81. "Talk to Nation: President Outlines Rights Proposals," *Tuscaloosa News*, June 12, 1963.
82. Clark, *Schoolhouse Door*, pp. 169–170, 207.

support of South Carolina's governor and state officials is notable. Similarly, Rose's consideration of the University of Kentucky presidency could have resulted in an abrupt change in leadership that neither UA trustees nor President John F. Kennedy desired, and perhaps he would not have coordinated the Clemson meeting, ultimately leaving someone else to lead UA.

Rose remained at UA, however, and although scholars such as Clark have not given him credit, journalists in 1963 recognized his role in the peaceful admission of Black students. The *Birmingham News* said Rose "displayed that sureness of hand, that combination of administrative courage and restraint without which troubles could have become in some degree, at least, insurmountable." The newspaper encouraged readers to tell Rose "thank you." The *New York Times* also described Rose as a capable administrator who was more university spokesman than academic. *Time* magazine added, "Behind all this manifest preparation stands a determined and dynamic president, Frank Anthony Rose." Individuals said much of the same, one of whom wrote that if not for Rose, "the crisis of this past week would probably be a chapter in the history of the '60s instead of a footnote. I, for one, am glad it was not a 'chapter.'"[83]

Finally, Rose demonstrates that white southern presidents did not have to personally believe in racial equality to exercise the conviction needed to desegregate. It is more accurate to say the interests of presidents and trustees converged to protect the university. For instance, on June 12, 1963, immediately after UA's desegregation, Gessner T. McCorvey, president pro tem of the trustee board, shared his true feelings about the situation. "I just hope and pray that these Negroes have sense enough to conduct themselves in a way that will not be offensive to our people," McCorvey said. Even more grotesque, McCorvey said that if civil rights activists decided to block railroads and airport runways, he would be tempted to make sure America had the "best-greased" railroads in the world. He then told Governor George C. Wallace he handled desegregation "magnificently," adding, "your statements will undoubtedly make a lot of these people 'start thinking,' and I just wished to tell you how fine I think you conducted yourself throughout." McCorvey was a racist at heart.[84]

83. "The University's Honor," *Birmingham News*, June 9, 1963; "Middleman in Alabama"; "Alabama Quality," *Time*, June 14, 1963. For the "footnote" quote, see David Ellwanger to J. Jefferson Bennett, June 14, 1963, Bennett Papers, Box 4, Location 088–102, Folder: Segregation Congratulatory, UA.

84. On interest convergence, see Derrick Bell, "Brown v. Board of Education," pp. 518–533; Gessner T. McCorvey to Frank Rose, J. Jefferson Bennett, Alex S. Pow, J. Rufus Bealle, June 12, 1963; and Gessner T. McCorvey to George C. Wallace, June 12, 1963, Rose Papers; both in Box 7, Location 084–080, Folder: Board of Trustees Correspondence, UA.

In the end, Rose's perspective on Black people and civil rights was not terribly different. He genuinely felt Black leaders wanted to move too quickly with desegregation. Rose also believed the problem with Black people was that most of them refused to seek formal education and accept responsibilities, another statement that ignored the effects of racism. In fact, a month after UA desegregated, when the *New York Times Magazine* asked whether he was an integrationist or segregationist, Rose said, "I'm a realist." By August 1963, James A. Hood, one of the two Black students enrolled, withdrew from the university (Malone remained enrolled and graduated in 1965). Afterward, Rose said, "we have been seriously disappointed in the withdrawal of James Hood from the university, particularly after we spent so much money and put so many hours of counselling into his admission and his student life." More concerned with the $25,000 the university spent on desegregation, Rose found the campus environment less important than the financial cost of admitting Black students. His efforts to prevent violence were made in the name of the university, not racial equality. He proved, however, that presidents of some southern white state-supported institutions—unlike at Ole Miss—developed the procedures that maintained peace if, how, and when Black students enrolled, even if against the governor's wishes. Yet, a few months later and far from Alabama, a college president in New Jersey was also confronted by a southern white supremacist governor over racial equality—a confrontation that would have national implications.[85]

85. For Rose on the pace of desegregation, once again, refer to Rose to Chandler (the former Sara Kay Burner), April 9, 1963; On Blacks not accepting responsibility, see Frank A. Rose to Richard M. G. Lawson, July 30, 1963, Rose Papers, Box 6, Location 084–079, Folder: L–Correspondence, UA; Gertrude Samuels, "Alabama U.: A Story of 2 Among 4,000," *New York Times Magazine*, July 28, 1963. On James A. Hood withdrawing from the university, see "Hood's UA Departure Anti-climactic with Entry," *Birmingham News*, August 12, 1963; and Don Brown, "Hood Assisted His Own Undoing," *Birmingham News*, August 12, 1963.; On Rose's disappointment in Hood's withdrawal, see Frank A. Rose to S. Robert Johnston, August 19, 1963, Rose Papers, Box 6, Location 084–079, Folder: J–Correspondence, UA; Memorandum on Desegregation Expenses, no author, June 20, 1963, Box 6, Location 084–079, Folder: Integration Plans, UA.

6

"The Northern Outpost of Southern Culture"

FREE SPEECH AND CIVIL RIGHTS

"I DON'T THINK I want to be Princeton's Jackie Robinson," explained one Black prospective student in 1961. For him, attending Princeton University would be like breaking the color barrier in Major League Baseball, thus he enrolled at another college instead. This prompted Princeton administrators to make "a special effort" to understand why Black students decided to attend other institutions. What the Jackie Robinson comment and other responses demonstrated was that Princeton had not shaken its reputation from the Civil War era—an era when half of its students were white southerners. That all-white boys' club image was amplified as the nation grappled with the Black Freedom Movement. Therefore, as ideals from the past clashed with the burgeoning effort to recruit more Black students to Princeton, college presidents were confronted by an old but growing civil rights concern—free speech.[1]

By the mid-twentieth century, controversial speech was a normal aspect of many institutions' intellectual life. Even during the Cold War—at the height of anti-communist sentiment and suppression in the United States—many college presidents still did not interfere when communists and their allies were invited to campuses. For instance, through the 1950s into the 1960s, the likes of Alger Hiss, the former federal official once sentenced to prison for perjury related to aiding communists, and Gus Hall, leader of the Communist Party USA, spoke before college audiences. Their campus appearances were controversial, particularly to those external to the institutions, and furthered the

---

1. Martin Mayer, "How to Get into Princeton," *Princeton Alumni Weekly*, September 28, 1962, p. 9 (periodical hereafter cited as *PAW*).

common depiction of higher education as a leftist bastion; however, the spirited distaste over these speakers' presence was typically expressed only verbally.[2]

Racial unrest, however, forced college presidents to reconsider free speech. It was at once a foundational tenet of the academy and an igniter of mass disruption, and the threat of violence was not solely a southern problem. For example, Martin Luther King Jr., after being pelted with rocks during a peaceful demonstration in Chicago, said, "I have seen many demonstrations in the South, but I have never seen anything so hostile and so hateful as I've seen here today." Violence was a potential result of any demonstration for Black humanity, and the distinctive southern culture at Princeton exemplified these issues years before the Free Speech Movement occurred at the University of California, Berkeley. Historian Robert Cohen said of that movement, "This was the first revolt of the 1960s to bring a college campus the mass civil disobedience tactics pioneered in the civil rights movement. Those tactics, most notably the sit-in, would give students unprecedented leverage to make demands on university administrators, setting the stage for mass protests against the Vietnam War." Yet, Princeton had set the stage for Berkeley.[3]

Few universities offer a more robust look into the tension between free speech protections, civil rights, and potential violence than Princeton. Its roster of speakers in the 1950s through the early 1960s included Alger Hiss, Fidel Castro, Martin Luther King Jr., and Ross Barnett, governor of Mississippi. As an Ivy League institution, Princeton influenced the broader US higher education system, and President Robert F. Goheen's effort to diversify intellectual viewpoints and enroll more Black students made him a sought-after consultant on free speech.

A New President and Gradual Change

Robert Francis Goheen was hired as president of Princeton University at a time when demands for dramatic societal changes were increasing. Despite the university being somewhat isolated in central New Jersey, the blatant

2. On college presidents and trustees handling Hiss and Hall, see Trustees Statement on Alger Hiss, April 20, 1956, Office of the President Records: Robert F. Goheen Subgroup, Box 425, Folder 3, Princeton University Archives, Department of Rare Books and Special Collections, Seeley G. Mudd Manuscript Library, Princeton University (collection and location hereafter cited as Goheen Records and Princeton); and John Patrick Hunter, "Backs Free Speech for All at U.W.," *Capital Times*, November 10, 1962.

3. "Dr. King Is Felled by Rock: 30 Injured as He Leads Protesters," *Chicago Tribune*, August 6, 1966; Cohen, *Freedom's Orator*, p. 1.

hypocrisy of the United States portraying itself as a global leader in democracy while maintaining a system of legalized racial discrimination had a local impact. The trustees of the Ivy League institution were some of the nation's most influential men and were invested in the nation's well-being. As such, they assessed the future as Harold Willis Dodds retired as president, and in 1957, at age thirty-seven, Goheen became the youngest person to lead the all-male Princeton University since the eighteenth century.[4]

Goheen replaced Dodds, who was hired at age forty-five in 1933 and served as president for twenty-four years. Dodds led Princeton through the Great Depression, the attack on Pearl Harbor, World War II, and the McCarthy-inspired attacks on higher education. "The Dodds Era . . . has been the most trying, demanding 24 years ever to confront a Princeton president," opened an April 1957 *Daily Princetonian* article. When Dodds was hired, a journalist considered Princeton an institution "of rich sons and staunch conservatives," and as he retired just before turning seventy years old, Princeton remained largely the same.[5]

Like the nation's other colonial colleges, Princeton had a long history with race despite its student body remaining almost completely segregated through the 1930s. The university's history was tied to slavery and the Jim Crow practices of past university presidents. "Princeton, as a northern town and an elite university, was as segregated as any place below the Mason-Dixon Line for much of its history," historian Stefan M. Bradley explained. Accordingly, Black people had a presence on campus but mostly through menial roles, not as students, until 1945 when the V-12 Naval College Training Program assigned four Black cadets to Princeton. This was a notable shift—courtesy of the military—in Princeton's all-white student body.[6]

4. On Goheen being the youngest president hired at Princeton since the 1700s, see "On Academic Heights," *New York Times*, December 8, 1956.

5. Hamilton W. Meserve, "President Dodds Weathered Turbulent Times Marked by Economic, Political, Social Crises," *Daily Princetonian*, April 4, 1957 (newspaper hereafter cited as *DP*).

6. For a brief overview of race at Princeton before 1940, see Bradley, *Upending the Ivory Tower*, pp. 46–52. Scholars have discussed the strict, nearly all-white enrollments at elite northeastern colleges and universities. In addition to Bradley, see, e.g., Karabel, *The Chosen*; and Perkins, "The First Black Talent Identification Program." The faculty at these colleges were also all- or majority-white. In 1955, Princeton hired Charles T. Davis as its first Black professor. He was an assistant professor of English after teaching at New York University since 1948. For more, "Eight New Professors Here; First Negro Teacher Named," *DP*, September 14, 1955. Although focused less on race or racism, see Axtell, *The Making of Princeton University*, for a lengthier history of the university.

This environment was notably different from that of Goheen's early childhood. He was born in Vengurla, India, where his parents served as Presbyterian medical missionaries. Goheen's older cousin, William Hallock Johnson, was also the former president of one of the nation's oldest Black colleges, Lincoln University in Pennsylvania, founded in 1854 before the Civil War. Thus, by the time fifteen-year-old Goheen moved to the United States in 1934, he was accustomed to seeing his family serve others even if he personally did not comprehend racial inequality; however, after two years at the Lawrenceville School, a New Jersey prep school and a top Princeton feeder school, he enrolled as a freshman at the all-white Princeton in 1936.[7]

Four years later, in 1940, Goheen earned the Pyne Honor Prize, the highest honor the university bestowed upon an undergraduate. He followed his bachelor's degree with one year of graduate study at Princeton before leaving campus for a brief stint in the army. Goheen returned to Princeton in 1945, and three years later, he earned his PhD in classics on a Woodrow Wilson Fellowship. Then, in 1950, Goheen joined the classics department as an assistant professor and, in 1954, became director of the Woodrow Wilson National Fellowship Foundation located in Princeton. Almost the entirety of his adult life was spent at or near the university. Therefore, when hired as president in 1957, Goheen was already beloved by students and respected by his colleagues. Whitney Oates, chair of the classics department, said of Goheen, "He is one of the ablest men in the whole damn teaching profession." His hire was unanimously approved by the university trustees, and it came at an academic turning point for the university. Goheen's background uniquely qualified him to lead Princeton into the coming years of racial unrest that would soon spread across the nation.[8]

To be clear, the Princeton trustees' decision to hire Goheen was not made in a vacuum. There were changes occurring on other Ivy League campuses, and those external factors made it easier for the board to choose a young, energetic

7. For more on the Lawrenceville prep school, see Karabel, *The Chosen*, pp. 316–317. Regarding his cousin being president of a Black college, see Robert Goheen to Roger S. Firestone, March 8, 1963, Goheen Records, Box 296, Folder 7, Princeton. For childhood background, Goheen biographical sheets were retrieved and consulted from the Princeton University Archives.

8. On Goheen's career trajectory, see "On Academic Heights." For the Whitney Oates quote, see "One of the Ablest," *Time*, December 17, 1956. On the unanimous decision to hire Goheen, see Robert A. Selar, "Classics Professor, 37, Picked to Follow Dodds," *DP*, December 7, 1956. Bradley assessed that "Goheen's worldview was somewhat more liberal than that of his predecessors. In terms of the university's relationship to Black students, Goheen attempted to change the university's racially charged exclusionary image." For more, see Bradley, *Upending the Ivory Tower*, p. 58.

Goheen. Princeton's greatest rivals—Harvard and Yale—were located in urban areas and had been making notable changes throughout the 1950s. Harvard was the most successful of the three institutions in attracting Black students. For example, by the late 1950s, Harvard was using the National Scholarship Service and Fund for Negro Students and secured support from a private foundation to expand its efforts to recruit more Black students. Therefore, the Goheen hire was about having a capable, fresh leader and trying to keep Princeton competitive with the changing times. The all-white, conservative Princeton was no longer a viable model for long-term institutional progress and success.[9]

Goheen understood this context as well as anyone. He was an alumnus of Princeton and well aware of the alumni's influence on the direction of the university. Therefore, before attempting to change Princeton's social fabric, Goheen used his first year as president to strategically engage the group. By 1958, the percentage of alumni who made contributions consistently tallied at least 72 percent—the highest proportion of alumni giving among all US colleges and universities. Relatedly, in March 1958, Jeremiah S. Finch, dean of the college, returned from a southern speaking tour. He had visited Dallas, Houston, New Orleans, and Miami, and in each city, he addressed alumni during dinners attended by twenty-five to fifty men. Finch updated the southern alumni base on campus initiatives, such as "the need for diversity in types of education," and he also checked their pulse. Finch found the southerners were interested in the club system—Princeton's form of fraternities—more than any other issue.[10]

That summer, in August 1958, Ulysses S. Grant III, grandson of the former US president and decorated Union general, invited Goheen to serve on the advisory council for the Civil War Centennial Commission. The commission wanted Goheen's advice as it planned to commemorate the war. "The assistance asked of you will probably have to be rendered a patriotic service, rendered voluntarily, except possibly reimbursement of expenses for travel that may be directed by the commission," Grant explained. His request that Goheen serve on this commission is a testament to Princeton's placement in the middle of the Civil War because, at the time, roughly half of the Princeton student body hailed from southern states. That said, Goheen agreed to be in the nation's service.[11]

9. On Harvard leading among the Ivies in Black students, see Karabel, *The Chosen*, pp. 400–401.

10. On alumni giving rates, see Karabel, *The Chosen*, p. 295; "Finch Back from Tour of South," *DP*, March 4, 1958.

11. Ulysses S. Grant III to Robert Goheen, August 7, 1958; and Robert Goheen to Ulysses S. Grant III, August 13, 1958, Goheen Records, Box 125, Folder 2, Princeton.

"I accept with pleasure," Goheen said, "since from her founding Princeton, though a northern college, has enjoyed unusually close and fruitful ties with the South." He acknowledged the university's southern presence. Yet, in January 1959, when asked what Princeton would do as a university regarding the war centennial, an internal memo noted that Goheen wanted to "let it lie for a while." This represented the contradictory nature of the university. On one hand, celebrating Princeton's role in the Civil War was important to southern alumni donors while, on the other hand, promoting that ideology conflicted with the long-term goals of what Goheen believed to be the hallmark of a progressive campus—free speech.[12]

Goheen believed that hearing a variety of voices—conservative, liberal, and moderate—was key to a strong institution. An illustration of this occurred during his second year as president when, on April 20, 1959, Fidel Castro, the new Cuban prime minister; Joseph S. Clark (D-PA), a US Senator; and Dean Acheson, former US Secretary of State, delivered talks at Princeton. This was considered "one of the most hectic days in the memory of university officials." Acheson delivered a public talk in the Woodrow Wilson Conference Room that afternoon, gave another one to the graduate college that night, and concluded with a lecture to students enrolled in the Politics 202 class two days later. He discussed the US presidency and foreign policy. Clark, also a former mayor of Philadelphia, delivered a similar talk, "What's Wrong with Foreign Policy," at Whig Hall on April 20. He criticized the Dwight Eisenhower Administration for failing to explain the complexity and severity of the nation's problems; however, among these highly acclaimed speakers, Castro stole the show.[13]

In only his second month as prime minister, Castro was on a US speaking tour when he arrived in Princeton from Washington, DC, where he spoke to the National Press Club. Castro was a leader in the Cuban Revolution from 1953 until it ended in 1959, and his armed revolt against an authoritarian Cuban government raised concerns for Eisenhower. In fact, before the fall of Cuban ruler Fulgencio Batista in 1959, US federal officials were aware of Batista's

12. Goheen to Grant III; Memorandum from Dorothy P. Whitfield, secretary to President Goheen, January 5, 1959, Goheen Records, Box 125, Folder 2, Princeton. For more about Princeton's southern atmosphere, see William A. McWhirter, "On the Campus," *PAW*, January 26, 1962, p. 14; and Bradley, "The Southern-most Ivy," p. 111.

13. For an overview of the three speakers on campus, see Jose M. Ferrer III, "Castro, Acheson, Clark Appear Today: Rebel Addresses ACP," *DP*, April 20, 1959. On Acheson's lectures, see "Acheson Warns against Summit Meeting," *DP*, April 23, 1959; "Acheson Leaves Today," *DP*, April 22, 1959. On Clark's lecture, see John F. Hellegers, "Clark Hits Eisenhower for 'Failure to Lead,'" *DP*, April 21, 1959.

dictatorial leadership. That aside, the thirty-two-year-old Castro and his emergence as a revolutionary in Cuba stirred the interest of youthful American college students.[14]

Therefore, Goheen quickly agreed to have Castro speak at Princeton when alumnus Roland T. Ely, class of 1946, approached campus officials to ask if they were interested in hosting the premier from Cuba (Ely's cousin was a newly appointed Cuban government official). It was too great an opportunity for Princeton students to hear a global figure, and Goheen immediately organized a security meeting in Nassau Hall weeks before Castro's arrival. Goheen met with Frank C. Taplan, assistant to the head proctor on campus; Robert L. Johnstone, university business manager; and James H. Brown, the head of the Philadelphia region for the US State Department. The plan included a security sweep of the building where Castro would speak and up to fifteen officers on duty overnight to keep anyone from entering. Fifty-two uniformed New Jersey State Police officers would be on campus alongside eight undercover officers in plain clothes. Security was also assigned to Ely's home, where Castro would stay for the night before traveling to New York City to speak at the Present Day Club. Goheen also arranged for Castro to speak at the Lawrenceville School. It was a tight one-day schedule for someone the *Daily Princetonian* called "one of the most colorful figures ever to come to Princeton."[15]

Castro's presence had the campus abuzz. He addressed the American Civilization Program Seminar, whose 1959 theme was "The United States and the Revolutionary Spirit." Although only 170 people had tickets, almost as many without tickets found their way inside as more than 300 people huddled in the building to listen to the Cuban leader deliver an hour and a half talk about the power of democracy. "It is the most beautiful political and social idea," Castro told the attentive Princeton audience, "to give people freedom and to satisfy their [material] needs. It includes the right of living and the right of not dying of want."[16]

14. On Castro's previous stop being the National Press Club, see Ferrer III, "Castro, Acheson, Clark Appear Today"; Schoultz, *That Infernal Little Cuban Republic*, pp. 52–108. On the United States being aware of Fulgencio Batista's dictatorship, see pp. 85–86. For more on the Cuban Revolution, see Farber, *Origins of the Cuban Revolution Reconsidered*, particularly chaps. 2 and 3.

15. Jose M. Ferrer III, "The Story behind Castro's Visit Here: Ely Makes Trip to Cuban Palace," *DP*, April 17, 1959; Jose M. Ferrer III, "Castro Security Plan Elaborate: Plan Laid Early," *DP*, April 29, 1959; Jose M. Ferrer III, "Castro Schedules Address Here: Cuban Leader to Visit ACP Seminar Monday," *DP*, April 15, 1959.

16. Ferrer III, "Castro Schedules Address Here"; "Premier Praises Democracy: 'Most Beautiful Idea,'" *DP*, April 21, 1959.

He also professed that democracy should not be sacrificed, and in a sharp criticism applicable to the United States, he emphasized, "Free elections, free press, and free speech are all important, but all of this means nothing if man doesn't know how to write or is always hungry." The revolutionary leader vowed to lead Cuba toward an economic program without stripping its citizens of their individual freedoms, and he said Americans should support a social revolution similar to the one he led in his country. "A real revolution," Castro added, saying he was not interested in personal financial gain but only "the moral prize." The attendees gave a standing ovation at the end of his formal talk.[17]

Outside of the building awaited a much larger crowd. Roughly 1,500 students cheered along McCosh Walk, with some sitting in trees, prior to the talk. Although not scheduled to make any public appearances, the charismatic Castro capitalized on the moment created by the excited undergraduates who chanted, "Viva Castro!" One thousand undergraduate students were still outside cheering for Castro, who ordered his motorcade to stop. To the confusion of the state police, Castro offered a spontaneous address. He told the crowd of his hope "that undergraduates here and throughout the U.S. will support our country's young government." He also invited Princetonians to Cuba to celebrate the nation's Independence Day on July 26, the namesake of the Castro-led 26th of July Movement and anniversary of the first rebellion.[18]

Castro was later noted for being a supporter of the Black Freedom Movement and symbolically stayed at a Harlem hotel when he once visited the United Nations, and dozens of US college students traveled to Cuba during the early 1960s. Some conservative alumni, however, voiced their concerns to Goheen over Castro's welcomed appearance, but students raved about the visit months later. "After 14 months of accustoming himself to the duties of his new office, President Robert F. Goheen '40 this year began to initiate some of the reforms which he has been interested in effecting," wrote Jose M. Ferrer III in the *Daily Princetonian* during a June 1959 recap of the academic year. "The announcement of a $53 million capital fund drive to enable Princeton to expand physically and intellectually was the year's biggest action . . . . The year was also highlighted by the appearance of a number of dignitaries on campus. Headed by Dr. Fidel Castro . . . ," Ferrer concluded.[19]

17. "Premier Praises Democracy."

18. Jose M. Ferrer III, "Castro Violates Security Regulations, Speaks to Washington Road Throng: Cuban Hailed by 1500," *DP*, April 21, 1959; "Princetonians to Visit Cuba Castro Invites," *DP*, April 22, 1959.

19. On Castro's stay at Hotel Theresa in Harlem, see Biondi, *Black Revolution on Campus*, p. 23. Donna Jean Murch discussed how several California students traveled in 1962 under the

As notable as Castro's visit was, however, no speaker whom Goheen welcomed to Princeton garnered as much negative attention as those focused on civil rights and desegregation in the United States. In January 1960, Princeton's southern alumni grew upset over the upcoming March 1960 visit by the prominent minister and civil rights leader Martin Luther King Jr. He had previously been scheduled to speak at Princeton on February 8, 1959, two months before Castro, but that visit was canceled due to an attempt to assassinate him in New York City on September 20, 1958.[20]

The critics referred to King as a "revolutionary," complained about his efforts to challenge southern segregation, and opposed the rescheduled appearance to campus. However, Goheen supported dean of the chapel Ernest Gordon's decision to uphold the invitation, and two months later, on March 13, 1960, King spoke at the University Chapel. There, he stressed that racial challenges lay in the hands of the "oppressed and the oppressor." The challenge for the oppressed was disenfranchisement, but for the oppressor, King criticized white Americans' selfish desire to "maintain a preferential economic and political power structure." Before an overflow crowd, there was no campus or local opposition to King during his chapel address, but there was pushback in Princeton against his larger message of fighting racial segregation.[21]

The day before King's visit, on March 12, twelve Princeton undergraduates and one faculty member picketed the local F. W. Woolworth Store on Nassau Street across from campus. The small group drew little sympathy for their demonstration from Black or white customers; however, this act of solidarity with southern Black college students' lunch-counter sit-ins was chastised in town. A small group of high school students, who, some accounts said, were inspired by conservative Princeton upperclassmen, assaulted the picketers, and the high schoolers and demonstrators had a brief scuffle. Eventually, police officers dispersed the crowd of about two hundred onlookers who

---

Student Committee for Travel to Cuba. For more, see Murch, *Living for the City*, p. 109. For more on Fidel Castro and Cuba and the implications for the United States, see Patterson, *Grand Expectations*, pp. 427–428. The disagreement with Goheen welcoming Castro would continue for years such as, in 1963, Madame Nhu of Vietnam was reportedly booed when she spoke on campus and Castro's warm reception was used as an example of Princeton's newly developed liberal leaning. For an example, see R. W. Daugherty to Robert Goheen, October 17, 1963, Goheen Records, Box 424, Folder 11, Princeton; Jose M. Ferrer III, "Year of Positive Action for University," *DP*, June 20, 1959.

20. Robert Lukens, "King Appearance Challenged: Southern Alumni Protest," *DP*, January 20, 1960.

21. Lukens, "King Appearance Challenged"; "Overflow Chapel Crowd Hears Sermon by King," *DP*, March 14, 1960.

gathered around the commotion. The picket was planned to coincide with King's visit and aimed to "awake the academic community to the segregation situation." The more telling aspect of the Woolworth picket and King's chapel visit, however, was the reaction among Princeton students and alumni.[22]

Although one letter expressed shock at the violence from counterprotesters, most questioned the purpose of the Woolworth demonstration. An editorial in the *Daily Princetonian* acknowledged the group's right to demonstrate but suggested that "there must be a better way to promulgate one's ideas than the ludicrous display of motley marchers who demonstrated as Princeton's representatives." The editorial board suggested that southerners knew how outsiders felt about segregation. Therefore, a demonstration in Princeton was pointless. Letters to the editors expressed much of the same. Integrationists would never end segregation if they continued to force white southerners to desegregate, read a letter written by "A Southerner." The picketers were naive at best, read another letter, and they harmed the university's reputation, professed another. This widespread sentiment at Princeton verified the slow pace of change.[23]

Following King's visit, the southern lunch counter sit-ins and nonsouthern solidarity demonstrations expanded in scope throughout the rest of 1960. In October, King was arrested during a sit-in demonstration in Atlanta alongside Black college students, and the next month, Harvard alumnus and US senator John F. Kennedy was elected president of the United States after he campaigned in favor of stronger civil rights legislation. Shortly after his inauguration, in April 1961, the Kennedy-approved Bay of Pigs invasion failed to overthrow Castro as a communist leader, a stark contrast to his speech on democracy two years earlier. The next month, college students joined the Freedom Rides to challenge segregated highway facilities, and in the summer of 1961, more violence and arrests occurred as the Freedom Rides continued. By early 1962, demonstrations on nonsouthern campuses caught the attention of Goheen and other college presidents in the Northeast, Midwest, and West. The January 1962 sit-in at the office of University of Chicago president

22. R. Hunter Morey, "Picketing Proposed," *DP*, March 11, 1960. The quote on awakening the community can be found in Rhys Evans, "Nassau St. Pickets Attacked by Mob," *DP*, March 14, 1960. The Dean of Students report to the trustees also mentioned the Woolworth's picket. For more, see Report to the Trustees' Committee on Undergraduate Life, April 8, 1960, Goheen Records, Box 66, Folder 1, Princeton.

23. Jonathan Day and Jeffrey Miller, "Acts of Violence," *DP*, March 14, 1960; "A Better Way," *DP*, March 14, 1960; Anonymous letter to the editor, "A Southern View," *DP*, March 14, 1960; Frank G. Childers, "Naïve Academics," *DP*, March 14, 1960; Thomas Deupree and Pen Kavanagh, "Childishness," *DP*, March 14, 1960.

George W. Beadle and the February 1962 student vote on the student Freedom Riders at the University of California, Los Angeles, were just two examples.[24]

These events were controversial and angered many white Americans across the country, but despite that, Goheen welcomed King to Princeton again on April 29, 1962. Since his previous visit, King's civil rights leadership had only worsened his reputation among conservatives. Nonetheless, he was one of eight speakers at the Seventh Biennial Religious Conference under the theme, "Integration: Conscience in Crisis." The weekend conference also showed four films related to racial segregation as a "contradiction of American principles." There, King emphasized steady resistance to segregation in America. "Segregation is dying," he said. "The question is how expensive and costly the nation will make the funeral." The death of segregation, and at what cost, was also something that Goheen was interested in at Princeton.[25]

Free Speech Meets Race

As Goheen welcomed controversial speakers to campus, several states had or were implementing speaker bans. Mississippi state officials did so in the mid-1950s, and North Carolina did the same in 1963, much to the surprise of William Friday, chancellor of the University of North Carolina. This was part of elected officials' attempt to suppress what they considered radical viewpoints, and was often tied to individuals who championed racial equality. Therefore, supporting free speech at Princeton positioned Goheen—despite helming a private university—as a leader among college presidents as other academic leaders sought his advice.[26]

One of the more notable requests came in 1962 from University of California president Clark Kerr—two years before the speech controversies on the

24. These events are discussed throughout the previous chapters in this book, particularly the first three chapters.

25. John M. Jones, "Conference Urges Racial Effort: Agreement Not Complete," *DP*, April 30, 1962. To further contextualize how several whites linked communism and higher education desegregation efforts, see Williamson-Lott, *The Jim Crow Campus*. For more on the Bay of Pigs invasion, see Kornbluh, *Bay of Pigs Declassified*; and Rasenberger, *The Brilliant Disaster*.

26. On the Mississippi speaker ban, see the following: Barrett, *Integration at Ole Miss*, p. 32; Cohadas, *The Band Played Dixie*, pp. 41–42; Williamson-Lott, *Jim Crow Campus*, pp. 40–42. Regarding the North Carolina speakers ban, see Link, *William Friday*, pp. 109–127. For more on officials' attempts to ban speakers or dismiss campus employees, see Turner, *Sitting In and Speaking Out*, pp. 32–33; and Whittington, *Speak Freely*, pp. 3–4, 51.

Berkeley campus. "It would be very helpful if you could give me whatever information is available concerning your own procedures and policies in this field," Kerr inquired. "I am particularly interested in your policy with respect to members of the Communist Party or other known subversive groups, right or left." The straightforward request was simple but telling of Goheen's success welcoming Castro, King, and others to campus. Yet, Goheen's stance on free speech was met with a new challenge when Princeton started to act on racial equality.[27]

On January 17, 1962, Goheen held his first monthly press conference of the year, and admissions questions were prominent, given that a variety of opinions had emerged about Princeton admitting more Black students. That same week, undergraduate students attending the Woodrow Wilson School Conference on Race Relations passed a resolution recommending that the university adopt a recruitment policy that quantified the recruitment of Black applicants. This "energetic program of recruiting qualified American Negro students," as described by the students, won thirteen of the twenty-member conference's votes. "Although this conference believes that the university does not intentionally discriminate in considering the applications of Negroes," the student conference explained, "we believe that many qualified Negro students are not aware of the fair consideration which their applications would find here."[28]

Perhaps shallow in thinking that admissions fairness was the only reason Black students considered colleges, the students' conference statement was still noteworthy. That same academic year, Yale hired Charles McCarthy, a recent Yale graduate, to recruit more Black students, and other Ivy League institutions took note, especially considering that their campuses were overwhelmingly white despite not being formally segregated. At best, Princeton enrolled no more than seven US-born Black students at any time. That was fewer than the number of students from Asia or Africa. To solve this, the conference recommended that the admissions staff's next admitted class be "at least 2 percent" Black.[29]

27. On Clark Kerr consulting Robert F. Goheen on speech policies, see multiple letters to/from Kerr/Goheen, December 1962–January 1963, Goheen Records, Box 134, Folder 6, Princeton.

28. Michael S. Mathews, "Goheen Issues Statement in Furor over Admissions," DP, January 19, 1962; McWhirter, "On the Campus," p. 14

29. Mathews, "Goheen Issues Statement." Regarding the number of US-born Black students, see McWhirter, "On the Campus," p. 14. On the Charles McCarthy hire, see Karabel, The Chosen, pp. 380–381. For more on the proportion of white students at these institutions, see Synnott, The Half-Opened Door.

Several people quickly critiqued this idea. An official from the NAACP disagreed with a quota approach. So, too, did Goheen. "I strongly favor the admission of well-qualified Negro students to Princeton, as I do that of other students who bring to the campus a variety of religious, racial, and cultural backgrounds," the president said during the press conference. "However, I do not see how anyone can say what a desirable proportion might be for any identifiable group, whether it be Protestant or Catholic, United States citizen or foreign, white or Negro, etc." Goheen believed in the diversity of the academic experience, something administrators had consistently preached since Dean of the College Jeremiah S. Finch's southern tour in 1958. Therefore, there was no intention to start admitting Black students just to meet a quota. Instead, Goheen wanted "well-qualified" Black students. He knew they existed, but he wanted these Black students to be selected as individuals, not "social statistics."[30]

C. William Edwards, director of admissions, echoed the president's stance but went a step further. Whereas Goheen was opposed to a quota that measured how many Black students should be admitted, Edwards found it erroneous to start any program to recruit Black students. "It would be very wrong to separate the application of a colored boy from the rest," Edwards said reacting to the resolution from the conference on race. "The admissions process is a comparison among many qualified people." He added that Princeton does not discriminate in admissions, and there should be no ill feelings toward the university among Black applicants. "If there is any feeling that Princeton is not receptive to Negroes," Edwards said, "I do not know if it exists."[31]

Despite his belief, several people knew Princeton was "an admittedly southern-influenced school," and the university's recruitment methods reflected as much. The admissions staff recruited elite northeastern prep schools, which did not have many Black students, and Edwards's focus on qualified applicants missed an opportunity to investigate why so few Black people considered Princeton in the first place. Meanwhile, Goheen was more in tune with the real issue. It would require a shared effort among campus officials to implement the changes he sought.[32]

30. Robert Goheen Statement on Admitting Black Students, January 17, 1962, Goheen Records, Box 315, Folder 1, Princeton; Mathews, "Goheen Issues Statement."

31. "Plan to Increase Negro Enrollment Described as 'Wrong' by Edwards," DP, January 19, 1962.

32. For the "admittedly southern" quote, see McWhirter, "On the Campus," p. 14; Edwards's notion that recruiting and admitting Black students would lower academic standards was prevalent at the Ivies. For more, see Bradley, *Upending the Ivory Tower*, pp. 8–9; and Karabel, *The Chosen*, pp. 383–384.

A month later, on February 27, 1962, Dan Coyle, special assistant to Goheen, sent the president a memo signaling a change to come when he shared a biographical overview of E. Alden Dunham, class of 1953. The young alumnus would soon replace Edwards as Princeton's admissions director. Edwards was exhausted from recruiting and its challenges, and the push for more Black students added an additional layer to an already demanding job. Fittingly, Dunham was assistant to James B. Conant, former Harvard president, and he was a scholar of public education who had earned his doctorate from Columbia University while working full-time. In short order, Dunham was a worthy replacement and the best of both worlds: a Princeton graduate with experience at two Ivy League universities that were more successful at enrolling Black students.[33]

Now, with the transition in place, Edwards offered one last recommendation to Goheen as admissions director. He suggested that the university delay the official announcement about his resignation, saying it would be better to wait until after admissions letters to the next class were mailed. Institutions with competitive admissions did not want any abrupt changes as admitted students weighed their options, and Goheen agreed. "I am inclined to go along with this suggestion," the president told Coyle. "Will you see that Dunham knows of the reason for the delay, and then, in April, coordinate the specific time of the release with Bill Edwards." From there, members of Princeton's class of 1967 were notified of their acceptance, and as instructed, Coyle coordinated the press release after admissions letters were mailed.[34]

On April 23, 1962, the department of public information issued the release about the change in admissions leadership. Shortly after resigning, Edwards said, "Somebody has got to find a better answer than I know." Goheen saluted Edwards for the work he had done, but the future for Princeton admissions depended on someone new. "It is with deep regret that we have accepted Mr. Edwards's decision to relinquish the post he has filled with distinction," Goheen stated in the press release. He praised the outgoing admissions director's work during the postwar boom with its "ever-rising numbers of qualified applicants." Edwards, now age forty-eight, who had served as director since 1950 and worked in admissions since 1945, was replaced by the thirty-year-old

33. Dan Coyle to Robert Goheen, February 27, 1962, Goheen Records, Box 339, Folder 3, Princeton. Coyle's letter to Goheen noted that Dunham earned his doctorate in education in 1961. Dunham is also credited with giving James B. Conant, formerly Harvard president, the phrase "social dynamite" to describe the emerging issues in American cities. For more, see Karabel, *The Chosen*, p. 314.

34. Robert Goheen to Dan Coyle, March 16, 1962, Goheen Records, Box 339, Folder 3, Princeton.

Dunham. But in the transition, Goheen succinctly summarized the primary duty of the position. "Over the past 17 years," the president said, "Mr. Edwards has served as a roving ambassador for Princeton as well as a singularly effective spokesman for higher education."[35]

In July 1962, prep school and secondary school leaders were notified of Edwards's resignation, and informed that Dunham would now work "closely with you in the selection of students for Princeton" and "continue the cordial relations which we have enjoyed in the past with secondary schools throughout the country." By September, the concerns of the Princeton admissions staff as it pertained to their priority to recruit Black students became more prominent. This coincided with President Kennedy's meeting that fall with the academic leaders from five institutions, including Harvard and Yale, to discuss the nation's racial climate. Also, the University of Mississippi's September 1962 desegregation was a violent affair.[36]

Therefore, a *Princeton Alumni Weekly* article also discussed Princeton admissions. It explained how the university compared with other private colleges, especially since it was one of the "Big Three" universities that recruited nationally. However, the geographic challenge, unlike at Harvard or Yale, was Princeton's more suburban setting that offered students no urban escape. The feature article also discussed standardized test scores and interviewing techniques, and had a section titled "Priority for Negroes." The university's Civil War history, with its large southern presence, was noted, alongside the university's practice of not asking an applicant's race, but the number of Black applicants remained low because "reputations last long in education."[37]

This foreshadowed how little there would be to show for all this planning by the end of the 1962–63 academic year because admissions numbers for Black students remained stagnant. Dunham's first year as admissions director resulted in about the same number of Black applicants admitted as Edwards's final year. Among the 1,202 acceptance letters mailed in the spring of 1963, only eleven were to Black students—one more than the number admitted the previous year. Among those Dunham admitted, only five enrolled. The difference, however, was that Dunham's first year had a 13 percent increase in the number of applications Princeton received. Therefore, based on percentage, Princeton had done worse at admitting Black students after the publicly announced plan

35. On the Edwards "somebody" quote, see Mayer, "How to Get into Princeton"; Press Release, April 23, 1962, Goheen Records, Box 88, Folder 7, Princeton.

36. Memo to Headmasters and Principals of Secondary Schools, July 1962, Goheen President Records, Box 88, Folder 7, Princeton. On the meeting at the White House with President Kennedy, see Karabel, *The Chosen*, p. 381.

37. Mayer, "How to Get into Princeton."

to prioritize recruiting them. "Next year, though, will be different," Dunham assessed. "I think there has been a more conscious and obvious effort to encourage Negroes to apply."[38]

To accomplish more in 1963–64, Dunham acknowledged that the university's racial climate had to change. Regardless of how actively they recruited, he felt the university's "hostile" reputation meant the best Black students would always choose Ivy League institutions farther north. Until then, Princeton would continue to have more success enrolling Black students from African nations than those from the United States (five Nigerians were admitted as late as April 26, 1963).[39]

Dunham's 1962–63 admissions report to the faculty highlighted two reasons why it was necessary to increase the number of Black students. First, it would add diversity. "The addition of more American Negroes and other underprivileged groups to the campus would contribute to the diversity of the student body and enrich the residential experience of all," the report explained. There was also a moral obligation. "At this particular point in American history," Dunham said, "it behooves all educational institutions to do what they can toward upgrading the status of the Negro in our free society. Princeton has an opportunity and responsibility in this regard."[40]

The gist of Dunham's report was that Princeton could benefit from Black students and Black students could benefit from Princeton. Yet, Dunham also repeated what he emphasized when the admissions numbers were released: the "long southern tradition at Princeton" would steer Black students to Harvard or Yale instead. This fact was an issue throughout Goheen's first five years as president, but by the spring of 1963, it was heightened due to the gruesome violence against peaceful demonstrators. In Birmingham, Alabama, on May 3, 1963, the local authorities' use of police dogs and high-powered water hoses on children during a civil rights rally solidified what had been a lingering crisis for the Kennedy Administration and its image on

38. On the number of Black students admitted and enrolled, see Report to the Faculty, 1962–1963, Goheen Records, Box 88, Folder 8, Princeton. On how Dunham's first year compared with Edwards's final year recruiting Black students, see Thomas J. Bray, "On the Campus," *PAW*, April 26, 1963.

39. Bray, "On the Campus." For an update to Goheen on foreign students admitted, see W. Bradford Craig to Robert Goheen, April 26, 1963, Goheen Records, Box 88, Folder 8, Princeton.

40. Admission Committee Meeting Minutes, May 24, 1963, Goheen Records, Box 88, Folder 8, Princeton; Report to the Faculty, 1962–1963. By 1963, a small number of predominantly white, nonsouthern colleges started to recruit Black students. For more, see Kendi, *Black Campus Movement*, p. 27.

the global stage, and the violence of the South also reared its ugly head at Princeton in New Jersey.[41]

Four days later, on May 7, W. M. Miles, an attorney in Union City, Tennessee, and class of 1901 alumnus, contacted Dunham after he read the *Princeton Alumni Weekly* and saw the priority for more Black applicants. "This is the first time I ever heard that Negroes were given any priority in admission to Princeton," Miles wrote, "and I am writing to inquire just what this priority is, that is, the nature and extent of this priority." For him, priority meant "a Negro is given preference over a white person."[42]

Dunham responded optimistically to the note from Miles. Despite feeling the *Princeton Alumni Weekly* was "somewhat inaccurate," he told Miles the focus of the article was correct. Indeed, Princeton wanted more Black students. He explained:

> This is in an effort to broaden the diversity in the undergraduate body, for diversity in race, religion, and socio-economic background seems to me an important part of the educational process at a residential college like Princeton. Actually, I would like to see a great many more applications from qualified Negro applicants so that priority in the admissions process is not necessary.

Thoroughly committed to this goal, Dunham then encouraged Miles to join Princeton in its effort, and he welcomed any suggestions of "qualified Negroes" Miles might know. The southern alumnus, however, would not aid such an effort, and Miles quickly responded.[43]

"I am particularly pained to learn that Princeton would like to see a great many more applications from qualified Negro applicants," he said. In fact, Miles used this opportunity to share his disappointment in how things had changed during Goheen's presidency. He said a previous Princeton president once visited Nashville, Tennessee, and, according to Miles, said "Princeton was the northern outpost of southern culture." Therefore, the southern alumnus griped, "throughout Princeton's entire history, up until recently, there has always existed a southern atmosphere." In closing, Miles confirmed to

41. For the "long southern tradition" quote, see Report to the Faculty, 1962–1963; Foster Hailey, "Dogs and Hoses Repulse Negroes at Birmingham: 3 Students Bitten in Second Day of Demonstrations against Segregation," *New York Times*, May 4, 1963.

42. W. H. Miles to E. Alden Dunham, May 7, 1963, Goheen Records, Box 425, Folder 3, Princeton.

43. E. Alden Dunham to W. M. Miles, May 17, 1963, Goheen Records, Box 425, Folder 3, Princeton.

Dunham there was no chance he would ever help encourage Black students to apply to Princeton.[44]

There stood the challenge for Goheen and Dunham. By the end of the 1962–63 academic year, the resistance to civil rights advancements was vast. In the South, there was obvious violence. At Princeton, the resistance was passive but violent nonetheless. In fact, as Miles furiously refuted Dunham's request in May 1963, racist literature was distributed for several days on campus by neo-Nazis. The pamphlets were anti-Jew and anti-Black. One piece of literature read, "Negro blood destroyed the civilization of Egypt, India, Phoenicia, Carthage, Greece, and Rome. It will destroy America!" This represented the distinct streak of hatred for Black people engrained in the university. The pace of change was slow until things were brought to a crisis point, jeopardizing Goheen's support of free speech and goal of attracting more Black students.[45]

In the fall of 1963, the Whig-Clio Society, the campus debate union, invited Mississippi governor Ross Barnett to speak at Princeton. The previous fall, his defiance of federal directives to enroll James Meredith, a Black student, at the University of Mississippi led to a race riot on campus that resulted in two deaths and dozens of injuries. Afterward, the Mississippi campus was occupied by federal troops to maintain peace during the entire 1962–63 academic year. Therefore, Barnett's white supremacist views were in stark contrast to Princeton's active search for more Black applicants. This forced President Goheen to weigh his belief in free speech alongside his personal conviction that Princeton should enroll more Black students. The conflict was Goheen's most formidable challenge in convincing qualified Black students to apply.

For example, in September 1963, Dunham issued his Report to Schools on admissions that provided an overview of the incoming class of 1967. The average scores on standardized tests were shared, and the recently admitted freshmen had a higher average S.A.T. score than any class before 1958. Furthermore, twenty-one of the freshmen were named University Scholars, a recognition given to those with the most outstanding high school academic records. Among the entire class, most of the incoming students were from New York (141), New Jersey (131), and Pennsylvania (100), while Virginia (27), Florida (20), Texas (17), and Kentucky (10) were southern states with double-digit representation among the number of students enrolled. But most notably, the

---

44. W. M. Miles to E. Alden Dunham, May 20, 1963, Goheen Records, Box 425, Folder 3, Princeton. For more details on Princeton's social reputation, see Karabel, *The Chosen*, pp. 294–296. Karabel noted that "alumni were also a serious problem, for they contributed to the image—and the reality—of Princeton as a private club."

45. "Neo-Nazi Party Distributes Racist Literature on Campus," *DP*, May 8, 1963.

report was mailed to four thousand private and public schools, and on the first page was the section "Search for Negro Applicants."[46]

It was an upfront notice to prep school and secondary school officials. "Princeton is actively seeking qualified Negro applicants in an effort to insure the diversity mentioned earlier," the report read. "Efforts of school people in steering toward Princeton qualified Negroes will be appreciated. Regardless of race, applications from promising underprivileged boys are encouraged." This plan would be null and void, however, if Governor Barnett's visit turned violent or demonstrated that Princeton remained friendly toward white supremacists. Either outcome would prove unwelcoming to potential Black students.[47]

Barnett Speaks at Princeton

In the late hours of September 19, 1963, Dan Coyle was troubled and could not sleep. He felt it was one thing to have to overcome the southern traditions at Princeton but another to welcome Barnett, one of the most prominent white supremacists, to campus. With Barnett slated to arrive in less than two weeks, Coyle wrote Goheen about his anguish over the visit.

"I find it difficult to believe that any valid purpose will be served by the appearance of Governor Barnett," Coyle said. There was nothing—no university constituency, institutional responsibility, or governance obligation—more important than institutional leaders opposing the visit, and he believed the university's national development depended on it. Controversial speakers, Coyle said, did not bother him. In fact, he seemed to "thrive on it," but the Sixteenth Street Baptist Church bombing in Birmingham that killed four girls only days earlier left Coyle at a loss. "The travesty of 'Barnett in Princeton in October 1963' is difficult to reconcile to my way of thinking," Coyle reflected, "either with 'Princeton in the Nation's Service' or with the tragic realities of the day, particularly in the light of [Alabama Governor George] Wallace's aberrations and the Birmingham murders." His fears accurately captured what scholar Gerald Horne, a Black Princeton student in the 1960s, later recalled as the "tremendous global pressure" that forced academic leaders at white universities to seriously pursue Black students.[48]

46. Report to Schools, September 1963, Goheen Records, Box 88, Folder 8, Princeton. On 4,000 copies being mailed, see Mel M. Masuda, "Ivy Colleges Encourage Negro Applicants," *DP*, November 14, 1963.

47. Report to Schools.

48. Dan Coyle to Robert Goheen, September 19, 1963, Goheen Records, Box 425, Folder 2, Princeton. For the Gerald Horne quote, see Bradley, *Upending the Ivory Tower*, p. xii.

Goheen took note of Coyle's concerns. The two men agreed in principle that Barnett represented the worst of America and nothing that Princeton endorsed. Their personal convictions were clear on the matter of a more diverse student body, but Goheen also weighed the value of free speech alongside the violent rhetoric of segregation. On September 24, five days after Coyle's late-night letter, Goheen issued a public statement about Barnett's upcoming visit:

> As is well known, this university is strongly committed to the fair and equal treatment of all persons without regard to their race, color, or religion. The invitation to Governor Barnett to speak here the night of October 1st runs hard against this basic tenet of the university, and personally, I judge the invitation to be untimely and ill considered.

He continued:

> At the same time, we have no less a commitment to the principle of free inquiry and debate. It is pivotal to the very idea of a university. And it must be considered to include, I believe, the right of students to hear men with strong convictions speak on issues of public moment however distasteful on occasion the views of such speakers may be to many of us.

Goheen did not believe in Barnett's views nor did any aspect of those views align with university policies, but he would not halt his appearance unless there was the threat of violence. Thus, safety precautions were made with local and state law enforcement. "But I am confident that our students and the people of this community can listen to extremist views, even of the distasteful character of those held by Governor Barnett, with due self-restraint," Goheen's statement concluded. "Perhaps Governor Barnett can learn something in New Jersey. I hope so."[49]

The next day, on September 25, Goheen fielded questions during a press conference. He explained that administrators were not informed of the Barnett invitation, and upon investigation, Goheen explained that "a few individuals" invited the governor without the approval of the Whig-Clio council as well. Other press conference questions focused on potential protesters, and Goheen said people have the right to protest Barnett. The press conference also highlighted the local relevance of the governor's visit because the town of Princeton had its own racial issues. There was a recent statement signed by five hundred town residents demanding fair housing, and from nearby Trenton,

49. Robert Goheen Statement, September 24, 1963, Goheen Records, Box 425, Folder 2, Princeton.

the state capital, a newspaper used the phrase "Ivy League Ghetto" to describe the deplorable housing conditions for Black Princeton residents. In response, Goheen weighed in, sharing his "belief in open housing and opposition to discriminatory housing." His statement on Barnett and subsequent press conference comments sparked swift reactions from several alumni, community leaders, faculty, and students, and over the next week, leading up to Barnett's October 1 appearance, the range of responses were indicative of the tensions on campus.[50]

Fritz Machlup, a faculty member in the department of economics, was "delighted" by Goheen's statement that was both released on September 24 and published the following day in the student newspaper. "I have now carefully reread the statement as published in the *Daily Princetonian* and find my first impression unchanged: it is in every respect an admirable pronouncement." Similarly, Norman M. Thomas, class of 1905 and a socialist party member, criticized Michael A. Pane, president of the Whig-Clio debate society, for the Barnett invitation. He called the invitation an example of "extraordinary social irresponsibility." Thomas believed Barnett's visit would be "taken as a kind of accolade of approval of the governor by a great university," and he wished Pane had withdrawn the invitation as Yale students had rescinded their fall of 1963 invitation to Alabama's segregationist governor George C. Wallace.[51]

Five university chaplains also found the invitation "a deep insult to a great many members of the Princeton community." Like Goheen, the chaplains supported free speech. There had been on-campus speakers in the past who espoused racist views, but their regret over Barnett was different. "A year ago, the Oxford riots took two lives," the chaplains said. "Medgar Evers was murdered less than four months ago. Thousands of Mississippi citizens seeking freedom and justice live in daily fear of their lives. The duty of their state to lead and protect them has been betrayed by their governor." Additionally, Princeton Borough mayor Henry S. Patterson II said: "I expect and urge that his stay in Princeton be marked, as far as Princeton is concerned, by the community ignoring him." In all, there was a sizable sense of opposition to Barnett, but this level of support for Goheen's statement was overpowered by the wave of criticism he received.[52]

---

50. Frank Burgess, "President Asserts Hall Officials Mismanaged Barnett Invitation: Did Not Notify Nassau Hall," *DP*, September 26, 1963.

51. Fritz Machlup to Robert Goheen, September 25, 1963, Goheen Records, Box 425, Folder 3, Princeton; Norman Thomas to Whig-Clio Society president, September 25, 1963, Goheen Records, Box 425, Folder 3, Princeton; "Thomas Raps Barnett's Visit," *DP*, September 27, 1963.

52. Chaplains' Statement, September 26, 1963, Goheen Records, Box 425, Folder 3, Princeton; Charles Creesy, "Chaplainry Asks General Boycott," *DP*, September 26, 1963.

Some critiques took on a tone more sympathetic to southern segregationists. For instance, a *Daily Princetonian* editorial disagreed with Barnett's views, but said "it could very well be a valuable experience for any undergraduate who hears him." In fact, the editorial board argued, "in this period of unrest and uncertainty on civil rights, the injection of an alien viewpoint is sound, from an intellectual, if not a civil order, point of view." Similarly, Jacques Bramhall III, a freshman who had been enrolled for only ten days at that point, was surprised by Goheen's treatment of Barnett. "Mr. Barnett's personal feelings towards the Negro are in no way important," Bramhall wrote. "The stand he takes on the question of integration is a stand forced on him by his belief in states' rights." But few responses to Goheen's condemnation of the governor were as gentle as the aforementioned. The defenders of Barnett were sterner.[53]

Ronald A. Walsh, a New Jersey native living in Jackson, Mississippi, defended the governor. "I am distressed that you, as the head of one of the country's finest universities, would deny a platform," Walsh told Goheen, "to the elected head of a segment of United States citizens." Jno C. Batte, also from Jackson, called Goheen's statement on Barnett contradictory. "Am surprised to see the communist speakers all over the North speaking to student bodies and no fuss about them," he said. John H. Morrell, an executive field underwriter for Phoenix Mutual Life Insurance Company in Hartford, Connecticut, also complained that universities opposed segregationists but allowed communists. "We are either a democracy where both sides of any subject may be heard or a police state where we are afraid of minority opinion," Morrell assessed. "There is no middle ground."[54]

Some even encouraged Barnett not to visit Princeton for fear of exposing himself to Goheen and New Jersey Governor Richard Hughes, calling both cowards. R. Paul Ramsey, a professor of religion, exhausted by the legal or moral debate over Barnett, said, "The more bad reasons I hear why he should not be heard, the more I rather approve his having been invited." Richard M. Asche, associate editorial director of the *Daily Princetonian* and self-professed "northern liberal," wrote a column urging the campus to be more considerate of Barnett. Typically, he said, nonsoutherners' approach to desegregation has been "We are right, and we'll ram it down their throats." And Kendall Blake, a freshman, added: "Right or wrong, Mississippi is never given the opportunity to be heard

53. "Barnett's Visit," *DP*, September 25, 1963; Jacques Bramhall III, "The Civil Rights Issue," *DP*, September 27, 1963.

54. Ronald A. Walsh to Robert Goheen, September 24, 1963; Jno C. Batte to Robert Goheen, October 1, 1963; John H. Morrell to Robert Goheen, September 30, 1963; all in Goheen Records, Box 425, Folder 3, Princeton.

nationally in her own words, but her actions and thoughts are always interpreted to others by those who are just as hate-filled and prejudiced as they
claim Mississippians to be." In the end, the newspaper received twenty letters
about Barnett's visit, and that did not include the letters written directly to
Goheen.[55]

Broadly speaking, it was the voices of those at the center of the struggle for
Black freedom that best captured the real issues of the moment. Ruth Lesis,
secretary of the League for Opportunity and Equality, acknowledged the value
of free debate but informed Goheen about the League's plan to organize a
peaceful protest against Barnett. Her rationale: "The mere presence of an individual who is so diametrically opposed to the best interests of our Negro
community is an effrontery to the divinity of the Negro race." For the writer
of an anonymous letter, a self-identified "Negro American," the racism in
Princeton was enough. "Inviting Ross Barnett to Princeton goes beyond mere
'academic inquiry,'" the letter read. "It borders on contempt for the Negro
community of Princeton."[56]

Most apropos, the day after Goheen's statement was released, Malcolm X,
the famed Black Islamic leader, was on the Princeton campus for a coffee hour
discussion with the faculty and students in the Near Eastern Program, and he
also weighed in on the Barnett controversy. "There is no distinction between
Barnett and Rockefeller," Malcolm X said, indicating that southern segregationists and northern philanthropists both benefit from racism. "There is as
much discrimination in New York as Mississippi," he added, while noting that
racism in New York came "with a smile."[57]

Goheen also knew racism had no regional boundaries. In fact, it was white
liberals' pronounced tolerance of Barnett's speech that frustrated him the
most. It was not only a question of free speech. There was also the real issue of
Black Americans being denied educational opportunity, jobs, and even being
murdered simply because of their race. Now, Princeton would have a leading

55. Charles E. Daul to Ross Barnett, September 27, 1963, Goheen Records, Box 425, Folder
3, Princeton; R. Paul Ramsey, "Ramsey Letter," DP, September 30, 1963; Richard M. Asche,
"Confessions of a Northern Liberal," DP, October 1, 1963; Kendall Blake, "Learn from Barnett,"
DP, October 1, 1963. On the editorial page, DP staff noted the influx of letters received about
Barnett's visit, and there were too many for all of them to be published. See "Barnett Letters,"
DP, September 30, 1963.

56. Ruth Lesis to Robert Goheen, September 30, 1963; Anonymous "Negro American" Letter to Robert Goheen, September 29, 1963; both in Goheen Records, Box 425, Folder 3,
Princeton.

57. Frank Burgess, "Malcolm X Declares West 'Doomed': Muslim Accuses President, Scorns
Washington March," DP, September 27, 1963.

segregationist on campus, and people were more upset over Goheen's assertion that the Barnett invitation was a bad idea than racism itself. In a letter to Reverend Rowland Cox, one of the campus chaplains, Goheen expressed his frustration. "I must confess," he said. "If the time, energy, and emotion, which this issue has consumed from so many parties this past week had been directed to concrete efforts to improve the rights and opportunities of underprivileged people in this area, it would seem to me to have been more profitable for all concerned." Goheen was perplexed, but he remained committed to his goal of admitting more Black students and addressing local racial problems, even on the eve of Barnett's controversial visit to Princeton.[58]

At 5:40 p.m., on October 1, 1963, Governor Barnett landed at McGuire Air Force Base outside of Trenton. Goheen was in Washington, DC, attending the ACE board of directors meeting. This left Michael A. Pane, a senior and president of the Whig-Clio, and about twenty other undergraduates to greet the governor upon his arrival. Absent were any official representatives from the university, elected state officials, or Air Force officers to welcome Barnett and his party of twenty other people, including some Mississippi state troopers, to New Jersey. Of course, the absence of a warm welcome did not matter to Barnett. Several segregationist governors knew how to put on a show for the cameras. Barnett used any occasion to offer a sharp jab at his opponents, and his appearance in New Jersey was no different. Thus, as he arrived, Barnett offered a witty one-liner on why he was visiting Princeton: "I wanted to see what the greatest southern college in the North was really like."[59]

Barnett's quip aside, his visit was a serious matter for the university's head security officer H. Walter Dodwell, whose task was to protect the governor in transit to and from campus. Therefore, all roads through campus were closed to vehicle traffic at 3 p.m., nearly three hours before the governor landed. New Jersey state police officers made their way to campus that afternoon, and some set up near Alexander Hall, where Barnett would speak. Ten state troopers stayed backstage and seventy-five others were on campus to escort Barnett safely to the hall.[60]

This police presence had merit. That evening, before Barnett's 8:30 p.m. speech, 3,500 people had jammed into Dillon Gym for an hour-long civil rights rally. The demonstrators included those affiliated with Princeton as well as

58. Robert Goheen to Rowland Cox, September 27, 1963, Goheen Records, Box 425, Folder 3, Princeton.

59. On Goheen's previously planned meeting in Washington, DC, see Burgess, "President Asserts Hall Officials Mismanaged"; Fred Stuart Jr., "Barnett Gets Small Greeting at McGuire Air Force Base," *DP*, October 2, 1963.

60. Stuart, "Barnett Gets Small Greeting."

others from other New Jersey cities such as Newark, New Brunswick, and Trenton. Reverend A. D. Tyson of Princeton's Mount Pisgah African Methodist Episcopal (AME) Church opened the rally, at which Bayard Rustin, assistant to Roy Wilkins (NAACP executive director) and organizer of the August 1963 March on Washington for Jobs and Freedom, also spoke. Rustin applauded the university for inviting Barnett, but questioned whether Barnett would grant Martin Luther King Jr. the same freedom to speak at the University of Mississippi. Furthermore, the rally turned its attention toward local affairs, and speakers urged the thousands in attendance to take stronger civil rights actions in Princeton. From there, the rally crowd marched—while holding signs that read "Human Rights over States Rights" and "Barnett Speaks at Princeton, Can King Speak at Mississippi"—to Alexander Hall to await Barnett.[61]

When Barnett arrived, the demonstrators hurled boos followed by singing "We Shall Overcome," but once backstage, he said he was "not in the least afraid of the mob demonstration." He added, "They are Americans and have a right to express their views." Inside the 1,246-seat Alexander Hall, a capacity audience awaited Barnett. Local and national media were on campus, but only photographers, no television cameras, were allowed inside. Due to overcrowding, his address was also played outdoors on loudspeakers that, inadvertently, drowned out the civil rights protesters gathered outside. Once Barnett was on stage, his talk was sporadically interrupted with a range of responses, from hisses and boos to catcalls and applause, as he critiqued the Kennedy Administration's proposed civil rights bill. "There are too many selfish, mealy-mouthed, pussyfooting, fence-riding politicians who are selling the American people down the river for their own personal ambition and gain," Barnett professed. "Freedom is being destroyed. Liberty is being destroyed," the governor said. Dismissing the horrors of slavery and the continued violence against Black citizens, he called the pending civil rights bill "infinitely more dangerous to the Republic than any offered in the past." Barnett also questioned the federal government's opposition to state rights, but the most gruesome of his comments focused on racial segregation: "I oppose the integration of the races because everywhere it has been practiced it has resulted in the mongrelization of the races." In the end, even with an opposing civil rights rally on campus, Barnett said he made "a few converts" in Princeton.[62]

61. Charles Creesy, "Crowd Sings Rights Anthem," *DP*, October 2, 1963. Several primary sources reference individuals from Newark, Trenton, and New Brunswick who attended the rally or Barnett's talk. For one, see Marge Cowenhoven to Dan Coyle, September 27, 1963, Goheen Records, Box 425, Folder 2, Princeton.

62. Creesy, "Crowd Sings"; Stuart, "Barnett Gets Small Greeting"; James Markham, "Princeton Braces for Barnett; Dodwell Expects No Trouble: Radio Networks to Cover Speech," *DP*,

Journalists' assessments of Barnett's effectiveness varied over the next two days. "We should all be gratified that the events of the evening transpired as successfully as they did and without serious incident," William D'O. Lippincott, dean of students, told the *Daily Princetonian* beneath the headline "End Barnett Visit Without Violence." Other headlines included the *New York Times*'s "Princeton Crowd Hisses Barnett," while the *Trenton Evening News* stated "Barnett Cowers Before Mob, Glows on Princeton Rostrum." The *New York Post* focused its coverage on the twenty people in Barnett's traveling party. The *Newark Evening News* opened with a description of the number of New Jersey state troopers needed to escort the visiting governor. The *New York Herald Tribune* emphasized how often the audience laughed at Barnett. Lastly, the *Philadelphia Inquirer* noted that Barnett was booed fifteen times but applauded thirty-two times, concluding it was "a not surprising ratio at a school which traditionally draws a large segment of its students from the South." Although each outlet varied in its focus, these northeastern newspapers similarly depicted Barnett as a joke and spectacle with a large entourage.[63]

To no surprise, southern journalists' coverage of Barnett's visit differed from that of their counterparts in the Northeast. In Jackson, Mississippi, the *Clarion Ledger* ridiculed the New Jersey audience. "This crazy mixed-up campus didn't know from nothing Tuesday night," the article read. The report acknowledged that most Princeton students inside Alexander Hall were attentive to Barnett's speech, but said it was the NAACP that "ran its rowdy course" and "showed extreme discourtesy to the campus group who had Gov. Barnett for its guest." It was the NAACP, presumably mostly from Trenton, that attempted to "crash the party" at Princeton because there were so few Black students enrolled. Fortunately, the *Clarion Ledger* explained, the governor was comfortable with demonstrators "even in such so-called seats of culture as the campus of this distinguished university."[64]

An editorial in Mississippi's *Vicksburg Evening Post* said much of the same. There, the editorial board called "the actions of many" at Princeton "a new low in discourtesy." Regardless of political views, the Mississippi journalists were appalled that a governor would be booed and subjected to taunts. "It is rather

---

October 1, 1963. For the liberty and freedom quote, see the following wire story: "Princeton Boos and Shoves Barnett," *Stanford Daily*, October 8, 1963. For the "infinitely more dangerous" quote, see George Cable Wright, "Princeton Crowd Hisses Barnett," *New York Times*, October 2, 1963. Regarding all other direct quotes, see James Markham, "Governor Fears Police State Rule," *DP*, October 2, 1963.

63. John H. Glick, "End Barnett Visit without Violence," *DP*, October 3, 1963; Frank Burgess, "Crowd Reaction Mixed in Press," *DP*, October 3, 1963.

64. Purser Hewitt, "Barnett Instructs New Jersey Crowd," *Clarion-Ledger*, October 2, 1963.

significant, too, that at Princeton, particularly, the demonstrations against the governor were mainly mounted by those outside the university, who led in the protest." To many southerners, American universities were under attack by outsiders. Mississippians especially felt this way following the forced desegregation of the University of Mississippi in late 1962. "Discourtesy in the extreme was shown, not to Governor Barnett, but to the state of Mississippi and to the basic principles of free speech and constitutional government," the editorial concluded. The irony of Mississippi journalists' disdain is that James W. Silver, a professor at the University of Mississippi in the early 1960s, said the southern white press fanned the flames of hate.[65]

As Barnett departed New Jersey, Goheen soon returned to campus from the ACE meeting in Washington—and to a mailbox full of conservative reactions to the Barnett situation. On October 2, three students—Edward J. Sylvester, Thomas B. Young, and Lynn Klotz—questioned why Goheen's statement "brought the wrath of heaven on the immorality of Gov. Ross Barnett" but said nothing about Malcolm X's appearance. The trio considered Barnett "a rabble-rousing, immoral demagogue, interested only in the personal profit he can make from a time of trouble." However, to them, "Malcolm X would be a Ross Barnett if he were white." The students shared their grievance with Goheen, believing that the administration was selective about which speakers to condemn and which ones students needed to hear. They asked: "Since when is the purpose of a university to determine to whom it will listen and to whom it will not?"[66]

The same day, C. W. Miles, class of 1933 from Union City, Tennessee, asked similar questions. During the previous spring, his father, W. M. Miles, wrote to Dunham about prioritizing Black students in admissions. Now, C. W. Miles found Goheen and Princeton students' actions toward Barnett too "disgraceful" for his tastes. "I know that you won't believe this," he told Goheen, "but the time will come when you and a great many other integrationists will witness the beginning of the fall of this republic when it becomes a mongrel race of half-breeds, as that is exactly what this integration problem will result in, if we have full integration." C. W. Miles, like his father told Dunham, felt Princeton was losing its southern atmosphere and its dignity. The majority of alumni sons like C. W. were nearly always admitted. Therefore, the push for more Black students also offended many alumni who feared their son's slot would be given

---

65. "Discourteous in the Extreme," *Vicksburg Evening Post*, October 2, 1963. On the white press and its role in racial violence, see Silver, *The Closed Society*, pp. 28–35.

66. Edward J. Sylvester, Thomas B. Young, and Lynn Klotz, "Malcolm X and Ross Barnett," *DP*, October 2, 1963.

to a Black person. In turn, C. W. Miles said his financial contributions would end, and he hoped his son would attend the University of Mississippi instead.[67]

Likewise, Charles R. Jacobs, a Chicago native who resided in Brookhaven, Mississippi, also protested Goheen's treatment of Barnett. Jacobs had no ties to Princeton, but he felt his unique experience as a Midwesterner living in the South gave him an understanding that Goheen did not have. "I believe that most northerners misunderstand the so-called segregationist," Jacobs explained. "The liberal press has painted a picture of a segregationist as a bigoted crackpot wearing a white sheet and probably a lynch rope hung over his shoulder." But segregation, he clarified, was not that. In schools, for instance, segregation was a conscious effort to isolate Black children with "backgrounds that, for the most part, are so immoral and unmoral" that they should not interact with white youth. "I'm sure that the type of Negro you come in contact with at Princeton," Jacobs attested, "is very different from the masses of that race."[68]

As the week after Barnett's visit continued, so did expressions of resentment of Princeton from across the nation. On October 3, Walter S. Cahall from Rosemont, Pennsylvania, told Goheen, "It was quite a shock to me to learn that Princeton is so low class, so communistic, so unfair." He felt Goheen and others had fallen for the Kennedy Administration's ploy to use civil rights to get the Black vote. "Princeton, from now on in my book, and of millions of others, is just a leftist dump." The same day, Gale Steele from Chattanooga, Tennessee, wrote, "Princeton has many, many students from the South, and they should be respected and their parents not insulted." A day later, on October 4, W. R. Cole Jr., from Louisville, Kentucky, said the anti-Barnett demonstrators caused "poor publicity for Princeton University," and by October 7, members of conservative student clubs at Princeton launched a new political journal to "combat the over-emphasis on liberal interpretation of events by the academic community." Despite the barrage of pro-segregation and anti-Black responses, these conservative voices were drowned out by a pro–civil rights sentiment, much as the Alexander Hall outdoor loudspeakers masked the civil rights demonstration on the night of Barnett's talk.[69]

67. C. W. Miles to Robert Goheen, October 2, 1963, Goheen Records, Box 425, Folder 3, Princeton. On alumni sons being largely admitted, see Bray, "On the Campus," p. 4; and Karabel, *The Chosen*, pp. 315–316. James W. Silver also noted how some southern social and political leaders were Ivy League educated. For more, see Silver, *The Closed Society*, pp. 25–26.

68. Charles R. Jacobs to Robert Goheen, October 2, 1963, Goheen Records, Box 425, Folder 3, Princeton.

69. Walter S. Cahall to Robert Goheen, October 3, 1963; Gale Steele to Robert Goheen, October 3, 1963; W. R. Cole, Jr. to Robert Goheen, October 4, 1963; all located in Goheen Records, Box 425, Folder 3, Princeton; "Conservatives Start Journal," *DP*, October 7, 1963.

The southern governor's presence inspired action among those sympathetic to civil rights causes. Articles about the day Barnett arrived at Princeton were paired with news coverage about the local borough mayoral candidate Minot C. Morgan's civil rights platform. "What little progress there has been in the field of civil rights in recent years in Princeton has been the result of the labors of dedicated individuals and volunteer groups," Morgan said. He also demanded that elected officials support such efforts. Relatedly, on October 2, Tyson of Mount Pisgah AME Church thanked Dean Lippincott on behalf of the Princeton Association for Human Rights for his cooperation with the civil rights rally. The campus support made the demonstration a success and permitted local Black residents to share their voices. "It allowed our citizens to express themselves peacefully, and through working together, the community was strengthened," Tyson said. In short, as the Daily Princetonian appraised the moment, "The outcry over the appearance of Governor Ross Barnett focuses attention sharply on Princeton's own segregation problem."[70]

The campus rally that greeted Barnett also "criticized past admissions discrimination and undergraduate apathy about the race problem," and it attracted students from Rutgers University, Newark State College, and Douglass College as participants. Some Princeton students considered his speech boring and a better fit for "an audience of flag-waving rightists or ardent racists." But what was most notable was the behavior exhibited by students from elsewhere. "We often malign our fellow students at Rutgers and Douglass and somehow consider ourselves superior," an editorial read in the Daily Princetonian. "But the conviction and dignity the hundreds from those schools displayed should force us to re-examine our stereotyped assessments." The editorial concluded: "They, not we, understand the joy, the expectation, the humor, the dedication that fuel the Negro's rightful cause." White students' awareness of free speech was linked to their understanding of social issues, which is what Goheen had spent years attempting to convey through the earlier controversial speakers. Now, there was an awakening among a significant portion of the Princeton student body, and there was also a fire within Goheen.[71]

70. "Rights Become Election Issue," DP, October 1, 1963; Albert D. Tyson, Jr. to W. D. Lippincott, October 2, 1963, Goheen Records, Box 425, Folder 3, Princeton; Dale Lasater, "Segregated Housing: Local Problem," DP, October 2, 1963.

71. On the admissions discrimination and student apathy critique, see Creesy, "Crowd Sings." At Newark State College, students enrolled in a civil rights class contacted Goheen's office about tickets to attend Barnett's talk: see Marge Cowenhoven to Dan Coyle, September 27, 1963, Goheen Records, Box 425, Folder 2, Princeton; "The Lesson of Barnett," DP, October 3, 1963. For more on white students, free speech, and civil rights, see Jo Freeman, "From

Goheen took the following weeks to catch up on Barnett-related correspondence. He personally thanked individuals for their role in ensuring safety of the campus. There was a note to Dominic R. Capello, superintendent of the New Jersey State Police, for his "excellent staff work." He shared his gratitude with H. Walter Dodwell, campus head security officer, for how well his team "shouldered the heavy responsibilities" associated with the Barnett visit. Goheen also sent similar letters of thanks to Princeton township mayor R. Kenneth Fairman and Princeton borough mayor Henry S. Patterson.[72]

But he was less courteous when he responded to C. W. Miles of Union City, Tennessee. It was Miles, the class of 1933 alumnus who, following Barnett's visit, informed Goheen that he would no longer contribute to Princeton. Miles's two-page rant against Goheen also concluded that he did "not expect an answer from this letter," but the president sent a sharp response. Goheen defended the students' behavior toward Barnett. He then questioned the governor's actions regarding the University of Mississippi and Miles's own aptitude as an attorney:

> My own deeply-felt disapproval of Governor Barnett stems from his open defiance of the laws of the United States, his actions so purely conducive to public violence, and his interference, as a governor, in the affairs of a university. The last, be it noted, was in violation of the Constitution of his own state. I find it difficult to understand how an attorney who practices law can condone open defiance of law by a public official.

Goheen also enclosed Dunham's 1963 Report to the Schools with its "Search for Negro Applicants" section on the cover. That closed the president's rebuttal to the disgruntled alumnus.[73]

This was the beginning of a more assertive Goheen as it pertained to racial equality. In all likelihood, if Barnett had not come, this strong stance on civil rights would have remained limited to Goheen's immediate administrative circle, but the governor's appearance and the adjacent civil rights rally

---

Freedom Now! to Free Speech: The FSM's Roots in the Bay Area Civil Rights Movement," in Cohen and Zelnik, *The Free Speech Movement*, pp. 73, 79–80.

72. Robert Goheen to Dominic R. Capello, October 4, 1963; Robert Goheen to H. W. Dodwell, October 4, 1963; Robert Goheen to R. Kenneth Fairman, October 4, 1963; Robert Goheen to Henry S. Patterson, October 4, 1963; all located in Goheen Records, Box 425, Folder 3, Princeton.

73. C. W. Miles to Goheen, October 2, 1963; and Robert Goheen to C. W. Miles, October 8, 1963; both in Goheen Records, Box 425, Folder 3, Princeton.

propelled several students to actively engage in civil rights activism. It also mobilized Goheen, and for the rest of the 1963–64 academic year, Princeton launched its first campaign in university history to address racial inequality.

Goheen: No More Lip Service

Just south of Princeton, after Barnett visited Princeton, University of Pennsylvania (Penn) administrators were evaluating an upcoming campus visit by George C. Wallace, the white supremacist governor of Alabama. The pending visit worried Chester E. Tucker, vice president for development and public relations at Penn, and he soon contacted Princeton's administrative vice president, Edgar M. Gemmell, to get his advice and insight. At Princeton, Gemmell described Barnett's talk as an opportunity to "form more friendly bonds and relationships with the Negro community here than ever before." Barnett's invitation was initially seen as a "slap in the face" to Princeton's Black community, and this prompted Goheen and others to meet with Black leaders. "Here on the campus we cooperated fully with their effort to engage in an orderly demonstration against Barnett's views with the understanding that they were not protesting against his right to speak," Gemmell explained to Tucker. "If we had not had the advance planning sessions with local Negro leadership, I suspect that we might have had a nasty mess on our hands." Although Penn, like Yale, eventually withdrew Wallace's invitation to speak on campus, citing the worsening "racial situation in Philadelphia" as the reason, for Tucker, Gemmell's advice was a blueprint for how to engage controversial speakers.[74]

On October 9, 1963, as Tucker and Gemmell discussed how to handle southern governors, Goheen emphasized the importance of desegregation in his remarks to the Whig-Clio Society, the debate group that had hosted Barnett only a week earlier. Before them, he gave opening comments to the society's Princeton Senate (the venue where opposing sides, the Whigs and the Clios, debated a particular topic), and civil rights were the topic of the night. "It seems highly significant, and certainly in keeping with the traditions of the society, that tonight you are debating in this hall—and on this campus—the Kennedy Administration's proposed civil rights legislation," said Goheen, who himself was a former Whig-Clio trustee. "There is, I think, no issue more pressing or more basic to the well-being of country at this particular juncture."

---

74. Chester E. Tucker to Edgar M. Gemmell, October 8, 1963; Edgar A. Gemmell to Chester E. Tucker, October 10, 1963; Chester E. Tucker to Edgar M. Gemmell, October 11, 1963; all in Goheen Records, Box 425, Folder 3, Princeton. On Wallace's speaking tour, see Permaloff and Grafton, *Politics and Power*, p. 200.

Indeed, he believed the civil rights struggles were the central societal issue, and he displayed this belief in the coming weeks.[75]

There was no more defining moment for Goheen than the one that occurred four days after the Whig-Clio's Princeton Senate. On Sunday, October 13, he shared the stage at the Princeton Playhouse with Reverend Tyson. The two men discussed the town's segregation issues during a fundraiser and showing of the film "Gone Are the Days." The film satirized race relations in its story of a Black minister who wanted to build an integrated church in the Deep South. Sponsored by the Princeton Association for Human Rights, proceeds went to the Elizabeth Taylor Byrd Fund designed to support and help local Black children enroll in college.[76]

Before a capacity audience of 1,200 people, Goheen delivered a passionate challenge to the town and campus. His thirty-minute talk focused exclusively on racial equality and what he called "The Revolution of 1963." He said, "the American Negro seeks justice in the sense of an equal chance both to share in and contribute to the total well-being of his community, his region, and his nation." There were vast economic and educational hurdles Black people faced, and it would require years to address those issues. Yet, those were not valid reasons to not work to improve race relations. "Even as we recognize these obstacles and these failings, surely, we must recognize also the no longer excusable, no longer postponable, no-longer-to-be-met-with-lip-service need to break through them to attain for Negroes no less than whites fair share in the rights and opportunities which this nation affords," Goheen said.[77]

In this spirit, he said it was time for a Second Princeton Plan (in 1948, the Princeton Plan for School Integration became a national model) that would address housing inequality, employment opportunities, equitable education, and fair treatment in public accommodations. Goheen then explained that the university real estate office no longer listed properties where there was evidence of discrimination. Goheen was also ready to ensure that campus contractors had fair employment practices and that university-owned properties were open to all races. From there, he challenged residents, those affiliated with the university or not, to do the same. "Let us dedicate ourselves tonight to the need for a far greater and more taxing response . . . to the achievement in this community of equal and open opportunities in all areas," Goheen

75. Notes for Whig-Clio Talk, October 9, 1963, Goheen Records, Box 315, Folder 3, Princeton; "Goheen's Address Will Open Senate," *DP*, October 9, 1963.

76. "Rights Movie at Playhouse," *DP*, October 10, 1963; Press Release, October 5, 1963, Goheen Records, Box 296, Folder 7, Princeton.

77. "Gone Are the Days" speech, October 13, 1963, Goheen Records, Box 315, Folder 3, Princeton.

urged. "This is no less than what the time and the Negroes' fair claim to justice demand of us all." This talk struck a chord with Princetonians, who interrupted his speech four times with applause, especially when he spoke about his plan to remove local properties that discriminated from the university's housing list. Furthermore, the event raised $2,200 for the fund.[78]

The next day, on October 14, the *Daily Princetonian* launched its series on undergraduate opinion on the civil rights movement. In a national survey of students, a range of questions were administered, and the student newspaper separately presented the results of respondents at southern and border-state universities and those in the Northeast, Midwest, and the West. The student journalists did not interrogate regional nuance or define border state versus southern state, but the results were telling for Goheen and others interested in civil rights. There were stark differences in that 77.7 percent of students in the South favored segregation compared with only 14.9 percent from other regions. Similarly, 67.4 percent of those in the South felt "the Negro is asking for too much change, too soon in his ongoing civil rights drive," while 42 percent of nonsoutherners felt the same. These differences soon gave way to similarities as both groups—nonsoutherners (92.7 percent) and southerners (93.8 percent)—were in favor of Governor Ross Barnett's visit to Princeton on October 1. Likewise, both nonsoutherners (82.5 percent) and southerners (85.3 percent) largely opposed quota systems for Black people.[79]

For some Princeton students, or at least those on the student newspaper staff, civil rights issues were a southern versus nonsouthern problem; however, Goheen knew that white supremacists and their sympathizers were everywhere. Navigating the southern alumni was more about ideology than geographic location. For instance, the day before Barnett's arrival, John H. Morrell from Hartford, Connecticut, lambasted Goheen for his statement on Barnett, and weeks after the governor's visit, Barry J. Howard from North Merrick, New York, wrote to the *New York Times Magazine* to express his displeasure with how Princeton treated the governor.[80]

Goheen's public declaration of intent to eradicate racial discrimination did not halt conservative resistance. In fact, it may have outright inspired it. That said, his suggested Second Princeton Plan still needed to maneuver past the lingering effect of Barnett's visit. In the October 15 issue of the *Princeton Alumni*

78. "Gone Are the Days"; on the audience reaction, see "Goheen Calls for Action on Equal Opportunities," *DP*, October 14, 1963.

79. Mel M. Masuda, "Most Southerners in 'Prince' Poll Oppose Segregation," *DP*, October 14, 1963; Mel M. Masuda, "South, North Groups Oppose Quotas," *DP*, October 16, 1963.

80. Morrell to Goheen, September 30, 1963; Barry J. Howard, Letter to the Editor, *New York Times Magazine*, December 1, 1963.

Weekly, an article acknowledged that "the large fact of the governor's presence would sit before that potential and so hard-to-find Negro applicant whom Admissions Director E. Alden Dunham would be trying to convince to come to Princeton."[81]

This point was not lost on Dunham who, on October 21, bluntly shared as much with Goheen. The admissions director had just returned to campus from a two-week trip to visit prep schools when he thanked Goheen for his actions while he was away recruiting. "I have just read the text of your talk before the civil rights group on October 13. I think it is excellent and wonder if a wider distribution of it may be in order," Dunham told Goheen. "Also, I enjoyed reading your hard-hitting letter to Mr. Miles in Tennessee (October 8). Last year, he blasted me in a letter for showing interest in Negro students." Dunham appreciated Goheen's willingness to fight back against racists and execute initiatives to address racial discrimination. Those public declarations were key to shifting the Princeton culture. The president's actions gave permission to other areas of campus (e.g., admissions, real estate, human resources) to think similarly as it pertained to race, but further action would require the university trustees' support at the next board meeting.[82]

On a Friday morning, October 25, 1963, the trustees and administrators met in the Faculty Room of Nassau Hall. Princeton was not without its share of notable men on its trustee board. Alumnus Allen W. Dulles, former director of the Central Intelligence Agency, from Washington, DC, was in attendance. So, too, was alumnus John D. Rockefeller III, the oldest son in a multigeneration philanthropist family, from New York City, among other influential corporate, government, and judicial leaders. Before this group, Goheen delivered the president's report as was customary for trustee board meetings, and he focused on alumni, free speech, and the university's responsibility to Black people.[83]

Goheen first discussed the need to further educate Princeton alumni because several of them did not understand the institution's prominence as a university. The university needed to protect its national reputation while alumni, after seeing Goheen's changes, were mostly engrained in protecting a semblance of their student experience. Next, Goheen discussed how five national or international figures had visited campus before the end of October 1963, and another four were scheduled for November with more planned

81. James M. Markham, "On the Campus," *PAW*, October 15, 1963.

82. E. Alden Dunham to Robert Goheen, October 21, 1963, Goheen Records, Box 339, Folder 3, Princeton.

83. Board of Trustees Meeting Minutes, October 25, 1963, Goheen Records, Box 66, Folder 4, Princeton.

for future semesters. Among the five, Barnett posed the most difficulties. Goheen told trustees the amount of time Gemmell, Lippincott, and Coyle spent explaining the importance of free speech and conversing with local Black leaders. Goheen also discussed the various perspectives seen in media coverage as nonsouthern journalists reported that the Barnett audience was controlled and southern journalists noted the crowd was rowdy. Lastly, and most importantly, Goheen drew the trustees' attention to the role of the university regarding Black people. He then read the first paragraphs of his October 13 talk at the Princeton Playhouse to "make his personal conviction on this matter very clear."[84]

Goheen told the trustees that his own beliefs and his conduct as president were intertwined. Therefore, the president's office would focus on equality for Black people as long as he led the university. His ideas included summer institutes for underprivileged youth, similar to an existing program at Yale, or an affiliation with a Black college. The University of Michigan and Tuskegee Institute in Alabama had a partnership and Colgate University was planning one with Lincoln University in Pennsylvania. Dunham also communicated with the United Negro College Fund (UNCF) to share ideas and resources with independent prep schools. All of these potential programs meant one thing to Goheen: an opportunity for more Black people to attend college whether at Princeton or elsewhere. It was clear where he stood. He made no deviation from any previous statement, letter, or speech. Afterward, Harold H. Helm, board chair, echoed his satisfaction with the desire to advance the university's national stature, and no other trustee interfered with Goheen's goals. He had the board's approval.[85]

The following week, on October 29, Goheen wasted no time publicly explaining his actions related to fighting racial discrimination. It was revealed that two married Black undergraduates were living in university housing reserved for a limited number of graduate students. When confronted about the irregularity, Goheen said: "Sometimes, as here, it is necessary to treat people unequally in order to afford them equal opportunities." On November 4, Goheen explained how the civil rights unrest awakened the administration to do more for US-born Black students. "For the past decade, we have been terribly concerned with what we could do for the students from underdeveloped countries," he said. "It took a shock to make us realize our problems at home."[86]

84. Ibid.

85. Ibid. For more on Goheen-approved programs for Black students, see Bradley, *Upending the Ivory Tower*, pp. 58–61.

86. Charles Creesy, "Administration Explains Policy of Negroes' Housing Privileges," *DP*, October 29, 1963; "Goheen Defines Parietal Rules, Negroes' Housing, Admissions," *DP*, November 4, 1963.

The next day, it was reported that Goheen and Kenneth M. Rendall Jr., manager of university housing, had removed two local property owners from the university's housing list due to discrimination. Two days after that, on November 7, Goheen committed university personnel to "advance the movement toward open and equal opportunities for Negroes" across university accommodations, housing, admissions, and employment. Specific to employment, Ricardo A. Mestres, financial vice president and treasurer, said the university was in talks with three building contractors regarding fair employment. The next week, on November 14, J. Merrill Knapp, dean of the college, noted that Ivy League university registrars had formed a committee to recruit more Black students. "Everyone realized at the time the committee was formed last year that they had to do more than just talk about attracting capable young Negroes," Knapp explained. "They had to actually do something about it."[87]

That call to action was most pronounced a week later, on November 22, 1963, when US president John F. Kennedy was assassinated in Dallas. The *Daily Princetonian* captured the moment in its headline, "Kennedy Met National Needs, 'Sounded the Call to Action.'" Any program that a college or university had adopted related to civil rights had answered Kennedy's call. Since the 1960 presidential election, he had pushed for stronger civil rights legislation and battled southern governors, including Ross Barnett, who had just criticized Kennedy during his Princeton talk. The death also hit close to home for Goheen, who was personally acquainted with Kennedy. In 1958, for example, Goheen during his first-year as Princeton president sat between then–US senator Kennedy and trustee Rockefeller III during a luncheon at the Shoreham Hotel in Washington, DC. Goheen considered Kennedy's death a byproduct of racism and hatred: "In shock and sorrow, we have come to see that the events in Dallas were symptomatic of widespread currents of hate and callousness and bigotry, seething blindly and destructively through many parts of the American society and endangering all we hold to be reasonable and right and dear." Yet, in shock and sorrow, campus administrators pressed forward.[88]

In December 1963, Goheen and Dunham planned to discuss Black student recruitment during the next trustee board meeting, and in January 1964,

87. Mel M. Masuda, "Owners Taken off Housing List," *DP*, November 5, 1963; "Talks Set on Hiring Practices," *DP*, November 7, 1963; Masuda, "Ivy Colleges Encourage Negro Applicants."

88. For the Kennedy assassination coverage, see the second issue of *DP* published on November 22, 1963; Robert Goheen Statement to Faculty Meeting, December 2, 1963, Goheen Records, Box 315, Folder 3, Princeton. On Kennedy and Goheen being acquainted, see the cover of the February 16, 1962, issue of the *PAW*.

Dunham presented to trustees the benefits of Black students. First, their enrollment was of national interest to provide leadership for future generations of
Black people, and secondly, Black students brought needed diversity and en-
riched all students. As board chair, Helm acknowledged Dunham's job would
be unpopular. He then encouraged other areas of campus to relieve the pressure on the admissions director and instructed other trustees to form a subcommittee to determine how the board could help. That same month, the
university announced its new summer program for forty youths from "disadvantaged urban environments."[89]

Then, in February 1964, Goheen met with other college presidents at the
Carnegie Corporation offices in New York City to investigate the long-term
undertaking to work with Black colleges. As a university with national stature,
Princeton was positioned to shape racial practices throughout higher education. Goheen's efforts soon started to come to fruition, a testament to which
was class of 1930 alumnus Burton T. Wilson's letter from Washington, DC, on
February 25, 1964. In response to the summer program, Wilson said: "When
this program becomes a reality, we can all feel we have indeed participated in
the nation's service."[90]

Conclusion

Robert F. Goheen at Princeton demonstrated the role college presidents
played in providing free speech protections for campus and, by extension, academic freedom for faculty. This role was underscored by the October 1963
campus appearance of Ross Barnett, the segregationist governor of Mississippi. This particular free speech controversy highlighted the transformations
occurring throughout higher education. As historian Stefan M. Bradley, author of *Upending the Ivory Tower*, noted, "The number of black students who
attended Princeton did not increase significantly until after 1963." Although a
variety of social changes and watershed moments in American history occurred that year, the racial makeup of Princeton was unlikely to have changed
the way it did if Goheen had attempted to have the student society rescind the
invitation to Governor Barnett in late 1963. There was something to be learned

89. Robert Goheen to E. Alden Dunham, December 10, 1964, Goheen President Records,
Box 66 Folder 4, Princeton; Board of Trustees Meeting Minutes, January 10, 1964, Goheen
Records, Box 66, Folder 5, Princeton; "University News," *PAW*, January 21, 1964.

90. On the Carnegie meeting, see Mina Rees to Robert Goheen, January 7, 1964, Goheen
Records, Box 176, Folder 7, Princeton; and Robert Goheen to Mina Rees, January 15, 1964,
Goheen Records, Box 176, Folder 7, Princeton; Burton T. Wilson, "Negro Applicants," *PAW*,
February 25, 1964.

from Barnett, despite his conflict with Goheen's personal views, because of what Mississippi and the broader South represented. In fact, Mario Savio, leader of the Berkeley Free Speech Movement in 1964, said his Mississippi experience transformed his perspective. "I had to go to Mississippi . . . ," Savio recalled about the summer of 1964. "So I went and I had my touch with reality."[91]

Goheen understood this reality. His tenure as president required a great degree of patience because he knew the traditions and culture of Princeton and its long history of a southern presence, in both ideals and actions, required negotiating. Southern alumni could not be immediately dismissed, regardless of how Goheen felt about racial segregation, but the admissions practices that relied on alumni networks were unreliable if Princeton was going to expand its intellectual offerings. These dynamics required a gradual push to diversify the student body and address local discrimination. Therefore, by supporting Barnett's right to speak, Goheen ventured into unchartered territory. At Yale University, in 1963, provost and acting president Kingman Brewster asked a student group to withdraw its invitation to segregationist governor George C. Wallace due to potential violence. Similarly, at the University of Pennsylvania, President Gaylord P. Harnwell and other administrators weighed Wallace's scheduled November 1963 lecture until law students withdrew their invitation. The situation at Princeton was different.[92]

Considering Princeton's prominence in higher education, Goheen's willingness to engage controversial speakers went a long way toward broadening the question of free speech and race. Goheen demonstrated the tensions between a college president's personal convictions and their formal duties as an academic leader. As demands for racial equality increased, college presidents at nonsouthern colleges and universities revisited what, if anything, they were doing to address racism. In 1960, only one Black student enrolled as a freshman at Princeton, and the same was the case with the freshman class entering in 1961; however, Goheen maintained his goals, and Princeton secured twenty Black applicants in 1963 and seventy-two in 1964. By 1968, Princeton counted forty-four Black students among the incoming freshman class. Even some white alumni, such as Charles Puttkammer, class of 1958, started to question other aspects of Princeton, and he felt recruiting Black students was important

91. Bradley, *Upending the Ivory Tower*, p. 58; Mario Savio, "Thirty Years Later: Reflections on the FSM," in Cohen and Zelnik, *Free Speech Movement*, p. 64.

92. On the University of Pennsylvania and George Wallace, see this chapter's previously cited exchange between UPenn's Chester E. Tucker and Princeton's Edgar M. Gemmell. For a brief account on Yale University and George Wallace, see Peter Savoley, "Free Speech, Personified," *New York Times*, November 26, 2017.

but Princeton also had to overcome a reputation of discrimination that went back to Woodrow Wilson's presidency at the university. In the end, Goheen's approach to speech and race distinguished him as a model for other presidents—including Clark Kerr at the University of California—and demonstrated that condemning racist speech was not enough, but instead, campus initiatives must align with touted values. The question about race moving forward, however, was how Princeton's effort to recruit more Black students would fit within the array of new affirmative action programs on college campuses.[93]

93. On the Black student admissions totals, see Karabel, *The Chosen*, pp. 393–394; Charles Puttkammer, "Negro Applicants," *PAW*, January 28, 1964. Puttkammer also authored a report, *Negroes in the Ivy League*, in 1962. On Woodrow Wilson as Princeton's president, see Bradley, *Upending the Ivory Tower*, p. 50. For more about Princeton since the Woodrow Wilson presidency, see Axtell, *The Making of Princeton University*.

7

"A Truly Influential Role"

COLLEGE PRESIDENTS DEVELOP
AFFIRMATIVE ACTION PROGRAMS

"I WRITE YOU personally to seek your help in solving the grave civil rights problems faced by this nation," read a letter from US president John F. Kennedy. It was July 12, 1963, when Kennedy sought the assistance of Carl E. Steiger, head of the University of Wisconsin Board of Regents. Racism disenfranchised Black citizens across multiple facets of life. Furthermore, the persistent violence of white supremacists toward Black people only magnified the hypocrisy of American democracy. Perhaps most pressing, racial discrimination in employment and education were linked, and there were no indications that race relations would improve for future generations. President Kennedy was forced to make good on his campaign promises, but the question became how. Thus, he turned to the leaders of the nation's colleges and universities for the answer. "The leadership that you and your colleagues show in extending equal educational opportunity today," Kennedy told Steiger, "will influence American life for decades to come."[1]

College presidents were called upon to develop programs that would help rectify racial inequities in society. The presidents of Black and white colleges and universities worked to address those issues and, combined, outlined ambitious affirmative action initiatives that were applicable to all of higher education. Across the nation, a broad array of programs were implemented: race-based admissions practices at white institutions, summer institutes for Black college faculty, advanced graduate-level training for Black college faculty,

---

1. John F. Kennedy to Carl E. Steiger, July 12, 1963, Fred Harvey Harrington Papers, Box 40, Folder: Civil Rights–Human Rights Institute–Anti-Poverty–Sam Proctor, UW-Madison Archives (collection, folder name, and location hereafter cited as Harrington Papers, Civil Rights–Sam Proctor, and UW). Kennedy also became consumed with addressing poverty after reading reviews of Michael Harrington's *The Other America*, published in 1962. For more, see Herbert Mitgang, "Michael Harrington, Socialist and Author, Is Dead," *New York Times*, April 2, 1989.

exchange programs between faculty and students at Black and white colleges, and research institutes focused on race, among other initiatives. Academic leaders pursued an imaginative, far-reaching educational opportunity platform that meant more institutions could serve the millions of disenfranchised Black people living in apartheid America, and Kennedy endorsed these programs; however, the motivations behind such efforts differed between the presidents of Black and white colleges and universities.

The programs focused on the nation's Black institutions were quickly deserted by white academic leaders, who were responsible for dismantling the system-wide plan, as they reneged on supporting initiatives that aided all of higher education. Those white leaders were motivated by publicity and private foundation support and seized affirmative action as an opportunity to concentrate on their specific institutional goals (e.g., enrolling more Black students) rather than on system-wide cooperation. At the University of Wisconsin (UW), where US president John F. Kennedy first encouraged such programs, President Fred Harvey Harrington was especially active in developing affirmative action programs. Harrington's actions demonstrate that a combination of factors, not just the racial unrest of the 1960s, inspired white college presidents to act. This narrowing from system-wide to individual goals ultimately omitted Black colleges, revealing how presidents developed affirmative action and left a lasting impact on higher education.

Tragedy Meets Opportunity

On Friday, July 27, 1962, at 8:15 a.m., UW president Conrad A. Elvehjem suffered a heart attack in his Bascom Hall office. He was rushed to Madison General Hospital where, an hour later, he was pronounced dead, with his wife, Constance, and son, Robert, at his bedside. Suffering from a "sudden coronary occlusion," Elvehjem's death shocked the campus since he had participated in a Telstar demonstration the previous afternoon. It was the tragic end to a tumultuous four-year presidency, which was embroiled in conflicts with student demonstrations, budgetary issues, and administrative turnover, but his untimely death also presented an urgent opportunity. The board of regents did not have the luxury of time for a long, drawn-out national search for Elvehjem's successor, but they needed someone who could manage burgeoning social and political changes occurring across the nation.[2]

2. "Elvehjem Dies: Suffers Heart Attack This Morning in Office," *Daily Cardinal,* July 27, 1962 (newspaper hereafter cited as *DC*); "Heart Attack Ends Career of UW's Conrad Elvehjem," *Wisconsin State Journal,* July 28, 1962 (newspaper hereafter cited as *WSJ*).

Four days later, on August 1, 1962, Fred Harvey Harrington accepted the UW presidency. Harrington had joined the university in 1937 as an instructor of history. In 1940, he briefly left Wisconsin for a position at the University of Arkansas before returning in 1944. By 1947, he was promoted to full professor and served as chair of UW's history department from 1952 to 1955. After a yearlong research leave in Europe supported by Fulbright and Ford Foundation grants, Harrington became special assistant to UW president Edwin B. Fred, who retired in 1957. As a result, in 1958, Harrington was seriously considered by the regents to replace Fred, but they hired Elvehjem instead. Therefore, Harrington was a natural successor to Elvehjem, having served as vice president of the university under him.[3]

This was important, considering how divisive the regents' decision was to hire Elvehjem in 1958. Edwin B. Fred was a bacteriologist, and Elvehjem's similar academic background as a world-renowned biochemist may explain why his presidency started without universal support. In the 1950s, as postwar higher education enrollments increased and Cold War interests were prioritized, academics and industry leaders debated the emphasis on the physical sciences. Elvehjem's selection was considered another slight against the humanities and social sciences. "Dr. Elvehjem is undoubtedly aware of the widespread apprehension which has existed over the selection of another physical scientist to head the university at a time of increasing concern over the neglect of the social sciences," assessed an April 1958 editorial in the *Capital Times*, a local daily newspaper. "Because of the growing realization of the seriousness of the great gap between our social science and our physical science, Dr. Elvehjem's administration is going to be under unusually close scrutiny."[4]

In addition to the scholarly divide, in March 1960, during Elvehjem's second year as president, UW students held a civil rights rally in solidarity with Black students in the South. Elvehjem was booed when he critiqued the students' protest methods, offered unsolicited advice, and called the students' behavior inconsistent. In 1961, Governor Gaylord Nelson publicly criticized Elvehjem for his failure to get state legislators to approve the university's budget request and, by 1962, more turmoil swirled as three senior administrators—the dean of the medical school, the dean of letters and science, and Harrington (then

3. John Patrick Hunter, "Hint Harrington to Head U: Predict Offer by Regents," *Capital Times*, July 28, 1962 (newspaper hereafter cited as *CT*).

4. "Some Advice about Education for Dr. Elvehjem to Ponder," *CT*, April 17, 1958.

vice president)—were fired, resigned, and accepted a position at another university, respectively.[5]

This was the administrative situation when the fifty-year-old Harrington assumed the presidency. The day after Elvehjem's passing, on July 28, 1962, the executive committee for the board of regents requested that Harrington return to Wisconsin from Japan, where he was teaching a seminar at the University of Kyoto. After the seminar, he was supposed to assume the presidency of the University of Hawaii. Yet, Harrington accepted the UW regents' request. In a statement published in the *Honolulu Advertiser* and reprinted in the *Wisconsin State Journal*, Harrington reneged on the Hawaii presidency with "a great deal of reluctance." He added:

> The death last Friday of the president of the University of Wisconsin Conrad A. Elvehjem, the man under whom I served, and the institution with which I have been associated for 20 years has presented a crisis which representatives of the Wisconsin faculty, the deans, and the Wisconsin regents today convinced me, demand my services here.

Hawaii's board agreed to release Harrington from his contract, but there was disappointment. "Your glee in Wisconsin at his appointment came as a shock to Hawaii," wrote Chonita Newport of Honolulu, citing travel expenses accrued by the university. "Let us hope that the University of Wisconsin will consider repaying the latter to the people of Hawaii. And, to Dr. Harrington, thanks for nothing!" But a few angry responses from Hawaii were hardly noticed in Wisconsin.[6]

5. Regarding the Wisconsin students' civil rights rallies, see "Plan Sympathy March to Square Thursday," *DC*, March 1, 1960; "SLIC May Await Vote by Senators," *DC*, March 2, 1960; "Many Faculty Give Protest Solid Support," *DC*, March 2, 1960; John Patrick Hunter, "500 Attend Campus Protest over Negro Mistreatment: Rally Is Orderly and Enthusiastic," *CT*, March 4, 1960; "Further Action Planned at Rally," *DC*, March 4, 1960. Also see Levin, *Cold War University*, pp. 113–114. On the university budget request, see John Patrick Hunter, "Nelson Says U.W. Has Failed to Sell Budget to Public," *CT*, December 15, 1960. Regarding the administrative issues, see John Patrick Hunter, "U. of Oregon May Call Harrington," *CT*, February 22, 1961; "Oregon U. Eyes Fred Harrington for Presidency," *WSJ*, February 22, 1961; "L&S Dean Ingraham Resigns: Charges Culture Unbalance," *DC*, April 11, 1961; "Faculty Praises Dean Ingraham," *DC*, October 3, 1961; Samuel C. Reynolds, "Bowers Fired as Dean on Regents' 8–1 Vote," *WSJ*, October 21, 1961.

6. "Dr. Harrington Reluctantly Asks Hawaii Release," *WSJ*, August 1, 1962; "A Word from Hawaii," *Milwaukee Journal*, August 15, 1962. On Harrington's age, see Hunter, "Hint Harrington to Head U."

Noting his physical stature—standing six feet, four inches tall—Wisconsin journalists considered Harrington a "big man" fit for a big job. Farther north in the state, the *Appleton Post-Crescent* said Harrington entered the job "with the richest training of any man who has occupied the presidential chair in Bascom Hall in half a century." Now, he was tasked with picking up one of Elvehjem's greatest challenges: negotiating the university's budget. The university needed a spokesperson who could articulate to the governor and state legislators the institution's financial needs. This was an area in which Governor Nelson considered Elvehjem to have been lacking. Harrington's fluid speaking ability gave the university community "the most confidence in its new leader." His view as a historian, too, would be key to his understanding of the administration's past snafus and using that viewpoint to lead the university. There was excitement and optimism about Harrington, and the president's office hummed with a new tone.[7]

Harrington's selection received "universal approval." One editorial called him "a popular choice," and he was revered as a historian as well as being a "fine administrator." His personality was also notable. "He also possesses an attribute highly necessary in these days of weird collegiate behavior—a good sense of humor," read one newspaper report. He was described by friends "as a natural leader, no matter what the group or the situation." A native of New York, he earned his undergraduate degree at Cornell and his doctorate from New York University, and at UW, he was a "quick-wired, decisive administrator" and a scholar whose "rapid-fire lectures were always delivered without notes." A mere week after Elvehjem's death, the regents had executed "the smoothest succession of command in the modern history of the school."[8]

By October 1962, Dean of Students LeRoy Luberg had provided Harrington with updates on campus issues relevant to the president's office. The updates included background on the Human Rights Committee, Civil Rights Committee, and campus budget. Regarding human rights, Luberg explained that campus fraternities and sororities wanted the freedom to initiate new members regardless of their "race, creed, or national origin." This was especially important since the Delta Gamma sorority chapter at Beloit College in Beloit, Wisconsin, was reprimanded by its national headquarters because they initiated a Black student. As for civil rights, Luberg told Harrington that he had

7. John Wyngaard, "UW's President-Designate Brings Historians View to Leadership," *Appleton Post-Crescent*, August 5, 1962; Hunter, "Nelson Says U.W. Has Failed."

8. "A Popular Choice," *Monroe Evening Times*, August 2, 1962; "Harrington Described as Natural Leader: New UW President Regards University as One of Four Best in Entire Nation," *Appleton Post-Crescent*, August 3, 1962; Wyngaard, "UW's President-Designate."

met with students and wondered if they could set a "pattern of quiet demonstrations." Meanwhile, the student senate volunteered to help with the budget concerns by footing the bill for a banquet for legislators. Once Harrington got a handle on matters privately, he started to articulate his hopes and plans for the university publicly.[9]

On October 1, 1962, Harrington's first faculty address emphasized his desire for the UW faculty to exercise its rights and responsibilities. To him, a strong faculty led to a better president, regents, and overall university. "I believe in this strong faculty role, just as I believe in academic freedom and the right of professors to speak," he said. His goal for the faculty members was for them to take on roles as policy leaders on campus, such as joining university-wide committees beyond their respective departments or units. The night before Harrington's call to action, a white mob had gathered at the University of Mississippi to prevent James Meredith from enrolling as the first Black student at that institution. The violence in Mississippi between supporters of segregationist governor Ross Barnett and of US president John F. Kennedy unfolded on international television and radio airwaves. The result: two people were killed and scores more were injured by the morning of October 1. Several Mississippians, including many faculty, had not voiced their disagreement with Barnett. Therefore, it is no coincidence that Harrington challenged the UW faculty to speak out willingly on issues.[10]

Three weeks later, on October 21, Harrington delivered his inaugural address titled, "The University and the State." He envisioned a university immersed in the "free and democratic search for truth and for new ways to improve the lot of mankind." Thus, the rapid, postwar campus growth paired well with Harrington's expectation that a bigger and better UW would serve the state better than ever before. After that address, on November 10, Harrington told the board of directors of the UW Alumni Association that he backed free speech, including radical speakers. "We think they ought to come here; we think that part of the business of education is to listen to all points of views," he explained. "I can't believe the students are going to turn to communism by listening to Gus Hall [leader of the Communist Party USA]. I think they will

9. Leroy Luberg to Fred H. Harrington, October 11, 1962, Harrington Papers, Box 22, Folder: Students, Dean of, Luberg, L. E., UW; John Patrick Hunter, "Beloit Sorority Suspended: U.W. May Close Unit," CT, July 12, 1962.

10. "Harrington Backs UW Faculty Rights," WSJ, October 2, 1962. Harrington's support of academic freedom is noteworthy for this time period. It represents a stark contrast to events at the University of Mississippi. For more on that university's chancellor, John Davis Williams, see chapter 4 of this book. For a comprehensive history of the conflicts between race and academic freedom in the South, specifically from 1955 to 1975, see Williamson-Lott, Jim Crow Campus.

learn to fight communism by listening to him." Within his first months as president, Harrington had urged faculty to exert themselves and allowed students to welcome a range of speakers to campus. Whereas Elvehjem once cautioned students about potential violence at a civil rights rally, Harrington welcomed dialogue around the most pressing issues of the day.[11]

Harrington encouraged the university faculty to insert themselves into policy discussions inside and outside of the classrooms. He did not oppose conflicting views if they resulted in greater good for the university, the state, and the nation. He also wanted a presence beyond campus, and on December 14, he was elected to the board of the Johnson Foundation in Racine, Wisconsin. That move foreshadowed the civil rights opportunities ahead of him and other college presidents.[12]

During the winter break, a press release dated December 28, 1962, arrived from University of Michigan vice president Wilbur K. Pierpont. The release noted that the Michigan regents agreed to comply with John F. Kennedy's President's Committee on Equal Employment Opportunity (PCEEO) request for statistics on university employees from "minority groups." The request was sent to entities, including universities, with federal government contracts, and Pierpont sent a copy of the press release to the other Big Ten universities, the University of Chicago, and the University of California. It was information-only for Michigan's peer institutions regarding this particular request from the Kennedy Administration, but it also indicated a larger shift in the federal government's expectations for universities and equal opportunity for Black people.[13]

College Presidents Implement Racial Programs

In 1963, Harrington joined a national movement among college presidents to develop an array of programs their universities would undertake to help ameliorate the nation's racial crisis and answer the Kennedy Administration's request. Elected in November 1960, Kennedy had campaigned on the need for

11. "The University and the State" (inaugural address), October 20, 1962, Biographical File: Fred Harvey Harrington, UW; John Patrick Hunter, "Backs Free Speech for All at U.W.," *CT*, November 10, 1962.

12. Harrington Elected Johnson Foundation Trustee, press release, December 14, 1962, Biographical File, Fred Harvey Harrington, Folder: Harrington, Fred H. Professor of History, UW.

13. Michigan Regents Press Release, December 21, 1962, Harrington Papers, Box 40, Folder: Civil Rights including "underprivileged"–"Negroes"–etc. (folder hereafter cited as Civil Rights), UW; Wilbur E. Pierpont to Select Group of Academic Leaders, December 28, 1962, Harrington Papers, Box 40, Folder: Civil Rights, UW.

stronger federal civil legislation, ultimately defeating the Republican Richard Nixon, who largely avoided discussing the sit-ins and other civil rights demonstrations. Kennedy was also unlike his predecessor, Dwight Eisenhower, who believed in states' rights; however, the first two years of the Kennedy Administration mirrored much of the same political hesitancy on racism as Eisenhower. In March 1961, Kennedy signed Executive Order 10925 instead of calling outright for a Congress-approved bill. The order was focused on employment and issued specific requirements of government contractors. "The contractor will take affirmative action to ensure that applicants are employed, and that employees are treated during employment, without regard to their race, creed, color, or national origin." This was the first time a federal government document used "affirmative action," a phrase coined by Hobart Taylor, a Black attorney in the White House, and the order established the PCEEO, a group limited to an advisory role without a budget or the authority to enforce the order. Otherwise, Kennedy did not push for the stronger civil rights bill because of known resistance from the southern members of Congress.[14]

Throughout 1962, academic leaders made gradual efforts to expand educational opportunities for Black students. For instance, Yale hired Charles Mc-Carthy, a recent graduate, to recruit Black students. This hire occurred during the 1961–62 academic year, shortly after Executive Order 10925 was signed and, in 1962, during the annual meeting of Ivy League admissions officers, the seven other institutions sought to learn more about McCarthy's work at Yale. The discourse gave rise to the Cooperative Program for Educational Opportunity, an initiative where Ivy League institutions and Seven Sisters women's colleges expanded their applicant pools by recruiting Black students. In the fall of 1962, Kennedy called a meeting at the White House with the academic leaders of five leading universities, including Harvard and Yale, asking them to help "make a difference" on race. About the same time, Kennedy also welcomed Black college presidents to the White House as he endorsed the United Negro College Fund (UNCF).[15]

14. On Kennedy and affirmative action, see Anderson, *Pursuit of Fairness*, pp. 59–62; on Anderson's assessment of Eisenhower and race, see p. 51. In addition to Anderson's *Pursuit of Fairness*, several texts credit Executive Order 10925 as the first federal document to use the phrase "affirmative action." Two examples are Perry, *Michigan Affirmative Action Case*, pp. 6–7; and Cokorinos, *Assault on Diversity*, p. 17. To read the order, see John F. Kennedy, Executive Order 10925, March 6, 1961, US Equal Employment Opportunity Commission, https://www.eeoc.gov/eeoc/history/35th/thelaw/eo-10925.html (accessed April 10, 2019).

15. On the McCarthy hire, Kennedy's "make a difference" request, and the Cooperative Program for Educational Opportunity, see Karabel, *The Chosen*, p. 381; and Duffy and Goldberg,

The next year—1963—was pivotal in the fight to end segregation. Author and activist James Baldwin's *The Fire Next Time* was published that year as a vivid account of racism in America. In April, prominent minister and civil rights leader Martin Luther King Jr. joined other civil rights leaders to lead the Birmingham Campaign, a series of demonstrations against segregation in the Alabama city. While there, King was arrested and penned an open letter to white clergy from the Birmingham jail. King shared his disappointment with the "white moderate." The biggest hurdle for racial equality, King argued, did not come from overt racists in the White Citizens' Council or the Ku Klux Klan, but from the white moderates who criticized civil rights activists' methods more than segregation itself.[16]

Two weeks later, Black children joined the Birmingham demonstrations, and on May 2, hundreds were arrested. The following day, when the children continued, white Birmingham police officers infamously used high-powered water hoses and police dogs on the Black youth. The images were circulated around the world by prominent media outlets, putting more negative attention on US race relations. Furthermore, Alabama governor George C. Wallace vowed to do everything within his power to prevent the desegregation of the University of Alabama. Uncertain of what Wallace would do, and suffering damage to his personal and presidential reputation for failing to address the racial crisis, Kennedy delivered his noted civil rights address from the Oval Office on the evening of June 11, 1963. In it, Kennedy transformed the fight for civil rights from a legal argument into a moral one.[17]

Crafting a Class, p. 138. On Kennedy's meeting with the UNCF leaders, see Goodson, *Chronicles of Faith*, pp. 142–144.

16. The year 1963 is credited as one of the most pivotal in the American civil rights movement. On John F. Kennedy, race, and the events of 1963, see Goduti, *Robert F. Kennedy and the Shaping of Civil Rights*; Baldwin, *The Fire Next Time*. For a commemoration, see Kat Chow, "As 2013 Winds to an End, So Do the Tweets of 1963," *National Public Radio*, December 31, 2013, https://www.npr.org/sections/codeswitch/2013/12/31/258664831/as-2013-winds-to-an-end-so-do-the-tweets-of-1963 (accessed April 11, 2019); Martin Luther King Jr. to C. C. J. Carpenter et al., April 16, 1963, *Letter from a Birmingham Jail*, Martin Luther King Jr. Research and Education Institute, Stanford University, https://kinginstitute.stanford.edu/king-papers/documents/letter-birmingham-jail (accessed April 11, 2019).

17. Foster Hailey, "Dogs and Hoses Repulse Negroes at Birmingham: 3 Students Bitten in Second Day of Demonstrations against Segregation," *New York Times*, May 4, 1963; "Wallace Calls for Calm at University," *Birmingham Post-Herald*, June 10, 1963; Bill Shamblin, "Over 300 Newsmen to Get Red-Carpet Treatment by UA," *Crimson White*, June 9, 1963; "Classes Started, UA Quiet," *Tuscaloosa News*, June 12, 1963; "Talk to Nation: President Outlines Rights

Also in June 1963, Kennedy hosted a White House meeting and called upon more than two hundred leading educators to "expand opportunities for Negroes at all levels of the educational system." He contacted academic leaders again in July 1963, including Carl E. Steiger, president of the UW Board of Regents. The events in Birmingham and elsewhere led Kennedy to fear "the explosive situation in many of our great cities." Therefore, it was critical that academic leaders at UW help address their specific state and local issues in an effort to ease racial tensions and provide Black children and their families with better opportunities.[18]

"Equal opportunity for education and for employment is a phrase without meaning unless the individual is prepared to take advantage of it," Kennedy explained, adding that universities needed to provide programs to assist "both white and negro students and their families." Kennedy's plea focused on a national initiative while trying to ease the tension between the federal government and individual states:

Young people and adults alike who have been disadvantaged need special programs in both general and vocational education if they are to be ready for further formal education or for employment. I have proposed to Congress an expansion of federal support in these areas, but the main task, of course, has to be carried out by state and local educational systems and by public and private institutions.

In short, the stability of society depended upon higher education, and Kennedy personally invited academic leaders to accept their national responsibility.[19]

The letter from Kennedy placed a sense of urgency behind what Harrington and others at UW had already been exploring, both in terms of programs and research projects investigating the race problem. On July 22, 1963, a confidential memo was circulated among UW administrators that listed the Black faculty employed at the university, including the Milwaukee campus and extension centers, and their tenure status. At UW, most academic units had no Black faculty, and if they did, the majority were pre-tenure assistant professors or instructors. Only four Black faculty members—one of the two in the School

---

Proposals," *Tuscaloosa News*, June 12, 1963. For more on desegregating the University of Alabama, see chapter 5 of this book.

18. On the White House meeting with educators, see American Council on Education (ACE), *Expanding Opportunities: The Negro and Higher Education* (A Clearinghouse Report) 1, no. 1 (May 1964): 1–8 (report retrieved from Beadle Records, Box 189, Folder 4, SCRC); Kennedy to Steiger, July 12, 1963.

19. Kennedy to Steiger, July 12, 1963.

of Letters and Science on the Madison campus and three of the six at the Milwaukee campus—were tenured. The limited number of Black faculty was not uncommon considering that no Black scholars were "permanent faculty" at any US majority-white college or university until 1941.[20]

This information gathering served as a precursor for UW leaders working to address racial issues, and on August 2, the board of regents voted to "study the problem of minority groups in the university to see if the university is doing all it can to help them." The regents' resolution read:

> That the university administration, as President Harrington had suggested, be requested to examine the whole subject of civil rights and equal educa- tional opportunities with a view to determining whether the university is doing everything that it can do in this area and what further can be done.

For Harrington, the university had not been as bad as some institutions re- garding Black students, faculty, and staff. Therefore, the request from the White House was an opportunity to position the university as the leader among other colleges and universities when it came to providing educational opportunities to Black citizens. "We need not feel ashamed of the university's records," Harrington said. "But are we doing enough?"[21]

Several faculty and administrators responded to Harrington's question. C. H. Ruedisili, associate dean of letters and science, shared a 191-item inter- national student survey that he administered in the spring of 1963. Survey questions asked those students how often they had experienced discrimina- tion in finding housing, at local restaurants, at social events, and from faculty, among other aspects of campus life. "Although these data are not directly

---

20. Robert Taylor Memo on Black Faculty, July 22, 1963, Harrington Papers, Box 40, Folder: Civil Rights, UW. During the mid-twentieth century, it was common for the number of Black faculty at large nonsouthern universities to be in the single digits. According to Ibram X. Kendi, "Among prestigious institutions, two of the 'sanctuaries' for black professors were UChicago and UCLA, with no more than six." For more, see Kendi, *Black Campus Movement*, p. 27. James D. Anderson, a preeminent historian of Black education, noted that there were no per- manent faculty at white universities until 1941, and "by the mid-1940s, there were approximately 3,000 African Americans holding master's degrees and more than 550 with Ph.D.s." Therefore, Black scholars' limited employment was not for lack of qualified individuals. These scholars faced racial discrimination nationally. For his detailed overview of Black faculty, see Anderson, "Race, Meritocracy, and the American Academy"; also see Winston, "Through the Back Door."

21. On the regents' vote to study the racial problems and the Harrington quote, see "UW Will Strive for More Help to Minority Groups," *WSJ*, August 3, 1963. For the regents' resolution, see Clarke Smith to Fred H. Harrington, August 9, 1963, Harrington Papers, Box 40, Folder: Civil Rights–Sam Proctor, UW.

concerned with discrimination problems of Negroes, I believe that you will be interested in our results," Ruedisili offered to Harrington, noting that the findings were currently being coded.[22]

A week later, on August 12, Leon D. Epstein, a professor of political science, suggested that the university offer "special educational opportunities for Negro graduates of Wisconsin high schools." He thought a large-scale scholarship program and campus housing considerations for Black students was not only a good idea, but it was the responsibility of the university. "To meet this need is a task suited to the tradition of our state university," Epstein advised. The next day, Morgan Gibson, a professor of English at UW-Milwaukee, sent Harrington a copy of a statement condemning de facto school segregation in the Milwaukee public schools. The statement, which several UW-Milwaukee faculty signed, was a two-page manifesto that outlined what the faculty considered "a fair summary of the evils of de facto educational segregation."[23]

The same month, as UW faculty assessed what they could do to address racial inequalities, Samuel M. Nabrit, president of Texas Southern, a state-supported Black college in Houston, issued the first proposal for action for how colleges and universities could answer the Kennedy Administration's call. He prepared a draft report titled "Program for Negro Colleges" alongside Jerrold Zachari, a physicist at the Massachusetts Institute of Technology, and Stephen White, an officer for Educational Services Inc., also based in Massachusetts. The trio emerged from the federal government's Panel on Educational Research and Development. With Nabrit as a leading voice, the main priority for higher education, they argued, "should be given to upgrading the faculties and the level of teaching at Negro colleges, and . . . this should be done through a nationwide effort drawing intensively on the skills and resources of established universities." There was a long history of racism toward Black colleges dating back to the founding of those institutions, and to address this, the Nabrit-Zachari-White team suggested that wealthier, white institutions host summer institutes for Black college faculty to receive additional training and start faculty exchange programs during the academic year.[24]

Nabrit was keenly aware of the resource differences, particularly in infrastructure, between Black colleges and the established white institutions

22. C. H. Ruedisili to Fred H. Harrington, August 6, 1963; and Foreign Student Survey, Spring 1963 both in Harrington Papers, Box 40, Folder: Civil Rights, UW.

23. Leon D. Epstein to Fred H. Harrington, August 12, 1963; and Morgan Gibson to Fred H. Harrington, August 13, 1963; both in Harrington Papers, Box 40, Folder: Civil Rights–Sam Proctor, UW.

24. On the Nabrit-Zachari-White proposal, see Langer, "Negro Colleges," pp. 372–373.

because he earned his undergraduate degree at Morehouse College and earned his PhD at Brown University and became a biologist. Additionally, in 1963, Black faculty only represented 2 percent of all US faculty with a PhD, and due to the lack of access to graduate-level training, only 28 percent of Black college faculty held a PhD or equivalent degree (compared with 51 percent at majority-white institutions). This was important because Kennedy called for "special programs," but he did not specify what programs should be adopted. As a result, Nabrit and his colleagues proposed programs where a broad coalition of institutions worked together, and their proposal quickly gained momentum among mainstream universities.[25]

Within a month, academic leaders at white institutions started announcing how they were committed not only to enrolling more Black students but also to investing in the Black colleges that enrolled two-thirds of the nation's estimated 180,000 Black college students. On September 17, Roger W. Heyns, vice president for academic affairs at the University of Michigan, invited UW to send a representative to an October 1963 conference in Ann Arbor about "the Negro in higher education." The previous spring, academic leaders from less than a handful of Midwest universities had met at Wayne State University in Detroit to discuss the topic, but Heyns wanted a "larger representation" for the upcoming conference, and UW, each of its other Big Ten peers, Wayne State, and the University of Chicago were invited.[26]

The invitation was also sent two days after the deadly bombing of the Sixteenth Street Baptist Church in Birmingham took the lives of four Black girls. This surely was on the minds of many Americans, and it underscored President Kennedy's earlier comment to academic leaders about the volatile situation in the nation. Accordingly, Heyns requested that UW's representative be a senior member of Harrington's administrative team and that the person attend the conference with some position papers or statements on the topic. Harrington and Robert L. Clodius, vice president for academic affairs, agreed to designate Donald McNeil as the central administrator on "the Negro and civil rights question." Clodius then notified Heyns that McNeil, special assistant to Harrington, would represent UW, but he also posed a question. "Those of us with institutions in metropolitan areas that have a substantial Negro population also have a special responsibility that is not mentioned in your enclosure. Are

25. On Nabrit earning his PhD at Brown, see Anderson, "Race, Meritocracy, and the American Academy," p. 162. For more on the percentages of faculty with a PhD or equivalent degree, see Huyck, "Faculty in Predominantly White and Predominantly Negro Higher Institutions."

26. On the proportion of Black students enrolled at Black colleges, see ACE, *Expanding Opportunities*, pp. 2–3; Roger W. Heyns to Fred H. Harrington, September 17, 1963, Harrington Papers, Box 40, Folder: Civil Rights–Sam Proctor, UW.

not research and adult education and public service especially important for us public universities?"[27]

Clodius's question was fair considering UW's campus in Milwaukee was unlike the University of Michigan in Ann Arbor, but Heyns and other Michigan academic leaders were well ahead of Harrington, who was still at the information gathering stage. On May 31, 1963, the University of Michigan's Advisory Committee on the Negro in Higher Education submitted its report on potential "research and action programs" about Black students and faculty. Three days after Clodius asked Heyns about UW-specific considerations, University of Michigan president Harlan H. Hatcher used his annual address before faculty and staff to explain the university's planned actions related to the national racial crisis.[28]

On September 30, 1963, Hatcher told Michigan faculty and staff, "we are in a new period of social relationships. . . . One of the many illustrations that I might choose from our collective life is the area of race relations." Hatcher then informed the campus community about three new university programs "related to this problem." First, the university had "reexamined its responsibilities to high schools in which there are a substantial number of Negro pupils." He specifically mentioned consulting with a former assistant principal of a public school in Detroit. Hatcher also stressed the need for Michigan to "examine our own practices with respect to students from deprived backgrounds" and "that we do not induce unnecessary failures and consequent social losses through insensitivity to individual problems." This initiative—adopting race-based admissions practices—was similar to what the Ivies and Seven Sisters had already implemented on a modest scale. Programs like the National Scholarship Service and Fund for Negro Students had existed since 1948, and Rockefeller Foundation officers discussed a pilot summer program that brought Black youth to Dartmouth, Oberlin, and Princeton in early 1963, but what Hatcher proposed was more robust.[29]

27. Fred H. Harrington to Robert L. Clodius, September 23, 1963; Fred H. Harrington to Charles Vevier and J. Martin Klotsche, September 23, 1963; Robert L. Clodius to Roger W. Heyns, September 27, 1963; all in Harrington Papers, Box 40, Folder: Civil Rights–Sam Proctor, UW.

28. N. Edd Miller to Roger W. Heyns, Report of the Advisory Committee on the Negro in Higher Education, May 31, 1963, Harrington Papers, Box 40, Folder: Civil Rights–Sam Proctor, UW.

29. Harlan H. Hatcher, "State of the University Address," September 30, 1963, Harlan Henthorne Hatcher Papers, Box 57, Bentley Historical Library, University of Michigan. For more on the origins of affirmative action at the University of Michigan, see Johnson, "Managing Racial Inclusion"; and Johnson, *Undermining Racial Justice.* Another study of the history of the

Hatcher's next program was the conference Heyns had already invited other academic leaders to attend. Michigan would host a forum of the leading midwestern universities on how to increase the number of Black people employed by colleges and universities and develop a research program that would help "increase the flow of Negroes into professions, including college teaching." This initiative was in direct cooperation with the PCEEO. The final program Hatcher discussed echoed the Nabrit-Zachari-White proposal when he announced an exchange program between Michigan and Tuskegee Institute, a Black college in Alabama founded by Booker T. Washington. "Faculty members and administrators from Tuskegee will be here next month to visit with members of our faculty in the hope that we can help them in the development of a strong liberal arts program," Hatcher added.[30]

The plans that Hatcher shared in Michigan soon expanded across the nation. The next month, on October 17, more than forty educators met for the Conference on Expanding Opportunities for Negroes in Higher Education in Washington, DC, hosted by the American Council on Education. The meeting was focused on "the long-range problems facing Negroes in the civil rights struggle—primary economic problems that cannot be overcome without more education and greater skill." Four of the five prominent proposals that emerged from the conference attendees focused on Black colleges. Those four were opportunities for more graduate training at "reputable graduate schools" for Black college faculty, faculty exchange programs between Black and white institutions during the academic year, scholars at leading white universities teaching at Black colleges for brief periods, and additional

---

race-based college admissions nationally has assessed the different years that universities implemented affirmative action policies found, at Michigan, that "the Opportunity Awards Program recruited 70 students in 1964 and 64 students in 1965, and many (but not all) of them were African Americans who graduated from Detroit-area high schools." For more, see Stulberg and Chen, "The Origins of Race-conscious Affirmative Action," p. 41. Historian Linda M. Perkins described the NSSFNS as "the first talent identification program in the nation to identify and place Black students in predominately white institutions of higher education." For more, see Perkins, "First Black Talent Identification Program," p. 174. The NSSFNS provided financial aid for Black students. For more, see Duffy and Goldberg, *Crafting a Class*, p. 138. For more background on the NSSFNS, see Plaut, "Plans for Assisting Negro Students." On early discussions for a pilot program at Princeton, Dartmouth, and Oberlin, see Rockefeller Foundation, "The Long Road to College: A Summer of Opportunity," A Special Report, Spring 1965, Assistant to the President Records, Donald R. McNeil, Box 7, Folder: Rockefeller Foundation, UW; For more on the Princeton-Oberlin-Dartmouth program, see Willie, "Philanthropic and Foundation Support," p. 274; and Bradley, *Upending the Ivory Tower*, pp. 61, 149–150.

30. Hatcher, "State of the University Address."

mathematics and science training for Black college faculty—a nod to Cold War–era priorities. The one proposal not focused on Black colleges was about white institutions seeking and admitting more Black students, along with providing those students with "adequate housing" and scholarships.[31]

ACE called on "all members" of the US higher education system "to assume constructive and responsible roles within their respective communities, institutions, and organizations in efforts to improve race relations and equalize educational opportunity." Lawrence E. Dennis, head of ACE's Commission on Academic Affairs, said: "Our long-term goal, equality of educational opportunity, means fully integrated higher education. But the interim goal must be improving Negro colleges." Indiana University president Elvis J. Stahr Jr. led ACE's eight-member Committee on Equality of Educational Opportunity. Following the conference, an ad hoc committee was formed to organize and plan the summer institutes for Black college faculty. Four Black college presidents were on the committee: Nabrit (Texas Southern), Samuel D. Proctor (North Carolina A&T), Stephen J. Wright (Fisk), and Martin D. Jenkins (Morgan State). The other members were Heyns, Zachari, J. C. Warner, president of Carnegie Tech; and Mina S. Rees, committee chair and a dean at City University of New York.[32]

The following Monday, October 21, the University of Michigan hosted the Inter-University Conference on the Negro in Higher Education. There, Michigan academic leaders officially announced the Michigan-Tuskegee exchange program before their midwestern peers, private foundation officers, and federal government officials. In doing so, Michigan officials demonstrated that affirmative action meant the most well-resourced universities had an obligation to aid and strengthen the Black colleges that southern state legislators and federal officials had largely ignored and discriminated against since their inception. Yet, while McNeil was in Ann Arbor for the Inter-University Conference, Harrington was traveling to New York City.[33]

The next day, on October 22, the presidents of Association of American Universities (AAU) member institutions met at the University Club in New York. The AAU was a consortium of the leading research universities and Harrington, Hatcher, and Stahr were in attendance among thirty-six other leading college presidents and ACE president Logan Wilson. During the meeting,

---

31. Susanna McBee, "Educators Seek Ways to Help Negroes," *Washington Post*, October 18, 1963; ACE, *Expanding Opportunities*.

32. McBee, "Educators Seek Ways"; ACE, *Expanding Opportunities*.

33. On the Michigan-Tuskegee program being announced during the Inter-University Conference on the Negro in Higher Education, see Park, "Planting the Seeds," p. 120.

Princeton president Robert F. Goheen brought attention to the previous week's ACE conference in Washington, DC, and Stahr's committee, "which will concern itself with what higher education can do in the interest of civil rights." Goheen "expressed the hope Mr. Stahr could speak to this subject at the next meeting of the Association," and Stahr welcomed "suggestions from members as to what the committee might consider."[34]

Momentum behind strengthening Black colleges swelled with the endorsement of ACE and the interest of the AAU, and by late 1963, publicity soon circulated in the media as the *New York Herald Tribune* called the Michigan-Tuskegee exchange agreement a "big brother" program. By this point, many of the nation's most influential white college presidents were absorbed in determining how their institutions could join the broad-reaching educational opportunity agenda, but on November 22, 1963, their need to act on civil rights was further propelled into reality following the assassination of US president John F. Kennedy in Dallas, Texas. Shortly afterward, on December 6, Harrington went before the UW regents to announce the university's "five-point program to help disadvantaged minorities."[35]

Although the five programs were actually still in the planning phase, the university strategically issued a press release noting that the Johnson Foundation in Racine—the same foundation Harrington joined as board member in December 1962—awarded a $30,000 grant to UW. The grant would aid a program designed to counsel disadvantaged high schoolers and encourage them to continue their education. Specifically, the program would identify talented students who were less likely to attend college and introduce those students to "remedial and enrichment courses" from high school through their first two years of college. Wisconsin's three-year program was estimated to cost $150,000, and the Johnson Foundation's grant was a modest but notable gift toward its launch. Like Michigan leaders working with Detroit public schools, UW planned to partner with the Milwaukee schools to identify twenty-five students for the program. "The talent search must pervade every segment of society," said H. F. Johnson, trustee board chair of the Johnson Foundation. "The job is to identify promising high school students and show that continuing education is a 'must' in a rapidly changing society." This gave Harrington the green light he needed as he reminded the regents of the possibilities ahead.

34. Association of American Universities Fall Meeting Minutes, October 22–23, 1963, Beadle Records, Box 46, Folder 5, SCRC.

35. "Colleges Adopt 'Big Brother' Plan," *New York Herald Tribune*, October 27, 1963; John Patrick Hunter, "U.W. Plans Exchange with Southern Negro Colleges," *CT*, December 7, 1963; David Bednarek, "UW Plans Programs to Help Minorities," *WSJ*, December 7, 1963.

"The Johnson Foundation grant makes it possible for us to move ahead rapidly in a program that long has been overdue," he said. "We have the chance now to show the way."[36]

Another program Harrington shared was a faculty and student exchange program with Black colleges in the South. Similar to the Michigan-Tuskegee partnership but larger, UW's program planned to launch simultaneously with multiple Black colleges—North Carolina A&T, North Carolina College, and Texas Southern. This mirrored what Nabrit and colleagues had advocated for in August 1963. Wisconsin's three other programs included the establishment of the Institute of Human Relations on the UW-Milwaukee campus, professional development institutes held in Madison for Black college faculty, and a research consortium focused on racial issues.[37]

The five programs were expected to address racial issues, including those on campus. For example, in 1964, UW enrolled only eighty-two US-born Black students out of a total 24,275 on the Madison campus. The twenty-six from Illinois were the most from a single state, leaving the university officials embarrassed that only twenty-one Black Wisconsin residents were enrolled at the university (92,000 Black people lived in the state, according to the 1960 census). "Originally, we had figured that the number of Negroes on the Madison campus was about 300–500," said McNeil, special assistant to Harrington and lead campus administrator on Blacks in higher education, "but a recent survey indicates a more accurate estimate would be fewer than 100."[38]

The program for the youth, however, would address the lack of Black students because it was aimed at preparing more Black children in the state's urban centers to enroll at UW. On the other hand, the other initiatives would require Harrington to reach beyond state boundaries. This was especially the case for the institute dedicated to "minority group programs" and the exchange program with Black colleges, and Harrington and McNeil needed two things to move them from the planning stage to implementation: the institute needed the human capital of a dynamic leader, and the exchange program

---

36. Hunter, "U.W. Plans Exchange"; Bednarek, "UW Plans Programs"; Johnson Foundation Grant (press release), December 6, 1963, Harrington Papers, Box 40, Folder: Civil Rights–Sam Proctor, UW. For more on academic leaders' hopes for these programs, such as "to eradicate the vestiges of racism," see Rooks, *White Money/Black Power,* pp. 14–15.

37. Hunter, "U.W. Plans Exchange"; Bednarek, "UW Plans Programs."

38. On Wisconsin Black enrollment and employment, Stu Chapman, "'U' Must Upgrade Education of Negroes, McNeil Asserts," *DC,* May 7, 1964; and David Gordon, "U.S. Negroes at UW Total under 100 Now: McGrath Makes Survey," *WSJ,* June 5, 1964. For the total enrollment, see Enrollment Report, Fall 1963, Office of the Registrar, University of Wisconsin, https://registrar.wisc.edu/enrollment-reports/ (accessed April 4, 2019).

needed financial capital. To achieve this, the two men embarked on parallel tasks: Harrington worked to cultivate a relationship with a Black college president in the South while McNeil did the same with private foundations.

Poaching Black Talent for White Use

By New Year's Day of 1964, the system-wide affirmative action programs were widely accepted, but motives varied between Black presidents and white presidents. Harrington soon focused on UW-specific goals and set aside the broader idea of strengthening Black colleges, but he set his eyes on those institutions for other reasons. If the proposed Institute of Human Relations were to succeed, he reasoned, some of the Black brilliance at Black colleges was better suited in Wisconsin.

On January 23, 1964, Harrington did not mince words in his three-page letter to Samuel DeWitt Proctor, president of North Carolina A&T. It opened: "Dear Sam, we want you to join us and provide university, state, and national leadership in the human relations field." A month earlier, Harrington had announced UW's five-point program without much planning, but he personally took the lead in finding a director for the institute. Harrington immediately made his case to Proctor, who was well regarded nationally. In 1955, Proctor had been invited to Alabama by Martin Luther King Jr. during the Montgomery bus boycott. That same year, he became president of Virginia Union, a Black college in Richmond, and led that institution through the turmoil of Ku Klux Klan violence in response to the students' involvement in desegregation efforts. He left Virginia Union in 1960 to become president of North Carolina A&T, where a student sit-in at a whites-only lunch counter ignited the national student civil rights uprising in February 1960. His résumé in the field of civil rights made Proctor the ideal director of the Institute of Human Relations. "This is a real career for you, Sam, one of great national importance," Harrington told Proctor. "We know you are doing vitally important work as the president of a predominantly Negro institution. We believe, however, that this Wisconsin role provides even larger opportunities for you—so large that we cannot even state them adequately here."[39]

Harrington's plea, however, did not persuade Proctor to jump at the opportunity to come to Wisconsin. Two weeks later, on February 10, since Proctor did not accept the position in Milwaukee, Harrington humbly followed up with Proctor. He admitted he must have done the esteemed Black leader a

---

39. Fred H. Harrington to Samuel D. Proctor, January 23, 1964, Harrington Papers, Box 40, Folder: Civil Rights–Sam Proctor, UW. For more on Proctor, see Bond, *The Imposing Preacher*.

disservice. "I think we have failed to set up our Human Rights position so as to show you its maximum possibilities." For Harrington, that must have been the problem. His ambition for UW's place in the national conversation about racial issues must not have been clearly articulated to Proctor. How else, then, would Proctor have not accepted by now? He and his team at UW needed to regroup, but first, they needed to repackage the director position to make it more appealing. "Wait for us, do," Harrington said, asking for Proctor to be patient. "We need you, and we think that you can render a greater national and international service with us than in Greensboro. We feel this deeply, and want to discuss this with you after we have rethought our own position." Harrington hoped a new pitch would be so appealing that Proctor would realize UW provided a larger platform than North Carolina A&T. In the meantime, he promised Proctor that he would follow up by the end of February.[40]

Harrington's initial request and subsequent backtracking revealed the ideology guiding white college presidents. Harold M. Rose, a Black geography professor at UW-Milwaukee, summarized the presumptive, supremacy-minded beliefs of Harrington and other whites: "The general assumption that the southern Negro institutions are inferior has played an important part in prompting this co-operative effort." Professor Charles V. Willie, a Black professor at Syracuse University in 1964, later assessed that "Although probably not intended, the phrase 'strong colleges,' or 'good colleges,' or 'prestigious colleges,' or 'selective colleges' turned out to be synonyms for the phrase 'predominantly white colleges.'" Considering this, Harrington genuinely believed it reasonable for Proctor to leave the presidency of a Black college to serve as the director of a new institute located on a secondary campus at UW.[41]

As promised, on February 26, Harrington reached out to Proctor. This time, it was for past business. He enclosed a check reimbursing Proctor for his January 8–9, 1964, visit to Wisconsin regarding the exchange program with the three Black colleges, including North Carolina A&T. But Harrington also used the brief letter to reiterate his belief in Proctor: "We are going to keep in touch with you and will get you some day." For Proctor, however, there were a number of reasons for his delayed acceptance of the Wisconsin position. Harrington's

40. Fred H. Harrington to Samuel D. Proctor, February 10, 1964, Harrington Papers, Box 40, Folder: Civil Rights–Sam Proctor, UW.

41. Rose, "Teacher-Exchange Programs," pp. 319–320; Willie, "Philanthropic and Foundation Support," p. 275. The belief that Black colleges were inferior or second-rate institutions also extended to the Black students being recruited from urban centers. At the Ivies and the midwestern public universities, admitting Black students often involved a debate over those students' academic ability. For examples, see Williamson, *Black Power on Campus*, pp. 59–60; and Karabel, *The Chosen*, pp. 383–384.

arrogance was a small part, but Proctor was also preoccupied with a commitment to the Peace Corps. For years, his career had swung between academic leadership and public affairs. In fact, Proctor took a leave of absence in 1963 from the presidency at North Carolina A&T to serve as an executive in the Peace Corps. Thus, by the time Harrington started courting Proctor, he had just returned to Greensboro from Africa and remained uncertain of his future duties with the Peace Corps.[42]

Therefore, on March 2, Proctor assured Harrington that it was no fault of their own that he had not accepted the offer to join in "the important work of the University of Wisconsin." It was a matter of Proctor needing to be sure the Peace Corps no longer needed his services. Once released from those duties, he said he would be ready to accept "permanent work," the kind of job that would allow him to be stationary for the next twenty years until retirement. Until then, Proctor only promised Harrington that he would keep in touch.[43]

This note from Proctor arrived as Harrington was tending to other aspects of UW's five-point plan. On March 10, Harrington was in Washington, DC, and testified before the US Senate regarding Senate bill 2490. At the initiation of Senator Vance Hartke (D-IN), the bill would increase the amount of loans authorized for financial aid, and it would establish scholarship and work-study programs, ultimately increasing support for more Americans to attend college. This aligned with Harrington's goal for UW to take the lead in expanding educational opportunities. In fact, he testified on behalf of the Association of State Universities and Land-Grant Colleges. Harrington supported the bill, which was also backed by the American Association of University Professors and other educational associations.[44]

Upon his return to Madison, Proctor's letter about his yet-to-be-determined Peace Corps status left Harrington confused about the next move. He was uncertain if Proctor had just completely removed himself from consideration, or if he was simply asking for more time. This led Harrington to turn toward

42. Fred H. Harrington to Samuel D. Proctor, February 26, 1964, Harrington Papers, Box 40, Folder: Civil Rights–Sam Proctor, UW. Regarding Proctor and Peace Corps, see Kelley, *Profiles of Five Administrators*.

43. Samuel D. Proctor to Fred H. Harrington, March 2, 1964, Harrington Papers, Box 40, Folder: Civil Rights–Sam Proctor, UW.

44. On Harrington's Senate testimony, see Samuel D. Proctor to Fred H. Harrington, March 21, 1964, Harrington Papers, Box 40, Folder: Civil Rights–Sam Proctor, UW. For the bill's description, see US Congress, Senate, *To provide assistance for students in higher education by increasing the amount of authorized loans*, 88th Cong., 2nd sess., March 10, 1964, S. Doc 2490. For Harrington's testimony, see US Congress, Congressional Record, *New Sponsors for Education Bill*, 88th Cong., 2nd sess., March 10, 1964.

Donald McNeil for insight. "This certainly seems to say that he wants to come with us," Harrington assessed. He then asked McNeil, "But when? We can wait, but how long?" As Harrington and McNeil attempted to figure out Proctor's intentions, the next day, March 19, UW-Milwaukee vice provost Charles Vevier sent Harrington an update from his end. A committee on the Milwaukee campus had compiled names for the institute director. Under Vevier's directive, the committee was "to do nothing but investigation and not negotiation." The thirteen potential candidates—five Black and eight white scholars— would serve as the talent pool since, by this point, Proctor seemed unlikely to accept the position. Vevier's only question was, What was Harrington's preference in contacting the other candidates for the director position.[45]

Just as the director search appeared to be moving forward, on March 21, Proctor sent Harrington an unsolicited note regarding Harrington's March 10 testimony before the US Senate. By this point, three weeks had passed since Proctor's letter to Harrington on March 2 about his Peace Corps uncertainty. Harrington had not yet responded to that letter, and Proctor used the recent testimony to send a follow-up. Proctor expressed his appreciation to Harrington for his work in Washington, DC, representing not only UW but all land-grant colleges, like North Carolina A&T. "We could not have a better proponent of the interests of American college students than that tall, intelligent, handsome president of the great university at Madison."[46]

Again, Harrington consulted with McNeil about Proctor's ambivalence. McNeil suspected Proctor simply wanted to keep his options open, especially with 1964 being an election year and that the Peace Corps would likely be impacted by who was elected president of the United States. In turn, McNeil told Harrington "if we could uncork a really big grant from [the] Ford [Foundation], we might get Sam pronto," but that had not happened. Therefore, McNeil felt the search for the director must continue even if it meant going with a "second-level" person. Until then, McNeil said, "I don't see how at this moment, though, we can hold the job open for him." Harrington agreed, telling McNeil, "Correct, we cannot wait for Sam Proctor." Soon after, the committee forwarded a list of finalists that did not include Proctor to Vice Provost Vevier on the Milwaukee campus. The University of Wisconsin, however, still had other business with Proctor despite his not accepting the institute director position.[47]

45. Fred H. Harrington to Donald McNeil, March 18, 1964, Harrington Papers, Box 40, Folder: Civil Rights–Sam Proctor, UW; Charles Vevier to Fred H. Harrington, March 19, 1964, Harrington Papers, Box 40, Folder: Civil Rights–Sam Proctor, UW.

46. Proctor to Harrington, March 21, 1964.

47. Donald McNeil to Fred H. Harrington, March 25, 1964, Harrington Papers, Box 40, Folder: Civil Rights–Sam Proctor, UW; Fred H. Harrington to Donald McNeil, March 27, 1964,

Harrington replied to Proctor on March 27, thanking him for his "fan letter" about his Senate testimony, but he focused more on the exchange program at this point instead of courting Proctor for the director position. He informed Proctor that the program was developing as scheduled despite "a rumbling or two" from the white colleges in North Carolina calling UW a "carpet bagger," referencing the derogatory Reconstruction-era term for northerners who exploited the post–Civil War South. Harrington assured Proctor that he had written to William Friday, president of the University of North Carolina (UNC), about such concerns. Friday had attended the previous fall's AAU meeting in New York and was abreast of the efforts undertaken by nonsouthern presidents, but there were still worries that southern legislators might punish Black colleges for collaborating with nonsouthern institutions. The perception that Harrington was considered a northern opportunist needed to be addressed. Thus, Harrington made sure Proctor knew UW had a plan and someone working to ensure that the exchange program would succeed. Simply put, Harrington said: "Don McNeil will watch all of this."[48]

White Presidents, Black Programs, Green Dollars

As Harrington attempted to persuade Proctor to come to Wisconsin, McNeil had his charge to solicit private foundations. In September 1963, Harrington designated McNeil as UW's lead administrator on racial initiatives. Yet, civil rights efforts were also highly contested, and many elected officials avoided agreeing to support programs with racial preferences. Unlike the Cold War initiatives that received generous funding, race programs did not garner the same support. This was one of the most blatant contradictions underlying the special programs Kennedy called for before his death, but no federal legislation had been passed to finance those initiatives. Therefore, private dollars

---

Harrington Papers, Box 40, Folder: Civil Rights–Sam Proctor, UW; R. W. Shortreed to Charles Vevier, April 11, 1964, Harrington Papers, Box 40, Folder: Civil Rights–Sam Proctor, UW.

48. Fred H. Harrington to Samuel D. Proctor, March 27, 1964, Harrington Papers, Box 40, Folder: Civil Rights–Sam Proctor, UW. Professor Harold M. Rose observed that "The extent to which participation spreads will depend largely on the success of initial programs and on the barriers to participation that may be raised in state legislatures, North and South, by boards of trustees and by local communities." For more, see Rose, "Teacher-Exchange Programs," p. 320; This was a decades-old belief, and Noliwe M. Rooks has similarly assessed southern white resistance following the Civil War: "At the time, southern whites feared that education for Blacks would provide African Americans with the means to eventually upset white supremacy. As a result, many whites in the South resisted northern efforts at educational reform." For more, see Rooks, *White Money/Black Power*, p. 103.

were needed to support the disadvantaged youth initiatives, exchange programs with Black colleges, race institutes, and related programs.[49]

On January 30, 1964, UW officials announced that they would host the
second Inter-University Conference on the Negro in Higher Education at
Wingspread, a conference center owned by the Johnson Foundation in Racine.
The previous fall, the University of Michigan hosted a one-day gathering, but
UW planned to hold a two-day conference that would begin on February 17
with three featured speakers: Hobart Taylor, executive vice president of the
PCEEO, who had coined the phrase "affirmative action" three years earlier;
Lawrence E. Dennis, head of ACE's Commission on Academic Affairs; and
McNeil. Among the topics on the conference agenda were testing procedures,
advanced training and summer institutes for Black college faculty, and expanding graduate-level admissions. Additionally, representatives were invited from
each Big Ten university, the University of Chicago, Roosevelt University in
Chicago, and Wayne State University in Detroit as well as Black colleges North
Carolina A&T and Texas Southern. Most notably, the officers from major private foundations were also invited. For McNeil, this was the ideal group to
have assembled for UW to take the lead among universities seeking to remedy
the nation's racial ills.[50]

Between the announcement and the actual conference, McNeil sent private
foundations a proposal for the faculty-student exchange between UW and the
three Black colleges—North Carolina A&T, North Carolina College, and
Texas Southern. The proposal emphasized the goals of the university. "The
University of Wisconsin is deeply committed to the cause of aiding minority
groups," the proposal stated. "By action of the Regents of the University, a
general policy of participation in movements to help the disadvantaged has
been established. On both the Milwaukee and Madison campuses, efforts are
being made to build into various departments professors who have research
and teaching interests in minority problems." McNeil shared the proposal
widely leading up to the conference. The Carnegie Corporation, Ford Foundation, and Rockefeller Foundation were a few of the groups on his list. Since
the turn of the century, many of these foundations or their namesakes' philanthropic dollars had been used, for better or worse, toward Black education, and
McNeil sent a resounding message to the foundations: "From top to bottom

49. John David Skrentny explained that, in the early 1960s, arguing for racial preferences was
a political risk for elected officials. For more, see Skrentny, *Ironies of Affirmative Action*, pp. 2–3.
On Wisconsin's plan to use private funds, see Hunter, "U.W. Plans Exchange."

50. Inter-University Conference (press release), January 30, 1964, Harrington Papers, Box
40, Folder: Civil Rights–Sam Proctor, UW.

of the university structure, Wisconsin is committed to this cause." This set the tone for the Inter-University Conference.[51]

At the conference, McNeil delivered the opening address welcoming sixty college administrators, faculty members, education association representatives, and private foundation officers. "It is hoped that this conference will provide an action blueprint for any institution to follow," he said. "We can start any place—preschool through graduate school and adult education—and do some good." Then, Dennis from ACE emphasized that Black people's success in higher education was a national issue. In turn, ACE was committed to developing a clearinghouse and coordinating center with the goal of offering advice to Black colleges and private foundations on how best to spend funds to support educational opportunity initiatives.[52]

Taylor, the third and lone Black keynote speaker, said universities must train more Black people for the job market. "I think the universities have a job to produce people, just as the corporations have a job to hire people," he said. "We are not talking simply about what's moral and what's right and humane. We're talking about national growth and the national economy as well." Modest race-based admissions practices may have started among private northeastern institutions, but the effort to "upgrade" Black education was led by the midwestern universities, and would force the Ivy League institutions and the stronger southern white universities to follow suit, according to Taylor. The University of Michigan's Roger Heyns agreed. As vice president for academic affairs, he believed that for any university to be effective, its leaders must be willing to put in significant effort, not gestures, and this meant hiring adequate staff or assigning staff to coordinate an institution's efforts.[53]

Immediately after the conference, Frank Bowles, program director of the Ford Foundation's education division, wrote to McNeil saying he enjoyed the conference. He then suggested that a smaller subgroup of academic leaders—a combination of McNeil and Heyns from Michigan alongside a couple of Black

51. There were dozens of letters to/from/about private foundations. One example, quoted in this paragraph, is Donald McNeil to Fred H. Harrington, February 3, 1964, Harrington Papers, Box 40, Folder: Civil Rights–Sam Proctor, UW. Several scholars have documented the support of white philanthropists for Black education. Broader historical surveys, see Anderson, *Education of Blacks in the South*; Anderson and Moss, *Dangerous Donations*; and Rooks, *White Money/Black Power*. For amounts spent by white philanthropists, see Anderson, "The Case of Mississippi," p. 298; Perkins, "First Black Talent Identification Program," p. 177; Willie, "Philanthropic and Foundation Support," pp. 272–274; Park, "Planting the Seeds," pp. 120–121.

52. David Bednarek, "Upgrading Negroes' Education Is Sought," *WSJ*, February 19, 1964; David F. Behrendt, "Negro's Education Is Hit as 'Lagging,'" *WSJ*, February 18, 1964.

53. Bednarek, "Upgrading Negroes' Education"; Behrendt, "Negro's Education Is Hit."

college presidents—convene again. Bowles thought an "action program" could be discussed over another one- or two-day conference with a group of only six to eight people, and if travel expenses were an issue, he asked for McNeil to simply let the Ford Foundation know. McNeil told Harrington, "the Bowles reply, especially, is really promising and I plan to follow up immediately," and for the two UW leaders, this was the desired outcome of the conference as McNeil's work continued throughout March 1964.[54]

On March 6, 1964, McNeil spoke with the Rockefeller Foundation's Leland C. DeVinney, who wanted assurance that the university would stay within its $75,000 budget per summer institute. McNeil promised as much, confirming to DeVinney that the Rockefeller's potential $150,000 grant would support two summer institutes—one for further training of Black college faculty in biology held at the University of North Carolina–Greensboro and another in mathematics to be held in Madison. While he was awaiting Rockefeller officers' decision on a $150,000 gift, a similar conversation unfolded between McNeil and the Carnegie Corporation. With Carnegie Corporation leaders, McNeil's conversation focused on two grants of $70,000 each to support two institutes, $74,000 in additional funds for a third institute, and $40,000 for overhead expenses. In both cases, McNeil had Harrington's approval to promise the private foundations whatever was needed to secure the large grants.[55]

Robert L. Clodius, UW vice president for academic affairs, used the promise to secure grants to execute the university's intentions when, on March 19, he convened a special Committee on Cooperation with Negro Universities. The committee was formed "in anticipation of the establishment and funding of this [exchange] program," Clodius explained. The next day, McNeil shared a two-page report with Harrington that addressed how UW was answering the federal government's questions about the university's role in the nationwide anti-poverty program. The report from the university's ad hoc Committee on Minority Problems listed activities across the Madison, Milwaukee, and extension campuses as a supplement to the work of Robert Lampman, an economics professor at UW. Lampman had also served on the late President Kennedy's council of economic advisers, ultimately giving Harrington a direct line to Washington, DC. This kept the momentum going and private foundation officers interested.[56]

54. Frank Bowles to Donald McNeil, February 19, 1964; Donald McNeil to Fred H. Harrington, March 5, 1964; both in Harrington Papers, Box 40, Folder: Civil Rights–Sam Proctor, UW.

55. Donald McNeil Personal Note to Himself, March 6, 1964, Assistant to the President Records, Donald R. McNeil, Box 7, Folder: Rockefeller Foundation, UW.

56. Robert L. Clodius to select group of faculty (letter convened Special Committee on Cooperation with Negro Universities), March 19, 1964, Harrington Papers, Box 40, Folder: Civil

Through the remainder of the spring, McNeil juggled multiple conversations with foundation officers. At the end of March, McNeil sent Fred Jackson of the Carnegie Corporation a revised proposal for the exchange program. In April, the Marshall Field Foundation committed $30,000 to UW, specifically for the programs planned for the Milwaukee campus, and the Rockefeller Foundation approved $75,000 for a summer institute for fifty Black college mathematics professors. Harrington also went back and forth with Leslie Paffrath of the Johnson Foundation in Racine about other universities' projects for the disadvantaged, such as the Dartmouth ABC (A Better Chance) program, and directed McNeil to be in touch with Paffrath. In May, McNeil closed an agreement with Jackson at Carnegie while also soliciting Bowles at the Ford Foundation. McNeil told Bowles that UW was ready to assume "a truly influential role in the movement to upgrade Negroes in both North and South." McNeil's use of "upgrade" was nearly identical to what Princeton Director of Admissions E. Alden Dunham said in his 1962–63 admissions report to the faculty, in which he said "it behooves all educational institutions to do what they can toward upgrading the status of the Negro in our society." By the end of June 1964, McNeil announced that the exchange program with the three Black colleges was ready to begin, thanks to the $300,000 grant from the Carnegie Corporation.[57]

At about the midpoint of the decade, several other white institutions were finalizing or rebooting their exchange programs with Black colleges. For decades, there had been "small-scale" exchanges between individual professors in the Northeast, Midwest, and West and Black colleges, but the number of such programs increased in the mid-1960s. Michigan-Tuskegee was one of the earliest announced. By 1965, other recognized exchange programs included Brown University with Tougaloo College in Mississippi; Cornell with Hampton Institute in Virginia; Yale also with Hampton; Princeton with Lincoln University in Pennsylvania; Indiana University with Stillman College in Alabama; Dartmouth with Talladega College in Alabama; Pomona College with Fisk University in Tennessee; Haverford College with Livingstone College in North Carolina; the

Rights–Sam Proctor, UW; Donald McNeil to Fred H. Harrington, March 20, 1964, Harrington Papers, Box 40, Folder: Civil Rights–Sam Proctor, UW; Peter Passell, "Robert Lampman, 76, Economist Who Helped in War on Poverty," *New York Times*, March 8, 1997.

57. Donald McNeil to Fred Jackson, April 9, 1964; Donald McNeil to Robert L. Clodius, April 3, 1964; Leslie Paffrath to/from Fred H. Harrington, April 13 and 16, 1964; Fred H. Harrington to/from Fred Jackson, May 20 and 25, 1964; Donald McNeil to Frank Bowles, May 25, 1964; Fred Jackson to Donald McNeil, June 5, 1964; all in Harrington Papers, Box 40, Folder: Civil Rights–Sam Proctor, UW; Report to the Faculty, 1962–1963, Goheen Records, Box 88, Folder 8, Princeton Archives. On the $300,000 Carnegie Corporation grant, see David Bednarek, "UW to Exchange Faculty with Negro Colleges," *WSJ*, June 23, 1964.

University of Dubuque with Johnson C. Smith University in North Carolina; and Southern Illinois University with Winston-Salem State College; however, UW had the most ambitious program, with three Black colleges. Yet, ambition came with a cost, and in capitalist America, the Black colleges would end up paying the price as the system-wide goals for affirmative action were soon dismantled.[58]

Omitting Black Colleges from Affirmative Action

The initial affirmative action programs for higher education were broad in scope. Harrington joined his fellow college presidents across a cadre of institutions in agreeing that the better-resourced white colleges and universities needed to recruit more Black students and hire more Black faculty, and that those same institutions also had a responsibility to help strengthen the nation's Black colleges. In fact, most programs initially proposed under the umbrella of affirmative action focused on Black colleges. Yet, when these programs were launched, an undercurrent of self-serving motives emerged among white college presidents that ultimately limited the effectiveness of the programs geared toward Black colleges before they even started.

For example, in February 1964, when UW hosted the second Inter-University Conference on the Negro in Higher Education, representatives from each of the nine state-supported Big Ten universities attended; however, absent among those invited were two private institutions—Northwestern University and the University of Chicago. An unidentified conference organizer told the *Milwaukee Sentinel* that the absence of academic leaders from the two universities was "shocking." The first conference—held in Ann Arbor, Michigan, in October 1963—had representation from Northwestern and UChicago. Yet, in February 1964, neither sent personnel to help brainstorm toward the collective effort to help Black people. This was particularly notable since Northwestern enrolled fewer than thirty Black students, the vast

---

58. The scope of formal exchange programs or other initiatives with Black colleges varied. Some were more modest, and both contemporary scholars and those from the 1960s differ in the exact number. For more, see Branson, "Interinstitutional Programs," pp. 470–476; Rose, "Teacher-Exchange Programs," p. 320; Park, "Planting the Seeds," p. 117; ACE, *Expanding Opportunities*, p. 8; Bradley, *Upending the Ivory Tower*, pp. 148–149; Williamson, *Black Power on Campus*, pp. 60–61. In this study of the University of Illinois, Williamson noted that one exchange program with a Black college emerged from the College of Education, not the university at large. Scholar Robert L. Allen has written extensively about challenges faced by Black citizens and US capitalism. For more, see Allen, *Black Awakening in Capitalist America*. This important historical text also discusses the "paternalistic racism" of the 1960s. For more, see pp. 163–164. Regarding affirmative action, specifically, see Allen, "The Bakke Case."

majority of whom were athletes, and no more than 2 percent of UChicago students were Black. "They claim they're not disinterested, they're only too busy," the same conference organizer stated. "But getting them here, where we're working out plans, is the guts of the program."[59]

It certainly was not that UChicago or Northwestern administrators were uninterested. At UChicago, on September 17, 1963, associate dean of the college Warner Wick and vice president Lowell T. Coggeshall discussed "The University and the Negro." There was some soul searching between the two men as Wick admitted that the dismal number of Black students enrolled was not a financial issue because UChicago could afford to finance the entire education of poor students regardless of race. "The real problem has been to find Negroes who both want to come to the university and have a good chance of surviving here," Wick told Coggeshall. As a result, the brightest Black students decided to enroll "at Harvard or MIT or Wellesley." Wick added that they needed to "spend a lot of time not only in identifying and recruiting candidates but also in counseling them about the best ways to prepare for the university and following their fortunes very carefully after they arrive."[60]

Wick also proposed the idea that the presidents of several peer institutions were proposing—a "cooperative arrangement" with Emory University and "the Atlanta Negro colleges." He closed: "We do this for institutions in South America and Nigeria, so why not here?" In short, they were interested in what the other midwestern universities were doing, and one week later, vice president Warner C. Johnson was designated to represent UChicago during the first Inter-University Conference; however, the interests of UChicago academic leaders changed between the October 1963 conference in Michigan and the one in February 1964 in Wisconsin.[61]

An incredible amount of insight into the programs proposed at UW can be gleaned from conversations that unfolded at UChicago. On October 25, 1963, Johnson returned from Michigan and informed UChicago provost Edward H. Levi that the conference was "interesting and I think worthwhile" but quickly surmised that the problems involved the state-supported universities "much more than they do private institutions." He told Levi he would share

59. David D. Gladfelter, "Educators Explore Negro Training," *Milwaukee Sentinel*, February 18, 1964; Historian Martha Biondi noted that, in 1965, twenty of Northwestern's twenty-six total Black students were student-athletes. For more, Biondi, *Black Revolution on Campus*, p. 81. On Chicago's percentage of Black of students enrolled, see Warner Wick to L. T. Coggeshall, September 17, 1963, Beadle Records, Box 189, Folder 3, SCRC.

60. Wick to Coggeshall, September 17, 1963.

61. Ibid.; Edward H. Levi to Roger W. Heyns, September 24, 1963, Beadle Records, Box 189, Folder 3, SCRC.

conference materials with someone likely more interested in the UChicago Division of the Social Sciences or Department of Education. Johnson believed there was no need to forward them to Levi or UChicago President George W. Beadle, and no one should attend any future meetings of midwestern universities on this topic. "I don't think we can ignore this matter in spite of the fact that our practices are above reproach," Johnson told the provost. "I feel we should adopt a position of being sympathetic, interested, and helpful whenever we can be of assistance."[62]

Johnson was certainly overconfident in his assessment that UChicago's engagement on questions about race were "above reproach." UChicago had its own racial issues with housing and urban renewal; however, Johnson felt the other universities were moving so quickly that "pitfalls" were inevitable. As a result, there were "many individuals [at state-supported institutions] who, given the opportunity, will take advantage of the situation and run with the ball so fast that all of us would find ourselves in an unfavorable and indefensible position."[63]

What Johnson had observed was that many white college presidents were seeking publicity for their Black programs. By this point, prominent private universities already received the bulk of national media attention, and UChicago had enjoyed much of the 1950s receiving positive press for its urban renewal efforts. President Beadle, Levi, Johnson, and other senior administrators at UChicago understood the power of positive publicity. In fact, in 1963, after UChicago was featured in *Time* and *Newsweek*, Beadle told Carl W. Larsen, director of public relations, the publicity was "worth a million in endowment." Relatedly, on January 29, 1964, the *Wall Street Journal* published a feature article about white colleges and universities recruiting more Black students. By 1964, this was a common effort among private and state-supported institutions from the Northeast to the West. Yet, the article named only private institutions: Princeton, Yale, Wellesley, Dartmouth, Oberlin. It also identified southern private institutions, such as Duke, Davidson, and Tulane, as seeking Black students for the first time. No state-supported universities were mentioned. [64]

The underlying truth in Johnson's assessment was that the ideas discussed among academic leaders were tainted by self-serving motives and a half-hearted

62. Warren C. Johnson to Edward H. Levi, October 25, 1963, Beadle Records, Box 189, Folder 3, SCRC.

63. Warren C. Johnson to Edward H. Levi, December 11, 1963, Beadle Records, Box 189, Folder: 4, SCRC.

64. George W. Beadle to Carl W. Larsen, May 31, 1963, Beadle Records, Box 263, Folder 1, SCRC; Lawrence L. Lynch, "Many Colleges Offer Extra Financial Aid to Recruit Negroes," *Wall Street Journal*, January 29, 1964.

belief in the broader goals and vision for affirmative action. For example, Harrington confided to two UW colleagues that "the exchange program has not started yet; but already some of the predominantly white institutions in the South are worried about 'carpet baggers.'" Harrington understood this was important to Proctor because leading a state-supported Black college left no room to anger white southerners, and he promised the Black leader that he would contact UNC president William Friday about the "carpet bagger" concerns.[65]

In reality, however, Harrington was actually dismissive of Black colleges. On March 25, 1964, Harrington told Friday that he wanted UW's efforts "to pay more attention to the North and to the Negroes and other deprived citizens of the northern states." Also, regarding the exchange programs with Black colleges, Harrington said, "I personally at first was rather doubtful about this approach since I thought that integration would eventually wipe out the 'predominantly Negro' label." Harrington did not believe Black colleges would exist in a desegregated society, but he said private foundation officers and southern Black and white academic leaders believed Black colleges "will be with us for a long time." Therefore, Harrington gently framed the exchange programs as something the private foundations "seem to be interested in going ahead on" and "the foundations are interested and moving fast." It was the foundation officers that were pushing the Black college programs, he explained. Yet, he omitted telling Friday that Donald McNeil, his assistant, was simultaneously soliciting Ford, Rockefeller, Carnegie, and other foundations to support UW's exchange program with three Black colleges. Harrington did not want to create a public rift between UW and a fellow AAU member because he was most interested in publicity.[66]

For instance, on June 15, 1964, McNeil asked Robert Taylor, a journalism professor, what more he could do to secure national media exposure. McNeil was frustrated that the Brown University–Tougaloo College exchange program was announced in *Time* magazine and "other newspapers around the country." Before Brown and Tougaloo were featured, he had spoken with a *Time* reporter who "seemed to think there was a possibility of doing a story solely on Wisconsin," but that did not materialize. Instead, it was Brown that earned the national spotlight. He confessed to Taylor that "we—whether anybody realizes it or not—are doing more than any institution in the country."

65. Fred H. Harrington to Jack Barbash and C. H. Ruedisili, March 25, 1964, Harrington Papers, Box 40, Folder: Civil Rights–Sam Proctor, UW; Harrington to Proctor, March 27, 1964.

66. Fred H. Harrington to William Friday, March 25, 1964, Harrington Papers, Box 40, Folder: Civil Rights–Sam Proctor, UW.

He admitted that what UW had accomplished thus far "isn't much, but compared to the others, it is a great deal." McNeil then explained to Taylor all the programs in the works at UW: the youth program in Milwaukee, the summer institute for Black college faculty in mathematics, the exchange program with three Black colleges, and the research studies. "It seems we would have a pretty good story to tell," McNeil assumed. "Do you suppose this is worth pursuing to get us a decent spread in *Time* or *Newsweek*? It would help me immeasurably with Ford and other foundations, government agencies, and [Peace Corp director Sargent] Shriver's new poverty outfit." Perhaps Samuel D. Proctor also realized that UW officials were partly motivated by publicity and the finances of private foundations; thus, he notified Harrington in May 1964, declining the offer to lead the Institute of Human Relations.[67]

On June 16, the day after McNeil inquired about media placement, he and Harrington welcomed representatives from the three Black colleges in the exchange program to the Madison campus. During a press conference as part of the two-day meeting, the Black educators mentioned how southern white institutions were now interested in working with them. Glenn F. Rankin, dean of instruction at North Carolina A&T, said President Friday at UNC had recently suggested a cooperative program between the institutions. John S. Lash, an English professor at Texas Southern, mentioned that Rice University and the University of Houston were having discussions about similar programs. Meanwhile, Cecil L. Patterson from North Carolina College added that Duke University was considering exchange opportunities. The *Wisconsin State Journal* published an article on page 10, and the *Capital Times* published a front page article after the first day of the event, but only a brief and no photo for the second day.[68]

A week later, on June 22, 1964, UW opened its Mathematics Institute. It was one of five summer institutes held concurrently across the nation for Black college faculty. The other institutes included physics at Princeton; history at Carnegie Tech; English at Indiana; and biology at UNC-Greensboro. The Rockefeller Foundation spent $150,000 to host the UW and UNC-Greensboro institutes and the Carnegie Corporation added $255,000 to support the others. At UW, the institute offered "courses devoted to the consideration of concepts

67. Donald McNeil to Robert Taylor, June 15, 1964, Assistant to the President Records, Donald R. McNeil, Box 8, Folder: Negro Intra-University Activities, UW; on Taylor's academic appointment, see "Distinguished Professor Taylor Dies," *University of Wisconsin News Service*, February 11, 2013, https://news.wisc.edu/distinguished-professor-taylor-dies/ (accessed April 11, 2019); Samuel D. Proctor to Fred H. Harrington, May 16, 1964, Harrington Papers, Box 40, Folder: Civil Rights–Sam Proctor, UW.

68. David Bednarek, "UW Plan Affects South Schools," *WSJ*, July 17, 1964; "Exchange Program Is Lauded," *CT*, July 18, 1964.

and approaches that can be used effectively in college mathematics courses, particularly those at the freshman level." In one regard, Harrington may have halted the "carpet bagger" concerns and helped pushed southern academic leaders to slightly raise the segregated curtain. Yet, publicity was limited, and one year later, UW administrators found themselves still disappointed in the lack of publicity behind their efforts.[69]

On June 18, 1965, McNeil shared with Harrington a recent Rockefeller Foundation report. The special report was titled, "The Long Road to College: A Summer of Opportunity," and featured Princeton, Oberlin, and Dartmouth. "As you know, what galls me is that we were in the game very early," McNeil complained to Harrington. "But again, the private colleges had the inside track." The nearly fifty-page report featured a descriptive narrative about Black children from disadvantaged backgrounds simply needing an opportunity. The foundation discussed the camaraderie the Black children developed as they summered at the exclusive colleges. "All three colleges kept their charges running hard all day," read the report, documenting the experience of the Black high schoolers. "All the youngsters were delighted with the college students who lived with them. . . . Often they became heroes to the youngsters, most of whom had never known a college student."[70]

The report was self-congratulatory and oblivious of Black life in America. Even something as simple as assuming most of the Black high schoolers were unfamiliar with a single college-going or college-educated person blatantly ignored the fact that the teachers and principals at Black schools had graduated from college. Nonetheless, it was something Harrington desired for UW. "The Rockefeller booklet on Negroes really is shameful. So much credit for so little," he said. "I haven't wanted too much publicity because we have accomplished so little (even though we have done more than most). But this fall we might consider a book like this on all our action programs."[71]

69. For more about the summer institutes, see A Report on the Conference on Programs to Assist Predominantly Negro Colleges and Universities, April 18–19, 1964, Goheen Records, Box 176, Folder 8, Princeton Archives. In April 1964, a meeting was held at the Massachusetts Institute of Technology (MIT) and financed by the Carnegie Corporation featuring dozens of Black college presidents, administrators, and faculty. The purpose of the two-day meeting was to discuss the details of the upcoming summer institutes; ACE, *Expanding Opportunities*.

70. Donald McNeil to Fred H. Harrington, June 18, 1965, Assistant to the President Records, Donald R. McNeil, Box 7, Folder: Rockefeller Foundation, UW; Rockefeller Foundation, "The Long Road to College."

71. Fred H. Harrington to Donald McNeil, June 24, 1965, Assistant to the President Records, Donald R. McNeil, Box 7, Folder: Rockefeller Foundation, UW.

The institutional-minded interests of Harrington and other white college presidents ultimately caused the Black college partnerships to fall apart. The system-wide goals were dismissed for the institution-specific objectives for white campuses, and this was not just the case at UW. In April 1965, for example, a dean at Tuskegee expressed his displeasure with how the exchange program was unfolding at Michigan. Many aspects of the Michigan-Tuskegee cooperative left him "disappointed with the way the relationship has developed." Tuskegee academic leaders felt Michigan had not promoted the program to its campus. Also, there was a lack of contact with faculty at Michigan, which had not made an earnest effort to recruit Tuskegee students. "I thought that one of the important parts of the relationship was the development of opportunities for graduate study by our students," the Tuskegee dean complained, but Michigan's response was that Black college's academic leaders must have had a simple "misunderstanding" about the program.[72]

A few months later, Congress and other federal officials earmarked financial support for the "special programs" that the late President Kennedy called for in July 1963. For two years, the Samuel M. Nabrit–led proposal that white academic leaders adopted had not secured the federal funding anticipated, thus leaving the initial programming supported only by private foundations. Yet, on June 4, 1965, US president Lyndon B. Johnson delivered one of the most important public declarations in the history of affirmative action. At the commencement ceremony for Howard University in Washington, DC, Johnson said, "Much of the Negro community is buried under a blanket of history and circumstance. It is not a lasting solution to lift just one corner of that blanket. We must stand on all sides and we must raise the entire cover if we are to liberate our fellow citizens." Johnson's point about "all sides" accurately captured the broad affirmative action goals that Nabrit, president of Texas Southern, had proposed two years earlier. Race-based admissions practices at white institutions were only one side of that figurative blanket. Strengthening Black colleges' financial standing, physical infrastructure, and faculty and student access to educational resources were its other sides.[73]

72. For the quotes between Tuskegee and Michigan officials, see Park, "Planting the Seeds," pp. 123–125. Park suggested the Michigan-Tuskegee program "probably lacked the level of administrative support expressed in official memos and press releases," (p. 125) and "For Michigan, the program appears to have been motivated by feelings of benevolence, self-interest, and perhaps a degree of public relations as well" (p. 130).

73. On the Nabrit proposal not receiving federal funding, see Harrington to Friday, March 25, 1964; Lyndon B. Johnson, To Fulfill These Rights, Howard University Commencement Address, June 4, 1965, http://www.lbjlibrary.net/collections/selected-speeches/1965/06-04-1965 .html (accessed March 5, 2019).

Following Johnson's signing of the landmark Civil Rights Act of 1964 and Voting Rights Act of 1965, the Higher Education Act of 1965 added to the promise of a broader commitment to Black higher education. Within the act, the purpose of Title III—"Strengthening Developing Institutions"— was to

> assist in raising the academic quality of colleges which have the desire and potential to make a substantial contribution to the higher education resources of our Nation but which for financial and other reasons are struggling for survival and are isolated from the main currents of academic life.

The act authorized $55 million to "carry out the provisions of this title." Also, despite the act not specifically naming Black colleges in its definition of "developing institutions," Title III's purpose extended to the "establishment of cooperative arrangements under which these colleges may draw on the talent and experience of our finest colleges and universities, and on the educational resources of business and industry, in their effort to improve their academic quality." By the late 1960s, however, the sentiment behind the self-serving motives and doubt about Black colleges that white academic leaders whispered among themselves emerged publicly.[74]

In 1966, Harold M. Rose, a Black geography professor at UW-Milwaukee, had seen enough of UW administrators' actions to offer a bold prediction about exchange programs with Black colleges:

> The potential of exchange programs is well worth the effort of establishing them if goals are sharply defined and participating colleges and universities make a sincere attempt to advance education by removing some of the handicaps which have confronted Negro college graduates in the past.

He then added: "It will be necessary for some Northern institutions to examine their motives carefully, in order not to seek participation in co-operative programs from a sense of righteousness or false pride." There were other concerns as well: would faculty at the white institutions be available or willing to spend a term at a southern Black college; would the nonsouthern institutions

---

74. Higher Education Act of 1965, November 8, 1965, Higher Education Act of 1965, p. 1129. Historian Martha Biondi explained that the Higher Education Act of 1965 "increased federal aid to universities and created scholarships and low-interest loans, spurring colleges and universities to increase the admission of African American and other underrepresented students. This marked the beginning of a more significant Black student presence on many historically white campuses." For more, see Biondi, *Black Revolution on Campus*, p. 82.

hire full-time staff to coordinate the inter-institutional efforts; and did students see the programs as simply keeping Black colleges "within the bounds of the existing system" or as truly improving Black education?[75]

Black college presidents had ventured north on multiple occasions throughout the early 1960s with the earnest goal of working with their white counterparts on multiple programs that would enhance their institutions and also benefit the white institutions now welcoming Black students in bulk. The white institutions had the resources and Black institutions had the pedagogical understanding of what it meant to educate Black students. Yet, education scholar Charles V. Willie concluded that, in 1967, "Probably no other event caused black educators to mistrust white liberals more than the *Harvard Educational Review* article entitled 'The American Negro College' that was authored by Christopher Jencks and David Riesman." Jencks and Riesman admitted that some Black colleges—Fisk, Spelman, Hampton, Howard, Morgan State and a few others—were the "head of the Negro academic procession," but even those institutions "would probably fall near the middle of the national academic procession."[76]

Jencks and Riesman argued, "Underpaid as their faculty members are, many of them could not make as much elsewhere. Some, indeed, could not get any other academic job. Insecure and marginal, they become insistently pedantic." By 1968, Black college programs with white institutions were on the decline if not outright defunct. First, the private foundation officers turned their attention to other issues. "Higher education was deemphasized in favor of grade school and high school," wrote Willie, assessing the Rockefeller Foundation. "Social change as a goal of foundation grant-making activity was still a major concern. By the close of 1968, however, the Foundation was more interested in institutional change than in producing changes within individuals alone." The foundation was "becoming more directly involved with the problems of the urban ghetto . . . ," he added. About the same time, the Ford Foundation took an interest in African American Studies programs, but that too declined over time. White institutions all but abandoned their interest in Black college exchange programs and institutes and turned completely to admitting significant numbers of Black students. To white college presidents like Harrington, the initial investment in the development of Black institutions was

75. Rose, "Teacher-Exchange Programs," p. 324.

76. Willie, "Philanthropic and Foundation Support," p. 278; Jencks and Riesman, "The American Negro College," p. 25.

less attractive than the publicity gained by further diversifying their own campuses.[77]

Conclusion

College presidents were the architects behind affirmative action programs in higher education after federal officials turned toward them to help address the effects of racial discrimination. Therefore, a collaborative effort emerged among academic leaders who recommended a range of programs that would aid Black people and other disadvantaged groups. College presidents tasked admissions officers with identifying and recruiting Black youth from the public high schools they usually overlooked. They also rallied behind the Samuel M. Nabrit–led idea that white college presidents dedicate their intellectual and financial resources to helping strengthen the Black colleges. Combined, both efforts were designed to help Black people attain more educational opportunities regardless of geographic region or whether at a Black or white campus. Affirmative action at its initial implementation was broad in scope, but by the end of 1964, federal officials had not earmarked federal funding to support the Nabrit-Zachari-White proposal. This left the partnership universities to seek private foundation officers for support.[78]

The search for private funding positioned white college presidents to compete among themselves, ultimately leaving Black colleges as an afterthought. Black educators were often invited to brainstorm with white presidents over how to achieve the broad affirmative action goals; however, white academic leaders were more interested in using Black talent for their own institutions. The courtship of Samuel D. Proctor by Fred Harvey Harrington is just one example, and if not Proctor, Talladega College president Herman Long was also on UW's shortlist to become director of its proposed human relations institute. Additionally, white academic leaders' search for national publicity distracted them from actually planning the programs with Black colleges. For instance, in June 1964, UW officials were described as still "working out" details for its

---

77. Jencks and Riesman, "American Negro College," p. 26. On the private foundations changing focus, see Willie, "Philanthropic and Foundation Support," p. 282; and Rooks, *White Money/ Black Power*, particularly p. 83.

78. Numerous primary sources credit Samuel M. Nabrit, president of Texas Southern, with the initial idea behind the exchange programs and summer institutes with white institutions. Two such sources are ACE, *Expanding Opportunities*; and Harrington to Friday, March 25, 1964. In the latter, Harrington noted that federal officials had not committed the funds initially expected to support Nabrit's plan.

partnership with North Carolina A&T, North Carolina College, and Texas Southern even after they had held a press conference about the program.[79]

The most perverse outcome was that adopting affirmative action programs actually advanced the careers of several white presidents and their white contemporaries. In 1965, the same year Tuskegee officials questioned their exchange program, Michigan's Roger W. Heyns, vice president for academic affairs, accepted the chancellorship at the University of California, Berkeley. Michigan's N. Edd Miller, assistant vice president for academic affairs, also left to become the chancellor of the University of Nevada. From Wisconsin, in 1968, Donald McNeil was named chancellor of the University of Maine. Afterward, newspaper reports noted that McNeil was credited for UW's "shift from the emphasis on agriculture to wider areas of public concern, particularly poverty and aids to the disadvantaged." In summary, their engagement with programs for Blacks in higher education was beneficial to their careers while their urgent, yet self-serving, planning had lingering effects.[80]

Decades later, historians and journalists continue to document the campus revolts that Black students spearheaded at numerous white institutions in the late 1960s and early 1970s. Upon their arrival, the demonstrations unveiled the lack of preparation to welcome Black students to white campuses and also exposed the effects of the racist policies and practices that white college presidents developed. White college presidents, alongside aspiring presidents, made a series of calculated decisions that framed affirmative action to exclusively represent the interests of white colleges and universities—an outcome far different from its initial design.

79. On Talladega College's president being considered for Wisconsin, see Vevier to Harrington, March 19, 1964; Bednarek, "UW Plan Affects South Schools."

80. Dennis Hevesi, "Roger W. Heyns, 77, Head of Berkeley in the 60's," *New York Times*, September 14, 1995; Megan Akers, "Nena Miller, Education Advocate, Wills Bronze Statue to University," *Nevada Today*, May 4, 2012; "McNeil Named Chancellor at U of Maine," *WSJ*, December 14, 1968. For further reading on how affirmative action aided white Americans more generally, see Katznelson, *When Affirmative Action Was White*.

Conclusion

THE CAMPUS COLOR LINE discloses how the Black Freedom Movement shaped, and was shaped by, the actions of college presidents. Spanning a variety of regions and institutional types, this book uses the American college presidency as a way to explain the spectrum of social and economic struggles during the movement. Institutions of higher education have usually occupied a marginal position in accounts about this period, but this national study places colleges and universities and their academic leaders at the center. It considers both Black and white campus environments across regional boundaries to bring all institutional types into the same web of analysis. In doing so, this book presents an opportunity to compare the effectiveness of Black and white presidents managing institutions during racial crisis, and this approach is advantageous to better understanding the broader system of higher education vis-à-vis single institutions or presidents studied in isolation. In summary, our understanding of the Black Freedom Movement—one of the most dynamic social movements in American history—is enhanced by studying college presidents as a collective. Their involvement in molding racial policies and practices at the institutional, state, and national level bears witness to why college campuses have been the most fertile grounds for social change.

The decisions made by the presidents of state-supported institutions are insightful for answering longstanding questions about the role of higher education in society. The concept of education for the public good was embedded within concerns over autonomy in academic leadership, and this is evident at Black or white state-supported campuses. For example, at Black colleges, negotiations were made within the parameters of a segregated society. Black presidents of state-supported institutions occupied a complicated role during the Black Freedom Movement. Some of them ultimately sacrificed their public reputations because they only fought privately for Black liberation behind the scenes. Yet, many of them were instrumental in helping maintain control of their institutions, secure money from white legislators for out-of-state scholarship programs and other initiatives, fight back against racists, and support student demands—all racial policies and practices that often had to be negotiated quietly.

The leaders of state-supported institutions were also responsible for how higher education expanded during the postwar years. At a time when the nation's private institutions remained largely exclusive, the bulk of the public looked to access higher education through state colleges and universities. In such circumstances, the university system—one state institution with multiple branch campuses—became a means to both expand and limit who could access specific campuses. Those decisions had racial implications, as questions about whether the academic leaders of state-supported institutions were the ultimate decision makers on their own campuses rather than state-level elected officials. In turn, these decisions (or the lack thereof) positioned college presidents to grapple with and implement practices related to the state-supported university's ultimate role in advancing or stifling racial equality. Therefore, as Black citizens had long been discriminated against in terms of access to educational resources, presidents were a driving force behind varying decisions with racial implications on state-supported campuses.

At private institutions, college presidents also helped mold policies and implement practices that had a far-reaching impact on the struggles for Black freedom. The presidents of the most exclusive and, by default, influential private universities used their prestige to shape federal-level decisions. One prominent issue was federal housing policies. As major cities experienced postwar migration, formerly all-white or majority-white neighborhoods experienced significant demographic shifts. The tensions over these shifts were significant due to racism and the subsequent prevalence of housing discrimination, which caused widespread overcrowding. The presidents of private urban universities acted swiftly to lobby federal- and state-level officials to amend policies and development funding models to displace the growing Black communities near their campuses. Also, the housing crisis was directly linked to public health issues with implications pertinent to Black residents. This tension between large universities and neighboring nonwhite communities is fairly well-known history; however, *The Campus Color Line* demonstrates how this was accomplished and the related impact on broader struggles for Black freedom. In using the white media while leveraging personal relationships with federal officials, the academic leaders of private institutions used public agents to advance institutional goals at the sacrifice of Black residents' right to fair housing and much more.

Combined, this history of the Black Freedom Movement as seen through the actions presidents of state-supported and private institutions—both Black and white and southern and nonsouthern—highlights how deeply white supremacy has been embedded within higher education. White control was a foundational concept working for or against these presidencies. For instance, Black college presidents were essentially in a battle over the control of their institutions. Even when Black colleges had independent boards of trustees, there was a persistent effort by state officials to acquire control of those boards or, at a minimum, influence curricular decisions at Black institutions. Formal segregation is based on the premise that white people should control *all* colleges and universities, and this was the case for Black and white campuses in the South.

Outside of the South, whiteness was also centered across a variety of issues. Among the numerous examples presented throughout this book, one of the most prevalent is the formation of the original affirmative action programs in higher education. The programs initially geared toward enhancing Black college resources were dismantled by white academic leaders who envisioned their campuses as the best places to address racial inequality. Black talent was best served, they argued, by white institutions. This led to attempted raids of Black administrators and faculty from Black colleges to serve white purposes. This also empowered white scholars to launch studies and establish race-focused research centers about Black institutions but oftentimes not with Black scholars. These actions derived from one of the most prevalent white supremacist beliefs: that whites were best at advising Black colleges, and Black people generally, about how to rectify societal racial inequalities. In short, Blackness was valued as long as it was under white control.

The most intriguing aspect of these historic challenges is how they remain prevalent today. Black colleges are still subject to white critique. White state officials and Black academic leaders still have contentious funding battles, which are rooted within the legacy of segregation. Similarly, white-centered accrediting agencies disproportionately levy penalties among Black colleges. These associations hold an "equal" standard of evaluation, particularly when it comes to financial standing, without accounting for the vestiges of systemic racism. Furthermore, these challenges are exacerbated by the legacy of popular press media framing of these institutions. Just as Martin D. Jenkins understood differences in the coverage of events by the *Baltimore Afro-American* and the *Baltimore Sun*, Black presidents continue to gingerly engage media (including social media) in efforts to protect their institutions and the communities they serve. The contemporary takeaway about the historic campus color line is how have the implications of desegregation impacted Black presidents' use of, and perceived need for, networking among themselves to advocate for their institutions as a collective, not individually.

Another lingering challenge is the contradictory behavior of white academic leaders in a modern society that touts racial diversity as a value. Many university-run police departments on white campuses are criticized for the way officers engage Black students and local Black residents. This harks back to when the criminalization of Black youth was a tactic that white presidents used to justify urban renewal programs. Additionally, even when some white campus administrators want to serve as allies, there is evidence that internal mechanisms and organizational structures can hamper those efforts to aid racial equality. Perhaps most notably, when one recalls the relationships between college presidents and the Black Freedom Movement, is the prevalent violence of silence among presidents of white colleges—an issue that remains debated today. Today, as in the past, several academic leaders take no stance in public statements or speeches regarding racial unrest, and there is remarkable inaction among college presidents while students, staff, faculty, and local residents demand an end to racism.[1]

The decision to remain quiet during a racial crisis is telling because college presidents did not lead universities in isolation from racial unrest. In Philadelphia, University of Pennsylvania president Gaylord P. Harnwell was involved in the university's expansion as it benefited from urban renewal initiatives that displaced a disproportionate number of Black residents. He was present at the 1957 meeting alongside the University of Chicago's George W. Beadle, and Black people in West Philadelphia were on the losing end of urban renewal. They voiced their demands, but Harnwell's public addresses were silent on civil rights. Similarly, in Los Angeles, Norman Topping, president of the University of Southern California, spent the early 1960s fundraising and speaking at country clubs—in drastic contrast to Franklin D. Murphy, chancellor at the University of California, Los Angeles, who spent a sizable portion of his time attempting to advance racial equality on campus and in the city. But the silence of Harnwell and Topping at private universities was not just a product of institutional type. Even Harlan H. Hatcher from the University of Michigan remained quiet on racial inequality when he was invited to speak before white audiences in the South.[2]

On February 15, 1964, Hatcher visited Jackson, Mississippi, for the Sixth Annual First Federal Foundation Awards Program, courtesy of a personal invitation from Ole Miss chancellor John Davis Williams. Hatcher delivered a lengthy speech about service, titled "Salute to Leadership." He focused primarily on one's service to the country and service to one's neighbor. Yet, this

1. A recent study related to whiteness in higher education is Cabrera, *White Guys on Campus*.

2. This paragraph is focused specifically on the public opinions expressed, in speeches or formal statements, by the presidents of the University of Pennsylvania and the University of Southern California. For the most part, in a review of more than sixty speeches, these public addresses are vacant of even vague references to civil rights.

speech was given in Mississippi, and Hatcher did not mention the state's social ills and ill treatment of its Black residents. The irony is that Hatcher publicly disavowed racial violence when he visited Tuskegee, a Black college in Alabama, the next month.[3]

Clark Kerr, president of the University of California, also held his tongue when speaking in the segregated South. On April 28, 1964, Kerr spoke at the inauguration of John W. Oswald as president of the University of Kentucky. Previously, Oswald was vice president for administration at the University of California, and Kerr traveled south to celebrate his former colleague's new role. Arguably, the occasion did not warrant a reference to racism and its impact on higher education, and therefore, Kerr made no mention of racial unrest in the South or back in California. Yet, a week later on May 5, 1964, Kerr discussed "The University: Civil Rights and Civic Responsibilities" during the university's charter day ceremonies in Davis, California. There, he vowed not to reprimand California students who were arrested in the South for civil rights demonstrations. "A citizen, who is not also a student, would have no such second trial or second penalty," Kerr said. "It would be manifestly unfair to treat the citizen who is also a student differently from the citizen who is not also a student." Kerr went on to condemn racial segregation when, only a week earlier, he had remained silent on the same issue when speaking at Kentucky, which still maintained all-white athletics programs.[4]

College presidents have an obligation to speak out and act against racial injustice, and historical silence connects the long history of college presidents and race in higher education with today's issues. The college president—in terms of responsibilities to varying stakeholders—functions like an elected official. Rhetoricians and political scientists have compiled decades of research interrogating the words of current or former US presidents, governors, and other elected officials. Of particular relevance, scholars argue that an elected official's emphasis on a particular topic influences the general public's interests in those areas. There are some obvious differences in the scope of the US presidency and that of the college presidency; however, the consensus is that a public leader's words matter. That is why the history of college presidents and social movements over race is

3. Harlan H. Hatcher, "Salute to Leadership," speech, February 15, 1964, Harlan Henthorne Hatcher Papers, Box 57, Bentley Historical Library, University of Michigan (collection and location hereafter cited as Hatcher Papers and Michigan).

4. On Kerr at the University of Kentucky, see Clark Kerr, "Greetings" at John W. Oswald inauguration, April 28, 1964, Clark Kerr Personal and Professional Papers, Carton 29, Folder 66, Bancroft Library, University of California, Berkeley (collection and location hereafter cited as Kerr Papers and UC-Berkeley); Clark Kerr, "The University: Civil Rights and Civic Responsibilities" speech, Kerr Papers, Carton 29, Folder 15, UC-Berkeley.

significant. Campus initiatives geared toward racial equality are only as effective as the college president's clearly articulated acknowledgment that racism is a problem. Anything less is negligent of each institution's unique mission to educate, and it leaves a key question unanswered: What is the responsibility of college presidents in the fight for racial equality?[5]

———

On March 22, 1964, Michigan's Harlan H. Hatcher spoke in Tuskegee, Alabama. He had been invited to rural Macon County by Tuskegee Institute president Luther H. Foster. The two men's acquaintance had grown over the years as their respective institutions launched the Michigan-Tuskegee Program for Mutual Development. The partnership's highlights included additional graduate-level training for Tuskegee students, cultural exchanges such as Tuskegee's choir performing at Michigan, and collaborative research to address "problems of mutual interest," such as "the emerging role of the Negro in American life." Now, on this early spring Sunday, Hatcher stood before an overwhelmingly Black audience as the keynote speaker for the Tuskegee Founder's Day Program. In advance, Foster told Hatcher that any subject he chose would be appropriate. He was simply "delighted" that Hatcher was attending the celebration. Yet, as a Black academic leader, Foster did offer some suggestions. A brief tribute "to the life and contributions" of founder Booker T. Washington and thoughts on a present-day issue in education or human relations would suffice. Fittingly, Hatcher adhered to Foster's suggestion and discussed America's racial crisis. The previous year, Alabama had been placed in the national spotlight thanks to the use of police dogs and water hoses on peacefully assembled Black youth in Birmingham, the church bombings also in Birmingham, and the governor's standing in the schoolhouse door in Tuscaloosa, and Hatcher's thoughts were particularly fitting. "The 1963 revelations of our backwardness and inadequate progress in basic American freedoms will have a comparable impact upon race relations and the role of the Negro citizen among his fellow Americans," Hatcher said at Tuskegee. "Our world cannot again be the same."[6]

5. Regarding the study of rhetoric, particularly among public officials, see the following: Burden and Sanberg, "Budget Rhetoric"; Cohen, "Presidential Rhetoric"; Cohen and Hamman, "'The Polls'"; O'Loughlin and Grant, "Presidential Speeches." Regarding campus diversity agendas, see Harper and Hurtado, "Nine Themes in Campus Racial Climates"; Cole and Harper, "Race and Rhetoric."

6. Luther H. Foster to Harlan H. Hatcher, December 20, 1963; Harlan H. Hatcher, "Michigan and Tuskegee" speech, March 22, 1964; Hatcher mentioned the Michigan-Tuskegee program in

Unfortunately, more than a half-century after this speech, an appropriate question is, did American higher education remain the same? Incidents of racism tied to higher education remain prevalent today, and since the campaign and subsequent election of US president Donald J. Trump, data compiled by the US Department of Education noted that reported hate crimes increased by 25 percent from 2015 to 2016. Specifically, during November 2016, the month of the election, law enforcement data, including data collected by the Federal Bureau of Investigation, confirmed a notable uptick in hate crimes, including incidents targeting race, disability, religion, gender, and national origin. The arrival of the Trump Administration stirred intolerance on campuses, and no particular institutional type was immune. In February 2017, Howard University president Wayne A. I. Frederick was confronted by students at the historically Black university for meeting with President Trump, who has repeatedly spoken out against Black Lives Matter. "Welcome to the Trump Plantation. Overseer: Wayne A. I. Frederick," read a message written on a university sidewalk. The same year, in August 2017, Teresa Sullivan at the University of Virginia faced a white nationalist rally that ended violently in Charlottesville. A series of internal e-mails revealed a hesitance among Virginia academic leaders to condemn neo-Nazis and white supremacists by name. The university's public statements were described as "tepid." In an America that followed its first Black president in Barack H. Obama by electing a US president publicly supported by white nationalists, the pronouncement by Harlan H. Hatcher at Tuskegee in 1964 resounds today—our world should not be the same.[7]

The Campus Color Line contributes to an understanding of the broader meaning of the institutional and cultural structures that are distinctive aspects of American democratic society. It demonstrates how, too often, historians recognize the importance of individual institutions while missing the larger social and political significance of the totality of the range of institutions, from

---

his Founder's Day address at Tuskegee; for a lengthier account of the program, see Harlan H. Hatcher, "State of the University" address, September 30, 1963; all in Hatcher Papers, Box 57, Michigan.

7. Dan Bauman, "After 2016 Election, Campus Hate Crimes Seemed to Jump; Here's What the Data Tell Us," *Chronicle of Higher Education*, February 16, 2018; Anemona Hartocollis and Noah Weiland, "Campus Backlash after Leaders of Black Colleges Meet with Trump," *New York Times*, March 4, 2017; Jack Stripling, "'Et Tu, Teresa?' How Pressure Built for U. of Virginia to Condemn Racists," *Chronicle of Higher Education*, November 20, 2017; Morgan Gstalter, "David Duke Praises Trump for Tweet about 'Large Scale Killing' of White Farmers," *The Hill*, August 23, 2018, https://thehill.com/homenews/administration/403210-david-duke-praises -trump-for-tweet-about-large-scale-killing-of-white (accessed March 10, 2020).

smaller colleges to elite colleges and universities. Yet, college presidents across the entire higher education landscape were positioned to play a significant role in helping institutions navigate between the American ideals of equal opportunity and the brutal realities of hardened social disparities due to segregation. Thus, this book provides insights that can lead to a better functional understanding of higher education through its historical analysis of college presidents' evolving roles, responsibilities, limitations, and networks as leaders during a period of dramatic social breakdown. Today, we have entered into a similar moment of social breakdown. Many media outlets and the general public have likened the recent wave of racial unrest on college campuses to those of the mid-twentieth century. This is important regardless of whether today is truly a new civil rights era or continuation of ongoing struggles for Black freedom. This book examines a history ripe for the contemporary university president and for anyone interested in understanding how academic leaders can embrace the influence of their position and commit to racial justice—a commitment that is the hallmark of any institution *truly* dedicated to liberation.[8]

8. Regarding popular press comparisons to the civil rights movement, see the introduction for recent articles from news organizations, such as *The Hill, US News & World Report,* and others.

BIBLIOGRAPHY

Archival Collections

GEORGIA INSTITUTE OF TECHNOLOGY, GEORGIA TECH LIBRARY

Desegregation File
Edwin Harrison Papers
Student Council Papers

MORGAN STATE UNIVERSITY, EARL S. RICHARDSON LIBRARY, BEULAH DAVIS RESEARCH ROOM

Martin D. Jenkins Collection
Morris A. Soper, Morgan Christian Center, and Morgan Board of Trustees Papers
Morgan State College Bulletin Collection

NORTH CAROLINA STATE ARCHIVES

Luther Hartwell Hodges Collection
Terry S. Sanford Governor's Papers

PRINCETON UNIVERSITY, SEELEY G. MUDD MANUSCRIPT LIBRARY

Princeton Alumni Weekly Collection
Robert F. Goheen: Office of the President Records

UNIVERSITY OF ALABAMA, W. S. HOOLE SPECIAL COLLECTIONS LIBRARY

Frank A. Rose Papers: President's Office Files
J. Jefferson Bennett Papers

UNIVERSITY OF CALIFORNIA, BERKELEY, BANCROFT LIBRARY

Clark Kerr Personal and Professional Papers

UNIVERSITY OF CALIFORNIA, LOS ANGELES, CHARLES E. YOUNG RESEARCH LIBRARY

Franklin D. Murphy Papers
Office of the Chancellor–Administrative Files of Franklin D. Murphy
UCLA Students: Student Activism Materials

UNIVERSITY OF CHICAGO, UNIVERSITY OF CHICAGO LIBRARY, SPECIAL COLLECTIONS RESEARCH CENTER

George Wells Beadle Papers
Hyde Park Historical Society Collection
Hyde Park–Kenwood Community Conference Records
Office of Student Activities Records
Office of the President: Beadle Administration Records
Sol Tax Papers
Student Government Records

UNIVERSITY OF KANSAS, MEDICAL CENTER

KU Medical Center, Oral History Project

UNIVERSITY OF MICHIGAN, BENTLEY HISTORICAL LIBRARY

Harlan Henthorne Hatcher Papers

UNIVERSITY OF MISSISSIPPI, J. D. WILLIAMS LIBRARY, ARCHIVES AND SPECIAL COLLECTIONS

Board of Trustee Reports and Minutes
George Street Collection
J. D. Williams Collection
James Howard Meredith Collection
Murphey Wilds Collection

UNIVERSITY OF PENNSYLVANIA, UNIVERSITY ARCHIVES AND RECORDS CENTER

Gaylord P. Harnwell Papers
Office of the President Records: Gaylord Probasco Harnwell Administration

UNIVERSITY OF SOUTHERN CALIFORNIA, DOHENY MEMORIAL LIBRARY

Leonard Wines Papers

UNIVERSITY OF WISCONSIN, STEENBOCK LIBRARY

Assistant to the President Records: Donald R. McNeil
Chancellors and Presidents Records: Conrad Arnold Elvehjem Papers
Chancellors and Presidents Records: Fred Harvey Harrington Papers
Conrad Arnold Elvehjem Biographical File
Division of Student Affairs, Office of Dean of Student Affairs: Leroy Luberg File
Fred Harvey Harrington Biographical File

WISCONSIN HISTORICAL SOCIETY

Congress on Racial Equality Collection

Newspapers and Magazines

Baltimore Afro-American
Baltimore Sun
Birmingham News
Birmingham Post-Herald
Capital Times (Madison, WI)
Chicago American
Chicago Daily News
Chicago Defender
Chicago Maroon
Chicago Sun-Times
Chicago Tribune
Clarion-Ledger (Jackson, MS)
Commercial Appeal (Memphis, TN)
Crimson White (University of Alabama)
Daily Bruin (University of California, Los Angeles)
Daily Californian (University of California, Berkeley)
Daily Cardinal (University of Wisconsin–Madison)
Daily Princetonian
Detroit Free Press
Ebony
Hyde Park (IL) Herald
Jet
Los Angeles Examiner
Los Angeles Sentinel

Los Angeles Times
Milwaukee Journal
Milwaukee Sentinel
Mississippian (University of Mississippi)
Montgomery (AL) Advertiser
New York Herald Tribune
New York Times
Newsweek
San Francisco Chronicle
Time
Wall Street Journal
Washington Afro-American
Washington Post
Wisconsin State Journal

Secondary Sources

Abrahamson, Eric John. *Building Home: Howard F. Ahmanson and the Politics of the American Dream* (Berkeley: University of California Press, 2013).

Alinsky, Saul D. *Rules for Radicals: A Practical Primer for Realistic Radicals* (New York: Random House, 1971).

Allen, Robert L. "The Bakke Case and Affirmative Action," *Black Scholar* 9, no. 1 (September 1977): 9–16.

———. *Black Awakening in Capitalist America* (New York: Doubleday, 1969).

Anderson, Eric, and Alfred A. Moss Jr. *Dangerous Donations: Northern Philanthropy and Southern Black Education, 1902–1930* (Columbia: University of Missouri Press, 1999).

Anderson, James D. *The Education of Blacks in the South, 1860–1935* (Chapel Hill: University of North Carolina Press, 1988).

———. "Philanthropy, the State and the Development of Historically Black Public Colleges: The Case of Mississippi," *Minerva* 35, no. 3 (Autumn 1997): 295–309.

———. "Race, Meritocracy, and the American Academy during the Immediate Post–World War II Era," *History of Education Quarterly* 33, no. 2 (Summer 1993): 151–175.

Anderson, Terry H. *The Pursuit of Fairness: A History of Affirmative Action* (Oxford: Oxford University Press, 2004).

Arsenault, Raymond. *Freedom Riders: 1961 and the Struggle for Racial Justice* (Oxford: Oxford University Press, 2006).

Axtell, James. *The Making of Princeton University: From Woodrow Wilson to the Present* (Princeton, NJ: Princeton University Press, 2006).

Baker, R. Scott. *Paradoxes of Desegregation: African American Struggles for Educational Equity in Charleston, South Carolina, 1926–1972* (Columbia: University of South Carolina Press, 2006).

Baldwin, James. *The Fire Next Time* (New York: Dial Press, 1963).

Balto, Simon. *Occupied Territory: Policing Black Chicago from Red Summer to Black Power* (Chapel Hill: University of North Carolina Press, 2019).

Barrett, Russell H. *Integration at Ole Miss* (Chicago: Quadrangle Books, 1965).

Baum, Howell S. *Brown in Baltimore: School Desegregation and the Limits of Liberalism* (Ithaca, NY: Cornell University Press, 2010).

Bell, Derrick. "Brown v. Board of Education and the Interest-Convergence Dilemma," *Harvard Law Review* 93, no. 3 (January 1980): 518–533.

———. *Silent Covenants: Brown v. Board of Education and the Unfulfilled Hopes for Racial Reform* (Oxford: Oxford University Press, 2004).

Bell, William M. *Black without Malice: The Bill Bell Story* (Fayetteville, NC: self-pub., 1983).

Benjamin, Lorna Akua. "The Black/Jamaican Criminal: The Making of Ideology" (PhD diss., University of Toronto, 2003).

Bieze, Michael. "Booker T. Washington: Philanthropy and Aesthetics," in Marybeth Gasman and Katherine V. Sedgwick (eds.), *Uplifting a People: African American Philanthropy and Education* (New York: Peter Lang, 2005).

Biondi, Martha. *The Black Revolution on Campus* (Berkeley: University of California Press, 2012).

Blain, Keisha N. *Set the World on Fire: Black Nationalist Women and the Global Struggle for Freedom* (Philadelphia: University of Pennsylvania Press, 2018).

Bond, Alan L. *The Imposing Preacher: Samuel Dewitt Proctor and Black Public Faith* (Minneapolis: Fortress Press, 2013).

Boyer, John W. *The University of Chicago: A History* (Chicago: University of Chicago Press, 2015).

Bradley, Gladyce Helene. "The Education of Negroes in Maryland," *Journal of Negro Education* 16, no. 3 (Summer 1947): 370–374.

Bradley, Stefan M. *Harlem vs. Columbia University: Black Student Power in the late 1960s* (Urbana-Champaign: University of Illinois Press, 2009).

———. "The Southern-Most Ivy: Princeton University from Jim Crow Admissions to Anti-Apartheid Protests, 1794–1969," *American Studies* 51, no. 3/4 (Fall/Winter 2010): 109–130.

———. *Upending the Ivory Tower: Civil Rights, Black Power, and the Ivy League* (New York: New York University Press, 2018).

Branson, Herman R. "Interinstitutional Programs for Promoting Equal Higher Educational Opportunities for Negroes," *Journal of Negro Education* 35, no. 4 (Autumn 1966): 469–476.

Brown, Linda Beatrice. *Belles of Liberty: Gender, Bennett College, and the Civil Rights Movement in Greensboro, North Carolina* (Greensboro: Women and Wisdom Press, 2013).

Brown, Scot. *Fighting for US: Maulana Karenga, the US Organization, and Black Cultural Nationalism* (New York: New York University Press, 2003).

Brown-Nagin, Tomiko. *Courage to Dissent: Atlanta and the Long History of the Civil Rights Movement* (Oxford: Oxford University Press, 2011).

Buni, Andrew. "Murphy, Carl," in Rayford W. Logan and Michael R. Winston (eds.), *Dictionary of American Negro Biography* (New York: W. W. Norton, 1982).

Burden, Barry C., and Joseph Neal Rice Sanberg. "Budget Rhetoric in Presidential Campaigns from 1952 to 2000," *Political Behavior* 25, no. 2 (June 2003): 97–188.

Bynum, Thomas. *NAACP Youth and the Fight for Black Freedom, 1936–1965* (Knoxville: University of Tennessee Press, 2013).

Byrd, Harry Clifton. "Remarks by President H. C. Byrd of the University of Maryland," *Morgan State College Bulletin* 3, no. 10 (December 1937): 7–9.

Cabrera, Nolan L. *White Guys on Campus: Racism, White Immunity, and the Myth of "Post-racial" Higher Education* (New Brunswick, NJ: Rutgers University Press, 2018).

Campbell, Marne L. *Making Black Los Angeles: Class, Gender, and Community, 1850–1917* (Chapel Hill: University of North Carolina Press, 2016).

Canton, David A. *Raymond Pace Alexander: A New Negro Lawyer Fights for Civil Rights in Philadelphia* (Jackson: University Press of Mississippi, 2010).

Carey, Bill. *Chancellors, Commodores, and Coeds: A History of Vanderbilt University* (Nashville, TN: Clearbrook Press, 2003).

Carson, Clayborne. *In Struggle: SNCC and the Black Awakening of the 1960s* (Cambridge, MA: Harvard University Press, 1981).

Catsam, Derek. *Freedom's Main Line: The Journey of Reconciliation and the Freedom Rides* (Lexington: University Press of Kentucky, 2009).

Chafe, William H. *Civilities and Civil Rights: Greensboro, North Carolina, and the Black Struggle for Freedom* (New York: Oxford University Press, 1980).

Clark, E. Culpepper. *The Schoolhouse Door: Segregation's Last Stand at the University of Alabama* (Oxford: Oxford University Press, 1995).

Cohadas, Nadine. *The Band Played Dixie: Race and the Liberal Conscience at Ole Miss* (New York: Free Press, 1997).

Cohen, Jeffrey E. "Presidential Rhetoric and the Public Agenda," *American Journal of Political Science* 39, no. 1 (February 1995): 87–107.

Cohen, Jeffrey E., and John A. Hamman. "'The polls': Can Presidential Rhetoric Affect the Public's Economic Perceptions?" *Presidential Studies Quarterly* 33, no. 2 (June 2003): 408–422.

Cohen, Lizabeth. *Saving America's Cities: Ed Louge and the Struggle to Renew Urban America in the Suburban Age* (New York: Farrar, Straus and Giroux, 2019).

Cohen, Robert. *Freedom's Orator: Mario Savio and the Radical Legacy of the 1960s* (Oxford: Oxford University Press, 2009).

Cohen, Robert, and David J. Snyder (eds.). *Rebellion in Black and White: Southern Student Activism in the 1960s* (Baltimore: Johns Hopkins University Press, 2013).

Cohen, Robert, and Reginald E. Zelnik (eds.). *The Free Speech Movement: Reflections on Berkeley in the 1960s* (Berkeley: University of California Press, 2002).

Cokorinos, Lee. *The Assault on Diversity: An Organized Challenge to Racial and Gender Justice* (Lanham, MD: Rowman & Littlefield, 2003).

Cole, Eddie R., and Shaun R. Harper. "Race and Rhetoric: An Analysis of College Presidents' Statements on Campus Racial Incidents," *Journal of Diversity in Higher Education* 10, no. 4 (2017): 318–333.

Collier-Thomas, Bettye, and V. P. Franklin. *My Soul Is a Witness: A Chronology of the Civil Rights Era, 1954–65* (New York: Henry Holt, 1999).

Conant, James B. "Social Dynamite in Our Large Cities," *Crime & Delinquency* 8, no. 2 (April 1962): 103–115.

Crowe, David E. *Prophets of Rage: The Black Freedom Struggle in San Francisco, 1945–1969* (New York: Routledge, 2000).

Daniels, Maurice C. *Horace T. Ward: Desegregation of the University of Georgia, Civil Rights Advocacy, and Jurisprudence* (Atlanta: Clark Atlanta University Press, 2001).

Danns, Dionne, Michelle A. Purdy, and Christopher M. Span (eds.). *Using Past as Prologue: Contemporary Perspectives on African American Educational History* (Charlotte, NC: Information Age Publishing, 2015).

Dark, Okianer Christian. "The Role of Howard University School of Law in Brown v. Board of Education," *Washington History* 16, no. 2 (Fall/Winter 2004/2005): 83–85.

Davis, John W. "The Negro Land-Grant College," *Journal of Negro Education* 2, no. 3 (July 1933): 312–328.

Davis, Margaret Leslie. *The Culture Broker: Franklin D. Murphy and the Transformation of Los Angeles* (Los Angeles: University of California Press, 2007).

de Graaf, Lawrence B., Kevin Mulroy, and Quintard Taylor (eds.). *Seeking El Dorado: African Americans in California* (Seattle: University of Washington Press, 2001).

Dittmer, John. *Local People: The Struggle for Civil Rights in Mississippi* (Urbana: University of Illinois Press, 1994).

Douglas, Ty-Ron M.O., Dena Lane-Bonds, and Sydney Freeman Jr. "There Is No Manual for University Presidents: An Interview with Andrea Luxton, President of Andrews University," *Journal of Negro Education* 86, no. 3 (Summer 2017): 368–380.

Doyle, William. *An American Insurrection: The Battle of Oxford, Mississippi, 1962* (New York: Doubleday, 2002).

Drake, St. Clair, and Horace R. Cayton. *Black Metropolis: A Study of Negro Life in a Northern City* (New York: Harcourt Brace, 1945).

Du Bois, W.E.B. "A Negro Student at Harvard at the End of the 19th Century," *Massachusetts Review* 1, no. 3 (Spring 1960): 439–458.

———. *The Souls of Black Folk* (New York: Modern Library, 2003). Originally published in 1903.

———. *The Talented Tenth*," in *The Negro Problem* (New York: James Pott, 1903).

Duffy, Elizabeth A., and Idana Goldberg. *Crafting a Class: College Admissions and Financial Aid, 1955–1994* (Princeton, NJ: Princeton University Press, 2014).

Dundjerski, Marina. *UCLA: The First Century* (Los Angeles: Third Millennium Publishing, 2011).

Dunne, Matthew William. "Next Steps: Charles S. Johnson and Southern Liberalism," *Journal of Negro History* 83, no. 1 (Winter 1998): 1–34.

Durham, Joseph. "Dr. Martin D. Jenkins Succeeds Dr. D. O. W. Holmes," *Morgan State College Bulletin* 14, no. 6 (June 1948): 4–7.

Duster, Alfreda M. *Crusade for Justice: The Autobiography of Ida B. Wells* (Chicago: University of Chicago Press, 1970).

Eagles, Charles W. *The Price of Defiance: James Meredith and the Integration of Ole Miss* (Chapel Hill: University of North Carolina Press, 2009).

Edelman, Marian Wright. *Lanterns: A Memoir of Mentors* (New York: HarperCollins, 1999).

Eisiminger, Skip. *Integration with Dignity: A Celebration of Harvey Gantt's Admission to Clemson* (Clemson, SC: Clemson University Digital Press, 2003).

Endersby, James W., and William T. Horner. *Lloyd Gaines and the Fight to End Segregation* (Columbia: University of Missouri Press, 2016).

Evans, Stephanie Y. *Black Women in the Ivory Tower, 1850–1954* (Gainesville: University Press of Florida, 2007).

Ezra, Michael. "Organizations Outside the South: NAACP and CORE," in Michael Ezra (ed.), *Civil Rights Movement: People and Perspectives* (Santa Barbara: ABC-CLIO, 2009).

Fairclough, Adam. *Teaching Equality: Black Schools in the Age of Jim Crow* (Athens, GA: University of Georgia Press, 2001).

Farber, Samuel. *Origins of the Cuban Revolution Reconsidered* (Chapel Hill: University of North Carolina Press, 2006).

Farmer, Ashley D. *Remaking Black Power: How Black Women Transformed an Era* (Chapel Hill: University of North Carolina Press, 2017).

Faulkner, Lawrence K. "Frank A. Rose and the Influences of His Administrative Leadership" (EdD diss., University of Alabama, 2015).

Favors, Jelani M. *Shelter in a Time of Storm: How Black Colleges Fostered Generations of Leadership and Activism* (Chapel Hill: University of North Carolina Press, 2019).

Fine, Sydney. *Expanding the Frontiers of Civil Rights: Michigan, 1948–1968* (Detroit: Wayne State University Press, 2000).

Fish, John Hall. *Black Power/White Control: The Struggle of the Woodlawn Organization in Chicago* (Princeton, NJ: Princeton University Press, 1973).

Flowers, Deidre B. "The Launching of the Student Sit-in Movement: The Role of Black Women at Bennett College," *Journal of African American History* 90, no. 1 (Winter 2005): 52–63.

Frederick, Jeff. *Stand Up for Alabama: Governor George Wallace* (Tuscaloosa: University of Alabama Press, 2007).

Gaillard, Frye. *Cradle of Freedom: Alabama and the Movement that Changed America* (Tuscaloosa: University of Alabama, 2004).

Gaines, Kevin K. *American Africans in Ghana: Black Expatriates and the Civil Rights Era* (Chapel Hill: University of North Carolina Press, 2006).

Gasman, Marybeth. "Perceptions of Black College Presidents: Sorting through Stereotypes and Reality to Gain a Complex Picture," *American Educational Research Journal* 48, no. 4 (August 2011): 836–870.

Gilpin, Patrick J. "Charles S. Johnson: An Intellectual Biography" (PhD diss., Vanderbilt University, 1972).

———. "Charles S. Johnson and the Race Relations Institutes at Fisk University," *Phylon* 41, no. 3 (1980): 300–311.

Gilpin, Patrick J., and Marybeth Gasman. *Charles S. Johnson: Leadership beyond the Veil in the Age of Jim Crow* (Albany: SUNY Press, 2003).

Gilpin, Patrick J., and O. Kendall White. "A Challenge to White, Southern Universities—An Argument for Including Negro History in the Curriculum," *Journal of Negro Education* 34, no. 4 (October 1969): 443–446.

Givens, Jarvis R. "There Would Be No Lynching if It Did Not Start in the Schoolroom": Carter G. Woodson and the Occasion of Negro History Week, 1926–1950," *American Educational Research Journal* 56, no. 4 (August 2019): 1457–1494.

Goduti, Jr., Philip A. *Robert F. Kennedy and the Shaping of Civil Rights, 1960–1964* (Jefferson, NC: McFarland, 2013).

Goldstone, Dwonna. *Integrating the 40 Acres: The Fifty-year Struggle for Racial Equality at the University of Texas* (Athens: University of Georgia Press, 2006).

Gonda, Jeffery D. *Unjust Deeds: The Restrictive Covenant Cases and the Making of the Civil Rights Movement* (Chapel Hill: University of North Carolina Press, 2015).

Goodson, Martia Graham (ed.). *Chronicles of Faith: The Autobiography of Frederick D. Patterson* (Tuscaloosa: University of Alabama Press, 1991).

Graham, Frances D., and Susan L. Poulson. "Spelman College: A Place All Their Own," in Leslie Miller-Bernal and Susan L. Poulson (eds.), *Challenged by Coeducation: Women's Colleges Since the 1960s* (Nashville, TN: Vanderbilt University Press, 2006).

Gribben, Alan. *Harry Huntt Ransom: Intellect in Motion* (Austin: University of Texas Press, 2008).

Grossman, James R. *Land of Hope: Chicago, Black Southerners, and the Great Migration* (Chicago: University of Chicago Press, 1989).

Haar, Sharon. *The City as Campus: Urbanism and Higher Education in Chicago* (Minneapolis: University of Minnesota Press, 2011).

Haney-Lopez, Ian. *Dog Whistle Politics: How Coded Racial Appeals Have Reinvented Racism and Wrecked the Middle Class* (Oxford: Oxford University Press, 2015).

Hanks, Lawrence J. *The Struggle for Black Political Empowerment in Three Georgia Counties* (Knoxville: University of Tennessee Press, 1990).

Hargrave, Edythe. "How I Feel as a Negro at a White College," *Journal of Negro Education* 11, no. 4 (October 1942): 484–486.

Harper, Shaun R., and Sylvia Hurtado. "Nine Themes in Campus Racial Climates and Implications for Institutional Transformation" in S. R. Harper and L. D. Patton (eds.), *Responding to the Realities of Race on Campus: New Directions for Student Services* (San Francisco: Jossey-Bass, 2007).

Harrington, Michael. *The Other America: Poverty in the United States* (New York: Macmillan, 1962).

Henderson, Harold Paulk. *Ernest Vandiver: Governor of Georgia* (Athens: University of Georgia, 2008).

Hine, Darlene Clark, and Kathleen Thompson. *A Shining Thread of Hope: The History of Black Women in America* (New York: Broadway Books, 1998).

Hirsch, Arnold R. *Making the Second Ghetto: Race and Housing in Chicago, 1940–1960* (Chicago: University of Chicago Press, 1983).

Hofstadter, Richard. *Anti-Intellectualism in American Life* (New York: Knopf, 1963).

Hollars, B. J. *Opening the Doors: The Desegregation of the University of Alabama and the Fight for Civil Rights in Tuscaloosa* (Tuscaloosa: University of Alabama Press, 2013).

Holmes, Dwight O. W. "Inaugural Address of Dwight O. W. Holmes," *Morgan State College Bulletin* 3, no. 10 (December 1937): 17–26.

Horne, Gerald. *Fire This Time: The Watts Uprising and the 1960s* (Boston: Da Capo Press, 1997).

Houck, Davis W., and David E. Dixon (eds.). *Rhetoric, Religion, and the Civil Rights Movement, 1954–1965* (Waco, TX: Baylor University Press, 2006).

Hurston, Zora Neale. *Dust Tracks on the Road* (Philadelphia: J. B. Lippincott, 1942).

Huyck, Earl E. "Faculty in Predominantly White and Predominantly Negro Higher Institutions," *Journal of Negro Education* 35, no. 4 (Autumn 1966): 381–392.

Jelks, Randal Maurice. *Benjamin Elijah Mays, Schoolmaster of the Movement: A Biography* (Chapel Hill: University of North Carolina Press, 2012).

Jencks, Christopher, and David Riesman. "The American Negro College," *Harvard Educational Review* 37, no. 1 (April 1967): 3–60.

Jenkins, Martin D. "Enrollment in Institutions of Higher Education of Negroes, 1940–1941," *Journal of Negro Education* 10, no. 4 (October 1941): 718–725.

———. "Enrollment in Institutions of Higher Education for Negroes, 1947–48," *Journal of Negro Education* 17, no. 2 (Spring 1948): 206–215.

———. "Holmes, Dwight [Oliver Wendell]," in Rayford W. Logan and Michael R. Winston (eds.), *Dictionary of American Negro Biography* (New York: W. W. Norton, 1982), pp. 320–321.

———. "Negro Higher Education," *Journal of Negro Education* 5, no. 4 (October 1936): 666–670.

Johnson, Matthew. "Managing Racial Inclusion: The Origins and Early Implementation of Affirmative Action Admissions at the University of Michigan," *Journal of Policy History* 29, no. 2 (2017): 462–489.

———. *Undermining Racial Justice: How One University Embraced Inclusion and Inequality* (Ithaca, NY: Cornell University Press, 2020).

Jolly, Jennifer L., and Justin Bruno. "Paul A. Witty: A Friend of Gifted Children," *Gifted Child Today* 33, no. 4 (October 2010): 14–17.

Jones, Ida. "Purpose, Progress, and Promise: Morgan State University, in Celebration of 150 Years," *Morgan Magazine* 1 (2017): 2–19.

Jones-Wilson, Faustine C., et al. (eds.). *Encyclopedia of African-American Education* (Westport, CT: Greenwood Press, 1996).

Karabel, Jerome. *The Chosen: The Hidden History of Admissions and Exclusion at Harvard, Yale, and Princeton* (Boston: Houghton Mifflin, 2005).

Katznelson, Ira. *When Affirmative Action Was White: An Untold History of Racial Inequality in Twentieth-Century America* (New York: W. W. Norton, 2005).

Kean, Melissa. *Desegregating Private Higher Education in the South: Duke, Emory, Rice, Tulane, and Vanderbilt* (Baton Rouge: Louisiana State University Press, 2008).

Kelley, Carrye Hill. *Profiles of Five Administrators: The Agricultural and Technical College History-Digest* (Greensboro, NC: Agricultural and Technical College, 1964).

Kelley, Robin D. G. *Hammer and Hoe: Alabama Communists During the Great Depression* (Chapel Hill: University of North Carolina Press, 1990).

Kemper, Kurt Edward. "The Smell of Roses and the Color of the Players: College Football and the Expansion of the Civil Rights Movement in the West." *Journal of Sports History* 31, no. 3 (Fall 2004): 317–339.

Kendi, Ibram X. (formerly Ibram H. Rogers). *The Black Campus Movement: Black Students and the Racial Reconstruction of Higher Education, 1965–1972* (New York: Palgrave Macmillan, 2012).

K'Meyer, Tracy E. *Civil Rights in the Gateway to the South: Louisville, Kentucky, 1945–1980* (Lexington: University Press of Kentucky, 2009).

Kornbluh, Peter. *Bay of Pigs Declassified: The Secret CIA Report on the Invasion of Cuba* (New York: New Press, 1998).

Lambert, Frank. *The Battle of Ole Miss: Civil Rights v. States' Rights* (Oxford: Oxford University Press, 2010).

Langer, Elinor. "Negro Colleges: Long Ignored, Southern Schools Now Courted by Major Universities and Foundations," *Science* 145, no. 3630 (July 24, 1964): 371–373, 428, 430.

Lassiter, Matthew D. *The Silent Majority: Suburban Politics in the Sunbelt South* (Princeton, NJ: Princeton University Press, 2006).

Layboure, Wendy Marie, and Gregory S. Parks. "Omega Psi Phi Fraternity and the Fight for Civil Rights," *Wake Forest Journal of Law & Policy* 6, no. 1 (2016): 213–301.

Lee, Chana Kai. *For Freedom's Sake: The Life of Fannie Lou Hamer* (Urbana: University of Illinois Press, 1999).

Lefever, Harry G. *Undaunted by the Fight: Spelman College and the Civil Rights Movement, 1957–1967* (Macon, GA: Mercer University Press, 2005).

Lesesne, Henry H. *A History of the University of South Carolina, 1940–2000* (Columbia: University of South Carolina Press, 2001).

Levin, Matthew. *Cold War University: Madison and the New Left in the Sixties* (Madison: University of Wisconsin Press, 2013).

Lindsey, Treva B. *Colored No More: Reinventing Black Womanhood in Washington D.C.* (Urbana: University of Illinois Press, 2017).

Link, William A. *William Friday: Power, Purpose, and American Higher Education* (Chapel Hill: University of North Carolina Press, 1995).

Lovett, Bobby L. *The Civil Rights Movement in Tennessee: A Narrative History* (Knoxville: University of Tennessee Press, 2005).

Lyman, Richard W. *Stanford in Turmoil: Campus Unrest, 1966–1972* (Stanford: Stanford University Press, 2009).

Marable, Manning. "Black Studies and the Racial Mountain," *Souls* 2, no. 3 (Summer 2000): 17–36.

Mays, Benjamin E. *Born to Rebel: An Autobiography* (Athens: University of Georgia Press, 1987). Originally published in 1971.

McGirr, Lisa. *Suburban Warriors: The Origins of the New American Right* (Princeton, NJ: Princeton University Press, 2001).

McWhorter, Diane. *Carry Me Home: Birmingham, Alabama: The Climatic Battle of the Civil Rights Revolution* (New York: Simon & Schuster, 2001).

Meredith, James. *Three Years in Mississippi* (Bloomington: Indiana University Press, 1966).

Michaeli, Ethan. *The Defender: How the Legendary Black Newspaper Changed America* (Boston: Houghton Mifflin Harcourt, 2016).

Moore, Natalie Y. *The South Side: A Portrait of Chicago and American Segregation* (New York: St. Martin's Press, 2016).

Moore, Winfred B., Jr., and Orville Vernon Burton (eds.). *Toward the Meeting of the Waters: Currents in the Civil Rights Movement of South Carolina during the Twentieth Century* (Columbia: University of South Carolina Press, 2008).

Morris, Aldon D. *The Origins of the Civil Rights Movement: Black Communities Organizing for Change* (New York: Free Press, 1984).

———. *The Scholar Denied: W. E. B. Du Bois and the Birth of Modern Sociology* (Berkeley: University of California Press, 2017).

Moye, J. Todd. *Let the People Decide: Black Freedom and White Resistance Movements in Sunflower County, Mississippi, 1945–1986* (Chapel Hill: University of North Carolina Press, 2004).

Muhammad, Khalil Gibran. *The Condemnation of Blackness: Race, Crime, and the Making of Urban America* (Cambridge, MA: Harvard University Press. 2010).

Murch, Donna Jean. *Living for the City: Migration, Education, and the Rise of the Black Panther Party in Oakland, California* (Chapel Hill: University of North Carolina Press, 2010).

Nash, George. *The University and the City: Eight Cases of Involvement* (New York: McGraw-Hill, 1973).

Nickerson, Michelle, and Darren Dochuk (eds.). *Sunbelt Rising: The Politics of Space, Place, and Region* (Philadelphia: University of Pennsylvania Press, 2011).

Norrell, Robert J. *Up from History: The Life of Booker T. Washington* (London: Belknap Press, 2009).

O'Loughlin, John, and Richard Grant. "The Political Geography of Presidential Speeches, 1946–87," *Annals of the Association of American Geographers* 80, no. 4 (December 1990): 504–530.

O'Mara, Margaret Pugh. *Cities of Knowledge: Cold War Science and the Search for the Next Silicon Valley* (Princeton, NJ: Princeton University Press, 2005).

Ownby, Ted. *The Civil Rights Movement in Mississippi* (Jackson: University Press of Mississippi, 2013).

Park, Laurel. "Planting the Seeds of Academic Excellence and Cultural Awareness: The Michigan-Tuskegee Exchange Program," *Michigan Historical Review* 30, no. 1 (Spring 2004): 117–131.

Parks, Gregory S., and Wendy Marie Layboure. "The Sons of Indiana: Kappa Alpha Psi Fraternity and the Fight for Civil Rights," *Indiana Law Journal* 91, no. 4 (Summer 2016): 1425–1472.

Parsons, Kermit C. "Universities and Cities: The Terms of the Truce between Them," *Journal of Higher Education* 34, no. 4 (April 1963): 205–216.

Patterson, James T. *Brown v. Board of Education: A Civil Rights Milestone and Its Troubled Legacy* (Oxford: Oxford University Press, 2001).

———. *Grand Expectations: The United States, 1945–1974* (Oxford: Oxford University Press, 1996).

Perkins, Linda M. "The First Black Talent Identification Program: The National Scholarship Service and Fund for Negro Students, 1947–1968," *Perspectives on the History of Higher Education* (December 2012): 173–186.

Perlstein, Daniel. "Minds Stayed on Freedom: Politics and Pedagogy in the African American Freedom Struggle," in William H. Watkins (ed.), *Black Protest Thought and Education* (New York: Peter Lang, 2005).

Permaloff, Anne, and Carl Grafton. *Politics and Power in Alabama: The More Things Change...* (Athens: University of Georgia Press, 2006).

Perry, Barbara A. *The Michigan Affirmative Action Case* (Lawrence: University Press of Kansas, 2007).

Perry, David C., and Wim Wiewel (eds.). *The University as Urban Developer: Case Studies and Analysis* (New York: Routledge, 2015). Originally published by M. E. Sharpe in 2005.

Pfeiffer, S. I. (ed.). *Handbook of Giftedness in Children: Psychoeducational Theory, Research, and Best Practices* (New York: Springer Publishing, 2008).

Pitre, Merline, and Bruce A. Glasrud (eds.). *Southern Black Women in the Modern Civil Rights Movement* (College Station: Texas A&M University Press, 2013).

Plaut, Richard L. "Plans for Assisting Negro Students to Enter and to Remain in College," *Journal of Negro Education* 35, no. 4 (Autumn 1966): 393–399.

Pratt, Robert A. *We Shall Not Be Moved: The Desegregation of the University of Georgia* (Athens: University of Georgia Press, 2002).

Rabby, Glenda Alice. *The Pain and the Promise: The Struggle for Civil Rights in Tallahassee, Florida* (Athens: University of Georgia Press, 1999).

Ramón, Ana-Christina, and Darnell Hunt (eds.). *Black Los Angeles: American Dreams and Racial Realities* (New York: New York University Press, 2010).

Ransby, Barbara. *Ella Baker and the Black Freedom Movement: A Radical Democratic Vision* (Chapel Hill: University of North Carolina Press, 2003).

Rasenberger, Jim. *The Brilliant Disaster: JFK, Castro, and America's Doomed Invasion of Cuba's Bay of Pigs* (New York: Simon & Schuster, 2011).

Reddix, Jacob L. *A Voice Crying in the Wilderness: The Memoirs of Jacob L. Reddix* (Jackson: University Press of Mississippi, 1974).

Robinson, Jo Ann Gibson. *The Montgomery Bus Boycott and the Women Who Started It* (Knoxville: University of Tennessee Press, 1987).

Rodin, Judith. *The University and Urban Revival: Out of the Ivory Tower and Into the Streets* (Philadelphia: University of Pennsylvania Press, 2007).

Rooks, Noliwe M. *White Money/Black Power: The Surprising History of African American Studies and the Crisis of Race and Higher Education* (New York: Beacon Press, 2007).

Rorabaugh, W. J. *Berkeley at War: The 1960s* (Oxford: Oxford University Press, 1990).

Rose, Harold M. "Teacher-Exchange Programs: Academic Co-operation between Northern and Southern Institutions," *Journal of Higher Education* 37, no. 6 (June 1966): 319–324.

Rothstein, Richard. *The Color of Law: A Forgotten History of How Our Government Segregated America* (New York: Liveright, 2017).

Roznowski, Tom. *An American Hometown: Terre Haute, Indiana, 1927* (Bloomington: Indiana University Press, 2009).

Sanders, Crystal R. "Pursuing the 'Unfinished Business of Democracy': Willa B. Player and Liberal Arts Education at Bennett College in the Civil Rights Era," *North Carolina Historical Review* 96, no. 1 (January 2019): 1–33.

Sanders, Katrina M. *"Intelligent and Effective Direction": The Fisk University Race Relations Institute and the Struggle for Civil Rights, 1944–1969* (New York: Peter Lang, 2005).

Sansing, David G. *Making Haste Slowly: The Troubled History of Higher Education in Mississippi* (Jackson: University Press of Mississippi, 1990).

Sartain, Lee. *Borders of Equality: The NAACP and the Baltimore Civil Rights Struggle, 1914–1970* (Jackson: University Press of Mississippi, 2013).

Schoultz, Lars. *That Infernal Little Cuban Republic: The United States and the Cuban Revolution* (Chapel Hill: University of North Carolina Press, 2011).

Schrum, Ethan. *The Instrumental University: Education in Service of the National Agenda after World War II* (Ithaca, NY: Cornell University Press, 2019).

Sides, Josh. *L.A. City Limits: African American Los Angeles from the Great Depression to the Present* (Berkeley: University of California Press, 2004).

Silver, James W. *Mississippi: The Closed Society* (Jackson: University Press of Mississippi, 2012). Originally published in 1964.

Skrentny, John David. *The Ironies of Affirmative Action: Politics, Culture, and Justice in America* (Chicago: University of Chicago Press, 1996).

Smith, C. Fraser. *Here Lies Jim Crow: Civil Rights in Maryland* (Baltimore: Johns Hopkins University Press, 2008).

Smith, Gerald L. *A Black Educator in the Segregated South: Kentucky's Rufus B. Atwood* (Lexington: University Press of Kentucky, 1994).

Sorrells, William. *The Exciting Years: The Cecil C. Humphreys Presidency of Memphis State University, 1960–1972* (Memphis, TN: Memphis State University Press, 1987)

Spencer, John P. *In the Crossfire: Marcus Foster and the Troubled History of American School Reform* (Philadelphia: University of Pennsylvania Press, 2012).

Stanford, Karin L. *African Americans in Los Angeles: Images of America* (Charleston, SC: Arcadia Publishing, 2010).

Stewart, Jeffrey C. *The New Negro: The Life of Alain Locke* (Oxford: Oxford University Press, 2018).

Stulberg, Lisa M., and Anthony S. Chen. "The Origins of Race-conscious Affirmative Action in Undergraduate Admissions: A Comparative Analysis of Institutional Change in Higher Education," *Sociology of Education* 87, no. 1 (2013): 36–52.

Suddler, Carl. *Presumed Criminal: Black Youth and the Justice System in Postwar New York* (New York: New York University Press, 2019).

Sugrue, Thomas J. *Sweet Land of Liberty: The Forgotten Struggle for Civil Rights in the North* (New York, Random House, 2009).

Synnott, Marcia Graham. *The Half-Opened Door: Discrimination and Admissions at Harvard, Yale, and Princeton, 1900–1970* (Westport, CT: Greenwood Press, 1979).

Taylor, Keeanga-Yamahtta. *Race for Profit: How Banks and the Real Estate Industry Undermined Black Homeownership* (Chapel Hill: University of North Carolina Press, 2019).

Taylor, Quintard. *In Search of the Racial Frontier: African Americans in the American West* (New York: W.W. Norton, 1998).

Terborg-Penn, Rosalyn. *African American Women in the Struggle for the Vote, 1850–1920* (Bloomington: Indiana University Press, 1998).

Thelin, John R. *A History of American Higher Education*, 2nd ed. (Baltimore: Johns Hopkins University Press, 2011).

Theoharis, Jeanne, and Komozi Woodard (eds.). *Freedom North: Black Freedom Struggles Outside the South, 1940–1980* (New York: Palgrave Macmillan, 2003).

Tilford, Earl H. *Turning the Tide: The University of Alabama in the 1960s* (Tuscaloosa: University of Alabama Press, 2014).

Trachtenberg, Ben. "The 2015 University of Missouri Protests and Their Lessons for Higher Education Policy and Administration," *Kentucky Law Journal* 47 (2018–19): 61–121.

Turner, Jeffrey A. *Sitting In and Speaking Out: Student Movements in the American South, 1960–1970* (Athens: University of Georgia Press, 2010).

Tuttle, William M., Jr. *Race Riot: Chicago in the Red Summer of 1919* (Urbana: University of Illinois Press, 1970).

Walker, Vanessa Siddle. *Hello Professor: A Black Principal and Professional Leadership in the Segregated South* (Chapel Hill: University of North Carolina Press, 2009).

———. *The Lost Education of Horace Tate: Uncovering the Hidden Heroes Who Fought for Justice in Schools* (New York: New Press, 2018).

Wallenstein, Peter. (ed.). *Higher Education and the Civil Rights Movement: White Supremacy, Black Southerners, and College Campuses* (Gainesville: University Press of Florida, 2009).

Washington, Booker T. *Up from Slavery* (Garden City, NY: Doubleday, 1901).

Wechsler, Harold. *The Qualified Student: A History of Selective College Admission in America* (New York: Wiley, 1977).

Wheatle, Katherine I. E. "'Ward of the State': The Politics of Funding Maryland's Black Land-Grant College, 1886–1939" (PhD diss., Indiana University, 2018).

White, Derrick E. *Blood, Sweat, and Tears: Jake Gaither, Florida A&M, and the History of Black College Football* (Chapel Hill: University of North Carolina Press, 2019).

Whittington, Keith E. *Speak Freely: Why Universities Must Defend Free Speech* (Princeton, NJ: Princeton University Press, 2018).

Williams, Rhonda Y. *The Politics of Public Housing: Black Women's Struggles against Urban Inequality* (Oxford: Oxford University Press, 2004).

Williamson, Joy Ann. *Black Power on Campus: The University of Illinois, 1965–75* (Urbana: University of Illinois Press, 2003).

———. *Radicalizing the Ebony Tower: Black Colleges and the Black Freedom Struggle in Mississippi* (New York: Teachers College Press, 2008).

———. "'This Has Been Quite a Year for Heads Falling': Institutional Autonomy in the Civil Rights Era," *History of Education Quarterly* 44, no. 4 (Winter 2004): 554–576.

Williamson-Lott, Joy Ann. *Jim Crow Campus: Higher Education and the Struggle for a New Southern Social Order* (New York: Teachers College Press, 2018).

Willie, Charles V. "Philanthropic and Foundation Support for Blacks: A Case Study from the 1960s," *Journal of Negro Education* 50, no. 3 (Summer 1981): 270–284.

Wilson, Edward N. "The Predecessors of Morgan State College: A Study of Growth and Achievement," *Morgan State College Bulletin* 6, no. 1 (January 1940): 3–16.

Winling, LaDale C. *Building the Ivory Tower: Universities and Metropolitan Development in the Twentieth Century* (Philadelphia: University of Pennsylvania Press, 2017).

Winston, Michael R. "Through the Back Door: Academic Racism and the Negro Scholar in Historical Perspective," *Daedalus* 100, no. 3 (Summer 1971): 678–719.

Witty, Paul A., and Martin D. Jenkins. "Intra-race Testing and Negro Intelligence," *Journal of Psychology* 1 (1936): 179–192.

Wolters, Raymond. *The New Negro on Campus: Black College Rebellions of the 1920s* (Princeton, NJ: Princeton University Press, 1975).

Woodson, Carter G. *The Mis-Education of the Negro* (Washington, DC: Associated Publishers, 1933).

Zinn, Howard. *SNCC: The New Abolitionists* (Boston: Beacon Press, 1964).

A NOTE ON THE TYPE

This book has been composed in Arno, an Old-style serif typeface in the classic Venetian tradition, designed by Robert Slimbach at Adobe.